Developments in Russian Politics 8

Edited by

Stephen White

Richard Sakwa

and

Henry E. Hale

DUKE UNIVERSITY PRESS   DURHAM   2014

This edition published in the United States in 2014 by
DUKE UNIVERSITY PRESS
Durham, NC 27708

Published in Great Britain in 2014 by
PALGRAVE MACMILLAN
Houndmills, Basingstoke, Hampshire RG21 6XS

Library of Congress Cataloging-in-Publication Data
Developments in Russian politics 8 / Stephen White, Richard
Sakwa, and Henry E. Hale, eds. —Eighth edition.
pages cm
Includes bibliographical references and index.
isbn 978-0-8223-5799-5 (cloth : alk. paper)
isbn 978-0-8223-5812-1 (pbk. : alk. paper)
  1. Russia (Federation)—Politics and government—1991–
I. White, Stephen, 1945– II. Sakwa, Richard. III. Hale,
Henry E., 1966–
DK510.763.D48 2014
947.086—dc23
2014017563

Printed in the United States of America on acid-free paper ∞

Contents

    Kathryn Hendley

    The heritage of Soviet law   145
    The institutional structure of the Russian legal system   147
    The Russian legal system in action   149
    Russians' expectations of the legal system   151
    Prospects for the rule of law in Russia   154

10 A Federal State?   157
    Darrell Slider

    Putin's vertical of power   159
    Interactions between governors and the president   165
    Federal agencies in the regions and the problem of
       decentralization   169

11 Managing the Economy   173
    Philip Hanson

    The changing environment of Russian economic policy   175
    Economic policies and policy-making, 2000–13   180
    Conclusions   190

12 Society and Social Divisions in Russia   192
    Svetlana Stephenson

    Rise in inequalities   193
    New consumerism and social distinctions   195
    Social divisions, the welfare state and pathologization of
       the poor   199
    Social networks and patrimonial structures   201
    Exclusionary processes   203
    Social divisions and civil society: towards new civic
       solidarity?   207

13 Foreign Policy   211
    Margot Light

    The domestic context of Russian foreign policy   211
    Russian policy towards the 'near abroad'   217
    Russian policy towards the 'far abroad'   224
    Future prospects   230

List of Illustrative Material

Map

Tables

Figures

Boxes

Preface

Russia is – by a considerable margin – the world's largest country. It spans two continents and nine (until 2010, eleven) time zones. It has one of the world's largest economies, and one of its most formidable concentrations of military might. It is a founding member of the United Nations, with a permanent seat on its Security Council, and a member of the various groupings of the world's leading industrial nations. So Russia matters, even if it no longer represents an ideological challenge to the Western system of government. And it matters very much who controls this vast territory, with its abundance of natural resources: how its leaders are chosen, what influences them, and how the country they lead interacts with the rest of the global community.

We have assembled a new team to explore such issues in this eighth edition of *Developments in Russian Politics*. As always, it is largely a new book: partly because it reflects the return of Vladimir Putin to the Russian presidency and far-reaching changes in the wider society, but also because it draws on a new set of contributors. Five of them appear in this *Developments* volume for the first time; others have taken on new subjects; and the remaining chapters have been entirely rewritten and updated. So this is, in substance, a new book. But it has the same objective as its predecessors: to provide an accurate and up-to-date analysis of the contemporary Russian system with a special emphasis on the issues that are currently most topical and which are likely to be of the greatest interest to other scholars as well as to the university and college students for whom it is primarily intended.

We start, as we must, by placing contemporary Russian politics within a longer-term perspective, and then move to the core institutions of the Russian state: the political executive (including the presidency and government), the legislature, the electoral system, and the political parties. Further chapters consider the wider relationship between Russians and their political system: the patterns of voting behaviour that have become established over more than twenty years of competitive politics, the protest politics that has become more prominent since the last edition of this book, and political communication in electronic as well as more conventional forms. We also consider the extent to which a rule of law has been able to develop that might place some limits on the exercise of central authority, and how far the federal system prescribed in the constitution is a political reality.

We move on to policy formation: in the economy, as slowing growth rates pose new challenges; in a changing and increasingly divided society; in foreign affairs; and in defence and security. A final chapter places the entire system within wider debates about 'democratization' and considers the trajectory of change. We conclude, as in earlier editions, with a guide to further reading and a comprehensive list of references.

We complete this book as Vladimir Putin settles firmly into his third term as president, and what may be the start of a longer period that would allow him to remain in office up to 2024. We hope the pages that follow will help to set out more clearly the nature of the office he once again controls, and the kind of challenges he will confront in the years to come.

STEPHEN WHITE
RICHARD SAKWA
HENRY E. HALE

Notes on the Contributors

Vladimir Gel'man is Professor in the Department of Political Science and Sociology at the European University at St Petersburg and Finland Distinguished Professor in the Aleksanteri Institute at the University of Helsinki. He has written extensively on contemporary political developments in Russia, with an emphasis on electoral and party politics, regional and local government, in journals such as *Europe-Asia Studies*, *Post-Soviet Affairs*, *International Political Science Review*, *Democratization*, and others. His recent publications include edited volumes, *The Politics of Sub-National Authoritarianism in Russia* (with Cameron Ross, 2010) and *Resource Curse and Post-Soviet Eurasia* (with Otar Marganiya, 2010). His current research focuses on analysis of political regime dynamics in post-Communist Russia in theoretical and comparative perspective.

Henry E. Hale is Associate Professor of Political Science at George Washington University. His books include *Great Expectations: Patronal Politics and Regime Dynamics in Eurasia* (forthcoming) and *Why Not Parties in Russia? Democracy, Federalism, and the State* (2006). He regularly spends time on the ground in Russia, including as a visiting fellow at the Carnegie Moscow Center for the fall 2012 semester. His current research focuses on political party development, political regime dynamics, and ethnic politics.

Philip Hanson is Associate Fellow of the Russia and Eurasia Programme at Chatham House, London, and an Emeritus Professor of the Political Economy of Russia and Eastern Europe at the University of Birmingham. His work includes an economic history of the USSR from 1945 to 1991 (*The Rise and Fall of the Soviet Economy*, 2003), a study of patterns of regional economic change in Russia, and a series of shorter papers including *Putin Again: Implications for Russia and the West* (with others, 2012). Past appointments have been at the Foreign and Commonwealth Office in the United Kingdom, the UN Economic Commission for Europe, Radio Liberty, and Michigan, Harvard, Kyoto and Södertörns universities. he is curently working on contemporary Russian economic policy and business–state relations.

Kathryn Hendley is William Voss-Bascom Professor of Law and Political Science at the University of Wisconsin-Madison. She has written extensively on Russian legal reform in journals such as *American Journal of Comparative Law, Europe-Asia Studies, Law & Social Inquiry, Law & Society Review, Post-Soviet Affairs,* and *Slavic Review.* She has been a visiting scholar at the Kennan Institute and the Woodrow Wilson International Center for Scholars in Washington, DC, the Program in Law and Public Affairs at Princeton University, and the Kellogg Institute for International Studies at Notre Dame University. She was a Fulbright Scholar at the New Economic School in Moscow in 2011–12. Her current research focuses on the role of law in the everyday lives of Russians.

Margot Light is Emeritus Professor of International Relations at the London School of Economics and Political Science. Her publications include *Putin's Russia and the Enlarged Europe* (with Roy Allison and Stephen White, 2006), Russia and Europe and the process of EU enlargement, in *The Multilateral Dimension in Russian Foreign Policy*, edited by Elana Wilson Rowe and Stine Toresen (2009), and 'The Export of Liberalism to Russia', in *After Liberalism? The Future of Liberalism in International Relations,* edited by Rebekka Friedman, Kevork Oskanian, and Ramon Pacheco Pardo (2013).

Jennifer G. Mathers is Senior Lecturer and Head of the Department of International Politics at Aberystwyth University. Her publications include *The Russian Nuclear Shield from Stalin to Yeltsin* (2000), the co-edited volume *Military and Society in Post-Soviet Russia* (with Stephen L. Webber, 2006), 'Nuclear Weapons in Russian Foreign Policy: Patterns in Presidential Discourse 2000–2010' in *Europe-Asia Studies* (2012) and 'Women and State Militaries' in *Women and Wars: Contested Histories, Uncertain Futures*, edited by Carol Cohn (2012). Her current research focuses on the intersection between internal and external dimensions of Russian security.

Ian McAllister is Distinguished Professor of Political Science at The Australian National University. His most recent books are (as co-author) *Conflict to Peace: Society and Politics in Northern Ireland Over Half a Century* (2013), *The Australian Voter* (2011) and (also as co-author) *Political Parties and Democratic Linkage* (2011). He has been director of the Australian Election Study since 1987. He is a Fellow of the Academy of Social Sciences in Australia and a corresponding member of the Royal Society of Edinburgh. His scholarly research covers comparative political behaviour, post-communist politics and Northern Ireland and Australian politics.

Sarah Oates is Professor and Senior Scholar at the Philip Merrill College of Journalism at the University of Maryland, College Park, USA. The author of several books on media and democratization, including *Revolution Stalled* (2013), she is currently working on a research project funded by the Google Data Analytics Social Science Research programme from the Economic and Social Research Council. This research work with colleagues at the University of Glasgow compares how voters in different countries create their own information agendas through online search.

Thomas F. Remington is Goodrich C. White Professor of Political Science at Emory University. He is author of *The Politics of Inequality in Russia* (2011), *The Russian Parliament: Institutional Evolution in a Transitional Regime* (2001), *The Politics of Institutional Choice: Formation of the Russian State Duma* (with Steven S. Smith) (2001) and other books and articles on Russian and post-communist politics. His current research focuses on the politics of social policy in Russia and China.

Graeme B. Robertson is Associate Professor of Political Science at the University of North Carolina at Chapel Hill. Graeme is the author of *The Politics of Protest in Hybrid Regimes: Managing Dissent in Post Communist Russia* (2011) and numerous articles on protest politics in Russia and elsewhere. He is currently working on a major project looking at the Russian opposition in the aftermath of the 2011–12 protest cycle.

Richard Sakwa is Professor of Russian and European Politics at the University of Kent at Canterbury and an Associate Fellow of the Russia and Eurasia Programme at Chatham House. He has published widely on Soviet, Russian and post-communist affairs. Recent books include: *Postcommunism* (1999), the edited volume *Chechnya: From Past to Future* (2005), *Contextualising Secession: Normative Aspects of Secession Struggles* (2003), co-edited with Bruno Coppieters, *Russian Politics and Society* (4th edn 2008), and *Putin: Russia's Choice* (2nd edn 2008). His book on *The Crisis of Russian Democracy: Factionalism, Sovereignty and the Medvedev Succession* was published in 2011. In 2014, he published *Putin and the Oligarch: The Khodorkovsky – Yukos Affair* and his study *Putin* Redux: *Power and Contradiction in Contemporary Russia*.

Darrell Slider is Professor of Government and International Affairs at the University of South Florida, in Tampa. He is the author of a number of works on Russian regions, elections, federalism and decentralization, including most recently a chapter on regional governance in Graeme Gill and John Young's co-edited *Routledge Handbook of Russian Politics and*

Society (2012). He is currently working on the issue of corruption and the low 'quality of government' in Putin's Russia.

Svetlana Stephenson is Reader in Sociology at London Metropolitan University. She is the author of *Crossing the Line: Vagrancy, Homelessness and Social Displacement in Russia* (2006) and *Youth and Social Change in Eastern Europe and the Former Soviet Union* (with Charles Walker, 2012). She has also published in a series of journals including *Criminal Justice Matters*, *Journal of Youth Studies*, *Sociological Review*, *Europe–Asia Studies*, *International Journal of Comparative Sociology*, *Slavic Review*, *Social Justice Research and Work, Employment and Society*. Her research has involved studying disadvantaged groups in Russia and their social organization, as well as perceptions of social justice and human rights in a comparative context. Her current research focuses on the Russian criminal gangs.

Stephen White is James Bryce Professor of Politics at the University of Glasgow in the UK. He is also visiting professor at the Institute of Applied Politics in Moscow, and has held appointments at the Johns Hopkins Bologna Center and Grinnell College, Iowa. He was the chief editor of the *Journal of Communist Studies and Transition Politics* until 2011, and co-edits the *Journal of Eurasian Studies*. His recent books include *Understanding Russian Politics* (2011) and *Russia's Authoritarian Elections* (with others, 2011). He is also the author of a forthcoming study of relations between Russia, Ukraine, Belarus and 'Europe' (with Valentina Feklyunina, 2014), and is currently working with a group of colleagues on the relationship between social inequality and political instability in Russia and China. He was elected a Fellow of the British Academy in 2010.

John P. Willerton is Associate Professor of Political Science at the University of Arizona, Tucson. He is the author of *Patronage and Politics in the USSR* and numerous articles and chapters dealing with various facets of Soviet and post-Soviet Russian domestic politics and foreign policy. His current research focuses on post-Soviet political elites, the Russian federal executive, semi-presidentialism in France and Russia, and Russia's relations with the Commonwealth of Independent States and former Soviet republics. He is also engaged in a project that deals with Putin and Russia's search for a national idea.

List of Abbreviations

ABM	anti-ballistic missile
CFE	conventional forces in Europe
CIS	Commonwealth of Independent States
CPRF	Communist Party of the Russian Federation
CPSU	Communist Party of the Soviet Union
FAR	Fatherland-All Russia
FNPR	Federation of Independent Trade Unions of Russia
FSB	Federal Security Service
GDF	Glasnost Defence Foundation
GDP	gross domestic product
GONGOs	government-organized non-governmental organizations
IMF	International Monetary Fund
KGB	Soviet security police
LDPR	Liberal Democratic Party of Russia
MERT	Ministry of Economic Development and Trade
MFA	Ministry of Foreign Affairs
MVD	Ministry of Internal Affairs
NATO	North Atlantic Treaty Organization
NGOs	non-governmental organizations
ODIHR	Office for Democratic Institutions and Human Rights
OHR	Our Home is Russia
OSCE	Organization for Security and Cooperation in Europe
OVR	Fatherland-all Russia party
PA	presidential administration
PFIGs	financial–industrial groups
RF	Russian Federation
RSPP	Russian Union of Industrialists and Entrepreneurs
RSFSR	Russian Soviet Federative Socialist Republic
SPS, URF	Union of Right Forces
USSR	Union of Soviet Socialist Republics
VKP(b)	All-Union Communist Party (Bolsheviks)
WTO	World Trade Organization

Legend:
- Frontier of Russia
- Frontier of Federal Districts
- Frontier of other units of administration
- Republic
- Autonomous Region
- Autonomous District
- Territory
- Region
- Federal City

BALTIC SEA

BARENTS SEA

KARA SEA

NORTH-WESTERN FEDERAL DISTRICT

Kaliningrad

Murmansk

KARELIA

St Petersburg
Leningrad

Pskov

Novgorod

Archangel

Nenets

Tver'

Vologda

KOMI

Yamal-Nenets

Smolensk

Moscow
Moscow

Yaroslavl
Ivanovo
Kostroma

CENTRAL FEDERAL DISTRICT

Bryansk

Kaluga

Vladimir

Kirov

Komi-Permyak

Khanty-Mansi

Orel

Tula

Ryazan'

Nizhnii Novgorod

MARI EL

UDMURTIA

Perm'

Kursk

Lipetsk

Penza

CHUVASHIA

TATARSTAN

BASHKORTOSTAN

Sverdlovsk

Krasnoyarsk

MORDOVIA

Voronezh

Ul'yanovsk

Saratov

Samara

Chelyabinsk

Kurgan

Tyumen'

Tomsk

BLACK SEA

Krasnodar

Rostov

Volgograd

Orenburg

Omsk

Novosibirsk

Kemerovo

AGYDEYA

KARACHAI-CHERKESSIA

KABARDINO-BALKARIA

NORTHERN OSSETIA-ALANIA

INGUSHETIA

CHECHNYA

Stavropol

KALMYKIA

Astrakhan

CASPIAN SEA

DAGESTAN

Altai

KHAKASIA

ALTAI

SOUTHERN FEDERAL DISTRICT

VOLGA FEDERAL DISTRICT

URALS FEDERAL DISTRICT

Map by András Bereznay; www.historyonmaps.com

Map of The Russian Federation under the 1993 Constitution

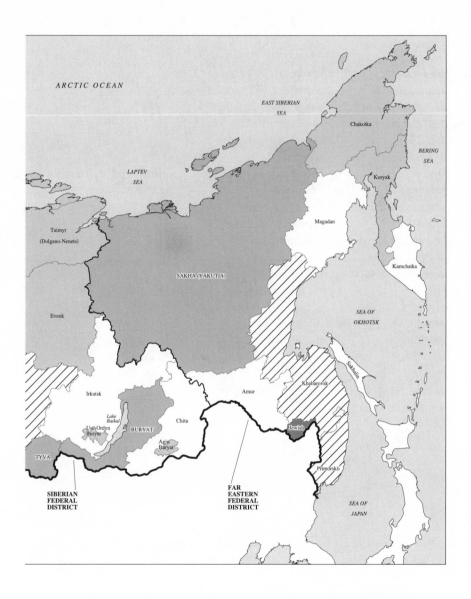

ARCTIC OCEAN

EAST SIBERIAN
SEA

Chukotka

BERING
SEA

LAPTEV
SEA

Koryak

Taimyr
(Dolgano-Nenets)

Magadan

Kamchatka

SAKHA (YAKUTIA)

Evenk

SEA OF
OKHOTSK

Irkutsk

Khabarovsk

Amur

Lake
Baikal

Ush-Ordyn
Buryat   BURYAT   Chita

Jewish

Agin
Buryat

TYVA

Primorskii

**SIBERIAN
FEDERAL
DISTRICT**

**FAR
EASTERN
FEDERAL
DISTRICT**

SEA OF
JAPAN

Glossary

advokat	lawyer
arbitrazh	commercial (courts)
deesposbnyi	capable
dedovshchina	bullying
demokratizatsiya	democratization
doverennye	trusted
Duma	lower house of Federal Assembly (parliament)
glasnost	openness
kompromat	smear tactics
krai	territory
perestroika	restructuring
poryadok	order
nomenklatura	list of party-controlled posts
oblast	region, province
obshchestvennye	social or public (organizations)
okrugs	districts
polpred	presidential envoy
siloviki	security and intelligence officials
soviet	council
ukazy	presidential decrees
uskorenie	acceleration
zastoi	stagnation

Chapter 1

Politics in Russia

RICHARD SAKWA

Russia re-emerged as an independent state in 1991, yet even to this day some basic issues about its national identity and political character remain deeply contested. It was certainly not going to be easy to create a capitalist democracy from scratch, but few could have predicted quite how dramatic and contradictory the whole process would be. Everything had to be created anew, including the party and parliamentary systems, legally defensible property rights, a new class of entrepreneurs, and especially the constitutional framework and the rule of law. Above all, the balance of power between the executive (president) and parliament provoked violent conflict. In addition, Russia needed to find a new role in the international system, one that corresponded to its own vision of itself as a great power but which also took into account the concerns of its new neighbours, the former Soviet republics that were now independent states, as well as the existing balance of power at the global level.

In the years since the collapse of communism there have been enormous achievements, yet the process remains incomplete and contradictory. The Soviet legacy of an enormous security apparatus, a vast dependent bureaucracy and an over-extended welfare system remains a potent force in politics, as do the rather more intangible factors of attitudes and political culture. The new Russian political elite remain steeped in the mores and prejudices of the Soviet era. This is coming up against an increasingly impatient younger generation, a growing proportion of whom have grown up in the post-Soviet years and for whom communism is something to be read about in the history books.

The transformation of the economy and polity, moreover, has spawned new interests and concerns, demanding a more open political system and genuine accountability by the authorities towards the institutions of representative democracy and subordination not only to the black letter but also to the spirit of the constitution. These demands spilled out into the streets in December 2011, in protest against the widespread fraud in the parliamentary elections in that month. The rebirth of an active opposition in turn revived competitive politics. The regime could no longer rule on its own. It was clear that the tortuous development of Russian politics and society had entered a new stage, the features of which will be analysed in this book.

The Soviet system

It is impossible to understand contemporary Russia without some understanding of what went before. In particular, in the space of less than a century two major political systems collapsed. The Russian Empire, ruled by the Romanov dynasty from 1613, was unable to withstand the strains of the Great War, which Russia entered in July 1914 in alliance with France and Great Britain. The abdication of Nicholas II, in February 1917, brought to an end the Romanov dynasty after 300 years in power. During the next eight months Russia tried to fight a war while making a revolution, and while it was notably unsuccessful in the first endeavour it shocked the world with the second. The Provisional Government in 1917 at last began to fulfil the potential of the long-gathering Russian revolution. Since at least 1825 and the Decembrist movement there had been growing pressure for the introduction of limited and accountable government, and now genuine constitutionalism had finally arrived. (The entire sequence of leadership from Nicholas II to the present is set out in Table 1.1.)

Only six months after the fall of the autocracy, on 7 November (25 October in the Old Style calendar), the radical Bolshevik Party under the uncompromising leadership of Vladimir Il'ich Lenin came to power. It was too late for the new authorities to stop the planned elections to the Constituent Assembly and the Bolsheviks found themselves in a minority in the new body. This was the first genuinely democratically elected legislature in Russian history, with 370 seats to the Socialist Revolutionary Party, and 175 for the Bolsheviks. The Assembly met for 13 hours, from 4 pm to 5 am, on 18–19 January 1918 (5–6 January, Old Style). Early in the morning, when the guard was 'tired', the Assembly was dissolved never to meet again. Thus Russia's first major experiment in democracy ended in a dismal failure. Three years of brutal Civil War ended in a Bolshevik victory, and the stage was set for one of the greatest experiments in political and social engineering in history. The dominant rule of the Communist Party was now established by Lenin, and once victory in the Civil War of 1918–20 was assured, development became the priority of Soviet power rather than more general emancipatory goals. For Joseph Stalin, who after a struggle following Lenin's death in 1924 achieved dictatorial power, accelerated industrialization became the over-riding aim, accompanied by the intensification of coercion that peaked in the

Table 1.1   *Tsarist, Soviet and Russian leaders*

Date	Name of leader
1894–17	Nicholas II
1917–24	Vladimir Il'ich Lenin
1924–53	Joseph Vissarionovich Stalin
1953–64	Nikita Sergeevich Khrushchev
1964–82	Leonid Il'ich Brezhnev
1982–84	Yurii Vladimirovich Andropov
1984–85	Konstantin Ustinovich Chernenko
1985–91	Mikhail Sergeevich Gorbachev
1991–99	Boris Nikolaevich Yeltsin
2000–08	Vladimir Vladimirovich Putin
2008–12	Dmitry Anatolevich Medvedev
2012–	Vladimir Vladimirovich Putin

terror of the 1930s. Victory in the Great Patriotic War of 1941–45 over Nazi Germany and its allies appeared to vindicate all the sacrifices of the early Soviet period, yet the prevalence of terror remained.

A first step towards destalinization was taken following Stalin's death in 1953 by his successor, Nikita Khrushchev, in his 'Secret Speech' of 25 February 1956 at the Twentieth Party Congress. Khrushchev provided a devastating critique of the man – Stalin – but failed to give a systemic critique of how he had been able to commit so many crimes for so long. During the long reign of Leonid Brezhnev (1964–82) the question of the political renewal of the Soviet system was placed firmly on the back burner. The Prague Spring in Czechoslovakia in 1968 tried to introduce 'socialism with a human face', but the attempt to renew the communist system by establishing a more humane and democratic form of socialism was crushed by Soviet tanks in August of that year. The attempt to establish a new form of 'reform socialism' raised issues that would later be taken up by Gorbachev, but by then it was too late. Instead, the last years of Brezhnev's rule gave way to what later was called the period of stagnation (*zastoi*) as the high hopes of the period of *détente* with the West gave way to an intensified and extremely dangerous renewed phase of the Cold War.

Already in 1983 Yuri Andropov, who had headed the KGB since 1967 and then briefly took over as General Secretary of the CPSU between Brezhnev's death in November 1982 and his own death in February 1984, posed the fundamental issue: 'We do not know the country we live in'. Andropov's response was a programme of 'authoritarian modernization', including the intensification of labour discipline, the struggle against corruption and the restoration of a more ascetic form of communist morality. On Andropov's death, the Brezhnevite Konstantin Chernenko managed to claw his way to power for a brief period despite his many illnesses. Chernenko's death in March 1985 finally allowed a new generation to assume the reins of leadership.

For 74 years, between 1917 and 1991, the Soviet Union sought to create an alternative social order based on its own interpretation of Marxist thinking combined with a Leninist understanding of the need for a dominant party. The Soviet system endured far longer than most of its early critics thought possible, but ultimately in 1991 came crashing down. The legacy of the failed experiment lives on in Russia today. The Union of Soviet Socialist Republics (USSR) was established in December 1922 as a union of allegedly sovereign republics to give political form to the diversity of the new republic's peoples and nations, and this was then given juridical form in the adoption of the Soviet Union's first constitution in January 1924. The system worked as long as there was a force standing outside the ethno-federal framework, the All-Union Communist Party (Bolsheviks) (VKP(b)), renamed the Communist Party of the Soviet Union (CPSU) at the Nineteenth Party Congress in 1952. With the launching of *perestroika* (restructuring) by the new General Secretary of the CPSU, Mikhail Gorbachev, in 1985, the Party gradually lost its integrative capacity as its own internal coherence dissolved, precipitating by late 1991 the disintegration of the state. In other words, there was a two-fold process, each with its own distinct logic but devastating when they came together, namely the *dissolution* of the communist system and the *disintegration* of the country.

Perestroika: from rationalization to disintegration

The appointment of a reforming General Secretary of the CPSU in March 1985 set in motion a period of 'transition' that continues to this day. Even though Gorbachev came to power as Andropov's protégé, his programme of reform quickly transcended even a residual notion of 'authoritarian modernization'. In domestic politics full-scale reforms were adopted, while at the same time he sought to put an end to the Cold War with the West, a struggle that he increasingly considered both futile and damaging for all concerned. Gorbachev came to power with a clear sense that the old way of governing the Soviet Union could no longer continue, but his plans for change swiftly came up against some hard realities. He achieved some significant success in democratizing the Soviet system, but by 1991 the communist order was dissolving and the country disintegrating.

On a visit to Canada in May 1983, Gorbachev and the Soviet ambassador, Alexander Yakovlev (who was later to play a large part in shaping the reforms) argued that 'We cannot continue to live in this way'

(Remnick 1993: 294–5). Gorbachev came to power committed to modernizing the Soviet system. In the space of six years, perestroika moved through five main stages: initial attempts to *rationalize* the system included some ambitious economic goals, a programme known as 'acceleration' (*uskorenie*); the focus then moved to a phase of *liberalization*, including the rapid development of *glasnost* (openness), in which the country's tragic past was exposed in all its savagery and glory; fundamental political questions began to be addressed in the next phase known as *democratization* (*demokratizatsiya*), which began to transform the society and polity through relatively free and fair elections and the creation of a genuine legislature freed from CPSU control; but all this began to provoke the *dissolution* of the foundations of the communist order, as its past was discredited and the basis of its rule delegitimized; culminating in 1991 in a final stage of *disintegration* of the country itself. Once changes began they could not be limited by regime-led reform, and pressure for radical renewal became overwhelming. The attempt in August 1991 by a group of conservatives to hold back the tide of change precipitated the result that they had sought to avert: the total dissolution of the communist system of government and, by the end of the year, the disintegration of the USSR.

Gorbachev did not come to power with a clear set of policies; but he did have an attitude towards change to which he remained committed to the bitter end. He intended to achieve a modernization of the communist system through perestroika, and within that framework launched what he called a 'revolution within the revolution' to save the system and not to destroy it. Gorbachev understood that the system was suffering from major problems, including declining economic growth rates, social decay, excessive secrecy in scientific and political life, and the degeneration of the ruling elite into a venal and incompetent class. Gorbachev never repudiated the basic idea that the communist system remained a viable, and in some ways a superior, system to capitalist democracy. His aim was to provide Soviet communism with the dynamism enjoyed by capitalism, but without its defects. He certainly never set out to undermine what was called the 'leading role' of the Communist Party or to destroy the planned economy. Perestroika, he insisted, was 'prompted by awareness that the potential of socialism has been underutilized' (Gorbachev 1987: 10).

In the economic sphere he got off on the wrong foot right away: the policy of acceleration sought to achieve economic transformation and increased output at the same time, and in the event was unable to gain the long-term achievement of either. This was accompanied by an anti-alcohol campaign that deprived the country of nearly one-third of tax revenues. Equally, *glasnost* was intended at first not to be freedom of speech but to expose the failings of a corrupt bureaucracy, and thus to strengthen the Soviet system. However, openness soon became a devastating search for the truth about Leninist and Stalinist repression and took on a life of its own, escaping from the constraints that Gorbachev had initially intended.

Gorbachev's own views about the past were filtered through a romantic Leninism, believing in a supposedly more democratic and evolutionary late Leninist model of the New Economic Policy of the 1920s. By the end of 1987 *demokratizatsiya* (democratization) came to the fore, with the gradual introduction of multi-candidate elections accompanied by a relaxation of the Leninist 'ban on factions', the formation of groups in the Communist Party. Gorbachev's own views at this time were eloquently developed in his book *Perestroika: New Thinking for Our Country and the World* (1987), in which he talked of perestroika as a revolution both from above and below. The 'from below' element was by now taking hold in the form of thousands of 'informal' associations, representing the rebirth of an independent civil society.

The changes begun by Gorbachev began to out-run his ability to control them. The proliferation of *neformaly* (unofficial social associations) and an independent press reflected a distinctive type of negative popular mobilization against the old regime that proved very difficult to channel into positive civic endeavour. The establishment of the Democratic Union on 9 May 1988 marked the beginning of the renewed era of multiparty politics, but its radical anti-communism signalled that Gorbachev's attempts to constrain and control political pluralism within the framework of 'reform communism' would fail and the communist order would dissolve. In some non-Russian republics the informal movement took the form of popular fronts, with Sajudis in Lithuania one of the largest representing aspirations for national autonomy and, later, independence. Once the genies of political pluralism and national self-affirmation were out of the bottle, they would take on a life of their own.

The high point of Gorbachev's hopes that a humane and democratic socialism could replace the moribund system that he inherited was the Nineteenth Party Conference in June–July 1988, where he outlined a programme of democratic political change and a new role for the USSR in the world. Soon after, in September, institutional changes weakened the role of the Party *apparatus*, and constitutional changes in November created a new two-tier parliament, with a large Congress of People's Deputies meeting twice a year selecting a working Supreme Soviet. The first elections to this body took place in March 1989, and revealed the depths of the unpopularity of Party rule. The early debates of the parliament riveted the nation, as problems were openly discussed for the first time in decades. The Congress stripped the Communist Party of its constitutionally entrenched 'leading role' in March 1990, and at the same time

Gorbachev was elected to the new post of president of the USSR. His failure to stand in a national ballot, and thus demonstrably gain the support of the people, was a fundamental mistake. Lacking a popular mandate, he was sidelined by those who did – above all Boris Yeltsin, who became head of the Russian Congress of People's Deputies in May 1990 and then went on to face a popular ballot in June 1991 to become Russia's first president.

What was called the 'nationalities question' now threatened the integrity of the country. Although Gorbachev was responsive to calls for greater autonomy for the 15 union republics making up the USSR, he had no time for any talk of independence. Through an increasingly desperate attempt to negotiate a new Union Treaty Gorbachev hoped to transform what was in effect a unitary state into a genuinely confederal community of nations. These hopes were dashed by Lithuania's declaration of independence on 11 March 1990, followed by that of Georgia and other republics in 1991. In foreign affairs, Gorbachev advanced the idea of 'new political thinking' (NPT), based on the notion of interdependence and a new cooperative relationship with the West. On a visit to the European Parliament in Strasbourg in September 1988, he talked of the establishment of a 'common European home', but it was not clear what form this would take. By 1989, the Eastern European countries in the Soviet bloc took Gorbachev at his word when he called for change and, from the autumn of that year, one after another of the communist regimes collapsed. The fall of the Berlin Wall in November 1989 marks the symbolic end of Soviet power in Eastern Europe, deeply affecting a KGB operative in the German Democratic Republic at the time, Vladimir Putin. Gorbachev facilitated the unification of Germany, although he is much criticized for failing to guarantee in treaty form the demilitarized status of the eastern part of the new country and of Eastern Europe in general. The enlargement of NATO to fill the perceived security vacuum would be one of the most controversial issues of the post-communist era.

At home, resistance to Gorbachev's policies grew to the point that a group prepared to seize power in a coup. The specific issue was the planned signing of the new Union Treaty on 20 August 1991, but the plotters were also concerned about economic disintegration and the loss of political control. For three days in August (19–21) Gorbachev was isolated in his dacha in Foros in the Crimea, while his nemesis, Boris Yeltsin, emerged much strengthened. Yeltsin had been elected president of Russia with 57 per cent of the vote on 12 June 1991, and thus he had the popular legitimacy to speak for the country. The image of Yeltsin standing on a tank outside the Russian White House (the seat of its government) has come to symbolize the high point of unity between the people and the Russian leadership. In the days following the coup, Yeltsin put an end to Communist rule by banning the Party in Russia. Attempts to save the Soviet Union in the last months of 1991 failed. The pressure for increased sovereignty for republics grew into demands for independence, and following the creation of the Commonwealth of Independent States (CIS) on 7–8 December, comprising Russia, Ukraine and Belarus, the USSR was clearly on its last legs. The CIS was broadened on 21 December to include most (with the exception of the Baltic republics and Georgia) former Soviet states. Gorbachev formally resigned as president on 25 December 1991, and on 31 December the USSR formally ceased to exist.

Gorbachev's reform of the Soviet system provoked its demise. The debate over whether the Soviet Union could have been reformed while remaining recognisably communist continues to this day (Cohen 2004). Gorbachev's perestroika clearly showed the system's evolutionary potential, but this was an evolution that effectively meant the peaceful transcendence of the system it was meant to save. From one angle, Gorbachev's reforms were a great success. By 1991, the country had become relatively democratic, staging the freest and fairest elections that the country has seen to this day, it was moving towards becoming a market economy, the union was changing into a confederation of sovereign states, and the Cold War had been overcome largely by Soviet efforts. However, the terminal crisis of the system in 1991 revealed deep structural flaws in Gorbachev's conception of reform and in the system's capacity for change while remaining recognisably communist in orientation. Gorbachev remained remarkably consistent in his commitment to a humane democratic socialism with a limited market in a renewed federation of Soviet states. However, his attempts to constrain the process of change within the framework of his preconceived notions soon crashed against some harsh realities: the aspirations for independence in a number of republics, notably of Estonia, Latvia and Lithuania, forcibly incorporated into the USSR by Stalin; the inherent instability of a semi-marketized system – it either had to be one thing or another, a planned or a market economy; and ultimately the lack of popular support for any socialism, irrespective of how humane or democratic it might have become. The attempt to reform the Soviet system exposed its many contradictions, and these ultimately destroyed the system and the country.

Post-communist Russia: the Yeltsin years

Russia entered the twenty-first century and the new millennium a very different country from the one that had entered the twentieth. The tsarist empire had disintegrated, the autocracy had been overthrown, the Soviet communist system had been and gone, and the USSR had also disintegrated leaving 15 separate successor republics. Independent Russia for the first time developed as something akin to a nation state rather than an as empire or part of a confederation. It was formally the 'continuer' state to the Soviet Union, and thus bore responsibility for the earlier state's treaty and debt obligations, but it also inherited a permanent seat in the United Nations Security Council (UNSC) and the nuclear weapons of the whole union. The economy was severely distorted by the Soviet planned economy and lacked private ownership of the means of production and the legal framework for a market order. Above all, the country now engaged in an extraordinary act of political reconstitution intended to establish a liberal democratic system. Democratic politics, defined as the procedural contest for political power and governmental accountability to a freely elected legislature and subordinate to the rule of law, accompanied by a public sphere of debate, criticism and information exchange, had finally arrived in Russia. Whether the so-called transition actually achieved democracy is another question, and one to which we shall return.

The Yeltsin administration was committed to Russia becoming a democratic market state allied with the advanced Western nations and integrated into the world economy. There was far less agreement, however, on how these three goals – democratization, marketization and international integration – were to be achieved. Bitter debates raged throughout the 1990s over all three, and aspects of these controversies will be discussed in later chapters of this book. On one thing, however, there was broad agreement: the borders of the Russia that emerged as an independent state in 1991 should not be changed, however unfair and arbitrary many considered them to be. Some 25 million ethnic Russians found themselves scattered across the 14 other newly independent states, yet Yeltsin's refusal to exploit the real and imagined grievances of the Russian diaspora to gain cheap political capital must forever stand as one of his major achievements (for a general review of Yeltsin's leadership, see Aron 2000; Colton 2008). Politics in the post-communist era would be in *Russia*, and not in some mythical re-established Soviet Union in whatever guise.

The nature of these *politics* is less clear. For the first two years following independence, Russian politics was wracked by the struggle to adopt a new constitution (Andrews 2002; Sakwa 2008a: chapter 3). The two-tier parliament that Russia inherited from the Soviet Union proved unworkable, and ultimately provoked an armed confrontation between the Congress of People's Deputies and the president in October 1993. Yeltsin sent in the tanks to dissolve the recalcitrant parliament, an event that stamped the mark of Cain on all subsequent developments. Yeltsin exploited the disarray among his opponents to strengthen the powers of the presidency, and the constitution was finally adopted in December 1993 in what set the pattern for flawed ballots. A new legislature was also elected, which in subsequent elections came to be dominated by the reconstituted Communists. Russia now gained a degree of political stability, although the legitimacy of the new polity was questioned because of the violence accompanying its birth and the flawed elections through which it was constituted. The constitution, nevertheless, is a fundamentally liberal document, proclaiming a range of freedoms that would be expected of a liberal democratic state, although the respective powers between parliament and president remain unbalanced. The presidency effectively stands outside the formal description of the separation of powers, and many of the ills of Russian democracy are ascribed to the excessively strong executive often dubbed 'super-presidential' (Fish 2001, 2005).

The presidency emerged as the guarantor not only of the constitutional order (as stated in the constitution), but also of a reform process that under Yeltsin was driven forwards with a single-mindedness that at times threatened to undermine democracy itself (Reddaway and Glinski 2001). This was an inverted type of 'Bolshevik' radicalism, seeking to establish the foundations of capitalist democracy in the shortest possible time. Fearing the revenge of the Communists, state property was disbursed in a chaotic process that did indeed create a new class of owners, but many deserved the title of 'oligarch' rather than entrepreneur. The pattern was set of entwined economic and political power that remains to this day, fostering corruption and a neo-Soviet economic statism. This was most vividly in evidence when it came to elections. Fearing that neo-communists and other opponents of moves towards the market and international integration would come to power in the 1996 presidential elections, Yeltsin toyed with the idea of cancelling them altogether. Instead, he drew on the resources of his new oligarch friends and launched an extraordinarily expensive propaganda barrage that propelled him to office for a second term. Later, President Dmitri Medvedev conceded that Yeltsin had not really won the election against his Communist opponent, Gennadii Zyuganov, but at the time no one was in a position to do anything about it. Although in ill-health for much of the time, Yeltsin dominated politics to the end of the decade (McFaul 2001).

Although Yeltsin formally remained committed to Russia's democratic development, several features undermined his ambition. The first was the unhealthy penetration of economic interests into the decision-making process. Rapid and chaotic privatization from the early 1990s gave birth to a new class of powerful economic magnates, the oligarchs. Their support for Yeltsin's re-election in 1996 brought them into the centre of the political process, and gave rise to the creation of what was known as the 'family', a mix of Yeltsin family members, politicians and oligarchs.

Most notorious of them was Boris Berezovsky, who used political influence as a major economic resource. Many others at this time exploited insider knowledge to gain economic assets for a fraction of their real worth. It was in these years that the empires were built of Mikhail Khodorkovsky (the Yukos oil company), Roman Abramovich (with Berezovsky at the head of Sibneft), Vladimir Potanin (Norilsk Nickel), Vladimir Gusinsky (the Media-Most banking and media empire), and many others (Fortescue 2006). Their heyday were the years between the presidential election of 1996 and the partial default of August 1998, and thereafter oligarchical power as such waned, although as individuals they remained important players.

The second feature was the exaggerated power of the presidency. Granted extensive authority by the 1993 constitution as part of a deliberate institutional design intended to ensure adequate powers for the executive to drive through reform, the presidency lacked adequate constraints. Too many decisions were taken by small groups of unaccountable individuals, notably in the case of the decision to launch the first Chechen war in December 1994. We will return to this question below, but associated with that is the third problem, the weakness of mechanisms of popular accountability. Although far from powerless, the State Duma (see Chapter 3) is not able effectively to hold the executive to account. This is related to the weakness of the development of the electoral (Chapter 4) and party system (Chapter 5). The fourth issue is the question of the succession. While all incumbent leaders try to perpetuate their power by ensuring a transfer to favourable successors, in Yeltsin's case the stakes were particularly high: he feared that a new president could mean a change of system in its entirety, with the possibility of personal sanctions being taken against him and his family. For this reason the Kremlin engaged in a long search for an individual who would ensure continuity and the personal inviolability of Russia's 'first president' (as he liked to style himself) and his associates.

Putin: the politics of stability

They found this guarantee in the person of Vladimir Putin. He was nominated prime minister on 9 August 1999, acting president on Yeltsin's resignation on 31 December, formally elected for his first term on 14 March 2000, for a second term on 14 March 2004, becoming prime minister on 8 May 2008 under the presidency of Dmitri Medvedev, and was re-elected to the presidency in March 2012. Putin respected the letter of the constitution, which stipulates a maximum of two *successive* terms, and now with the gap he was allowed two more terms, each now extended to six years. Theoretically, Putin could remain in power until 2024, at which point he would still only be 72 years old. Putin's accession to the presidency in 2000 did not at first represent a rupture in the constitutional system inherited from Yeltsin, but changes in leadership style, policy orientations and ideological innovations effectively marked the beginning of a distinct era. Putin's programme of 'normal' politics, accompanied by attempts to build a state based on 'order' and 'stability', represented a new stage in Russia's endlessly unforgiving attempts to come to terms with modernity (Sakwa 2008b).

Putin's approach was characterized by the pursuit of a politics of stability. The sharp polarization that attended Yeltsin's rule gave way to an explicitly consensual and 'centrist' approach. The nature of this centrism was not simply an avoidance of the extremes of left and right but sought to generate a transformative centrism on which a new developmental model for the country could be based. The new approach allowed the regime to reassert its predominance while establishing a framework for socio-economic transformation to continue. The regime adopted a pragmatic and technocratic approach that allowed society to get on with its business as long as it did not challenge the leadership's tutelary claim that it knew what was best for the country. A relatively coherent and durable new political order emerged.

While Putin was undoubtedly a reformer, his approach to change was no longer one of systemic transformation but of system management. In other words, he was a transactional rather than transformative leader. His speeches and interventions are peppered with the concept of 'normality'. The concept of normality suggests a certain naturalness of political debate and choice of policy options, relatively unconstrained by the formal imposition of ideological norms. This represented a type of depoliticization, reducing structured political choice and allowing the regime to rule on behalf of society. Putin's strategic goal of modernization of the economy was accompanied by the attempt to consolidate society. Although these goals were not always compatible, a common principle underlay both: the attempt to avoid extremes in policy and to neutralize extremist political actors. Putin's rule was technocratic and based on the exercise of administrative power. Putin's politics of stability was characterized by the refusal to accept changes to the constitution, the acceptance of the privatizations of the Yeltsin years, and the explicit repudiation of revolution as an effective form of achieving positive political change.

This echoed Putin's sentiments voiced in his *Russia at the Turn of the Millennium* in December 1999, where he noted that the communist revolutionary model of development not only had not delivered the goods, but could not have done so (Putin 2000: 212). Although regretting the breakup of the Soviet Union (but not the dissolution of the Communist system),

Putin never considered the restoration of anything resembling the USSR as remotely possible, let alone desirable. In his 25 April 2005 address to the Federal Assembly he called the break-up of the Soviet Union 'the greatest geopolitical disaster' of the twentieth century and a 'tragedy for the Russian people', but this did not mean that he sought to restore the old state. At the heart of Putin's politics of stability was the attempt to reconcile the various phases of Russian history, especially over the last century: the Tsarist, the Soviet and the democratic eras. In foreign policy, Putin insisted that Russia should be treated as a 'normal' great power. He insisted that Russia's foreign policy should serve the country's economic interests, a policy that was evident in debates over the union of Russia and Belarus.

At the heart of Putin's leadership was the reassertion of the constitutional prerogatives of the state (what he called the 'dictatorship of law'), accompanied by the struggle to ensure that that the regime did not fall under the influence of societal actors. In particular, the 'oligarchs' under Yeltsin had exercised what was perceived to be undue influence; this was now repudiated. Equally, the independent regional governors were reined in, and between 2005 and 2012 they were appointed by the Kremlin. The gap between the regime and the state became increasingly apparent as the 'dual state' became consolidated. The distinction between the constitutional state and the administrative regime is central to understand the contradictions of the Putin system (Sakwa 2010a, 2011). Putin claimed to be strengthening the state, but in practice this meant intensifying the tutelary prerogatives of the administrative regime. The regime increasingly became insulated from all political actors, including independent political parties and parliament. Accountability mechanisms were weakened, and what was gained in the ability of the government to act as an independent force was lost in its lack of interaction with society.

Putin's supporters advance the argument that stability and security should come before democracy. Russia, they suggested, should not be expected quickly to achieve a high-quality democracy, given its authoritarian past, its political culture and the weakness of civil society. Following the Beslan school massacre of 1–3 September 2004, Putin on 13 September announced a range of reforms to the state system, including the appointment of governors and wholly proportional parliamentary elections. The return to the themes of 'authoritarian modernization' reflected the intensification of 'managed democracy', the term used to describe the tutelary politics that had emerged under Yeltsin. Although Russia had formally gained all the institutions of a capitalist democracy, the spirit of pluralism and accountability was lacking. Democratization theory often assumes that once the authoritarian burden is lifted, society will automatically spring back into some sort of democratic shape.

However, in the Russian case the 'totalitarian' experience had devastated civil society and the foundations of liberalism, hence society itself has to become an object of the transition process. This tends to justify the displacement of sovereignty from the people to some agency that can carry out the necessary transitional measures, theoretically on behalf of the people who are considered not yet fit to govern themselves. In the Russian case this was the elite group around Yeltsin, and under Putin the administrative regime.

The term 'sovereign democracy' came to the fore in the period following the Beslan hostage crisis, but this was only part of a larger debate about democracy and Russia's place in the international system The key point was to achieve state sovereignty in the international system, accompanied by what Vladislav Surkov (at the time responsible for the management of political affairs) called the democratization of international relations (Surkov 2006: 31–2). By now the economic situation had improved, with the country registering an average of 7 per cent annual growth throughout Putin's first two terms as president, the standard of living was rising, poverty decreasing and Russia was becoming a consumer society on the Western model. The growing confidence based on domestic economic and political stabilization and windfall energy revenues was, paradoxically, accompanied by a deep-rooted insecurity about Russia's international position and domestic integrity. The 'orange' revolution in Ukraine in late 2004 saw massive movement that forced a third round run-off presidential contest between Viktor Yushchenko, favoured by the West, and Viktor Yanukovich, the candidate promoted by Russia. The Kremlin was deeply alarmed by what it considered to be the West's use of civil society to force regime change, and thus clamped down on Russian NGOs and popular mobilization.

An important aspect of Putin's politics was the tension between stability and order. This was a feature of Brezhnev's rule that in the end gave way to stagnation. Stability is the short-term attempt to achieve political and social stabilization without having resolved the underlying problems and contradictions besetting society. Thus Brezhnev refused to make the hard choices that could have threatened the regime's precarious political stability. Order in this context is something that arises when society, economy and political system are in some sort of balance. To a large extent an ordered society operates according to spontaneous processes, whereas in a system based on the politics of stability administrative measures tend to predominate. As Samuel Huntington (1968) noted, political order in changing societies sometimes requires the firm hand of the military or some other force that is not itself subordinate to democratic politics. Putin on a number of occasions explicitly sought to distance himself from this sort of tutelary politics, yet overall the *leitmotif* of his leadership was the technocratic assertion that the regime knows best. To achieve this, a system of 'managed democracy' applied administrative resources to manage the political process, undermining the spontaneous interaction of pluralistic political and social forces. This was in evidence as Putin managed the succession in 2007–08 to allow Medvedev to assume the presidency. The aim was continuity, and this was confirmed by Putin taking up the office of prime minister.

In 2008, Medvedev assumed the presidency, and although for the duration of his four years in the Kremlin he was constrained by the 'tandem' format of rule – since Putin took over as prime minister – he was nevertheless able to articulate a less tutelary approach to politics. Medvedev condemned 'legal nihilism', and stressed a rather more liberal path towards modernization. Medvedev rejected the term sovereign democracy, insisting that democracy did not need any adjectives. His article 'Russia, Forward!' of September 2009 provided a devastating critique. Russian social life was characterized as a semi-Soviet social order, 'one that unfortunately combines all the shortcomings of the Soviet system and all the difficulties of contemporary life' (Medvedev 2009). The fundamental question was whether Russia, with its 'primitive economy' and 'chronic corruption', had a future. Medvedev attacked not Putin but the system that Putin represented, a balancing act that blunted his message. This pusillanimity characterized his entire presidency, but although it is now common to disparage his achievements, the principles enunciated by Medvedev – for greater political pluralism, economic competitiveness and international engagement – are challenges that Russia objectively faces, whoever the leader.

The negative popular reaction to the 'castling' move of 24 September 2011 made this all the more visible. On that day it was announced that Putin planned to return to the presidency, swapping places with Medvedev, who would become prime minister. Russian politics appeared to have become an elite affair, with citizens little more than bystanders. The frustration burst out into mass demonstrations following what was seen as blatant fraud in the parliamentary elections in December, forcing the regime to move towards political liberalization. The registration of political parties became much easier, direct gubernatorial elections were restored, the electoral system was once again reformed and a degree of competitiveness returned to Russian politics. In other words, the programme enunciated by Medvedev was being implemented, although in very different circumstances to that originally envisaged. Following Putin's return to the Kremlin in May 2012 there was a period of 'tightening of the screws', but in the end mild political reform continued. Society had changed as a result of the prosperity of the Putin years, and an increasingly powerful popular constituency had emerged demanding inclusion in the management of public affairs, above all through free and fair elections.

Conclusion

The scope of transformation in post-communist Russia has been unprecedented. A monolithic society was converted into a pluralistic one, a planned economy was reoriented towards the market, a new nation was born, and the state rejoined the international community. None of these processes is complete, and by definition never can be. The reform process itself generated new phenomena that raise questions about the received wisdom of the political sciences and economics. There has been rapid divergence in the fate of post-communist countries, with the majority of Central and East European countries joining the European Union in May 2004 with a second wave in January 2007 and Croatia entering in June 2013. The 12 former Soviet states that at one time or another were grouped in the CIS look increasingly different from each other, although none has been able to establish a consolidated democracy.

The 'third wave' transitions, to use Huntington's (1991) term to describe the mass extinction of authoritarian regimes following the fall of the dictatorship in Portugal in April 1974, prompted a renewed interest in problems of democratization. The dissolution of communism encouraged political scientists to look again at the theoretical literature on democratization and to compare the transitions in the post-communist bloc with earlier transitions in Latin America and Southern Europe (O'Donnell *et al.* 1986). The insights garnered in the study of the democratization process elsewhere provide a theoretical framework to study the problem of the reconstitution of central political authority on principles of democratic accountability. The degree to which this literature has anything to offer when political regime change is accompanied by economic transformation, state and nation building and societal reconstruction remains a moot point (Bunce 1995).

The view that democracy is the inevitable outcome of post-communist transition is clearly mistaken. There is far too much that is contingent in processes of systemic change to allow any firm teleological view to be convincing. While about a hundred countries have set out on the path of democracy during the 'third wave', at most three dozen have achieved functioning democracies (Carothers 2002). The contrary view – that the legacy of communist and even pre-communist authoritarian political cultures, economies and social structures doom the attempt to build democracies where there had at best been weak traditions of pluralism, toleration and political competition – is equally misleading. Deterministic views of democratization leave out of account national political cultures, level of economic development, strategic concerns, leadership choices and elite configurations, economic dependencies and proximity to zones of advanced capitalist democratic development (above all the European Union). Rather than a *teleological* view about the inevitability of democracy, the *genealogical* approach takes into account concrete questions of political order, constitutionalism, state building, social structure and social justice, interacting with the practice of democratic norms and good governance (Sakwa 2012). Despite the efforts of political scientists, there is no agreement on one single factor that determines the success or failure of a democratization process.

The relationship between liberalism, democracy and constitutional order remains contested in the post-communist context. Instead of government being accountable to the representative institutions of the people and constrained by the constitutional state and its legal instruments, the government assumed an independent political existence. It is at this point that a politically responsible and accountable government becomes a regime; formal institutions are unable to constrain political actors and informal practices predominate (North 1990). The outward forms of the constitutional state are preserved, but legality and accountability are subverted. A set of para-constitutional behavioural norms predominate that, while not formally violating the letter of the constitution, undermine the spirit of constitutionalism. Para-constitutional behaviour gets things done, but ultimately proves counter-productive because it relies on the personal intervention of the leadership rather than the self-sustaining practices of a genuinely constitutional system. The regime is constrained by the constitutional state, but the system lacks an effective mechanism of accountability.

The contrast between the informal power relations established within the framework of regime politics, on the one hand, and the institutionalized competitive and accountable politics characteristic of a genuinely constitutional democratic state characterizes Russian politics. Particularistic informal practices have been in tension with the proclaimed principles of the universal and impartial prerogatives of the constitutional state. Under Yeltsin, personalized leadership came to the fore, with the power system and its oligarchical allies operating largely independently from the formal rules of the political system outlined in the constitution. Behind the formal façade of democratic politics conducted at the level of the state, the regime considered itself largely free from genuine democratic accountability and popular oversight. These features, as Hahn (2002) stresses, were accentuated by the high degree of institutional and personal continuity between the Soviet and 'democratic' political systems. A party-state ruled up to 1991, but the emergence of a regime-state in the 1990s created a system that perpetuated in new forms the arbitrariness of the old order. Under Putin, the regime-state consolidated its power but, as a result of changes in society and the elite, came under increasing challenge. Putin in his third term has to find more inclusive forms of political management, or his presidency could find itself the target of a popular movement of the sort that we have seen in the 'Arab spring' since 2011.

A democratic transition is usually considered to be over when democracy becomes the only game in town and where there is 'definiteness of rules and indefiniteness of outcomes'. Russia's transition is indeed over, but instead of democratic consolidation Russia's 'managed democracy' reversed the formula to ensure 'definiteness of outcomes and indefiniteness of rules'. Nevertheless, the scope for democratic development in Russia remains open. The government does seek to deliver a set of public goods, and it does not appeal to an extra-democratic logic to achieve them. The regime is legitimate precisely because it claims to be democratic. Putin's government is undoubtedly considered legitimate by the great majority of the Russian people, as evidenced by his convincing electoral victories and consistently high personal ratings. However, too much is settled not in the framework of competitive politics but within the confines of the power system, leaving government only weakly accountable to society and its representatives. Nevertheless, the sinews of constitutionality are developing, and politics is not yet entirely subsumed into the administrative order. It will take an active citizenry and political pressure from below and courage from the leadership to ensure that the promise of Russia's democratic development is fulfilled.

Chapter 2

The Hegemonic Executive

JOHN P. WILLERTON

The May 2012 return of Vladimir Putin to the presidency (with Dmitri Medvedev selected as prime minister) constituted the return of Russia's paramount leader to the country's top executive and decision-making position. Putin reassumed the presidency and immediately asserted himself as a strong and confident leader who would continue the policy programme and assertive posturing that had characterized his first presidency (2000–08). Putin had served four years (2008–12) as Russia's prime minister, the country's number two executive position, with a managerial portfolio entailing a vast range of complex governmental supervisory responsibilities. His tenure as prime minister was marked by a prominent public profile and the forceful promotion of policies that had been the hallmark of his own presidency. More than a year before his March 2012 election to the presidency, Putin began to assert himself on issues that generally fell within the purview of the president (most notably on Western intervention in Libya). If it was difficult to find a real difference in public posturing between Prime Minister Putin and President Medvedev, their points of emphasis and rhetorical style varied, and ever stronger suggestions emerged that Putin might return to the top executive position. Medvedev's September 2011 public endorsement of Putin to be the presidential candidate of their platform party, United Russia, signified that Putin would once again, both *de facto* and *de jure*, lead the governing Kremlin team and the entire country.

Russia has been led since 2000 by a large and varied constellation of political-elite elements closely associated with Vladimir Putin. Putin is arguably the only person who could hold together and manage a diverse coalition that includes interests and officials who might otherwise be at odds with each other. Coming to power in the wake of the economic morass and political–bureaucratic infighting of the 1990s, the Putin Kremlin team constructed a coherent domestic and foreign policy programme that earned Putin considerable public support throughout his first presidency. Indeed, supporters had pushed for a reform of the 1993 Constitution's two-consecutive-term limit to permit Putin to remain in

19

the presidency. But in 2007, Putin, bowing to constitutional limits, nominated his trusted protégé and then first Deputy Prime Minister, Dmitri Medvedev, to be the candidate of his platform party, United Russia. Putin's choice was not universally hailed among Kremlin team and United Russia members, and there was little doubt that Medvedev would struggle to lead a diverse coalition that was in fact based on his patron's career and political interests. But to no one's surprise, Medvedev, enjoying both Putin's endorsement and all the advantages that accrued to the country's governing party, easily won the March 2008 presidential election with over 71 per cent of the popular vote.

The four-year Medvedev–Putin 'tandemocracy' entailed a continuation of the Putin programme, albeit with Medvedev's presidential manner involving a softened rhetoric and seemingly more Western leadership style. This rhetoric and style left both opposition forces and Westerners more sanguine about the prospects for policy change, and in both the domestic and foreign arenas. In fact, the signature programmes of the first Putin presidency, from the four National Priority Projects (NPPs) to the Stabilization Fund, continued, even as they were adjusted to changing domestic conditions. Putin's 'dictatorship of the law' initiative was continued via Medvedev's 'legal nihilism' discussion. Essential features of the first Putin presidency, including the new tax system and revenue gathering means, the crafting of functional (balanced) budgets, reclaiming of national resources and controlling of foreign capital, were maintained or modestly adjusted. Few realities for the 2008–12 period involving Russia's domestic policies varied fundamentally from the realities of the preceding years. The same conclusion could also be drawn for Russian foreign policy, though the improved atmospherics coming from a seemingly more congenial President Medvedev cannot be denied. Overall, Prime Minister Putin's imprint was on all-important initiatives, though President Medvedev did leave a mark in his own priority areas (such as upgrading of the courts).

The first years of the second Putin presidency, from May 2012, build on the thinking and programmes of the preceding dozen years. What could be called a pro-active modernization thrust, grounded in both Soviet experience and the Russian socio-economic environment, focuses on the revitalization of Russia's military–industrial complex, with preference given to traditional economic priorities (such as the Baikal Amur and Trans-Siberian railways), but with openness to new investment foci (such as infrastructure of the Russian Far East). As highly pressing political and economic challenges had been addressed in the governing Putin team's first dozen years, new attention is given to what might be viewed as 'second tier', though important, policy concerns, including education, family, and youth issues. A more assertive foreign policy line, involving relations with former Soviet Union (FSU) states, the US, and dynamic developments in the Middle East (for example, Iran and Syria), also characterizes the second Putin presidency. Well into its second decade of governing, the Putin team is firmly in charge, with a hegemonic presidency, a powerful executive branch, and a strong federal government at the core of the twenty-first century Russian polity.

A paramount leader and the strong presidency

Vladimir Putin came to power in the complicated and troubling environment of the post-Soviet 1990s, and among the most important contributions he made to the evolution of the Russian polity was to restore the power of the presidency, the executive branch, and the federal state. In personality, leadership style and policy preferences, he proved able not only in meeting – but exceeding – public expectations, his 50 per cent approval rating at the time of his 2000 elevation to the presidency rapidly moving into the 60–70 per cent range throughout his first presidency. Indeed, Putin left the presidency in May 2008 at a remarkable 84.7 percent approval level (Itar-Tass, 30 April 2008), maintaining strong public support throughout his subsequent tenure as prime minister. Many observers noted Putin's good fortune in the timing of his first presidency, with record energy prices significantly boosting an economy that had only emerged from a lengthy depression during the 1990s. Yet at the heart of Putin's strong leadership was the reality that the institutionalized hegemonic presidency was joined with a decisive and energetic occupant: renewed state power was joined with dynamic leadership.

Putin's modest background and forceful leadership style fitted with Russian preferences in the post-Soviet era. Putin was born into a working-class family and was a product of the post-Stalinist period; he made a career in the Soviet intelligence services that entailed an elite education, travel and work abroad, and a broader awareness of both the Russian society and the outside world. His life experiences of the late Soviet and early post-Soviet periods left him subject to divergent and conflicting influences that were evident both in his rise to power and in his presidency. As an intelligence officer, Putin was well conditioned to a chain-of-command culture that emphasized loyalty and strict subordination, public order, and commitment to a strong state. Working as a key associate of the reformist St Petersburg mayor Anatolii Sobchak, however, he personally experienced the need for root and branch system change, and became sensitive to bottom-up societal pressures, notions of elite and governmental accountability, electoral procedures, and the messiness of democracy building (Hutchins 2012).

Vladimir Putin always exhibited an uncanny ability to express appreciation for past Soviet experience while simultaneously engaging post-Soviet thinking. In the run-up to his first presidential term, Putin's life and career experience provided him with a strong awareness of the complexities of system change and of governmental administration, and not only of commercial life but of civil society. Putin's institutional and policy preferences would be partly drawn from the Soviet past, but they would also rely on an evolving set of post-Soviet ideas and a willingness to make adjustments as dynamic conditions dictated. Moreover, Putin's 'trial and error' approach to policy-making bolstered his ability to adjust to dynamic domestic political and socio-economic realities. These preferences and skills have proven no less true of Putin's second presidency than of his first. Thus, the pro-active economic modernization programme of the second presidency builds on the substantial, broadly conceived reforms of the first presidential term (2000–04), while marking a more active programmatic thrust than the more tempered and piecemeal efforts of the second presidential term (2004–08). Similarly, the first presidential term expansion of state power in high-priority military–industrial sectors would contrast with the targeted privatization efforts of the second presidency.

Perspectives on Vladimir Putin, his leadership style, and his tenure both as a president and prime minister, have varied, with especially divergent judgements separating mainstream Russian elite and public perspectives from those of many Western observers. At the heart of Russian assessments have been widespread elite and public perceptions of significant domestic and foreign policy successes. Russians highlight the country's considerable economic growth, the evident rise in citizens' standard of living, and Russia's return as a major global player. Putin team initiatives reversed the conditions and developments associated with Russia's 'failing state'; the 'failing state' signifying a state that is losing its vibrancy and legitimacy as it fails to carry out the tasks or provide the services to which it is committed (Willerton, Beznosov and Carrier 2005). A combination of factors was responsible for this turnaround, but forceful political leadership must be included among them. This turnaround began and continued during the entire period since 2000, and this includes the presidencies of both Putin and Medvedev. But throughout this period, Putin was universally understood in Russia to be the country's paramount leader, and most Russians accordingly associated responsibility for policy successes with him, while Medvedev, whether as president or prime minister, was viewed as his accommodating associate. During the first presidency, Putin's modest style and 'samurai warrior' personal ethic won him considerable public sympathy (Solovyov 2008). Meanwhile, his willingness from the onset to tackle complex problems (such as taking on the influential oligarchs, beginning the process of reining in regional power barons, and crafting an intelligible tax programme), his ability to manage the bureaucracy while simultaneously strengthening the state and providing tangible returns to the population, predictably secured him consistently high marks. Indeed, the extent of Putin's authority – that is the legitimacy of his governance – was revealed in the second term (2004–08), when his government advanced unpopular reforms that trimmed the welfare state while Putin's popularity went unaffected. In the judgement of most Russians, as revealed in opinion surveys, Putin and his government delivered on most promises set out in the first presidency (leaving office with an 83 per cent approval rating according to the Levada Center).

Russians' confidence in Putin's leadership abilities continued during his four-year tenure as prime minister (2008–12), when the paramount leader maintained a high profile in tackling a wide array of domestic economic problems while presenting himself as a strong manager overseeing a diverse array of officials. Well-publicized encounters with industrial managers, high-visibility trips throughout the country, and lengthy sessions with interested publics enabled Putin to simultaneously exhibit his forceful manner and his detailed command of the wide range of issues on the country's agenda. Equally important were Putin's regular, lengthy presentations before the State Duma, not to mention his very active agenda of interactions with foreign leaders and luminaries. It is little surprise that Putin's public approval ratings were always a few ticks higher than those of President Medvedev: an important reality, since prime ministers and their governments are generally viewed much more negatively by a Russian public that lays the responsibility for most policy failings on these government authorities. Putin left the prime ministership in May 2012 with solid public approval ratings (65 per cent), a feat especially impressive when considering nearly all his predecessors failed to enjoy widespread public support upon the completion of their tenures.

Western observers' views of Putin and his leadership impact were and continue to be much more sceptical, and they often have been highly negative (e.g. Gessen 2012; Hill and Gaddy 2013). Enhanced power concentration and related decision-making 'streamlining', hallmarks of the Putin period, were seen as undercutting democratic principles, with the four-year interlude of a Medvedev presidency having no discernible impact on this over-riding Western judgement. A new corporatism enabling the state to dominate key industries was joined with the state's consolidation of control over the media and its enhanced ability to shape public opinion. Meanwhile, corruption continued to be widespread and appeared to include elements of the ruling Kremlin team itself. Putin himself had acknowledged that his regime's failure to address the country's endemic corruption had been the biggest failing of his first presidency, though Westerners questioned the seriousness of his regime's efforts. Finally, fledgling impulses for creating a Russian civil society had been undercut by the impact of the developments we have noted. Indeed, a vociferous minority of Russians would publicly express similar negative assessments of the Putin style and legacy, their opposition keenly evident in public demonstrations in Moscow and other urban centres in 2011–12. For most Western observers, the bottom line was a new authoritarianism, one that came with a more forceful foreign policy and that was grounded in Russia's re-emergence as a formidable energy-producing power (Mendras 2012).

While granting this gap in Russian and Western assessments, the Putin second presidency began with considerable domestic public support and a publicly articulated pro-active modernization programme that built on the initiatives of his first presidency while giving new attention to Russia's 'challenged regions' (such as the North Caucasus, Siberia and the Far East), social policies long needing action, a renewed emphasis on stream-lining state institutions, and revived attention to corruption. Much of Putin's thinking had been set out in a series of position papers issued during the early 2012 presidential campaign, and these – at times lengthy – expositions nicely set out a substantive framework that anticipated both the continuing and new policies of the second presidency. We give attention to these position papers and the policies that arose from them in the concluding section of this chapter, but suffice it to note that if Putin's discussion is at times surprisingly candid, it is also unapologetic and assertive. A muscular domestic political–economic programme is linked with an assertive foreign policy line, the result sure to reinforce many Russians' support and most Westerners' reservations.

Institutions of the federal executive

Russia's semi-presidential system is formally grounded in the 1993 Constitution, but its *de facto* logic stems in part from the Soviet experience, where the executive was divided between policy-making bodies housed in the Communist Party apparatus and policy-implementing bodies housed in the Soviet government. In a democratic setting, the semi-presidential system divides political responsibilities between a president (and related institutions), who is head of state and sets out the broad contours and directions of policy, and a prime minister and government, who are responsible for developing, implementing, and managing policies. Here the prime minister and other ministers who form the government are responsible to both the president and the national legislature. In most modern semi-presidential systems, it is the head of state, the president, who nominates the prime minister, who must enjoy majority support within the legislature. That support is ensured by the president nominating the leader of the majority party or coalition, with the prime minister then forming a government comprising ministers who must be approved by the legislature. The overall experience of the Putin period, from 2000 up to the present, fits with this institutional logic, with the pre-eminence of the presidency assured. The four-year Putin prime ministerial tenure, however, reveals the potential heightened importance of the head of government's position, especially when the prime minister enjoys a strong standing with the political elite and population.

The president

A vast array of institutions and officials comprise the federal executive, with the hegemonic presidency at the helm. Informal arrangements, involving various whirlpools of interest, bureaucratic elements, and groupings of personnel also structure the president's decision-making primacy. The federal presidency has been hegemonic not only because its position is constitutionally superior to that of other institutions, but because it has possessed independence and freedom of manoeuvre. Since 1992, the president, through decrees, legislative proposals, and vetoes, has been able to direct the decision-making process. While many of these formal abilities have not proven essential in the Putin period, when the president had strong elite and public support, and when his platform party dominated the parliament, they are available if needed. Meanwhile, the president is able to appoint and guide the work of the prime minister and government, with key cabinet members (such as the foreign, defence, internal affairs and justice ministers) appointed by and directly accountable to the head of state. The president is supported by a large set of agencies and officials that link him to all federal and major sub-federal institutions (see Figure 2.1).

While the Putin government did oversee some institutional changes that further bolstered the president's position (such as in nominating regional governors, rather than allowing them to be directly elected), these changes only modestly expanded the already advantageous position of the head of state. The 1993 Yeltsin Constitution specified that the president 'defines the basic directions of the domestic and foreign policy of the state', while the president also represents the country domestically and internationally (see Articles 80–93). As the head of state and commander-in-chief of the armed forces, the president has the right to declare a state of emergency and martial law, call for referendums, and even suspend the decisions of other state bodies if their actions violate the constitution or

Figure 2.1   *Major institutions of the Putin executive*

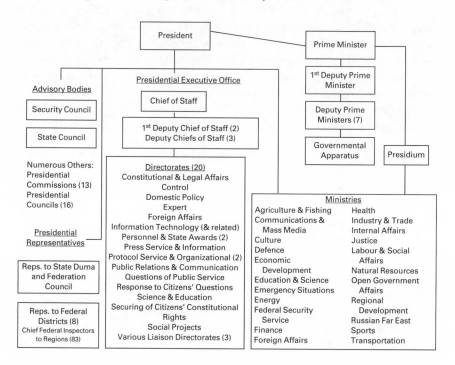

federal laws. Changes during the Putin leadership strengthened the president's ability to direct Russia's centre–periphery relations, in a country that is as vast as it is varied in its regional and ethnic composition.

Much decision-making initiative comes out of the presidential administration, but the president directs the federal government through the appointment and supervision of the prime minister and other ministers. The president, acting through the vast structure of supporting agencies, initiates legislation, reporting annually to a joint parliamentary session on his government's domestic and foreign policy. Especially Putin but also Medvedev have used such sessions, as well as annual lengthy press conferences, to promote their agendas and further consolidate their authority. Meanwhile, there are conditions under which the president can dissolve the lower house of the parliament, the State Duma, but these entail unusual circumstances that to date have not arisen. Likewise, the rival legislative branch has the formal ability to remove the president for malfeasance, but the procedures for impeachment are cumbersome and involve numerous federal bodies including the Constitutional Court and upper house of the parliament, the Federation Council. Since a two-thirds majority of the full membership of both houses is required to remove a president from office, the probability of ouster is low by any standard; the dominant position of the Putin platform party, United Russia, only further ensures the near-invulnerability of the head of state. The more compelling constraint on a president's tenure in office comes with the constitutionally mandated consecutive two-term limit, with Putin's 2008 decision to step down at this point, following President Boris Yeltsin's 1999 decision to retire after nearly two terms of his own, setting a precedent that is unlikely to change. The late 2008 Medvedev-initiated legislation to extend the presidential term to six (previously four) years means that a second two-term Putin presidency could last until 2024, making the term limit of little immediate significance.

An important, constitutionally permitted means by which the chief executive can manoeuvre unilaterally is through the issuing of presidential decrees (*ukazy*), which have the force of law. The Constitution (Art. 90) provides the president extensive leeway in issuing decrees to make institutional and policy changes, and while such decrees are inferior to laws, they are binding so long as they do not contradict the Constitution or federal laws. In the face of a massive state bureaucracy, with its numerous and often-conflicting ministries, there is a need for powerful top-down mechanisms such as presidential decrees to direct its activities. While policy-making decrees may be over-ridden by parliament, a two-thirds vote of both chambers is needed, and this is highly unlikely to occur, not only given the parliament's highly fragmented structure and the weakness of the party system, but the strength of President Putin's party, United Russia. In the past, most notably during the Yeltsin period, decrees had a significant impact on Russian politics, and Putin relied on them during his first term to advance important initiatives (such as the establishment of the country's (then) seven macro-districts and restoration of the system of presidential envoys, efforts to 'normalize' Chechnya, and energy and economic reforms). Yet as the Putin team further strengthened its position, including within the federal legislature, decrees became less critical and Kremlin initiatives were advanced through legislation. This continued during the Medvedev presidency, but even with United Russia's diminished position within the State Duma following the December 2011 elections, President Putin has advanced his agenda via legislation and not decree.

Presidential administration and advisory bodies

As Figure 2.1 reveals, a vast presidential administration supports the activities of the country's chief executive and supervises the implementation of presidential decisions. Originally built on the organizational resources of the Soviet Communist Party central apparatus, this extensive set of institutions is composed of dozens of agencies and includes approximately

3,000 full-time staff members: a number suggesting it is larger than the comparable support structure of the US president. The 20 directorates that are at the heart of the presidential administration, reorganized during the Putin presidency and continuing under Medvedev and in the second Putin presidency, reflect the decision-making and supervisory interests of the federal executive. The complex and often hidden manoeuvrings of the varied organizations and informal groups of officials constitute a sort of 'checks and balances' system within the federal executive. Since the Russian Constitution is silent on the functioning of this administration, it is up to each president to structure and manage it according to his own power and policy needs. Elite and public expectations of a chief executive being able to direct this administration – along with the federal government and the political process overall – are critical to positive evaluations of strong leadership. Occasional ruptures during the Medvedev presidency (for instance, the president's public squabble with Finance Minister Alexei Kudrin, which led to that powerful minister's September 2011 resignation) reflected the challenges of managing a large presidential team, with Medvedev's own public standing suffering as a result. Doubtless, management of the presidential administration is central to President Putin's ability to govern, but his tenure – past and present – has never entailed public evidence of team member disputes or insubordination, a reality that reinforces his authority both within the governing elite and the country.

Management of the presidential administration requires a team of reliable subordinates, and Putin has had this throughout his two presidencies. Critical is the head of the presidential administration, the president's chief of staff, who oversees both administrative and personnel matters and operates as a sort of *éminence grise* of the federal executive. Medvedev held this post during the middle of Putin's first presidency, while the current chief of staff, Sergei Ivanov, is another senior protégé who – like Medvedev – has held a variety of top positions in the governing team. Ivanov's experience and connections make him a key figure, not only in linking the president to the extensive set of institutions below, but in connecting the president to the government, Prime Minister Medvedev, and senior government officials. There is some irony in considering these juxtaposed officials, as both Ivanov and Medvedev were the leading candidates to succeed Putin to the presidency in 2008. Drawn from different elements in the Putin team (see Figure 2.2 below), Ivanov and Medvedev had divergent career paths, built associations with Putin in different ways, and have been associated with, and articulated, contrasting perspectives on Russia's development and appropriate policies: Ivanov is associated with more conservative statist views, Medvedev with more reformist Western ideas. Today they are both senior members of the governing team, with Ivanov's organizational prowess making him especially suitable to be the chief of staff, while Medvedev's managerial experience makes him an appropriate head of government.

Other top presidential administration personnel, notably the first deputy chiefs of staff, Vyacheslav Volodin and Aleksei Gromov, similarly bring significant past work experience with Putin to these senior organizational posts. Volodin has proven to be an especially important Putin protégé, bringing a straightforward and tough approach to personnel and policy matters that has enhanced team discipline with more sophisticated Kremlin manoeuvring *vis-à-vis* the opposition. Dozens of top functionaries who head directorates and agencies beneath these senior officials also bring considerable experience and ongoing work relationships with the president and prime minister.

Figure 2.1 also indicates that the federal executive includes numerous presidential representatives within most federal and sub-federal organizations, with these representatives serving as liaisons to coordinate those bodies' actions with presidential preferences. Especially notable are the presidential representatives to the eight federal districts, and the chief federal inspectors to the 83 regions, officials directly linking the federal executive to the most important administrative units of Russia's vast periphery. The federal executive also includes numerous advisory bodies that deal with selected policy areas while formally linking the president and his executive team to other institutional actors. These bodies also do not have a constitutional status, they operate at the president's pleasure, and similar to the presidential administration can be reorganized or abolished as the chief executive sees fit. Several of these bodies have now accrued some institutional history, encompass senior officials, and facilitate the president's handling of high-level policy matters. This is true of the Security Council, formalized under the 1993 Constitution, which deals with foreign and security issues and includes the prime minister, relevant ministers, and the heads of the federal districts. Meanwhile, the State Council (created in 2000) includes the heads of Russia's 80-plus regions and is the main institutional setting where regional leaders can deal directly with the president.

Prime minister and government

The president's power and authority has also been traditionally grounded in his direct influence over the prime minister and cabinet, which form the government and define the 'basic guidelines of the government's activity'. The constitution does not specify which ministries shall be formed, leaving it to the president and prime minister to make the desired choices, but it does identify the policy areas with which the government will deal. The government crafts the federal budget and implements fiscal and monetary policies. It is responsible for the conduct of the economy and has oversight of social issues. The government implements the country's foreign and defence policies, administers state property, protects private property and public order, and ensures the rule of law and civil rights.

At the government's helm stands the prime minister, who is nominated by the president and must be approved by the Duma. While the Duma can remove the government through the passage of two 'no confidence' votes within three months, there are political constraints on the parliament doing so; while the Duma for its part must be dissolved by the president if it does not approve his prime minister designate three times in a row. Traditionally, the prime minister's power is grounded in presidential approval rather than parliamentary support. The position and power of Prime Minister Medvedev, while formally nominated by President Putin and approved by an overwhelming vote of the State Duma (299–144, with support from United Russia and the Liberal Democratic Party), is grounded in the strong support given to him by President Putin, even granting the assessment by many that Medvedev is an experienced manager and thoughtful politician. Prime Minister Medvedev's ability to advance the Putin agenda is certainly bolstered by the presence of a vast array of Putin protégés and allies in top governmental and presidential posts.

Having served as president, Dmitri Medvedev's past experience in the presidential administration and federal government has yielded a nuanced knowledge of both policies and high-level elite politics that is valuable to a prime minister. A lawyer-academic who first met Putin while working in the St Petersburg government of reformist mayor Anatolii Sobchak, he moved to Moscow shortly after Putin became prime minister (1999), and during the first Putin presidency Medvedev held a number of highly influential positions; especially notable was his service as head of the presidential administration (2003–05), first deputy prime minister (2005–08), and his chairmanship of Gazprom (through most of 2000–08), the world's most powerful energy conglomerate. Well attuned to the intricacies of Kremlin politics, Medvedev supervised the four national priority programmes (agriculture, education, health care, and housing), negotiated Russia's energy disputes with Ukraine and Belarus, and even rallied support for Serbia in the dispute over Kosovo's independence in the midst of his 2008 presidential campaign. If his presidency had proven unexceptional (his championing of judicial reform a notable exception), he was nevertheless well-positioned to manage a complex constellation of political–institutional forces led by his mentor, President Putin.

The prime minister chairs the Cabinet of Ministers, which oversees the state bureaucracy and has both political and law-making functions. Individual ministers set objectives for their ministries, craft their own subordinate bodies' budgets and oversee policy implementation, but do not have independent power bases. While most ministers report to the prime minister, five 'power' ministries (Foreign Affairs, Defence, Internal Affairs, Justice, and Emergency Situations) are directly accountable to the president. The prime minister's power over the ministries is further consolidated through the Cabinet Presidium, led by the prime minister and including the first and deputy prime ministers and other senior ministers. The Presidium coordinates and manages the government's work and, with it including three of the power ministers (foreign, defence, and internal affairs) who also report directly to the president, it reinforces the interconnected executive supervisory roles of the president and prime minister. The institutional arrangements and responsibilities of the federal executive are becoming increasingly routinized, as both Presidents Putin and Medvedev have exhibited similar preferences in the setting out of ministerial portfolios during the past administrations. Putin now has in place a vertical, top-down administrative arrangement which he contends streamlines the policy process.

The composition of the Medvedev government as of early 2014 includes many top officials drawn from past Putin and Medvedev presidential administrations and governments, encompassing not only reliable managers but experienced political watchdogs. Influential holdovers such as 1st Deputy Prime Minister Igor Shuvalov, 'troubleshooter for the North Caucasus' Deputy Prime Minister Dmitri Kozak, and Foreign Minister Sergei Lavrov, are joined by Medvedev protégé, Justice Minister Aleksandr Konovalov. Upcoming officials such as Deputy Prime Minister (for industry and energy) Arkadii Dvorkovich, Deputy Prime Minister (for the military–industrial complex) Dmitri Rogozin, and the macro-economic planner Minister of Finance Anton Siluanov are among the promising younger members. Meanwhile, one-time influential figures such as long-serving Finance Minister, Aleksei Kudrin (2000–11), and Kremlin insider and former United Energy Systems (UES) chair and current head of the Russian Nanotechnology Corporation (Rusnano), Anatolii Chubais, continue to play important behind-the-scenes roles, if not in their direct dealings with Medvedev, then with the presidential administration and Putin. Overall, while acknowledging there are many nuances in fully appreciating this configuration of ministers, we can generalize that the reliable experience of veteran Kremlin team members and the promise of rapidly advancing technocrats are key factors explaining the composition of the Medvedev government.

The governing Putin team

Informal politics – the politics of personalities, career networks, regional and sectoral interests, and competing institutions – are central to the conduct of Russian politics, as they were in Soviet times. Central to the informal politics of the twenty-first century federal government is the constellation of forces comprising the governing Putin team. Analysis of informal politics is difficult: definitive evidence is often lacking, with the necessary interpretation always subject to sceptical judgement. We proceed cautiously in assessing contemporary Russia's informal politics, our focus being on the core elements and logic of an evolving Putin team that continues to govern Russia. In broadly characterizing these elements we may note their business-like manner, but an essential feature is loyalty to Vladimir Putin. The performance of a Putin team member may prove disappointing, but loyalty generally yields a continuing role in the governing elite. Thus, the one-time deputy prime minister and top Putin lieutenant Vladislav Surkov lost his post in May 2013 for reported work deficiencies, yet within just a few months returned to a top presidential support role as an aide dealing with the all-important North Caucasus regions of Abkhazia and Ossetia.

Considerations of space preclude a full-blown analysis of all the officials noted in Figure 2.2, but the major informal groups listed reflect the diversity of elements comprising the governing team. The so-called 'St Petersburg lawyers and economists' are a highly educated group of academics and specialists, trained and starting their careers in the northern capital, who have been central to the crafting and implementation of Russia's economic and political transformation. Generally educated in the late or immediate post-Soviet period, they ascended to federal importance under Putin, though older figures tied with them were important in the Yeltsin years (such as Anatolii Chubais). Here are officials often focused on the technical complexities of the country's economic and political overhaul. They are generally committed to a market economy, privatization, careful structuring of the state's role in the country's socio-economic life and full engagement of Russia with the global economy, but nested in a putatively democratic political system. We must distinguish another grouping, 'St Petersburg political–business elements', as these officials, also from Putin's hometown, have backgrounds more grounded in practical business experience and politics, but their policy preferences generally have been aligned with those of the St Petersburg lawyers and economists. Overall, while organizing officials into these groups, there are differences in background and articulated priorities: we must differentiate Gazprom chair Aleksei Miller from Russian Nanotechnology Corporation (Rusnano) head Chubais, and from politi-

Figure 2.2   *Major informal groups of the Putin team*

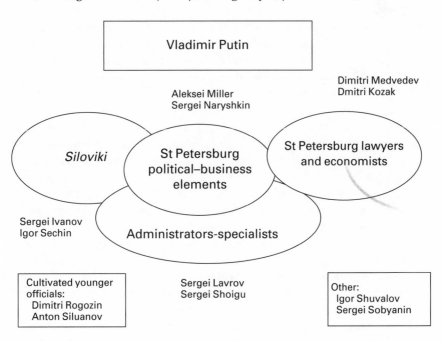

cian–businessman and now State Duma Speaker, Sergei Naryshkin. Likewise, the policy troubleshooter, Dmitri Kozak, who has assumed responsibility for the troubled North Caucasus Region (and the February 2014 Sochi Winter Olympics), brings tremendous 'hands on' political experience, while Justice Minister Konovalov is one Medvedev protégé who continues to be of influence as Medvedev moved from the presidency to the prime ministership. There may be personal-career rivalries among these elements, but it is difficult to assess such dynamics, while all of them appear committed to the governing Putin team's power and policy agenda.

The other major group in the governing Kremlin team is the *siloviki* (derived from the Russian word for power), officials from the intelligence–security services who have constituted a dominant force throughout the Putin period. It is challenging to accurately identify a common interest or shared set of perspectives for all *siloviki*, but many would conclude they have a natural preference for a strong state and less sensitivity to the nuances of the democratic system. *Siloviki* have presented themselves as disciplined professionals, they are generally highly educated, and some have brought past commercial experience to their government positions. A view of many in Russia, if not in the West, is that the *siloviki* are generally non-ideological, have a pragmatic law and order focus, and emphasize Russian national-state interests. The *siloviki* had been especially prominent in the first Putin presidency, their ranks at the senior level thinning by the beginning of the Medvedev presidency in May 2008. However, the presence of Sergei Ivanov, a long-time Putin protégé and lead *silovik*, as the presidential chief of staff is important. Long-time senior Putin lieutenant and *silovik*, Igor Sechin, now executive chairman of the integrated oil corporation, Rosneft, is the most visible of the *siloviki* who have gone on to assume leadership roles in corporations and state-holding companies. The positioning of such Putin loyalists in important business settings cannot be over-emphasized when considering the Putin team's priority attention to Russia's continued economic advancement in the 2010s.

Finally, as Figure 2.2 indicates, these groups should be juxtaposed not only to one another, but to the experienced administrators and specialists and younger cultivated officials who are making their mark in the second Putin presidency. Some ministers in the Medvedev government are holdovers from the previous regime, including seasoned officials not easily associated with a given career group (such as Foreign Minister Sergei Lavrov or Defence Minister Sergei Shoigu). These officials' credentials and past experience have provided them the personal connections and reputations that make them formidable figures. Shoigu, in particular, merits attention, as he not only had a successful past tenure as the Minister for Emergency Situations, but was tapped to be Moscow *oblast* governor, and then was called upon to assume the Defence Minister's portfolio when Putin protégé Anatolii Serdyukov was dismissed early in the second Putin presidency. Some of these officials bring an organizational prowess that makes them highly valuable to the decision-making process (such as Igor Shuvalov). Meanwhile, we must note there are cultivated younger officials who have rapidly moved up in the Putin period, who bring extensive experience and relevant troubleshooting skills to important areas (such as Dmitri Rogozin, in the military–industrial and foreign policy spheres, and Anton Siluanov in the area of macro-economic planning). Reviewing Figure 2.2, we can see that the constellation of figures responsible for executive branch and federal level policy-making is large, multifaceted, and spans both cooperating and competing elements. It reveals the complex interconnection of organization and personnel considerations. Putative 'conservative' groupings (such as *siloviki* Ivanov and Sechin) manoeuvre around 'liberal' groupings (like Medvedev and Konovalov), while other influential officials retain more independent positions (among them Sergei Sobyanin, one-time head of the presidential administration who became Mayor of Moscow in 2010). If not prone to simple explanation, this constellation of varied actors reinforces the conclusion that a priority concern for all

Russian chief executives must be the management of both institutions and personnel. By all appearances, Vladimir Putin continues to be successful in managing his second presidency team.

Complexities of a hegemonic executive

Putin's May 2012 return to the presidency surprised no one, but the circumstances that led to his return and that influenced the atmosphere of Russian politics as his second presidency commenced were highly challenging. We outside the Kremlin corridors of power will never know the calculations of Putin and Medvedev that led to the decision that Medvedev vacate the presidency in favour of his mentor. While some posited this had been a foregone choice from the earliest days of the Medvedev–Putin tandem, others were less certain. The Putin–Medvedev public explanation regarding the need for Putin's return to the presidency, however, certainly fits with the reality that United Russia and the Putin team were under considerable public pressure, that then-President Medvedev's public standing had significantly dropped over the course of his four-year tenure, and that only Putin had the public standing to help reverse United Russia's failing standing in the parliamentary election campaign – and for the United Russia candidate to decisively reclaim the presidency three months later.

Medvedev had easily won the presidency in March 2008 (71.2 per cent), and his public standing reached its zenith, at roughly 83 per cent, during and after the August 2008 war with Georgia. But from late 2008 onwards Medvedev's public standing slowly but consistently dropped, his approval ratings always a few ticks (or more) lower than those for his prime minister. Russians judged he did not have the gravitas or skills either to effectively navigate Byzantine-like Kremlin politics or to manage the behemoth Russian state. His Westernizing rhetoric, emphasizing among other things Russia's accelerating de-Sovietization without due consideration (in Russians' judgement) for the pluses of the Soviet experience, did not sit well with much of the public. Moreover, initiatives such as fighting crime by transforming the *militsiya* (police) to a *politsiya* (new name using the English), the over-blown claims around the payoffs of the Skolkovo high-tech research centre, and the optics surrounding the 'Hamburger Summit' with US President Barack Obama (June 2010), were just a few of the many Medvedev actions that suggested a political amateur. If the Kremlin elite and bulk of the population had been reassured by Putin's presence as head of government during the Medvedev presidency, then having Putin return as head of state and Medvedev serve as top administrator of the Putin programme seemed more natural for a governing team that would continue to guide the polity.

Table 2.1   *The Russian presidential election, 4 March 2012*

	Nominated by	Vote	%
Vladimir Putin	United Russia	45,602,075	63.60
Gennadii Zyuganov	Communist Party	12,318,353	17.18
Mikhail Prokhorov	Independent	5,722,508	7.98
Vladimir Zhirinovsky	Liberal-Democratic Party	4,458,103	6.22
Sergei Mironov	A Just Russia	2,763,935	3.85
valid vote		70,864,974	98.84
invalid vote		836,691	1.16
total vote		71,701,665	100.00
registered voters/			
ballots cast		109,860,331	65.27

The logic of the choice for Putin to replace Medvedev as United Russia's presidential candidate was borne out by both the December 2011 and March 2012 elections. Even granting irregularities in the 2011 parliamentary elections, United Russia still could not claim to have won a majority of the vote (gaining 49.3 per cent), and in all likelihood the United Russia share would have been considerably lower if the less respected Medvedev had been the presidential candidate (Medvedev's public approval ratings at the time hovering in the low-50 per cent range according to the Levada Center and VTsIOM). In contrast, Putin's March 2012 re-election with 63.6 per cent enabled him to avoid an embarrassing second round (see Table 2.1).

During Putin's May 2012 inauguration, even commentators on state-controlled television networks (such as NTV and RT, 7 May 2012) remarked on the serious domestic pressures that confronted the new president, on public expectations regarding an improving economy, the need for addressing the country's widespread corruption, and the necessity of ensuring citizens' continued improving material circumstances. While only a small minority of the population had taken to the streets in the mass demonstrations of 2011–12, the phenomenon of 'Putin fatigue' was palpable (as noted for instance by Levada Center deputy head Aleksei Grazhdankin and St Petersburg Politics Fund chair Mikhail Vinogradov, RIA-Novosti, 24 August 2012). Moreover, the political activist and Putin critic Aleksei Navalny's characterization of United Russia as a 'party of swindlers and thieves' found universal resonance, with highly advantaged United Russia candidates occasionally even falling to electoral challengers who publicly stoked the flames against the ruling elite. Public frustration even led to Putin's approval ratings dropping. After a dozen years in power, there was no mistaking that Putin and his team were fully responsible for Russian domestic realities, and they were under ever-greater public pressure to address problems they had to date failed to handle.

Developments of the second Putin presidency must be judged in light of these strong public concerns. A reconfigured team of both old and new faces brought the experience and expertise necessary to craft and implement a serious second Putin presidential programme. Actions and policies of the Putin team may be evaluated in the wake of the programmatic vision set out by Putin in the set of seven position papers issued in January–February 2012 during the presidential election. These position papers, published in major national newspapers, detail the wide array of issues facing Russia both domestically and internationally. Considered individually, they offer detailed analyses of major issue areas, from the state of the economy and society, to nationality matters, the ongoing need for political change, and foreign challenges and opportunities. Taken together, they provide a programmatic vision of then-candidate Putin. Most important initiatives and policies of the second Putin presidential team have been anticipated by the thinking and posturing set out in these seven position papers (Box 2.1), and they merit our attention as we reflect over Putin's authority and legacy. Many of these policy initiatives are explored more fully in the chapters that follow.

Central to the second Putin presidency programme are new measures to further reinvigorate and modernize the economy. These include big infrastructural and transportation projects (such as a Moscow–Kazan high-speed railway), and many explicitly tied to bolstering the economic efficiency of large metropolitan areas such as Moscow and St Petersburg. Putin's 'trial and error' approach is revealed in the accelerating privatization of state holdings (such as the aviation corporation *Sibir* and the industrial construction firm *Mosenergostroi*, both in 2013). Given the emphasis on education in a number of these Putin position papers, it is no surprise that education reforms (structural and curricular) and increased spending mark the second presidency, with related efforts to revitalize (and increase funding for) higher education as well as reorganize the Academy of Sciences. All of these initiatives are directly tied to the further energizing of the economy, with the revitalization of the military–industrial complex and even the reorganization of the military similarly touted.

The success of these developmental initiatives is doubtful without addressing the pervasive problem of corruption, and a surprise investigation into the defence ministry was but the most suggestive of a number of high-profile cases. Efforts to bolster governmental accountability and transparency may begin with legislation to distance government officials from private sector positions and property, but various other steps (such as pressing government institutions to put ever more material on the internet for public consideration) promote public

Box 2.1 Putin presidential campaign position papers, 2012

soft power

Position Paper	Primary concerns with policy implications
'Russia muscles up – the challenges we must rise up to face' 16 January 2012 (*Izvestya*)	Post-Soviet recovery phase over; Russia's re-emergence through a diversified innovation-based economy; create new sustained growth sources. Institute structure of social guarantees and safeguards for public; middle-class focus; social mobility with support for social NGO's and attention to poor; education renewal. Russian sovereignty in age of global transformation.
'Russia: the ethnicity issue' 23 January 2012 (*Nezavisimaya gazeta*)	Multi-ethnic state with Russian culture at core; education and media to socialize common cultural code, tied with civic patriotism; role of religion in education, social welfare, and the armed forces. Popular election of regional governors with bolstered multiparty system. Channel domestic migration with 'harmonious' inter-regional social infrastructure. Address ethnicity-related crimes amidst corruption with bolstered judicial system and effective law enforcement. Integration across the post-Soviet space.
'Economic tasks' 30 January 2012 (*Vedomosti*)	Russia's search for a new place in the global system. Upgrade cutting-edge technology, with priority sectors identified and labour productivity raised. Cautious privatization of state corporations and vertically integrated holding companies. Increased funding for and bolstered cooperation among research universities, Academy of Sciences, and the private sector. Continued focus on customs unions and trade zones. Shift from state regulation to market mechanisms. Anti-corruption efforts with accelerated tax reforms. Priority of balanced budget.
'Democracy and the quality of government' 6 February 2012 (*Kommersant*)	Restoring qualitative rights (e.g., employment, healthcare, and education). Streamlining electoral registration process; bolstered public involvement through consultative arrangements (with crowdsourcing); heightened information availability by authorities to public; 'internet democracy'; further development of 'public chambers'. Rethink regional-municipal and federal–regional relations. Limits on government-property ties (including executive branch controls). Transparency, accountability linked with fighting corruption.

'Building justice: a social policy for Russia' 13 February 2012 (*Komsomolskaya pravda*)	Safeguard social guarantees through bolstered economy. Heightened pay, enhanced education and professional standards for professionals. Raised worker participation in management; raised worker social mobility via professionalization. Fiscal prioritization of education and healthcare. New attention to the disabled. Reconsider state revenues and taxes in lessening inequality. Consistent incremental pension increases without raising the retirement age. Focus on day care and kindergarten; enhanced state benefits to students with heightened salaries for educators; Academy of Sciences and university streamlining with bolstered cooperation. Upgrading medical services with focus on outpatient treatment. Expanded housing with affordable (state guaranteed) mortgage arrangements.
'Being strong' 20 February 2012 (*Rossiiskaya gazeta*)	Modernize defence industry with strengthened strategic deterrent; focus on high-precision long-range conventional capabilities (with prioritization of weapons and systems specified). Emphasis on collective security arrangements. Streamlined organization with smaller brigade as main tactical unit; streamline command structure; continued strengthening of social-resource support for military personnel. Military service as social mobility engine, balanced with military as professional contract force. Upgrade defence contracting system; counter excessive defence sector protectiveness and corruption; bridging of defence and civilian sectors with intended competition among R&D projects and teams; promote private defence enterprises; university–state–private cooperation.
'Russia and the changing world' 27 February 2012 (*Moskovskiye Novosti*)	Russian behaviour nested in international organisations and law. Protect remaining Russian interests in mid-east. Expressed concern over foreign funded NGO's efforts in Russia. Weapons proliferation concern. Engagement of Asia-Pacific. Russia understood as an 'inalienable and organic part' of Europe and European civilization, with anticipated enhanced cooperation with Europe. 'Ebb and flow' relationship with US. Expand benefits of WTO accession. Enhanced government support for Russian entrepreneurs in foreign markets. Continuing priority attention to status of Russian minorities (e.g., in Baltics).

engagement along with public administration reform (including importing Western public policy administration experience). The system of consultative 'public chambers' will be further upgraded, their discussions expanded. These concerns are highlighted in several position papers. Meanwhile, the proposal is floated to return to the popular election of regional governors, and this is set for most regions (though with exceptions for the North Caucasus republics) by 2017. Overall, second- presidency Putin political initiatives appear directed to make the power vertical less rigid, although they are unlike to diminish its political effectiveness.

We also find initiatives focused on families and children. Looking beyond the high-visibility (in the West) adoption and anti-gay propaganda laws, the regime is building on the payoffs of the national priority programmes for improving the demographic situation, both in birthrate and adult mortality levels. The most tangible new efforts involve funding for and restructuring of public schools, including kindergarten expansion. Anti-tobacco and alcohol legislation is also tied to social well-being, while concrete efforts to consolidate and upgrade the system of matching employee–employer pension plans, while not raising the retirement age, are well-received by the public (as was Putin's criticism of Medvedev government officials who countenanced less funding and a higher retirement age).

Finally, these domestic initiatives have been joined by a more assertive foreign policy stance (for instance, on Iran and Syria) that enjoys widespread Russian elite and public support. Brought together, these initiatives and policies constitute an ambitious programmatic record that is building on the positions set out by then-candidate Putin. While their successful implementation is uncertain, their results will be critical to the eventual legacy of Putin as he moves through his second presidency.

An experienced paramount leader once again leads Russia, and he is supported by a varied team of protégés and allied interests who continue to dominate the political scene. No institutions or organized opposition elements threaten the ability of this Putin team to promote its agenda. But 'Putin fatigue' characterizes the mood of many Russians, and there is survey evidence from reputable agencies that Russians are impatient for material gains. In March 2013, a Levada Center survey found that 55 per cent of Russians did not want President Putin to be re-elected in 2018, as compared with only 22 per cent who did (United Press International, 11 April 2013). Putin and his team continue to be under serious domestic public pressure, and they need to deliver. If Putin's ideas and proposed programme are intended to address these popular concerns, only time will tell whether the Putin team will be successful. For the foreseeable future, the hegemonic presidency and executive will dominate Russian politics. But if a Putin presidency and executive have restored a strong state, they have done much less to build a vibrant democracy. Russians may settle for a strong state for the moment, but the Putin team will understand that in the longer term it is only economic prosperity that will protect them from 'Putin fatigue'.

Chapter 3

Parliamentary Politics in Russia

THOMAS F. REMINGTON

Changes in the status and role of Russia's parliament – known formally as the Federal Assembly – reflect the turbulent evolution of the post-communist political system. Mikhail Gorbachev's democratizing reforms of the late 1980s transformed the Soviet parliament from a ceremonial adornment of communist rule into an arena of stormy debate and tense political confrontation in the 1990s when Boris Yeltsin was president. In the 2000s, however, under presidents Putin and Medvedev, parliament has largely reverted to its Soviet-era role as a rubber stamp for the leadership's policy initiatives. In this transformation are reflected the hopes, contradictions, and failures of democratic reform. Still, while parliament is not the source of political legitimacy and authority for the state in Russia that it is in liberal democracies, neither is it quite the decorative window-dressing that it was in the Soviet era. Rather, parliament has become one of several sites in Russia's political system where bargaining and deal-making among organized interests take place. It also gives Putin and the government reliable majorities for their legislative agenda. Of particular importance is the dominant position of the United Russia party in parliament: United Russia serves as the mechanism for converting the political needs and ambitions of members of parliament into a solid bloc of voting support for the Kremlin. The transformation of parliament's place over the years since the communist regime ended tells us a great deal about the dynamics of power in Russia.

To understand the contemporary Federal Assembly, it helps to begin with a brief review of the status of elective representative bodies in the Soviet Union. Although they exercised little actual power, they symbolized the idea that the people were sovereign in the state. Legally, the Soviet political system rested on the fiction that state power resided in the hierarchy of *soviets* (or councils). Soviets were popularly elected bodies in which, according to Soviet doctrine, legislative and executive power were fused. Each village and town, region and republic, had its nominally elected soviet (elected in the characteristic, uncontested elections for which the regime was famous), while at the apex of the system, the USSR

42

Supreme Soviet was the equivalent of a parliament for the Soviet Union as a whole. At the same time, it was understood that actual political power lay with the Communist Party of the Soviet Union, which exercised power through the soviets and the executive bodies that were nominally accountable to the soviets. Therefore, the few votes that soviets were called upon to take were exercises in the unanimous affirmation of decisions that had been made by the Communist Party. Both Soviet political thought and practice rejected any notion of a separation of powers, and thus reinforced the older Russian tradition of an absolutist state.

This system changed markedly when Mikhail Gorbachev launched his political reforms in the late 1980s. Gorbachev used new expanded parliamentary structures and open elections as instruments for awakening popular political energies. His goal was to channel the country's newly active political life into a new set of legislative structures where he would be able to guide decision-making. Gorbachev created a cumbersome four-tiered parliament for the USSR, consisting of a huge Congress of People's Deputies, which elected a smaller, full-time parliament called the Supreme Soviet. In turn, the Supreme Soviet was guided by its Presidium, which was overseen by a chairman. The first election of deputies to this new parliamentary structure was held in 1989; in 1990, elections were held for the equivalent bodies at the level of the union republics and in regions and towns throughout the Soviet Union.

Gorbachev's strategy was to give *glasnost*, his policy of open political communication, an institutional base. He sought to incorporate many diverse groups into the new parliamentary arena while ensuring that he would have the ultimate power of decision over policy. But liberalization of politics under Gorbachev had unanticipated consequences. Not only did it mobilize radical democrats against defenders of the old order, it also encouraged coalitions of democrats and nationalists in the republics, including Russia, to rally around demands for national independence. As a result, the new USSR parliament and its counterparts at lower levels *represented* reasonably well the political divisions existing in the country between defenders and challengers of the old order. But they were woefully unsuited to *deciding* the grave policy questions that the country faced. They lacked even the most rudimentary institutional means to generate and debate coherent alternative policy options. They depended heavily on the executive to set their agendas and guide their decision-making. Sessions of the new USSR parliament, and the parliaments in the union republics and lower-level territories, were frequently the sites of passionate but inconclusive debate, dramatic walk-outs by embattled minorities, and deep frustration as the deputies found themselves unable to reach majority decisions on difficult issues. Little wonder that they were never able to resolve the most serious crises that the Soviet Union faced.

Gorbachev's awkwardly remodelled parliament did achieve some notable results, passing some major new legislation and stimulating the formation of proto-parties. But faced with the fundamental conflict between radical reformers and hardliners over market-oriented reform, the parliament simply ducked: it created a state presidency for the USSR, a curiosity that was logically incompatible with the principle of CPSU rule. Then it delegated extraordinary powers to President Gorbachev, who fell into a trap of his own making by constantly expanding his formal powers. What he failed to recognize at the time was that by doing so, he only encouraged the presidents of the union republics to follow suit at their own level of jurisdiction, thus deepening the disintegration of the Soviet state. The more power Gorbachev claimed for himself as president of the USSR, the less power he had in actuality, and the more he undercut the possibility that *any* central level institution – president, parliament or Communist Party – could have held the union together.

Boris Yeltsin and the crisis of 1993

The 1990–93 period was marked by the rise of Boris Yeltsin, who made Russia's parliament his initial base of power. Yeltsin led a coalition of radical democrats and Russian nationalists in a struggle for greater autonomy for Russia within the union. Yeltsin's own position was strengthened, rather than weakened, by Gorbachev's clumsy attempts to undermine him. In 1990, Yeltsin was elected by a narrow margin to the position of Chairman of the RSFSR Supreme Soviet, enabling him to use the parliament as his institutional base for challenging Gorbachev. In spring 1991, Yeltsin rallied a majority of deputies who endorsed his proposal for a powerful, directly elected Russian president. In June 1991, he was elected president of Russia in a nationwide election.

Establishing the presidency, however, led to a contest between the legislative and executive branches. The leadership of the parliament began to challenge Yeltsin for supremacy, claiming that the legislative branch was the supreme seat of state power. Yeltsin claimed that as popularly elected president, he embodied the Russian people's will. The August 1991 coup attempt further solidified his political position. The popular resistance to the coup in Moscow, Leningrad, and other Russian cities, and his own uncompromising opposition, gave Yeltsin a substantial political bonus. Many of his communist opponents in the Russian parliament lost their political bases through a series of presidential decrees which suspended, and later outlawed, the activity of the CPSU and confiscated its considerable property. In October 1991, at the Fifth Congress, Yeltsin sought and received special powers to enact economic reform measures by decree; he won the congress's consent to put off elections of local heads of government until 1 December 1992, and its approval of constitutional amendments giving him the right to suspend the acts of lower authorities in Russia if he found they violated the constitution and to suspend legal acts of the union if they violated Russian sovereignty; and the congress approved his programme for radical economic transformation. A few days later Yeltsin assumed the position of prime minister himself, named a new cabinet dominated by young economists committed to rapid liberalization, and issued a package of decrees launching the radical 'shock therapy' that is discussed in Chapter 11.

Making full use of his expanded powers, Yeltsin pursued his programme of reform throughout 1992. Although the impetus of 'shock therapy' fizzled out as the year proceeded, opposition to Yeltsin grew, and the majority in the parliament shifted further and further away from him. Yeltsin was also unable to win legislative approval for a new constitution that would formalize his powers *vis-à-vis* the government and the legislative branch. Under the old constitution, however, only the congress had the power to amend the constitution or adopt a new one. Confrontation between Yeltsin and the Congress–Supreme Soviet intensified. In March 1993, the congress attempted to remove Yeltsin from power through impeachment but fell slightly short of the necessary two-thirds majority. Yeltsin countered by holding a popular referendum on support for his policies in April, which gave him a surprisingly strong vote of confidence. However, the constitutional crisis continued to deepen.

Finally, on 21 September, Yeltsin issued decrees that lacked constitutional foundation but offered a political solution to the impasse. He shut down parliament, declared the deputies' powers null and void, and called elections for a new parliament to be held on 12 December. He also decreed that there was to be a national vote on the same date on the draft constitution that had been developed under his direction. In the December referendum, Yeltsin's constitution was approved. It has remained in force ever since.

Yeltsin's constitution created a two-chamber Federal Assembly. The upper chamber, the Federation Council, allocates two seats to each of Russia's constituent territories (called 'subjects of the federation'). Under the initial election law that Yeltsin put into effect, half of the 450 seats in the lower house – the State Duma – were to be filled by candidates elected from parties' electoral lists according to the share of votes that party received, so long as it won at least 5 per cent of the party-list votes. The other half of the seats were filled by plurality voting in 225 single-member districts. In the first election held under this plan, in 1993, voters were also given the opportunity to elect their two representatives to the Federation Council.

Not surprisingly, Yeltsin's draft constitution provided for a very strong presidency. The president could issue decrees with the force of law, and veto laws passed by parliament. Yet the constitution also provided for the 'separation of legislative, executive and judicial powers' (Article 10). Contradictions between the powerful presidentialist elements in the constitution and the principle of separation of powers have been resolved very differently at different times since the adoption of the constitution. Under Yeltsin, the president shared some power with the parliament; since Putin took office, however, parliament has been pushed to the sidelines of the political system. The changes in the balance of power between president and parliament reflect both changes in the organizational arrangements within parliament itself as well as shifts in the larger institutional environment in which parliament and president operate.

The first and second Dumas

One of the most important determinants of the balance of power between president and parliament is the outcome of elections. The first elections held under the new electoral system in 1993 gave no one political party or coalition a majority of seats in the Duma, although anti-Yeltsin forces held a clear majority. As a result, parliament fought Yeltsin over much of the legislation he proposed, with the result that Yeltsin sometimes simply bypassed parliament by issuing presidential decrees. Yet both Yeltsin and the parliamentary leadership generally sought to avoid the sort of mutually destructive confrontations that had brought the country to the brink of civil war in 1991 and 1993. Regular bargaining and consultation between the executive and legislative branches succeeded in working out compromises on numerous pieces of legislation.

This pattern continued in the second Duma, which sat from 1996 up to 1999. Yeltsin had decreed that the Duma elected in 1993 would serve for only two years and that elections would be held again in December 1995 for a new Duma that would serve a normal four-year term. The December 1995 election was characterized by a huge number of political groups running: 43 parties registered and ran lists, far more than could hope to win seats given the 5 per cent threshold rule for obtaining them. Four parties succeeded in winning seats on the party-list ballot, and they divided the 225 proportional representation seats among themselves.

The Communists and the factions allied with them came close to commanding a majority of seats in the new Duma. The Communists therefore became an indispensable member of many majority coalitions. However, their position was not secure. To win majorities, they generally needed to offer concessions to other factions or to moderate their policy stance. The Communists refrained from seeking full control over the chamber and largely abided by the previous working arrangements in such matters as the distribution of committee chairmanships among factions, and the practice of forming task forces and legislative commissions by recruiting members from all factions.

Likewise, President Yeltsin devoted considerable effort to bargaining with the Duma over legislation. Both the president and the government maintained permanent representative offices in the Duma, working closely with deputies to ensure the passage of key legislation. Altogether, around 100 executive branch officials were detailed to liaison duty with the Duma. Much of the bargaining within the Duma and between Duma and the executive took place out of public view; public attention instead tended to focus on the histrionic displays of temper on the floor and high-stakes brinkmanship between president and Duma. One of the most memorable confrontations between the branches came as the Duma tried to remove the president through impeachment. The deputies were well aware that removal of the president by means of impeachment was a long and complicated process of which a two-thirds parliamentary vote was only the first step, and that even if they succeeded in passing a motion to impeach, the odds of actually removing Yeltsin were remote indeed. In the event, Yeltsin deployed carrots and sticks to win over some of the opposition forces, and the motion failed.

Yet spectacular as this pyrotechnic display of president–parliament conflict was, it was already a sideshow by 1999. The polarization between democratic and communist forces, real enough in the early 1990s, had faded in importance by the end of the decade in guiding actual alignments in parliament. Although episodes such as the impeachment vote continued to attract public attention, actual parliamentary politics increasingly came to centre on distributive issues – how government spending should be allocated; on whom the burdens of taxes should be imposed; who should control the privatization of state enterprises; to whom access rights to the exploitation of lucrative mineral resources should be granted. The Duma became a central arena for wheeling and dealing among powerful organized interests, including firms, business associations, regional governments, federal ministries, and shadowy bureaucratic 'clans' linked to senior figures in the presidency and government. The fine details of legislation were the object of acute interest and vast sums of money were at stake, not a little of which wound up in the pockets of those drafting and voting on the legislation itself (see Barnes 2001).

The high point of parliamentary power occurred after the August 1998 financial crash. Yeltsin tried to bring back Viktor Chernomyrdin as prime minister, but the Duma adamantly refused to confirm him. After two tense confirmation votes failed, Yeltsin backed down and appointed

Yevgenii Primakov, a centrist acceptable to the Communists. The Duma confirmed him and Primakov formed a government reflective of the balance of power in parliament. With Yeltsin weakened both physically and politically Primakov began making the major decisions on economic policy. This was as close as Russia has yet come to parliamentary government, where the cabinet is made up of the majority coalition in parliament. This phase was short-lived, however; Yeltsin dismissed Primakov in May 1999, on the eve of the impeachment vote in the Duma.

The stormy era of confrontation between president and parliament ended in December 1999. Elections to the third Duma were held on 19 December; five days later the second Duma held its final session. On 31 December, Yeltsin resigned as president some months before the end of his second term. He was succeeded by his prime minister Vladimir Putin, whose powerful political appeal had been demonstrated by the remarkable electoral success of the party with which he was loosely affiliated, Unity, in the parliamentary election. Putin's accession to the presidency, combined with the outcome of the parliamentary election of December 1999, changed legislative–executive relations fundamentally. After January 2000, the Duma became an instrument for approving nearly any initiative offered by the president. This trend grew still more marked following the 2003 presidential election, when the president's allies gained an overwhelming majority in the Duma, and the president had succeeded in taming or suppressing nearly every source of independent political initiative in the country. At the same time, the Duma remained an arena for the resolution of distributive conflicts.

The third, fourth, fifth and sixth Dumas

Since 1999, United Russia (initially Unity) has dominated the Duma. Table 3.1 shows the strength of parliamentary parties in the third, fourth, fifth and sixth Dumas. The 1999 election gave the party most closely allied with Putin – Unity – a strong plurality in the Duma. Unity had to work to build majority coalitions that could pass legislation proposed by the president and government. Its success in forming a fairly reliable cross-factional majority coalition reflects the skill with which the presidential administration manipulated parliamentary politics.

Working in close cooperation with the president's parliamentary managers, Unity assembled a coalition of four parliamentary factions that coordinated voting on major legislation proposed by the president and government. Faction leaders could not always enforce party discipline (two of these factions were made up of deputies elected in single-member districts, who had to pay close attention to powerful local interests back home), but by drawing votes as needed from other factions, they ensured

Table 3.1   *Party factions in 3rd, 4th and 5th Duma convocations*

	3rd Duma (2000–2003)		4th Duma (2003–2007)		5th Duma (2007–2011)	
	Party list vote%	seats in Duma (%)	Party list vote%	seats in Duma (%)	Party list vote%	seats in Duma (%)
Unity/ United Russia*	23.32	18.4	37.4	68	64.3	70
OVR	13.33	10.2				
CPRF	24.29	20.2	12.65	11.56	11.57	13
LDPR	5.98	3.9	11.49	8	8.14	9
SPS	8.52	7.3	3.97	0	0.96	0
Yabloko	5.93	4.8	4.32	0	1.59	0
Motherland/ A Just Russia**	9.04	8.67	7.74	8		

*Unity merged with OVR in 2001 to form United Russia.
**A Just Russia formed in 2006 from the merger of Motherland, the Pensioners' Party and the Party of Life.

Abbreviations:
OVR = Fatherland–All Russia
CPRF = Communist Party of the Russian Federation
LDPR = Liberal Democratic Party of Russia
SPS = Union of Rightist Forces

that the president's legislative agenda almost never suffered a defeat and the president almost never had to veto legislation passed by parliament. As Table 3.2 indicates, only 76 per cent of the legislation that passed the Duma in third (final) reading was eventually signed by the president in the 1994–95 Duma (sometimes the president only signed after multiple rounds of veto and revision), and only 69 per cent of the legislation passed in the 1996–99 period. But since Putin took office, over 90 per cent of the bills passed by the Duma have been signed into law. The table demonstrates the enormous impact of the change from the Yeltsin to the Putin era: not only did the number of vetoes by the president or Federation Council plummet, beginning with the 2000–03 convocation, but the volume of legislation passed by the Duma also began rising rapidly, starting in 2004. In his end-of-term addresses, Speaker Gryzlov never failed to boast of the impressive productivity of the Duma. 'Parliament', he once famously observed, 'is not a place for political battles, for defending some sort of political slogans or ideologies. It is a place where people should engage in constructive, effective legislative activity' (*Gosudarstvennaya Duma: Stenogramma zasedanii*, 2003). Under his leadership, the Duma turned into a law-making machine, a role it has continued to play under Speaker Naryshkin (who succeeded Gryzlov in January 2012). Under

Table 3.2   *Passage rates for legislation, Russian State Duma, 1994–2007*

	First convocation: 1994–1995		Second convocation: 1996–1999		Third convocation: 2000–2003		Fourth convocation: 2004–2007	
	No.	As %	No.	As %	No.	As %	No.	As%
Total no. of bills considered in any reading	(na)		2133		2125		2713	
Laws passed (in 3rd reading)	464	100	1045	100	781	100	1087	100
Vetoed by president only	263	29.3	185	18	31	4	7	0.64
Vetoed by president + FC			113	11	10	1	3	0.28
Signed by president (of those passed in this period)	354	76	724	69	730	93	735	91.9

Source: Based on Analytic Reports of Russian State Duma, various years.

Naryshkin, in fact, the Duma has come to be called 'the mad printer'. Many close observers have noted that the rapid pace of work results in legislation that often needs to be amended because of ambiguous language, and deprives controversial laws of public understanding and approval. The government's own liaison to the Supreme Court, noting that Duma Chairman Gryzlov once boasted that in one term the Duma passed 632 new laws, observed that 'in my opinion, this is nothing to be proud of, this is a catastrophe!' (Kharat'yan 2013).

It is notable that whereas Yeltsin had often resorted to his decree powers to enact major decisions, Putin almost never does: thanks to his commanding base of support in the parliament, he is able to pass a far more sweeping legislative agenda than Yeltsin had proposed. Putin's early legislative achievements included significant reductions in taxes, legalization of a market for transactions in land, the foundations of a system of mortgage lending, sweeping changes in the pension system, overhaul of the labour market, major changes to federal relations, substantial liberalization of the judicial system, and breakups of major national monopolies. Painful as many of these changes were for the deputies to swallow, they ultimately passed them, albeit sometimes in modified form.

The 2003 elections produced a decisive victory for the president's forces and a humiliating defeat for the opposition both on the right and the left. The liberal democratic forces failed entirely to win party-list seats and the Communists' share of the party list fell by nearly half, while the party backed by the Kremlin, United Russia (the successor of Unity) took more than 37 per cent of the party-list vote. Together with deputies elected in single-member districts, United Russia wound up with two-thirds of the seats in the new Duma. No party had held so dominant a position in parliament since the late 1980s, and United Russia used its commanding majority to make sweeping changes to the way parliament was run. They replaced the old power-sharing, proportional arrangements of the previous three Dumas with a new majoritarian system in which their members held nearly all the committee chairmanships and seats on the governing Council of the Duma, and their leader was elected the Duma's chairman. And they quickly moved to impose a gag rule on their members, demanding that no member speak to the press without party approval.

But for all their ability to control the Duma, theirs was a pyrrhic victory, because the power to make policy decisions lay in the Kremlin. As total as United Russia's influence is in the Duma, the Kremlin's monopoly on policy-making is just as absolute. As a result, United Russia is completely dependent on the Kremlin for its power and privileges. Its base of support in society is thin, and it has identified itself completely with the interests of office-holders rather than offering a clear policy programme. This is a mixed blessing for the Kremlin. The party's effectiveness in delivering reliable majorities in parliament depends on its ability to win elections. Therefore, if the Kremlin were to withdraw its support from the party and its fortunes collapsed, the president and government might not be able to ensure such solid voting support in parliament. President Putin has repeatedly said that Russia needs a 'capable' (*deesposbnyi*) parliament and has tied that to the ability of United Russia to forge consistent, coherent majorities.

Putin's legislative agenda shifted after 2003. Modernizing economic reform took a back seat, while anti-terrorism legislation, generous increases in social spending, and the establishment of a number of new state corporations taking over ownership and control of many of Russia's most significant public and private industries occupied much more of the parliament's time. These pieces of legislation gave deputies, particularly those from United Russia, many opportunities to showcase their effectiveness in bringing benefits back to their home districts and to the powerful business lobbies that backed them. So although they ceded even more power to the executive branch (for example, supporting the law replacing direct elections of governors with a system of presidential nomination and greatly expanding the power of the security police to deal with terrorists), they also reinforced the popularity of United Russia with the electorate.

Preparations for the December 2007 Duma election proceeded amidst great uncertainty about the presidential succession. President Putin resolved many fears and doubts when he announced that he intended to run at the top of United Russia's list of candidates and to stay on in power – but not as president. The presidential administration pulled out all the stops to ensure a smooth and controlled succession. The first step was to guarantee a large victory for United Russia in the Duma election by methods that included manipulation of media coverage, massive funding for United Russia's campaign, disqualification of popular opposition politicians, and outright falsification of voting returns in many districts (see Chapter 4). The official results gave United Russia 64.3 per cent of the vote. Because this election was entirely based on proportional representation from party lists (there were no longer any single-member district mandates), and because the threshold to receiving seats was raised from 5 to 7 per cent, only four parties won representation. As in the fourth Duma, United Russia took three-quarters of the seats and full control of the Duma, and the party's leader, Boris Gryzlov, was once again elected speaker.

The 2011 elections yielded a much slimmer majority for United Russia. Its official total was just under 50 per cent but independent analysts calculated that the true vote share was closer to 35 per cent (Lyubarev 2012). It took a clear majority of seats and retained control over the Duma's calendar. As a result, United Russia continues to provide consistent majorities for the president's legislative agenda.

The Federation Council

The president and government also dominate the upper house of parliament, the Federation Council. Like the United States Senate, the Federation Council is designed as an instrument of federalism in that every constituent unit of the federation sends two representatives to it. Thus the populations of small ethnic-national territories are greatly overrepresented compared with more populous regions. Members of the Federation Council were elected by direct popular vote in December 1993 but since the constitution was silent on how they were to be chosen in the future, requiring only that one representative from the executive branch and one from the legislative branch from each region be members of the chamber, new legislation was required to detail how members of the Federation Council should be chosen. Under a law passed in 1995, the heads of the executive and legislative branches of each constituent unit of the federation were automatically given seats in the Federation Council, and this was the system in force between 1996 and 1999.

In 2000, new legislation was passed which provided that the governors and legislatures of the regions were to choose full-time representatives to occupy their regions' seats in the Federation Council. In 2012 ,the procedure was changed again, so that each regional legislature would elect one of its members to serve as a member of the Federation Council from the legislative branch while the executive branch's representative would be chosen by the governor from candidates that he or she identified before being elected. In practice, regardless of the formal procedure, since Putin took power, his advisors have had the final say on all decisions over the selection of members. The frequent changes in the procedures used to form the Federation Council reflect conflicting pressures over its role; many in the political elite think it should be popularly elected. The desire for greater legitimacy, however, is thwarted by the constitutional provision that its members must represent the legislative and executive branches of government in each region, and by the authorities' desire to guarantee a pliant and loyal body.

Because the Federation Council rejects the use of political factions to organize its deliberations, United Russia has only an informal status in the chamber. Nevertheless, the president and government guide its decisions closely. Under the constitution, some legislation is not required to be considered by the Federation Council, although the chamber can choose to take up any bill it wishes to consider and can initiate legislation. Actual voting in the Federation Council routinely produces lopsided majorities favouring the president's position; the chamber spends very little time on floor debate, since the decisions are agreed upon beforehand in consultations among committee chairs and the president's representatives. Federation Council members also spend a good deal of time in lobbying with federal government agencies on behalf of their home regions or business interests (Remington 2003).

The Federation Council has important constitutional powers. It approves presidential nominees for high courts such as the Supreme Court and the Constitutional Court. In addition, it approves presidential decrees declaring martial law or a state of emergency, and any actions altering the boundaries of territorial units in Russia. It must consider any legislation dealing with taxes, budget, financial policy, treaties, customs and declarations of war. In the Yeltsin period, the Federation Council defied the president's will on a number of issues. After President Putin entered office, however, the Federation Council lost its independence. Its members, although often caught between the conflicting imperatives of their home regions and the president's domination of the political system, have rarely had much difficulty deciding to take the president's side. The highly centralized nature of the current system means that it is far more costly to members to oppose the president than to side with the president against their home regions.

The legislative process in the Federal Assembly

Basic legislative procedure

The State Duma originates all legislation except in certain areas of policy that are under the jurisdiction of the upper house, the Federation Council. Upon final passage in the State Duma, a bill goes to the Federation Council. If the upper house rejects it, the bill goes back to the Duma, where a commission comprising members of both houses may seek to iron out differences. If the Duma rejects the upper house's changes, it may over-ride the Federation Council by a two-thirds vote. Otherwise it votes on the version of the bill proposed by the commission (see Figures 3.1–3.3). When the bill has cleared both chambers of the Federal Assembly, it goes to the president for signature. If the president refuses to sign the bill, it returns to the Duma. The Duma may pass it with the president's proposed amendments by a simple absolute majority, or over-ride the president's veto, for which a two-thirds vote of the entire membership is required. The Federation Council must then also approve the bill, by a simple majority if the president's amendments are accepted, or a two-thirds vote if it chooses to over-ride him.

Figure 3.1   *The legislative process: overview*

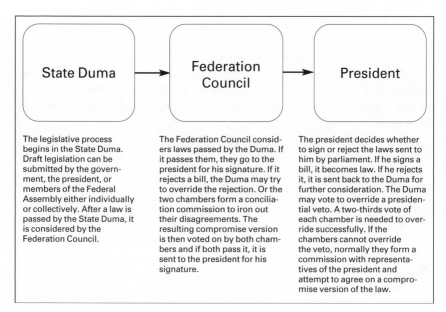

The legislative process begins in the State Duma. Draft legislation can be submitted by the govern- ment, the president, or members of the Federal Assembly either individually or collectively. After a law is passed by the State Duma, it is considered by the Federation Council.

The Federation Council consid- ers laws passed by the Duma. If it passes them, they go to the president for his signature. If it rejects a bill, the Duma may try to override the rejection. Or the two chambers form a concilia- tion commission to iron out their disagreements. The resulting compromise version is then voted on by both cham- bers and if both pass it, it is sent to the president for his signature.

The president decides whether to sign or reject the laws sent to him by parliament. If he signs a bill, it becomes law. If he rejects it, it is sent back to the Duma for further consideration. The Duma may vote to override a presiden- tial veto. A two-thirds vote of each chamber is needed to over- ride successfully. If the chambers cannot override the veto, normally they form a commission with representa- tives of the president and attempt to agree on a compro- mise version of the law.

Figure 3.2   *The legislative process: bill introduction*

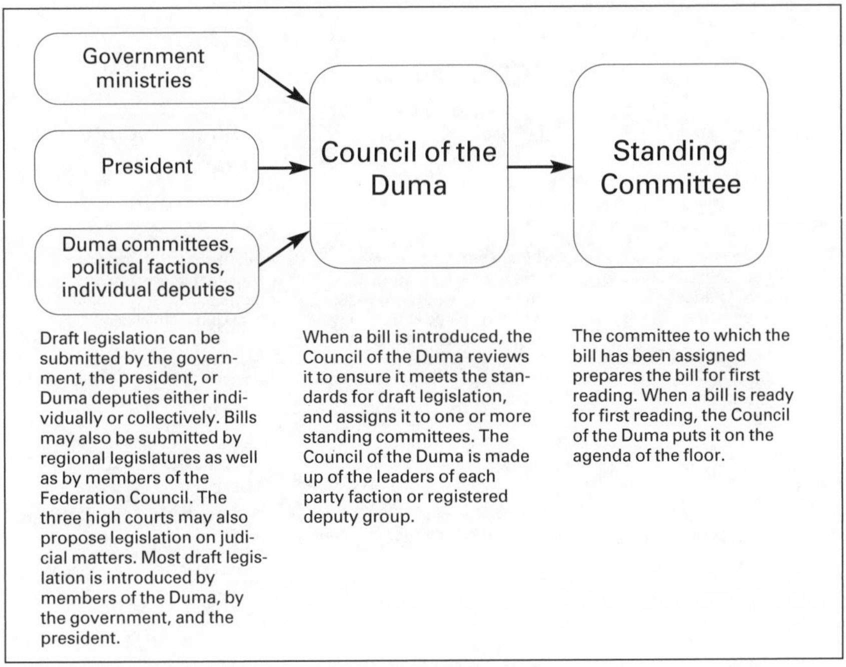

```
┌──────────────────┐
│   Government     │
│   ministries     │ ──────┐
└──────────────────┘       │
                           ▼
┌──────────────────┐   ┌──────────────┐      ┌──────────────┐
│   President      │──▶│ Council of the│ ────▶│  Standing    │
└──────────────────┘   │    Duma      │      │  Committee   │
                       └──────────────┘      └──────────────┘
┌──────────────────┐       ▲
│ Duma committees, │       │
│ political factions,│ ─────┘
│ individual deputies│
└──────────────────┘
```

Draft legislation can be submitted by the government, the president, or Duma deputies either individually or collectively. Bills may also be submitted by regional legislatures as well as by members of the Federation Council. The three high courts may also propose legislation on judicial matters. Most draft legislation is introduced by members of the Duma, by the government, and the president.

When a bill is introduced, the Council of the Duma reviews it to ensure it meets the standards for draft legislation, and assigns it to one or more standing committees. The Council of the Duma is made up of the leaders of each party faction or registered deputy group.

The committee to which the bill has been assigned prepares the bill for first reading. When a bill is ready for first reading, the Council of the Duma puts it on the agenda of the floor.

State Duma

The steering committee of the Duma is the Council of the Duma. The Council of the Duma makes the principal decisions in the Duma concerning the agenda and acts, on occasion, to overcome deadlocks among the political groups represented in the Duma. Until the sweeping changes of 2004, it was made up of the leader of each party faction or registered deputy group regardless of size, which served to diffuse political power in the chamber. Since 2004, however, it has been dominated by the United Russia faction.

All deputies in the Duma belong to the political faction tied to the party on whose list they were elected. Under new Standing Rules, they may not change factions (on pain of losing their seat). Each party that has won at least 7 per cent of the party-list vote is entitled to form a faction in the Duma made up of its elected deputies. The factions use the Duma as a means for showcasing their pet legislative projects, giving their leaders a national forum, obtaining organizational support for their party work, and providing service to their constituents. However, only the United Russia faction has any real power to shape legislation. It is so large and diverse that it has sub-divided into three internal policy forums, one with

Figure 3.3   *The legislative process: three readings*

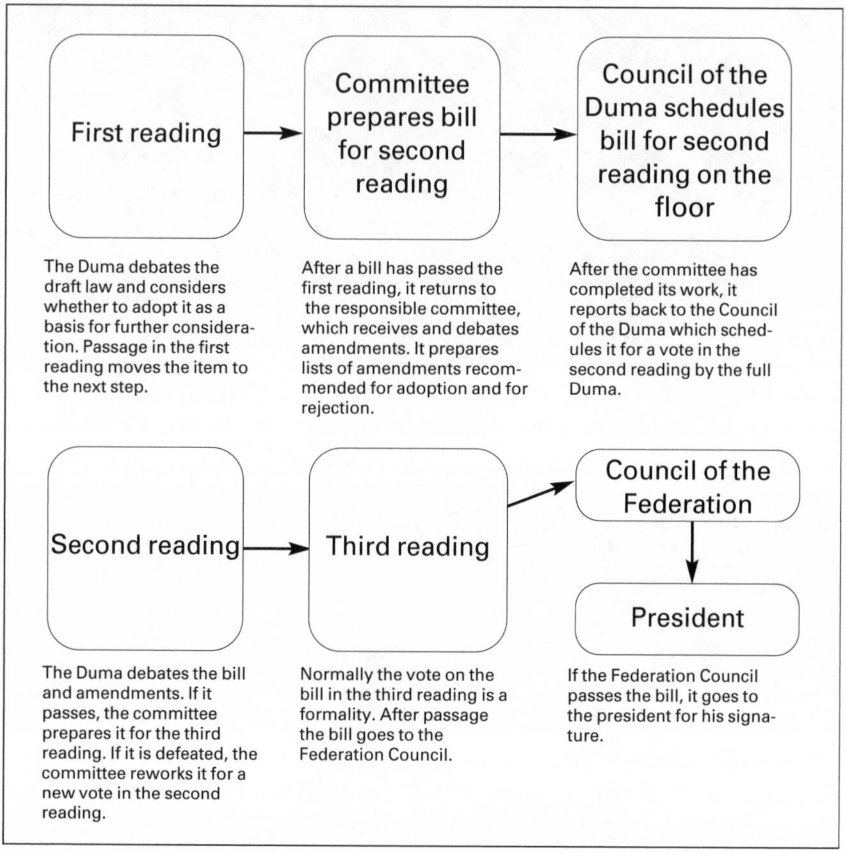

First reading	Committee prepares bill for second reading	Council of the Duma schedules bill for second reading on the floor
The Duma debates the draft law and considers whether to adopt it as a basis for further considera-tion. Passage in the first reading moves the item to the next step.	After a bill has passed the first reading, it returns to the responsible committee, which receives and debates amendments. It prepares lists of amendments recom-mended for adoption and for rejection.	After the committee has completed its work, it reports back to the Council of the Duma which sched-ules it for a vote in the second reading by the full Duma.
Second reading	Third reading	Council of the Federation / President
The Duma debates the bill and amendments. If it passes, the committee prepares it for the third reading. If it is defeated, the committee reworks it for a new vote in the second reading.	Normally the vote on the bill in the third reading is a formality. After passage the bill goes to the Federation Council.	If the Federation Council passes the bill, it goes to the president for his signa-ture.

a vaguely pro-market orientation, one broadly social-democratic, and the third focused on patriotic and moral values.

The Duma also has a system of standing legislative committees to handle legislation in particular issue jurisdictions. Each deputy is a member of one committee. The work of drafting and developing legisla-tion goes on in the committees, and committees report out legislation along with recommendations on amendments that have been proposed. Members join committees according to the issues areas in which they wish to specialize.

Formally, bills are considered in three readings (see Figure 3.3). In the first reading, the Duma simply decides whether or not to approve the bill's basic conception. If it passes, the bill goes back to the committee, which then sifts through the amendments that are offered. When the committee has agreed on its recommended version of the bill, it reports it out again to the floor for a second reading, and the whole chamber decides on which amendments to approve and which to reject. At that point the floor votes on the bill in its entirety, and sends it back to the committee for a final editing and polishing. The third reading gives the Duma's final approval to the bill, after which it goes to the Federation Council.

In recent years, a practice has evolved whereby much of the bargaining over legislation occurs before the first reading as the government discusses the proposed budget with its parliamentary allies before submitting the budget bill formally. Through the 'zero reading,' as it is called, deputies in the United Russia faction are able to reward their friends and supporters by such budget revisions – something much easier to do when oil revenues are swelling the budget.

Some deputies are lobbyists for particular interest groups. All those regarded as the most effective belong to the United Russia faction. One deputy is known as the champion of the insurance industry, another as the advocate for the legal profession, and several others are regarded as voices of the oil and gas industries. One is known as an effective lobbyist for Tatarstan. Such deputies cultivate close ties with allies in the presidential administration and government, and involve themselves actively in the legislative process to ensure that the details of legislation serve the interests of those they represent. Many have dozens of successful bills to their credit (Tsvetaeva 2011).

The relationship between the executive and the United Russia party illustrates the dynamics of a dominant party regime (Reuter and Remington 2009). In such a regime, rulers use the dominant party to control the political process. The party gives ambitious politicians an opportunity to build political careers. Thanks to their privileged access to the government, party politicians can reward the wealthy and powerful interests that back them, steering lucrative contracts or jobs their way. The party operates as a giant patronage machine. The rulers benefit by ensuring that politicians will be loyal to the authorities rather than competing against it. The party mobilizes support for the regime at the elections, and the authorities use all their powers of control over the media, money, election commissions, courts, police and the like, to make sure that opposition parties cannot make serious inroads into the ruling party's dominant status. In parliament, the dominant party organizes large, lopsided voting majorities to pass the executive's proposed legislation. In effect, politicians in the dominant party give up their political voice in return for access to the benefits of office. This allows them to pay back the business interests that have funded their election campaigns. On the other hand, the United Russia party offers little to the president and government other than reliable legislative support. The party is relatively unpopular in society, and heavily dependent on the administrative resources of the executive branch in winning legislative elections.

As a result of the new relationship between parliament and president established under Vladimir Putin, vetoes of legislation are rare but behind the scenes debate over legislation is routine. Sometimes a bill passes through all three readings in a matter of weeks or even days, but in other cases disagreements within the government or between the government and major social interest groups keep a bill bottled up for years. Bills can be slowed down by disagreements within the executive branch itself (as different ministries lobby for different versions of the legislation) or when the Kremlin changes United Russia's marching orders. Generally, however, the Duma remains on the sidelines over major national policy debates. The Duma does not exercise any influence over the basic directions of budget policy, for example. A difficult and protracted recent debate over reforming the pension system has taken place entirely within the executive branch, with the Duma simply left to ratify decisions that the president and government make. The Duma's role therefore is to supply secure legislative majorities for the executive branch when a policy takes the form of legislation. In return, Duma deputies enjoy a variety of perquisites, and some opportunity to modify the details of legislation.

The 1993 Constitution did not give the Federal Assembly a formal power of 'oversight' over the executive, such as the United States Congress has. Parliament, however, has other formal powers which it can use to monitor and check executive power if it is so inclined and if the executive allows it to do so. One of its instruments is the Audit Chamber, which reviews the accounts of state bodies including federal ministries, regional governments, and even private companies. Another is the practice of inviting government officials to parliament to respond to deputies' questions during a 'government hour'. Committees frequently organize hearings to gather public testimony on matters of public policy and assist in developing legislation. Parliament can also conduct investigations of allegations of executive branch misconduct. All of these powers, however, can only be exercised to the extent that parliament chooses to wield them and the executive branch consents to their being used. In the current period, when political power in the state is highly concentrated in the presidential administration, parliament's oversight power has been reduced to virtually nil.

The Federal Assembly in perspective

The ability of a legislature to exercise its constitutional prerogatives depends both on its own internal structures and on features of its institutional environment. One critical aspect of that environment in Russia is the degree to which the president dominates political processes. In the

1990s, Yeltsin's political and physical weakness, and his own fitful but sincere democratic instincts, allowed parliament to play a stronger role than has been the case under Putin and Medvedev. Putin changed these patterns immediately upon assuming power as president. He centralized and disciplined policy-making within the executive branch, and re-engineered the internal procedures of both chambers of parliament in such a way as to ensure him consistent and reliable majorities. In the Duma, this has come about through the domination of parliament by United Russia. In the Federation Council, Putin's reforms of 2000 deprived the Federation Council of any political independence, allowing him to shape the chamber's majorities as he chose. Thus neither chamber has the means or inclination to challenge the president. This state of affairs is not necessarily permanent, but a shift to a more balanced relationship between the branches would require deep changes on both sides. The president would need to give up much of the informal power he presently possesses, and parliament would need to win an independent political mandate from the electorate.

Over the past twenty years, parliament's role in the political system has changed fundamentally. In the early 1990s, parliament reflected the sharp polarization in the country, together with the grave debility of all the central political institutions. No one party held a majority in parliament, and the weakness of parliament and the president forced them to bargain with one another as best they could. After the August 1998 financial crash, Russia's political system even gravitated toward a parliamentary model for a period of several months. Under Putin, the authorities took pains to construct a lasting dominant party system built around United Russia. If United Russia's current dominance were ever to give way to a competitive party system, then parliament would again become a more important arena for deliberation. Likewise, if the mass media, national interest groups, and judicial bodies grew more autonomous, that would encourage members of parliament to stake out policy positions independent of the president. Finally, if a future president himself were to recognize that making the government more accountable to parliament would make it a more reliable and effective instrument for exercising power, Russia would see a more even balance in the distribution of power between the executive and legislative branches.

Chapter 4

The Electoral Process

STEPHEN WHITE

Elections had taken place regularly throughout the years of Soviet rule. Indeed, as Stalin told the constituency meeting that agreed to nominate him to the newly established Soviet parliament, they were the 'only genuinely free and democratic elections in the entire world': not simply were they secret, direct and universal, they were also free of the attempts to influence voters and distort their wishes that were a feature of elections in class-divided capitalist societies (1937: 1). The entire adult population had the right to vote; almost all of them exercised that right; and the successful candidates elected a new government when the parliament met for its first session shortly afterwards. Most of the deputies, certainly, were Communist Party members. But the constitution under which they operated was based on the principle of popular sovereignty, which placed all formal authority in the hands of the people as a whole. The only body that could adopt a law that was binding on all citizens was accordingly a body they had themselves elected.

These, however, were also 'elections without choice' (Hermet et al. 1978). There was no choice of party, because the Communist Party was the 'leading and guiding force of Soviet society' under Article 6 of the Constitution. And until the very end of the Soviet period there was no choice of candidate either, as the only bodies that had the right to make nominations were the Communist Party and the public organizations that it controlled. Indeed it was very difficult to avoid voting altogether, as the authorities engaged in a massive effort to collect ballots from citizens wherever they happened to be: from shepherds in distant pastures, passengers on long-distance trains, submariners in the ocean depths or cosmonauts in outer space. The results were correspondingly impressive: at the last national elections that were organized on this basis, in 1984, turnout was 99.99 per cent, and 99.94 and 99.95 per cent respectively were reported to have voted for the single list of candidates for each of the parliament's two chambers – a 'convincing demonstration', claimed the Politburo, 'of the unshakable unity of the Soviet people around the Communist Party and its leninist Central Committee' (*Pravda*, 8 March 1984: 1).

60

One of the successful candidates on this occasion was the future party leader, Mikhail Gorbachev. But a central element in the *perestroika* he initiated the following year was a far-reaching 'democratization' of the political system, and of the electoral system in particular. Under the existing system, he told a special party conference in the summer of 1988, as many as a third of the entire society were elected to various state and public agencies, but 'the great bulk of them were kept out of any real participation in the handling of state and public affairs'. The result was 'indifference, a slackening in the social activism of the masses, and the alienation of working people from public ownership and management' (XIX *Vsesoyuznaya* 1988: I, 46, 48). The conference agreed with Gorbachev that a 'substantive modernization of the existing electoral system' was necessary, including the 'listing of more candidates on the ballots than there are seats to be filled' (ibid.: II, 138). An entirely new election law, adopted in December 1988, was based throughout on these very different principles. The candidates themselves had to put forward a 'programme', so that voters could choose between them; and all votes had to be cast in a screened-off booth, putting an end to the open affirmation that had been the normal practice in the past. The first election that took place on this newly competitive basis, in March 1989, was a political earthquake: nearly 40 party and government leaders went down to defeat, and Boris Yeltsin, a former member of the Politburo who was now the Kremlin's most uncompromising opponent, won an overwhelming 89 per cent of the vote in Moscow (White 1991). It was perhaps the decisive moment in the process that led to the demise of the Soviet system itself.

It was less easy to characterize the system that took its place at the end of 1991. The new Russia, according to its 1993 Constitution, was a 'democratic federal law-based state with a republican form of government' (Art. 1). Ordinary citizens were the only source of legitimate authority, and their wishes found ultimate expression in the referendum and 'free elections' (Art. 3). But what were 'free elections'? Formally, elections in the new Russia satisfied every reasonable criterion: there was a choice of party and candidate; the various contenders had every opportunity to set out their programme before a national electorate, including publicly funded television broadcasts; and there was little obvious interference in the casting of ballots. But was this enough? Did the various contenders have approximately equal opportunities, or did some of them enjoy more media coverage and sometimes the direct support of the state itself? Were the election laws fair to all, or skewed to the advantage of contenders that enjoyed the favour of the Kremlin? How much direct falsification took place? And what did ordinary citizens make of it all?

Initially, international observers had been very positive about the electoral process in what was routinely described as a 'young democracy'. As late as 1999 the Organisation for Security and Cooperation in Europe (OSCE), which provided the most authoritative assessments of such matters, felt able to report that the Duma election of that year had 'marked significant progress in consolidating representative democracy' (OSCE 2000a: 2); the presidential election, shortly afterwards, had been a 'benchmark in the ongoing evolution of the Russian Federation's emergence as a representative democracy', within a legislative framework that was 'consistent with internationally recognized democratic standards' (OSCE 2000b: 2, 3). But international opinion became increasingly dissatisfied as a set of arrangements developed in which the Kremlin itself had clearly become the dominant participant (some, notably Urban 1994, had been more sceptical from the outset). And by the end of Putin's second presidential term in the early years of the new century there was general agreement that these were less 'free and fair' than a distinctive form that might perhaps be called 'authoritarian elections' – unlike democracy, which was a system in which 'parties lose elections', this was a system in which '*opposition* parties lose elections' (Schedler 2002: 47).

Transitions, it was pointed out, could lead anywhere: towards democracy, as it was understood in western countries, or towards new forms of authoritarianism that fell outside established categories (Carothers 2002 was a particularly influential statement of this view). Periodic elections provided 'at least a semblance of democratic legitimacy', but by placing them under 'tight authoritarian controls', a ruling group could hope to 'cement their continued hold on power' (Schedler 2002: 35–6). Genuine elections, by contrast, had to satisfy a number of rigorous conditions: they should be the means by which the society's most important decision-makers were chosen; alternatives must be freely available; parties and candidates must have unlimited access to the public sphere in order to communicate with the electorate; all adult citizens (except in special circumstances) must have the right to vote; they must be able to express their preferences, without constraint, through a secret ballot; votes must be counted honestly; and the winners must have effective decision-making authority. It was only when all of these conditions applied that an election could properly be regarded as 'democratic' (ibid.: 40–1).

In an authoritarian election of the Russian kind there was a whole series of mechanisms that made it difficult if not impossible to mount an effective challenge to the governing authorities (for a fuller account see White *et al.* 2012). For a start, the election laws themselves were changed repeatedly, and normally in a direction that was to the Kremlin's advantage. The changes that took place in 2005 were particularly significant, notably the elimination of the single-member constituencies that had previously accounted for half the seats in the Russian parliament and the restriction of the right to compete with nationally registered political

parties. The election itself was administered by commissions within
which Kremlin-aligned parties were normally dominant, and which could
be relied upon to reject any parties or prospective presidential candidates
that appeared likely to represent a serious challenge by (for instance) finding errors in their nomination papers. Media coverage was overwhelmingly biased, in tone as well as quantity, towards officially favoured
parties and candidates. And local officials competed with each other to
report the kind of results that would maintain or even improve their own
position, in much the same way they had competed to 'fulfil the plan' over
the long years of Soviet rule.

There was accordingly some surprise when the December 2011 parliamentary election led to a sharp fall in the share of the vote that was secured
by the Kremlin's favoured party, and then to a series of public demonstrations that were the largest expression of oppositional opinion that had been
seen since the end of Soviet rule. Putin was successfully returned to the presidency in March 2012, and if he served another two consecutive terms he
could be the country's chief executive until 2024. But the demonstrations
continued (even if the numbers diminished), and there was evidence from
elections at lower levels that the Kremlin was no longer in charge of the
representative process to the same extent that it had been in the recent past.
At the election to the Moscow mayorate that took place in September 2013,
the opposition activist, Aleksei Navalny, came second with a solid 27 per
cent of the vote, even though the Kremlin's preferred candidate, incumbent
Sergei Sobyanin, won an overall majority. And in Russia's fourth-largest
city, Ekaterinburg, another oppositionist and social reformer, Evgenii
Roizman, beat the United Russia candidate into second place.

The Kremlin, for its part, began to change the election laws again, but
this time in an apparently more liberal direction, back towards the mixed
system that had prevailed after 1993 and which, it seemed, would be fully
reintroduced in time for the next Duma election in December 2016 (see
Box 4.1). Other changes made it easier to establish a political party
(although this might also make it more difficult to organize a coherent
opposition), and the threshold for representation, which had been raised
to 7 per cent, came down again to 5 per cent. Still more important, there
was at least a qualified return to the direct election of regional governors,
which had been abolished in December 2004 following a hostage-taking
crisis in the North Caucasus. The crucial question, as the Putin presidency
entered its third term, was whether changes of this kind would be sufficient to maintain a stable relationship between regime and society or if a
more far-reaching accommodation would be required. Either way it was
likely that the electoral mechanism would be involved, not only as an
issue in itself but also because it set out the framework within which other
issues would have to be addressed.

Box 4.1   Duma election legislation since 1993: a summary

1993–2005: a mixed electoral system: 225 independent or party-sponsored deputies elected by simple majority in single-member constituencies, 225 elected by a national party-list contest with seats allocated proportionally to all that exceeded a 5 per cent threshold.

From 2005: all 450 seats, at future elections, to be filled by the national party-list contest; electoral blocs prohibited.

In 2007: a new threshold for representation, 7 per cent rather than 5 per cent, came into effect.

In 2009: a federal law allocated one seat to parties that received 5 or 6 per cent of the vote, and 2 seats each to parties that won 6 or 7 per cent.

In 2011: amendments approved lowering the threshold back to 5 per cent for elections to the Duma in 2016 and subsequent years.

In February 2014 further legislation restored the mixed system: 225 seats will as before be filled by a national party-list contest, and 225 by a series of contests in individual constituencies.

Sources: based on *Kommersant*, 1 March 2013: 2; and subsequent press reports.

Towards authoritarian elections

The new constitution of 1993, adopted in what was already a post-Soviet Russia, set out the basic principles that would apply at all future elections. Under the terms of article 32, all citizens have the right to elect and be elected to the organs of state power and local government and to take part in referendums except those who have been declared incapable of exercising their rights by a court, and prisoners. The 'multinational people' are the 'bearer of sovereignty and the only source of power in the Russian Federation', and they exercise this power both 'directly' and through elections to state bodies and local government (art. 3). The electoral process is regulated in more detail by a framework law, first adopted in its present form in 2002, which covers the 'basic guarantees' that apply to referendums and elections at all levels of the Russian system. Elections, according to the law, take place on the basis of a universal, equal, direct and secret ballot (art. 3), and the electorate includes all Russian citizens aged

Table 4.1 *Russian Duma elections, 1993–2011*

Date	*PL seats*	*SMC seats*	*% PL threshold*	*PL threshold*	*PL winners*	*Turnout (%)* 'voted'	*Turnout (%)* 'took part'
12 Dec 1993	225	225	5	13	8	n.d.	54.81
17 Dec 1995	225	225	5	43	4	64.38	64.73
19 Dec 1999	225	225	5	26	6	61.69	61.85
7 Dec 2003	225	225	5	23	4	55.67	55.75
2 Dec 2007	450	–	7	11	4	63.71	63.78
4 Dec 2011	450	–	7	7	4	60.10	60.21

Note: PL=party list; SMC=single-member constituency. Electors 'took part in the election' by receiving a ballot paper and 'took part in the voting' by casting a valid or invalid ballot.

Source: official communiqués of the Central Electoral Commission, incorporating subsequent corrections.

18 or over wherever they are resident, with the exceptions that have already been noted (art. 4).

Legislative power at the national level, as we saw in the previous chapter, is exercised by the Federal Assembly, which is the 'representative and legislative organ of the Russian Federation'. It consists of two chambers: a popularly elected lower house, the State Duma, roughly corresponding to the House of Commons in the United Kingdom or the House of Representatives in the United States, and an upper house, the Federation Council, sometimes described as a 'Senate', which is composed of representatives of the various republics and regions (there were 83 of these in 2014 and each had two representatives, which meant a total membership of 166). The Duma was initially elected for two years, and then four years at a time, but following constitutional amendments in 2008 it is now elected for a five-year term; this means that the Duma that was elected in December 2011 will serve until December 2016 (the entire sequence is set out in Table 4.1). The Russian President is also elected directly, initially for four years but since 2012 for six years at a time, which means that the next scheduled presidential election will take place in March 2018.

All of these processes are regulated in turn by more detailed legislation. The Duma, in the first instance, was elected in two separate ways: half of the 225 seats were filled by a national party-list contest, with seats awarded proportionally to all the parties that reached a 5 per cent threshold; the other 225 seats were filled by contests in single-member constituencies all over the country, with the result determined by simple majority. In principle, it was thought, a mixed electoral system of this kind would achieve an optimum balance between the need to reflect the concerns of individual localities while at the same time providing a programme of government for the country as a whole. The national party-list contest was expected to encourage political parties, which were still very weak. It would advantage pro-Kremlin reformers, who were the most likely to have a national profile. And some element of proportionality was needed, in the view of supporters of the new system, if there was to be an 'organized parliament' and not an assembly of individuals representing the varied and perhaps conflicting interests of their own constituencies (*Rossiya*, no. 35, 1993: 3).

There were elections to the Duma on this party list and constituency basis in 1993, 1995, 1999 and 2003. But in 2005 it was replaced by an entirely party-list system as part of a package of far-reaching changes that followed a hostage-taking emergency at a school in the town of Beslan in the northern Caucasus at the start of September 2004. This had ended in tragedy when President Putin ordered the armed forces to seize the building and more than three hundred lost their lives, half of them children. Speaking shortly afterwards, Putin claimed the incident had shown the need for the Russian government to be 'fundamentally restructured for the purpose of bolstering the country's unity and preventing crises'. This meant, first of all, that executive agencies at all levels should be reconstituted as a 'single system of authority', with leading officials in the republics and regions appointed on the basis of presidential nomination rather than direct election. Putin also believed it was 'essential, in the interests of strengthening the country's political system, that we adopt a proportional system of elections to the State Duma', and promised to expedite the necessary legislation (Putin 2004).

The shift to a wholly party-list Duma, in fact, had been under consideration for some time, and the entire package of changes (in the view of their opponents) was nothing less than an 'electoral counter-revolution' (Ivanchenko and Lyubarev 2007: 195). There had certainly been a 'lot of problems with the single-member deputies', explained a very senior member of the Presidential Administration in an interview that was not for attribution. They had been 'controlled by the governors, by the regional elite. It was harder to work with them'. The new system was one in which United Russia might win fewer seats, but this was an acceptable price to pay for a Duma that could be managed more easily, and for a proportional system that would on the whole be more transparent ('I mean, transparent for us', he laughed. 'For the Centre. Easier to control'). As things stood, added other officials, 'someone unexpected and undesirable might be elected'. And if enough of them were elected, 'the State Duma might become unpredictable in its behaviour'. Now awkward individuals could be excluded, and the whole system would 'work like clockwork' (White and Kryshtanovskaya 2011: 562, 563–4).

Other changes followed, which were also of a kind that was likely to advantage the Kremlin and its favoured parties and candidates. There had, for instance, been an 'against all' provision on the ballot paper at every federal election up to 2004, allowing voters to reject all the parties and presidential candidates on offer. It became increasingly popular, winning 4.7 per cent of the party-list vote in the 2003 Duma election and 12.9 per cent in the single-member constituencies; indeed it 'won' three of them, which meant that by-elections had to be held so that candidates could be found who were able to secure a larger total. There were even suggestions that 'against all' might reach the party-list threshold at the Duma election that was to follow, although it would hardly be able to take its seats. But in the event, the provision was withdrawn entirely in 2006 (McAllister and White 2008a). Another legislative change was the abolition of the minimum turnout requirement, in April 2007. There was clearly little likelihood that the turnout in a Duma election would fall below 25 per cent, which had been the minimum required; but it was not inconceivable that the turnout in a presidential election might fall below 50 per cent, which would have made the entire exercise invalid.

The 2007 Duma election, based on the new law, was a near-perfect example of what were already being described as 'authoritarian elections'. Several mechanisms were of particular importance, not least the legislative framework itself. For a start, the contest was (for the first time) restricted to nationally registered political parties, which meant parties whose establishment the Kremlin itself had authorized. Parties that were represented in the outgoing Duma had the right to put forward a list of candidates without additional formality; other parties had either to collect the signatures of 200,000 electors, or pay a deposit of 60 million roubles (about $2.5m). But if more than 5 per cent of the signatures were declared invalid, or if the number fell below the minimum once invalid signatures had been eliminated, the application as a whole would be rejected. Fourteen parties sought to register a list of candidates on this basis, seven of them by collecting signatures, but three were found to have included an excessive number of invalid signatures in their nomination papers and their applications were unsuccessful. It was the same when a former prime minister who was now in opposition, Mikhail Kasyanov, attempted to register as a presidential candidate in January 2008 (for whatever reason, supporters of oppositional parties and candidates always seemed to have worse handwriting than pro-Kremlin loyalists).

The campaign itself was heavily weighted in favour of the Kremlin by a further series of mechanisms. Access to the media, and particularly to national television, was a crucial resource in a country with an electorate of about a hundred million distributed across nine (originally eleven) time zones. Accordingly, it made a lot of difference that national television gave more coverage to Kremlin-sponsored parties and candidates, over and above the advantages that would in any case have been enjoyed by incumbents. Over the campaign period, it was established, United Russia had 19 per cent of prime-time news coverage on the authoritative First Channel (which is largely state-owned), 20 per cent on Rossiya (which is entirely state-owned), 19 per cent on the third most popular national channel, NTV (which is owned by state-controlled Gazprom Media), and 32 per cent on TV-Tsentr (which is owned by the Moscow city administration). Its main challenger, the Communist Party of the Russian Federation, had 2, 3, 2 and 1 per cent respectively. It was much the same in the 2008 presidential election, when the Kremlin's favoured candidate, Prime Minister Dmitri Medvedev, had between 26 and 43 per cent of prime-time news coverage on the same four channels and none of the other candidates had more than 7 per cent on any of them (White 2011: 536–7).

It could also be difficult when independent parties or candidates wished to organize a public demonstration. The former world chess champion Gary Kasparov, who was one of the leaders of the openly oppositional 'Other Russia' coalition, was among the dozens who were arrested by riot police when he took part in an anti-Kremlin meeting in Moscow in November 2007, his speech, according to western newspaper reports, interrupted by a 'screeching noise from loudspeakers on top of a nearby building'. In St Petersburg the following day 'scores of demonstrators were detained and some beaten ... as riot police broke up a protest over the Kremlin's lurch towards authoritarianism'; nearly two hundred were arrested, among them the Union of Right Forces leader Boris Nemtsov. Opposition leaders were repeatedly harassed by pro-Kremlin youth in the run-up to the poll – stalked by activists, their news conferences disrupted, and recordings of 'loud, maniacal laughter' played at their public meetings. One activist handcuffed himself three times to Kasparov's car; another tried to put a butterfly net over Nemtsov's head with a sign saying 'political insect'; others still pelted him with condoms (cited in White 2011: 542–3).

On polling day itself there were additional pressures, particularly for all who worked in state-funded institutions. Students were taken to the polling station in groups and given 'detailed instructions'; deans were on hand to record any absences; and academic staff themselves were told to 'vote for United Russia or face dismissal'. Voting in 'closed' institutions, such as hospitals, prisons and the army, was especially open to administrative pressures of this kind (White 2011: 544–5); but it was a much more general phenomenon. In Russia's third-largest city, Nizhnii

Novgorod, foremen went round the workforce at the city's massive vehicle plant telling them to vote for the ruling party and report back after they had left the polling station, or obtain absentee certificates and fill them out in front of their immediate superiors. 'Names would be taken, defiance punished.' Elsewhere in the city teachers handed out leaflets promoting 'Putin's Plan' and told children to lobby their parents. A number were 'threatened with bad grades if they failed to attend "children's referendums"'; at other schools parents were simply 'ordered to attend mandatory meetings with representatives of United Russia' (Levy 2008).

There were also more obvious violations of the election law, including ballot stuffing and multiple voting. In a particularly egregious case at a polling station in Moscow a group of nearly 70 had arrived together on a bus, declaring themselves to be temporary residents and demanding that their names be added to a supplementary register. It took more than an hour for the formalities to be completed, after which they were all allowed to cast a ballot. The same group, using the same bus, had reportedly appeared at five other polling stations in the same area; they had voted, according to observers, 'at least six times' (Buzin and Lyubarev 2008: 177). In another case, this time in Dagestan, a single voter had managed to vote five times using different forms of documentation (Kriger 2008: 9). Some of these were professional voters, who were doing it for the money; they could photograph the completed ballot paper on their mobile phone and collect the reward on their way out (Zalessky 2007: 17–18). But there were many other forms of inducement: pensioners in Novgorod, for instance, were offered expensive tableware to cast a ballot that had already been completed in favour of United Russia; party officials in Kemerovo were handing out free vodka and tickets to the local ice-hockey stadium (Kriger 2008: 8, 9).

The count was another opportunity to ensure the right result. Commission members, for instance, could swap the piles of votes for the various parties and then 'count them out in front of observers as if nothing had happened'. A 'modernized version of this method' was to attach a ballpoint refill to a finger and put a tick on the ballot papers that voters had forgotten to complete. Or alternatively, to spoil a ballot paper on which a vote had been cast for an anti-Kremlin party by adding another tick. Much more common, in the view of seasoned observers, was the identification of 'errors' in the first set of results, allowing a 'corrected' version to be prepared in which the results that were required could easily be inserted; observers might be forced to leave the room at this point, or not informed that a new protocol was being prepared (Zalessky 2007: 18). In other cases observers might be refused admission to the polling station in the first place, or forced to sit some distance from the voting booths. There were cases when the lights failed mysteriously for three or four minutes as the votes were being counted (*Zayavlenie* 2007); there were even cases in which observers who had drawn attention to ballot stuffing were themselves arrested and threatened with criminal prosecution (Buzin and Lyubarev 2008: 163–4).

An increasingly salient feature of the Russian electoral process was the proportion of voters who exercised their rights outside a polling station, and sometimes in advance of polling day. The election law allowed votes to be cast up to 15 days beforehand in 'inaccessible or distant localities, on ships that on polling day [were] at sea, [or] at polar stations', or at polling stations that were 'outside the boundaries of the Russian Federation'. The numbers were very small (just 0.2 per cent of the total in December 2007), but steadily increasing. Much larger numbers voted on the basis of absentee certificates, a procedure that was intended to cater for electors who were obliged to be elsewhere on polling day; more than a million took advantage of this facility in December 2007, about twice as many as had done so four years earlier and some 1.7 per cent of all the votes that were cast. And still larger numbers made use of mobile ballot boxes, by which election officials visited electors in their homes or hospital wards because their particular circumstances did not allow them to attend a polling station in person; more than four million voted on this basis in December 2007, and more than five million (7.5 per cent of the total) in March 2008.

The effect of each of these arrangements was to reduce the proportion of the electorate that cast their vote in a conventional polling station under the watchful eye of observers, and to drive up the proportion that cast their vote in circumstances in which the secrecy and indeed integrity of the ballot were much less likely to be secured. There were certainly many instances in which the facility appeared to have been abused. In Khabarovsk, for instance, an electoral commission itself was found to have completed 24 applications for the use of the mobile ballot box on behalf of the residents of a local old people's home, in an attempt to raise turnout levels; four of the supposed applicants later insisted they had made no such application, three could not have written anything at all as they were blind, and one had died the day before (Kriger 2008: 9). Elsewhere, there were cases where local electoral commissions set out themselves with mobile ballot boxes to find electors who had not yet exercised their democratic rights (Buzin and Lyubarev 2008: 105). Altogether, more than 5.7 million (8.3 per cent of the total) voted in one or other of these less closely regulated ways in December 2007, and more than seven million (9.4 per cent) did so in March 2008; in both cases these were larger proportions than ever before.

Free and fair?

The parliamentary and presidential elections that took place in 2011–12 raised many of these long-standing issues, but this time in the context of an active challenge to the Kremlin's authority. The formal provisions of the electoral law, once again, appeared to have been scrupulously respected. There was a choice of parties and candidates on the ballot paper. There were detailed regulations on the use of campaign funds, and on campaigning itself. And there was a substantial delegation of OSCE observers, unlike 2007 and 2008 when it had proved impossible to agree on the basis on which they would operate. The outcome was a clear victory for United Russia (Table 4.2), and then for Vladimir Putin in the presidential contest in March 2012 (Table 2.1); but there was no suggestion, even from oppositional politicians, that they had somehow 'stolen' their victories. Indeed the official results were very close to the final predictions of the major survey agencies, not all of which were Kremlin-friendly. How else could this be interpreted, asked the chairman of the Central Electoral Commission, than as independent confirmation of the validity of the entire exercise?

But there was a very different assessment from international monitors, including the team that was deployed by the OSCE's Office for Democratic Institutions and Human Rights. The Duma election, they accepted, had been 'technically well-administered across the country', but it had been 'slanted in favour of the ruling party', which had operated with the direct support of the state itself. It had not been administered impartially, the media had been biased, and state bodies had intervened improperly at various levels. All of this had 'not provide[d] the necessary

Table 4.2   *The Russian Duma election, 4 December 2011*

Party	Vote	Percent	Seats (%)
United Russia	32,379,135	49.3	238 (52.9)
Communist Party	12,599,507	19.2	92 (20.4)
Fair Russia	8,695,522	13.2	64 (14.2)
Liberal Democratic Party	7,664,570	11.7	56 (12.4)
7 percent threshold			
Yabloko	2,252,403	3.4	0
Patriots of Russia	639,119	1.0	0
Right Cause	392,806	0.6	0
Valid vote	64,623,062	98.4	
Invalid vote	1,033,464	1.6	
Total vote	65,656,526	100.0	
Registered voters/turnout	109,237,780	60.1	

Source: data from the Central Electoral Commission.

conditions for fair electoral competition'. Moreover, the quality of the election had 'deteriorated considerably during the count, which was characterized by frequent procedural violations and instances of apparent manipulation, including several serious indications of ballot box stuffing'. During the campaign the distinction between the state and the governing party had been 'frequently blurred by state and local officials taking advantage of their office or position to advance the chances of one party over the others', and there had been 'numerous credible allegations of attempts by local state structures to influence voter choice and to pressure them into voting for the governing party' (OSCE 2012: 3–4).

Not surprisingly, the Central Electoral Commission rejected these criticisms, a number of which (in its view) were at odds with the evidence of the final report itself, and there were certainly some features of the OSCE mission that qualified the authority of its conclusions. In the first place, there was no 'verdict' at all, either in the preliminary report that was issued the day after polling day or in the final report that appeared about a month later. Why, asked an indignant press conference that was attended by the author, had the mission felt unable to declare the elections free and fair, or otherwise? This would be a 'political statement' that was not a part of their remit, responded delegation leaders, and in any case much too summary an assessment of a large and complex exercise. But then why, journalists persisted, had the OSCE felt able to pronounce in exactly these terms on the elections that had taken place in Kazakhstan and Belarus? Why had there been no representation in parts of the country such as the North Caucasus, where the most outrageous falsification appeared to have taken place? (It was too dangerous to go there, apparently, and the foreign ministries of the member states who sponsored the delegation members had been unwilling to accept the risk.) How much weight, in any case, could be placed on the impressions of 262 foreign observers, more than a third of whom did not know Russian (*Vybory* 2012: 529), about an exercise that was taking place in nearly 96,000 polling stations spread across a seventh of the world's entire land surface?

Nor was this all: as there were many other international observers, some of them selected by the Russian authorities themselves. And not surprisingly, they came to rather different conclusions. In December 2011 the mission from the Commonwealth of Independent States was the largest with 208 observers, all of them Russian speaking. In its final report the mission concluded that the election had taken place in a 'calm atmosphere' and 'in accordance with the requirements of the electoral law of the Russian Federation'; there had been minor infractions, but 'none that could have influenced the results', and taken as a whole it had satisfied 'generally recognised democratic norms' (CIS 2011). The Shanghai Cooperation Organization also reported that voting had taken place in a 'free, transparent, democratic and well organized atmosphere' and in accordance with Russian legislation and the country's international obligations, all of which made it possible to declare the election 'democratic and legitimate' (SCO 2011). These missions were also working on the basis of an international convention, in this case a 'convention on standards for democratic elections' that had been signed by seven CIS member countries in Chisinau in 2002. Why should their conclusions be given any less credence than those of the international observers from the West, whose own practices were scarcely beyond criticism?

But the evidence of the streets was also difficult to disregard, in particular the wave of demonstrations that began on the evening of polling day in December 2011 and developed into the largest and most sustained that had been seen since the final years of the Soviet era (they are discussed in several other chapters of this book). The demonstration that took place on Bolotnaya Square in central Moscow on 10 December 2011, six days after the election itself, was the largest of all: according to police estimates, about 25,000 were involved; the BBC put the figure at 50,000; the organizers themselves claimed 150,000, in spite of temperatures that hovered around –20C. The largest numbers were in Moscow itself, but there were protests in more than 90 other Russian cities, and across the world (*New Times*, 12 December 2011: 3, 8–9). There were five key demands, so far as the Bolotnaya Square demonstrators were concerned: the immediate release of the 'political detainees' that had been arrested by the police; cancellation of the elections themselves; the resignation of CEC chairman Vladimir Churov; the adoption of new and more democratic legislation on parties and elections; and the conduct of 'new, open and honest elections' (ibid.: 5).

How representative were the demonstrators, and how widely supported were their demands? The survey evidence suggests that dissatisfaction with the Duma election was fairly widespread. Indeed, on the evidence of a post-election survey conducted by the Levada Center, which is the oldest and probably most respected of the Russian public opinion agencies, a relative majority thought it had been largely or at least somewhat dishonest, although there was a greater willingness to accept the outcome a month later (Table 4.3). A survey that was conducted for the author and associates by a different agency at the same time reached a very similar conclusion: that a narrow majority (52 per cent) thought the Duma election had been largely or entirely fair, but that a very substantial 39 per cent took the opposite view. And as Table 4.3 also makes clear, the proportion that thought the election had been dishonest was greater than it had been at the time of the previous Duma election in 2007. Nor was there much indication that this was a protest that was confined to the younger, well educated and affluent Muscovites who had attended the

Table 4.3   *How honest were the elections to the Russian State Duma?*

	Dec 2007	Dec 2011	Jan 2012
Entirely honest	16	5	8
Fairly honest	45	30	35
Not very honest	15	30	23
Completely dishonest	5	15	14
(No response)	18	20	19

Source: Levada Center data as reported in Gudkov *et al.* 2012: 29 (N=1,600; rounded percentages).

Bolotnaya Square demonstration in their fur coats. In fact, on the evidence of our January 2012 survey, it was the prosperous who were the most satisfied and the poorest who were the most likely to be alienated.

What, then, about the demands of the protestors? On the evidence of the Levada Center they were also widely supported, at least in general terms. In their post-election survey, in mid-December 2011, 44 per cent largely or entirely supported the demonstrators' demands, as compared with 41 per cent who were largely or entirely opposed. However, there was less support for the demonstrators' more specific demands, as they had been agreed at Bolotnaya Square. No more than a quarter thought the December election should be annulled and a new election called instead (27 per cent were in favour, but 52 per cent against). There was no more support for the demand that the CEC chairman Vladimir Churov should be dismissed (27 per cent were in favour, but 44 per cent opposed). And few were prepared to take part themselves in any new mass protest against electoral violations (16 per cent said they would 'definitely' or 'probably' become involved, but 74 per cent were either 'probably' or 'definitely' reluctant to do so) (Rose 2012a: 44–5). Not surprisingly, those who were most likely to believe the election had been unfair were the most likely to support the protest demonstrations, and vice versa.

Some conclusions

Clearly, opinions could vary, and change over time. There were also some ways in which the authorities could seek to accommodate the most widely shared concerns. There was no indication that they would be prepared to accept the demonstrators' central demand, which was the cancellation of the Duma election. But there were ways in which the electoral process could at least be modified so as to recover some of the public confidence it had evidently lost. One of these was already apparent at the presidential election in March 2012: web cameras, installed at great cost in nearly all polling stations, allowing the entire process to be monitored remotely. Another was the use of transparent ballot boxes, which made it possible to see if votes had been cast individually or in pre-completed batches. The presidential election, for these and other reasons, was widely seen as an improvement on the Duma election (60 per cent thought it had been largely or entirely honest, as against 27 per cent who took the opposite view) (Rose 2012b: 32). It had also been suggested that there should be a return to the mixed party list and constituency system, so that voters had a greater sense of a deputy who could represent their particular interests in the national legislature, and the election law was changed in this sense in February 2014.

All the same, the nature and significance of the disaffection that had followed the 2011 Duma election remained somewhat unclear. Why, for instance, had this particular election, at this particular time, given rise to such widespread popular dissatisfaction? Was it demonstrably more dishonest than the ones that had preceded it? Or was it simply *believed* to have been more dishonest? And if this was the case (as it appeared to be), how could that perception itself be explained? Was it the result of particular circumstances, such as the attack on the reputation of the ruling party – a 'party of crooks and thieves' – that had been made by the blogger Aleksei Navalny in the spring of 2011? Or the decision that was announced in September 2011 that Putin and Medvedev would be 'castling', with Medvedev returning to the premiership when Putin was re-elected president in a decision they had apparently made 'years earlier'? Or the prospect of a Putin presidency that might now extend until 2024? Or were long-term factors involved of a kind that were more generally employed in the social sciences, such as a slowdown in the rate of economic growth or changes in the wider society, such as a growing 'middle class'?

In the end, the electoral process was perhaps best seen as an important but not decisive element in this larger constellation of forces. As a mechanism, 'authoritarian elections' could often help to protect a ruling group from the fluctuations of popular sympathy that their counterparts in the liberal democracies had to confront. But they were hardly a complete guarantee. And the more the rules were amended, so as to eliminate at least the more obvious forms of abuse, the less protection they were likely to offer. Russians, over many centuries, had looked to the state to provide public order and social welfare. But if the state was no longer able to maintain its side of the bargain because growth rates were falling, or if there was widespread dissatisfaction for some other reason, it was unlikely authoritarian elections would provide enough legitimacy to compensate. Ultimately, there were only two choices: either a government that rested on the consent of the governed, or a government that maintained itself by force. The Putin leadership, it appeared, was attempting to find a path between them. It was not yet clear that one existed.

Chapter 5

Russia's Political Parties and their Substitutes

HENRY E. HALE

Many observers expected Russia to develop a competitive party system rapidly after the USSR broke apart in late 1991. Russia was democratizing, the argument went, and the experience of Western countries had given experts little reason to question Max Weber's classic aphorism that democracy was 'unimaginable' without parties (Weber 1990). Russian developments quickly challenged this view, however. A plethora of parties did spring up during the 1990s, with as many as 43 appearing on the parliamentary ballot in 1995 alone, but by the end of that decade their growth had stalled. Independent politicians continued to dominate the country's most important posts. For example, only 3 per cent of Russia's regional leaders, when running for re-election, chose to do so as party nominees between 1995 and 2000. Likewise, President Boris Yeltsin himself consistently declined to join any party after leaving the Communist Party of the Soviet Union (CPSU) in 1990.

In the 2000s, Russia's party system did finally begin to take shape, but with a major twist. Putin instituted a series of reforms that weakened the most important pre-existing parties and corralled a majority of the most influential independent politicians into a new pro-Putin organization called the United Russia Party. Since the late 2000s, the party has commanded majorities not only in the national parliament but also in nearly all regional legislatures, and virtually all governors have been affiliated with it. Despite this, United Russia's growth has never quite reached the point of complete dominance, even in the government. Current President Vladimir Putin agreed to serve as party 'chairman' 2008–12, but even during this period refused to call himself a party 'member,' preferring to keep his distance and periodically criticize it even as he often praised it. Some have asked, how strong can a party be if its own top patron will not fully commit himself to it? Moreover, there is evidence that the Kremlin (that is, Russia's president and his close associates) continues to keep a stable of other parties and party-like organizations 'in reserve' that can be used either to attack true opposition parties or perhaps one day replace United Russia if something goes wrong. In addition, the Kremlin frequently manipulates the party system by revising important laws in ways that help it survive different challenges.

How did this situation come about, and what does the answer tell us about how politics works in Russia? That is the subject of the pages that follow.

The building blocks of Russian parties

Why would any politician ever bother joining a party in the first place? One short answer is: a politician will join a party when that party gives the candidate a greater chance of getting elected than he or she would have as an independent. Parties in Russia, and arguably everywhere, generally offer candidates at least two kinds of advantages. First, they can provide a candidate with money, organization, connections, and other *resources* that can be used to campaign or otherwise win office. Second, they can connect a candidate with a set of ideas that the party has a *reputation* for pursuing, helping a candidate reach out to people who may support the party's ideas but who may not know anything about the candidate. Politicians who are rich in either resources or reputation, therefore, tend to be particularly successful party builders because they have something that other ambitious politicians want. These things, resources and reputation, are thus the building blocks of parties.

What building blocks were available to would-be party builders in Russia upon the USSR's demise? The only pre-existing party with any claim to have stood the test of time was the CPSU, but in the wake of the August 1991 coup attempt it was banned along with its Russian branch. Even in its heyday, it was mostly an instrument of control rather than a party geared for actually competing in free elections. Moreover, by 1991, its central Marxist ideas were widely discredited and it had been losing members since CPSU leader Mikhail Gorbachev started seriously reforming the Soviet system. Nevertheless, the party did leave behind some significant networks of true believers and people who had forged important personal connections that could eventually be reactivated for organizing a party.

Once Gorbachev began reforming the Soviet political system in earnest, and even before parties other than the CPSU were formally legalized in early 1990, a huge number of 'informal' organizations sprang up to promote various political causes. Flush with the opportunity to publicly pursue almost any political agenda openly, these associations were extremely diverse and generally small, often focusing on the pet issues of all and sundry politicians. Some of these grassroots groupings did begin to coalesce into larger associations, with the most prominent being Democratic Russia. During the late *perestroika* period, Democratic Russia looked like it could successfully rival the Russian branch of the declining CPSU and was able to mobilize hundreds of thousands of people in some of Moscow's largest streets rallies ever. But this was an extraordinarily motley movement, united almost solely by a common desire to end communist dictatorship. Once the USSR broke apart, it splintered and left little in the way of reputation and resources for future party builders to utilise.

By far the most important source of building blocks for Russia's first party system was the Soviet state. In fact, almost every non-communist politician who has built a truly successful Russian party gained his or her primary fame or other party-building resource through some connection with the state structures of the USSR or the Russian Federation. Upon reflection, this is not surprising: the Soviet state penetrated nearly all aspects of life in some way and explicitly sought to own or at least control all the means by which someone could accumulate political influence, including mass media, social organizations, and, as Marxist ideology dictated, economic resources (including all enterprises and banking institutions). Even after political liberalization removed most controls over political activity, the state remained overwhelmingly the greatest source of money, organization and media attention, which are among the most valuable building blocks for parties. Even after Yeltsin's governments privatized the bulk of Russia's economy in the 1990s, business (including the media it controlled) still remained highly dependent on aspects of the state for its profitability. All this meant that people within or connected to the state had major advantages in building the first non-communist parties. It also meant that people within the state continued to have tremendous resources that could be used against party-building projects that they did not like or to support parties that served their purposes.

The next section shows how this particular array of building blocks translated into the party system that dominated Russia in the 1990s as a necessary step for understanding United Russia's rise in the 2000s and the party system as it exists now in the 2010s.

The veteran parties: those first emerging in the early 1990s

Researchers have found that the outcome of a country's first multiparty elections, often called 'founding elections', can have a disproportionate long-run impact on how its party system develops (O'Donnell and

Schmitter 1986: 61–2). This is because the parties that win gain the visibility, opportunities to impact policy, and access to resources that political office brings. These gains, in turn, can be ploughed back into the party-building project, giving the initial winners a great advantage in future rounds. Winners also gain an advantage just for being seen as winners: voters and potential donors generally do not want to risk wasting votes or money on parties that will not be able to 'pay a return' on the investment by holding office (Cox 1997).

The specialists who initially authored Russia's current constitution in 1993, empowered after Yeltsin unilaterally abrogated the old constitution and called early elections late that year, were well aware of research on the importance of founding elections. They were also aware of other research indicating that the results of such elections would depend heavily on the election rules that they themselves chose. They thus chose the rules strategically in order to pursue certain concrete goals. One of these goals was to buttress the power of Yeltsin and his allies; another was to promote the development of a multiparty system. A complex set of compromises ultimately produced a system that was expected to have mixed effects on the party system (Hough 1998; McFaul 2001). It was to be dominated by a strong president, and here no special advantage was given to candidates who wished to run as party nominees.

The constitutional drafters did, however, plan for the parliament to spur party-system development. While an upper chamber (the Federation Council), as we have seen, was to represent regions on a largely non-party basis, half of the lower chamber (the State Duma) was to be elected through a competition between nationwide party lists with a 5 per cent threshold. This effectively reserved at least half of the Duma's seats for parties capable of winning this proportion of the nationwide vote. The other half of the Duma was to be chosen in 225 districts, with one deputy elected per seat. While parties could compete for these seats too, in fact independents frequently won them. Regional authorities were left the freedom to determine election rules for regional and local elections. This basic setup remained in place until the 2007 elections.

Since the first presidential election to take place under the new constitution did not occur until 1996, observers at the time saw the 1993 Duma elections as potentially being a founding election for Russia's post-Soviet party system. The passage of time reveals that these elections did have something of a 'founding' effect, but only in a specific sense: parties that failed to clear the 5 per cent threshold in the first or subsequent Duma races have almost all proven unable ever afterward to make it into parliament. The only parties capable of breaking into the Duma for the first time after 1993 have been those with the unusually strong backing of the state authorities. There are only two of these state-backed 'upstarts' in the parliament as of the start of 2014: the United Russia Party and the 'A Just Russia' Party. At the same time, success in 1993 proved no guarantee of long-term success. In effect, subsequent Duma elections served as what might be called 'weeding elections', successively winnowing down the field to the two veteran parties that are in the parliament today: the Communist Party of the Russian Federation (CPRF) and the Liberal Democratic Party of Russia (LDPR). The following paragraphs tell the story of the veteran parties, those first gaining traction in the founding elections of 1993. After that, we turn to the upstart parties. Readers are directed to Table 5.1 for summary information on Russia's most important parties from 1993 to 2014.

One-hit wonders

Among the eight parties to win official delegations ('fractions') in the party-list Duma elections of 1993, four were never able to repeat the feat on their own: the Agrarian Party of Russia (APR), the Women of Russia bloc, the Democratic Party of Russia (DPR, an early breakaway from Democratic Russia), and the pro-Yeltsin Party of Russian Unity and Accord (PRES). These all either disappeared or merged into other pro-Kremlin parties during the 1990s or 2000s.

The Communist Party of the Russian Federation

It is a common mistake to regard the CPRF as the direct continuation of the CPSU in Russia. In fact, Yeltsin banned the Russian branch of the CPSU in 1991 and confiscated its property. Even when the Constitutional Court effectively reinstated it at the end of November 1992, there was no longer any organization in place to reclaim its mantle. Instead, there was a wide variety of small Communist organizations that were led by little-known former officials that had formed after the ban, all now competing for at least a share of the inheritance. Moreover, it was a decidedly non-communist idea (at least, according to Karl Marx) that enabled a little-known former CPSU official, Gennadii Zyuganov, to wind up as the heir. This idea was nationalism. During 1991 and 1992, he crafted a distinct ideology of nationalist socialism that helped cement a broad alliance of former communists and hard-line non-communist Russian nationalists that proved able to mobilize tens of thousands in street protests. Such impressive displays of support, combined with fears that communism alone might not be potent enough to win many votes after the USSR's break-up, led key former CPSU leaders to hitch their wagons to Zyuganov's locomotive. This, then, was the origin of the Communist Party of the Russian Federation, which officially emerged in early 1993

Table 5.1 *Post-Soviet Russia's main parties*

Party	Main leaders	Years in Duma[1]	Main policy stands	Attitude to Kremlin	% loyalists in population 2012[2]	Party status 2014
United Russia[3]	Vladimir Putin, Dmitri Medvedev guarded pro-Westernism	1999–	Anti-communism, presidentialism,	Pro-Kremlin	32	Duma majority, Prime Ministership
CPRF	Gennadii Zyuganov	1993–	Socialism, nationalism	Anti-Kremlin	9	Duma minority
LDPR	Vladimir Zhirinovsky	1993 –	Nationalism, law and order	Loyal opposition	3	Duma minority
A Just Russia	Sergei Mironov	2003 –	Moderate leftism	Loyal opposition	3	Duma minority
Yabloko	Sergei Mitrokhin, Grigorii Yavlinsky	1993–2003	Democracy, social market, pro-Westernism	Anti-Kremlin	<2	Deputies in a few sub-national legislatures

Notes: [1] Official delegation earned in party-list competition. [2] According to the Russian Election Studies 2012 survey (Colton and Hale 2014), conducted right after the March 2012 presidential elections, using Colton's (2000) measure of 'transitional partisanship'. [3] Or its main predecessor, the Unity Bloc.

after the Constitutional Court had ruled it would be legal. The CPRF gained a surprisingly high 12 per cent in the party-list vote in the snap 1993 Duma election and became the only leftist party to clear the 5 per cent barrier. This consolidated its position as the primary heir to the CPSU legacy, and it quickly reintegrated many of the CPSU networks that had fallen apart in 1991.

The party reached the pinnacle of its influence in 1996, when Zyuganov took Yeltsin to a second round in the presidential contest of that year and failed only after Yeltsin's allies resorted to media manipulation and other methods of machine politics to achieve their patron's victory. The party also captured a large share of governorships and controlled many regional legislatures, especially in the 'red belt' of Russia's southwest. Then as now, the party was no longer calling for a return to full-blown communism, accepting a significant role for private enterprise and making democracy a central element of its platform. Rather ironically, the CPRF has actually been the primary source of political competition in Russia since the mid-2000s. Despite having its support nearly halved by a negative media campaign in the 2003 Duma campaign, it remained the only party with a large and independent following that had a hope of standing up to United Russia. Thus in the Duma and most sub-national legislatures, the CPRF is the party with the second-most seats. While in the 1990s it drew significant financing from big business, which hoped to minimize its losses should the CPRF happen to win, since the mid-2000s it has come to rely mostly on modest funding allocated formally or informally by state officials and on donations of time and money from its still-large pool of dedicated (if aging) members (Morar 2007).

The Liberals: divided and marginalized

Yeltsin's supporters repeatedly urged him to lead a party that could withstand the revival of the communists, but Yeltsin consistently refused, fearing that leading a party would alienate other voters and limit his room for political manoeuvre. That did not stop him from backing efforts by his key loyalists to build parties to support him, his market-oriented reforms, and his relatively pro-Western foreign policy orientation. In 1993, the new Russia's Choice party became the first 'party of power', backed by the administrative resources of the Russian presidency. Initially expected to win a large majority in the glow of Yeltsin's 1993 victory over 'hardliners' in the defeated Congress, its party list netted a shockingly low 16 per cent due to dissatisfaction with the ongoing economic collapse and Yeltsin's violent suppression of the parliament. Yeltsin effectively cut the party loose and it splintered, dropping out of the Duma altogether in

1995. It returned in 1999 by combining with a few fresher faces under the label Union of Right Forces (SPS) and by openly supporting the highly popular Prime Minister Putin for the presidency. The SPS ultimately flew too close to Putin's sun, however. Once Putin had adopted many of the market reforms the party had been pushing and the economy started actually to grow, it was the most clearly Putinite party, United Russia, that claimed and won the credit in voters' eyes and that also won the benefit of Kremlin election resources. It thus failed to repeat its 1999 success in 2003, and ultimately it dissolved, split between one group who chose to work with the Kremlin and another group, which either left party politics or joined various liberal microparties that have enjoyed little to no electoral success, even at the local level. The most significant is currently the Republican Party of Russia–Party of Popular Freedom (RPR–PARNAS), whose nominee in the 2013 Moscow mayoral election netted an impressive 27 per cent of the vote. But this success has not been repeated elsewhere and owed mainly to the fact that its nominee, Aleksei Navalny, was a charismatic politician. And Navalny has no plans to become a member of this party, instead leaning to becoming leader of a new one.

The Yabloko party followed a similar trajectory after 1993, though still exists as the largest liberal party (which is not saying much). It was founded by economist Grigorii Yavlinsky, who gained fame as a market reformer in the Yeltsin government just before the USSR's break-up. After Yeltsin abandoned Yavlinsky's reform plan for Gaidar's, Yavlinsky united pro-market, pro-Western and pro-democracy politicians who thought that Yeltsin had actually undermined these ideals by his methods, with the 1990s economic collapse being important evidence. These stands and Yavlinsky's personal appeal to highly educated voters helped earn Yabloko (an acronym for the party's founders that literally means 'apple') representation in every Duma between 1993 and 2003, winning 5–8 per cent on each occasion. Its undoing was its complicated relationship with the oligarchs, the Kremlin, and other liberal parties. Opposing the Kremlin, it softened its critique of Putin to avoid banishment. Opposing the oligarchs, it had to take money from some of them (including Yukos chairman Mikhail Khodorkovsky) to finance a viable campaign. Opposing Yeltsin's reforms and hence other important liberal parties, the latter responded by simultaneously attacking it and calling Yabloko the main obstacle to integration of the 'democratic' camp in Russia. Khodorkovsky's dramatic arrest on the eve of the 2003 election not only exposed Yabloko's relationship to this controversial figure, but also eliminated its main source of funding. The party has not recovered and can claim only a handful of loyalists as of 2014, though it did win a delegation in the St Petersburg legislature, its most visible political platform, and won enough votes (just over 3 per cent) in the 2011 Duma race to qualify for some limited state funding.

The Liberal Democratic Party of Russia (LDPR) of Vladimir Zhirinovsky

Vladimir Zhirinovsky first burst on to the national political scene in June 1991, during presidential elections for the Russian Republic of the not-yet-disintegrated USSR. The fact that someone could win 8 per cent of the vote and come in third place with his radical nationalist rants, calls for territorial expansion and authoritarian tirades shocked observers both inside and outside Russia. These observers found themselves even more shocked when Zhirinovsky's party, the famously misnamed Liberal Democratic Party of Russia, actually won the party-list Duma elections of 1993, scoring 23 per cent of the vote and humiliating the second-placed Russia's Choice.

While the LDPR might seem to be an example of a party rising up independently of state resources due to a charismatic leader, some research suggests that the party (the first non-communist formation to officially register in the USSR) was actually the product of a KGB attempt to use Zhirinovsky to discredit the whole idea of democracy and electoral politics (Wilson 2005: 23–6). Remarkably, in the Duma itself, the LDPR frequently votes with the Russian government despite its seemingly radical opposition rhetoric, leading to widespread speculation that it gets financial help from the Kremlin along with the dues and corporate donations it publicly acknowledges. This has not prevented the party from winning roughly 10 per cent of the party-list vote in every Duma election after its 1993 victory (most recently, 12 per cent) except 1999, when it still got 6 per cent. Its organization and brand are almost entirely centred on the personality of Zhirinovsky himself, whose brazen antics (from tossing a glassful of orange juice on to his reformist opponent during a televised debate to tugging on a female deputy's hair in parliament) are designed to entertain and grab attention more than to persuade. Disavowing both communism and liberalism in the process, he has proven consistently able to mobilize the support of both nationalists and people (especially poor males in small towns) who just want a way to register their dissatisfaction with the state of affairs in Russia – meaning that they do not vote for more independent opposition parties.

Party substitutes

The building blocks available to party builders were also available to people who had no intention of actually building parties, but still wanted to influence political outcomes in Russia. Thus alongside the 1993-vintage parties there quickly appeared what might be called 'party substitutes' (Hale 2006). These were types of political organizations whose bosses generally wanted to avoid the strings that would come attached to party membership (such as the need to adhere to an ideology or party rules that could limit one's room for manoeuvre), but who still wanted to get 'their people' elected to key state posts.

Regional political machines

One key type of party substitute was the regional political machines run by powerful governors. Russia's reform process gave regional authorities a great deal of latitude to design their own provincial state institutions and to influence the way local firms were privatized, if they were privatized at all. Many of the original 'governors', as they are widely called, used this opportunity to make sure that their bureaucracies or their cronies gained ownership of former Soviet enterprises during the 1990s reforms. These governors also set up extensive licensing and inspection procedures for firms not owned by their close associates, and very often also established effective control over local police, courts, election commissions, and other state bodies. The result was a series of regional political machines that had great power to get candidates that it favoured elected, by hook or by crook. While such governors during the 1990s would frequently pay lip service to political parties supported by the Yeltsin administration in order to secure subsidies, the vast majority acted very independently, almost always running for office themselves as non-party candidates. To win an election in Russia in the latter half of the 1990s, in fact, a candidate was usually better off gaining the support of a regional political machine than a party, though parties did win many battles.

Oligarchic corporate conglomerates

Another important sort of party substitute was a set of mega-rich and politically connected corporate conglomerates, led by figures popularly known as 'oligarchs' due to their influence on affairs of state. Corporations in virtually all countries engage in politics, usually by lobbying government or contributing to candidate campaigns. What made these politicized financial–industrial groups (PFIGs) special was that they often went straight to the electorate, recruiting their own candidates for office and supplying these candidates with their primary campaign organization and resources. This was profitable for PFIGs because the candidate once elected could be counted upon to vote for the corporate interest when needed, and this was most reliable when the candidate was not beholden to any party that might impose other claims on their loyalties. Thus major Russian firms like Gazprom and the Alfa Group, not to mention corporate groups with less than national scope, also provided ways for ambitious politicians to win office without having to bother joining a party.

The Kremlin

One might even interpret the Kremlin itself as being 'the ultimate party substitute' in Russia. Much like regional political machines could powerfully influence local politics, so could the Russian president and his administration have a major impact on national politics. In part, it could do so by putting pressure on regional political machines and PFIGs to support candidates backed by the president. For example, many PFIGs depended for their wealth on cushy deals with the government, and the president also had a great deal of control over budgetary and non-budgetary financial flows that could be directed toward or away from particular regional political machines. Moreover, the Russian state continued to own or otherwise control the two most-watched television networks during the later 1990s, which meant it could influence how campaigns were covered. This effect was greatest during presidential elections, when no individual PFIG or regional machine was big enough alone to guarantee a candidate's victory and when the Kremlin was likely to be most aggressive in mobilizing its resources. Yeltsin's presidential victory as an independent over the CPRF's Zyuganov in 1996 was a pivotal moment in the development of the Kremlin as a party substitute. The Kremlin could also directly intervene in regional-level elections to significant effect, though it was often unsuccessful when working against the vital interests of the local political machine. What this has meant is that incumbent presidents have at their disposal many resources for re-election that do not depend on any party. They thus prefer to maintain maximum flexibility by keeping some distance even from parties that support them, including United Russia. No Russian president has ever sought to be an actual member of any party while in office.

One consequence of all of this is that Russia's parties failed to dominate the political system in the 1990s not so much because they were objectively 'weak', but because they faced very strong competition from extremely powerful independents backed by regional political machines, PFIGs, and the Kremlin itself.

Parties originating in the Putin era: United Russia and A Just Russia

The most important party to appear in the Putin era, United Russia, might actually be thought of as a conglomeration of these party substitutes, increasingly tightly harnessed during the 2000s to Putin and the broad programme he advocated. This 'administrative' path to party development is not as abnormal as one might think, even in democracies. American Senator Martin Van Buren founded the Democratic Party in the United States, for example, largely by cobbling together a coalition of state political machines and recruiting Andrew Jackson to lead it and win the presidency in 1828 (Aldrich 1995).

In Russia, events took a different twist. Its Van Buren was Moscow Mayor Yuri Luzhkov, who recruited the popular former Prime Minister Yevgenii Primakov and successfully organized many of Russia's strongest regional political machines and corporate representatives under the label Fatherland-All Russia (FAR) in August 1999. But Luzhkov, unlike the original Van Buren, lost his struggle to capture the presidency for his team and himself personally. The battle in 1999–2000 was all the same so hard-fought and so close that it had the effect of terrifying Kremlin insiders who feared losing power.

The main lesson Kremlin insiders learned – one that still guides them today – is that while they want to maintain flexibility by being independent of parties, they ultimately needed a party of their own to defeat challenges from coalitions of party substitutes like FAR. In 1999–2000, the party that saved them was the Unity bloc, the precursor to United Russia that was formed less than three months before the December 1999 Duma election in a last-ditch effort to prevent what initially looked like a certain FAR victory. Contrary to a common perception, Unity was not initially created to be a true party of power. The first party of power, Russia's Choice, was seen as a failure, as was the second, the Our Home is Russia (OHR) party formed by Prime Minister Viktor Chernomyrdin after Yeltsin abandoned Russia's Choice. OHR won only 10 per cent of the vote in 1995 and lost almost all of its support after Chernomyrdin was sacked as prime minister in 1998. Kremlin insiders thus did not at the time expect a new party of power to have much chance of success, especially since Yeltsin was as unpopular as ever and the newly appointed Prime Minister Putin's ratings were still in single digits as of the late summer of 1999.

Instead, as the Kremlin official most directly responsible for overseeing the Unity project later admitted openly, Unity had only one purpose at its creation, an extraordinarily narrow purpose that was limited to a single election: to counter the campaign of FAR (Shabdurasulov 2008). It was mainly to be a diversion, a 'decoy party' designed to muddy the electoral waters, to make governors and oligarchs think twice before joining forces with FAR, and to provide an alternative framework in which governors left out of FAR (or leaving it) could publicly express this in return for Kremlin favours. While positioning itself as slightly to the right-of-centre ideologically, it mimicked FAR's emphasis on competence and pragmatism and included the well-respected Emergencies Minister (now Defence Minister) Sergei Shoigu atop its party list. Its platform was strikingly similar to that of FAR, one of whose representatives called it the 'purest plagiarism' (*Segodnya*, 4 October 1999). The governors who nominally supported Unity tended to come from regions that were the least successful and most dependent on the central government, and even they generally delegated only mid-level associates to appear on its party list (Hale 2004a).

Imagine Unity's creators' surprise when the party not only cleared the 5 per cent hurdle, but also got far more votes than FAR and came within one percentage point of the first-place CPRF! The party's informal Kremlin curator, Igor Shabdurasulov, could not contain his glee, calling Unity's performance a 'colossal breakthrough' and a 'revolution' (*The Moscow Times*, 21 December 1999). Between its last-minute creation in early October and the December balloting, Putin's popularity had soared after decisively sending troops into the rebellious Chechnya republic in retaliation for a series of terrorist bombings in Moscow and other cities, and state-controlled television had out-competed pro-FAR television and done severe damage to the reputations of Luzhkov and Primakov, tarred as corrupt and old. Both Luzhkov and Primakov then dropped out of the presidential race as it became obvious that Putin would win handily even in a completely fair contest.

Almost immediately after the December 1999 elections, state officials began encouraging the transformation of Unity from a one-off campaign tactic into a fully fledged party of power. A first step was to develop the party's formal organization and reputation. This began with the formation of Unity's official Duma delegation, which soon joined forces with a large number of independent deputies (and even some from other parties) who had been elected in the Duma's district contests. Interestingly, FAR's representatives, elected primarily as pragmatists who had planned on benefiting from a close association with those in power, were quick to do an about-face and join the new Unity-led coalition in the Duma. Indeed, Putin and his top Kremlin aides (especially deputy presidential administration chief Vladislav Surkov, emerging as the party's main strategist) were happy to extend this offer even to Luzhkov personally (who accepted) since FAR governors controlled some of the most powerful political machines in Russia. In early 2002, the merger between FAR and Unity was formally consummated under the new name of the United Russia Party.

As part of the same process, the Kremlin went about corralling Russia's party substitutes into the new party of power structure and reducing their ability and incentive to ever again organize a collective challenge to the incumbent authorities. Putin first stripped governors of most of their political autonomy through a variety of reforms (see Chapter 9), ultimately replacing gubernatorial elections for the period 2005–12 with a system whereby the Russian president nominated a candidate who then had to be confirmed by the local legislature, usually dominated by United Russia. Putin also moved decisively against the oligarchs to end their days as more or less autonomous political actors. Thus during his first term his prosecutors targeted two of the most prominent, Boris Berezovsky and Vladimir Gusinsky, effectively forcing them to leave the country and give up their control of key television networks to corporate owners more tightly under Kremlin control. Even more important was the demonstrative arrest in October 2003 of Mikhail Khodorkovsky, owner of the Yukos oil company and Russia's richest man, who on some interpretations had designs on the presidency himself and had been launching a large informal slate of Yukos candidates to run as independents in the 2003 Duma election. That arrest capped a major campaign to coordinate the political activities of both big businesses and regional political machines, directing their efforts to support United Russia candidates rather than to acting as party substitutes. Since that time, few big businesses have dared to give substantial backing to any party without the Kremlin's OK, and United Russia has had by far the biggest OK.

Putin and his supporters also made a series of changes in law during the 2000s that gave United Russia a tremendous advantage over its rivals. Only organizations that were officially categorized and registered as national 'political parties' were allowed to nominate candidates in Duma and party-list regional legislative elections, and the registration requirements were made increasingly strict. Whereas there were over 40 parties registered in 2003, by the end of the 2000s this number had dwindled to only seven. Other rules were explicitly intended to sift smaller parties out of elections: parties were barred from running together in coalitions for the Duma; state financing for parties was given out in proportion to their election performance; and the time for televised election campaigning was reduced to less than a month for parliamentary and presidential elections, benefiting parties that were already in government because their activities were covered by media as 'news'. As we saw in the previous chapter, Putin also replaced the mixed system of Duma elections with a party-list-only system, which increased the power of central party authorities relative to regional ones and eliminated the opportunity for party substitutes to compete directly in election. The threshold for winning seats in that competition went up from 5 per cent in 2003 to 7 per cent starting with the 2007 election. Another rule change reserved a significant portion of regional legislative seats for national parties, helping lead to United Russia's dominance in most regional legislatures.

The Kremlin has also helped ensure United Russia's rise by manipulating the set of available alternatives. Partly, this has been through pressuring or spreading damaging information about the party's true opposition. For example, a blistering documentary film 'Anatomy of Protest 2' shown on the NTV channel in October 2012 presented images of what it said was one small opposition party leader (Sergei Udaltsov) plotting with a Georgian politician to destabilize Russia (*Polit.Ru*, 17 October 2012). The authorities have also used less conventional means, including the establishment of what Andrew Wilson (2005) has called 'virtual parties', which the Kremlin intends to play the role of a 'loyal opposition' that will help create an appearance of contested elections and take votes from real opposition parties while not actually acting against the interests of the incumbent administration. Virtual parties are not a Putin-era invention. Some were created under Yeltsin, such as (reputedly) the Pensioners' Party, which first ran for the Duma in 1999 and is thought to have targeted the CPRF's base of loyalists. As hinted above, some say the LDPR is in fact Russia's oldest virtual party, though its leader argues otherwise.

The most prominent virtual party appearing in the Putin era is A Just Russia, one of the four parties that have official delegations in the Duma as of 2014. It has its roots in the Motherland bloc that was formed in 2003 through an alliance between the Kremlin and disgruntled CPRF allies who hoped to use the authorities' support for their own political gain at the Communists' expense. At the same time state media was depicting the CPRF as losing touch with true socialist values by accepting corporate money, as described above, these same media broadcast relatively positive portrayals of Motherland as a more authentic heir to communist ideals. Thus not only were CPRF voters given reason to doubt their old party, they were supplied an alternative that did contain some credible leaders, including the genuinely popular leftist economist Sergei Glazyev and the nationalist Duma deputy Dmitri Rogozin. The results were dramatic: during the final week of the campaign, the CPRF's ratings plummeted and Motherland's soared, surprising even its Kremlin supporters by reaching 9 per cent of the Duma vote. Once in the Duma, both Rogozin and Glazyev proved less than loyal to the Kremlin and were pushed out of the Motherland leadership. The new leaders then merged the party with the Pensioners' Party and a minor party founded by a close Putin associate, Federation Council Speaker Sergei Mironov. Mironov, not known for either leftist or nationalist views, then assumed the leadership of the new 'A Just Russia' party and tallied 8 per cent of the officially counted votes in the 2007 Duma election and 13 per cent in 2011. Some speculate that it is part of a Kremlin plan to eventually engineer a two-party system in Russia, with A Just Russia potentially waiting in the wings to capture leftist votes should United Russia's popularity decline.

Of course, the true opposition's difficulties should not all be blamed on Kremlin manipulation. For one thing, it would be a mistake (though a common one) to dismiss United Russia as being solely an administrative product that represents no ideas and has no genuine popular support. Independent surveys show that as many as 26 per cent of the population could be considered loyal to the party in 2004 and that this figure had grown to 30 per cent by 2008 and 32 per cent by 2012, despite a major crisis the party faced in 2011 (described below). Thus while there is strong evidence of at least some ballot box fraud – for example, an improbably high number of precincts reporting turnout figures corresponding to round numbers in the parliamentary elections of 2007 and 2011 – this is not the main story of its rise (*RFE/RL Newsline*, 29 February 2008; Shpilkin 2011).

Its popularity derives first and foremost from its close association with Vladimir Putin. The Unity and then United Russia fractions in the Duma have always characterized themselves as wholly supportive of Putin's agenda, and this was clearly a winning strategy since Putin has retained majority approval ratings throughout his eight years in the presidency. Survey results also provide strong evidence that Russian citizens tend to credit United Russia (as well as Putin) for improvements in the economy. Indeed, economic growth and popular presidents normally strengthen parties associated with incumbents and weaken opposition parties (Erikson *et al.* 2002). But the party does also stand out in voter minds for certain kinds of stands on important issues. It has been associated with a market economic orientation, opposition to communism, a guarded pro-Western foreign policy, and a tough stance on rebellious minority regions like Chechnya. Voters who support such positions, the survey evidence suggests (Colton and Hale 2014), have been significantly more likely to vote for United Russia than for other parties. It remains to be determined exactly how much of United Russia's success is due to the coercive power of Russian authorities and how much is due to the same kinds of things that make parties popular everywhere, including association with a successful leader, a growing economy, and widely supported policy positions. While Russia's shift to a more authoritarian system in the 2000s has clearly worked to United Russia's advantage, one could also argue that people would not have tolerated this authoritarian shift had there not been genuine popular support for Putin and his favourite party. Russian opposition parties have also made some serious strategic mistakes, as when Yabloko and the SPS seemed to spend more effort attacking each other than Putin in the 2003 Duma campaign in bids to become the dominant liberal party (Hale 2004b).

All this made possible another United Russia step toward reaching its peak of dominance in 2007–08: for the first time the party began to play an official role in presidential politics. Having previously never run as its nominee, outgoing President Putin agreed to head the party's list in the 2007 Duma campaign, an unprecedented move in Russian politics, ensuring that it won a huge majority of over two-thirds of the seats. Putin declined his Duma mandate after the election, electing to become prime minister instead. Second, Putin's choice to succeed him as head of state, First Deputy Prime Minister Dmitri Medvedev, then ran for president as a United Russia Party nominee, something neither Putin nor Yeltsin had ever done. Third, immediately after Medvedev succeeded Putin in office, Putin acceded to the post of United Russia chairman as well as prime minister. But despite all these moves, neither Putin nor Medvedev has yet proven willing to fully affiliate themselves with, and thus fully lend their authority to, United Russia by becoming 'members'. Their hesitancy indicates both that United Russia is not yet close – even after having existed for over a decade – to having the status of the old CPSU and that Kremlin insiders themselves see risks to their own power in taking this final step. They want, it appears, to make sure that the party remains an instrument of their personal leadership rather than an institution with its own interests and authority that could one day part ways with theirs or compromise their reputation.

United Russia beyond the 2011–12 political crisis

United Russia's rapid growth in authority plateaued after the 2007–08 election cycle. Especially with the major economic crisis of 2008–09 (see Chapter 11), the party's popular support started a gradual trend of decline, culminating in a noticeable drop in 2011. Rather than double-down and concentrate efforts on supporting United Russia, Putin and some of his strong supporters announced the creation in May 2011 of an 'All-Russian Popular Front'. While some speculated that Putin might be preparing to change party horses, the Popular Front was used instead as a loose umbrella organization that would simultaneously work closely together with United Russia at the same time that it drew in Putin supporters who for one reason or other were not part of United Russia. It did, however, serve as a bet-hedging mechanism, ready to be turned into a pro-Putin party quickly should support for United Russia utterly collapse. And this undercut United Russia's authority as Putin's primary political vehicle.

The crisis for United Russia came to a head in late 2011 (Hale 2011). The primary catalyst came when Prime Minister Putin and President Medvedev effectively botched the announcement on September 24 that the tandem-mates would trade offices, indicating that something like this had been planned all along and thereby making many voters feel like dupes. Both Putin and Medvedev suffered. The hopes many had nurtured that Medvedev was becoming an independent politician were crushed, and his authority was badly damaged. And not long afterward, Putin himself appeared actually to have been whistled at (booed) when appearing on a live-televised sporting event, signalling to many a major crack in his political Teflon. The pair's 'castling' (as it became widely known in Russia, referring to the chess term) also caused some technical campaign difficulties for United Russia: the party's campaign planning had been based on the idea that Putin would lead its party list as he had done in 2007, but the castling deal meant that the new party leader would be the politically emasculated Medvedev. Making matters worse, various officials attempted to salvage a strong election result for United Russia by resorting to various forms of manipulation, but these were often clumsy and blatant, causing a further decline in popular support. And with many party governors unpopular, in some regions party representatives were given permission to campaign against them, generating mixed incentives in the political machine. The label 'Party of Swindlers and Thieves', coined by opposition blogger Aleksei Navalny, stuck to it in the minds of many voters, sometimes involved by opposition and even virtual parties. Strikingly, even A Just Russia began attacking United Russia during the campaign. On the heels of scandal after scandal, the party stunningly failed even to claim a simple majority of the officially counted votes, netting just 49 per cent, and there was evidence that even this modest tally reflected fraud. Within a week of the election many tens of thousands were on the street protesting (see Chapter 7), launching a major movement that continued to rally large numbers of people well into 2012.

These events prompted the Kremlin to initiate a series of reforms that remain in place up to the present. These reforms have greatly changed the form of the party system, though its essence (domination by United Russia with minor roles for the CPRF, A Just Russia, and LDPR) remains the same. One reform was to greatly relax registration requirements for political parties. By late 2013, the Justice Ministry's official website listed 74 registered parties (Ministry of Justice 2013). While representing an advance in political freedom, this reform has nevertheless helped United Russia by facilitating the division of its opponents (Golosov 2012). The vast majority of parties registered under the new rules have been non-factors in the regional elections of 2012 and 2013. The Civic Platform Party organized by major businessman Mikhail Prokhorov (owner of the Brooklyn Nets NBA basketball team and the third-place finisher in the 2012 presidential election) shows some potential to win a significant number of regional and perhaps national parliamentary seats, though it remains too early to tell. Another post-2011 reform was to restore some kind of direct gubernatorial elections, though the Kremlin's candidates have won all of them and not significantly altered the balance of power among parties. The parliament has also restored a form of district-based elections for the Duma, which could lead to the return of party substitutes and other non-party candidates in the future, but how this will affect the party system will depend heavily on exactly how any such reform is designed. In the end, United Russia wound up weathering the storm just fine, retaining nearly a third of the Russian population as self-professed loyalists and close to 2 million members (Colton and Hale 2014; *Moskovskii Komsomolets*, 28 May 2013).

Conclusion

Russia has come a long way in forming a party system since the USSR disintegrated in 1991, but its development was not what observers initially expected. While a set of parties did emerge and grow during the 1990s based largely on political resources and reputation gained through connections to the state, their growth was stunted as Yeltsin-style privatization and overly strong executive authority led to the rise of party substitutes that often managed to out-compete parties for both candidates and votes. After Kremlin authorities nearly lost power to the Fatherland-All Russia coalition of party substitutes in 1999–2000, the newly elected President Putin began to transform Russia's party system by both reducing the power of party substitutes and organizing them around one increasingly dominant party, United Russia. As these efforts were all linked with a growing economy and a popular president, and as state-controlled television could ensure that voters made this link, United Russia reached a point of near-dominance in the political system that it has sustained into 2014.

At the same time, Putin has remained reluctant to tie his personal authority too closely to any party (even United Russia) since his mighty Kremlin power base has given him a great deal of room for political manoeuvre and which a strong party might limit. He thus prefers to be above the partisan fray, seen as the president of all the people rather than of any one party. Russia's political system is therefore not yet fully a party system, even a fully 'dominant party system'. There is even speculation that the authorities might still one day try to engineer a two-party system, perhaps pairing United Russia with either A Just Russia or the All-Russian Popular Front, though to date they have shied away from allowing other parties to challenge United Russia too vigorously for fear of fostering dangerous splits in the political machinery that keeps them in power. These calculations could change, however, should United Russia's support in the population take a nosedive. Russia's party system thus remains in flux and could take on quite different directions in the years ahead.

Chapter 6

Voting Behaviour

IAN McALLISTER

This chapter examines patterns of voting behaviour in Russia, using public opinion surveys to trace how these patterns have evolved over time. Early studies relied on the model of voting behaviour that dominated the first wave of democratization in the late nineteenth century. This model emphasizes stable parties competing around major social cleavages, with electoral choice being shaped by high levels of mass partisanship. It soon became clear that this 'group memberships' model of voting was not readily applicable to Russia, and that other factors were more important in shaping electoral choice. Accordingly, later voting studies have examined performance evaluations and the importance of political leadership as factors that shape voting choice. The picture of Russian voting behaviour that emerges is a complex one, with elements of group membership combined with performance evaluations, often mediated by political leadership.

The chapter is divided into five sections. The first section examines patterns of electoral participation since the early 1990s, while the second section covers the inheritance of authoritarian values among the electorate, reflected in nostalgia for a return to communism among the older generations. The remaining three sections cover the main explanations for voting behaviour, namely social group memberships, evaluations of performance, and political leadership. Confirming other research, the conclusion is that voters are motivated by making performance evaluations based on economic prosperity, with these evaluations being closely associated with the leadership of Vladimir Putin.

Electoral participation and dissent

As we saw in Chapter 4, election turnout in Russia and the other republics during the years of communist rule was consistently high, and much higher than in the same period in the established democracies (see, for example, Blais 2000; Franklin 2004). This was due, in part, to a desire on

97

the part of the authorities to show their greater popular legitimacy as compared with the West. It was also a consequence of practicalities, and while there was no formal obligation to vote, it was usually difficult to avoid; by 1984, as we have seen, turnout had reached 99.9 per cent. Such unbelievably high figures were typically the result of fraud and the common practice of voting on behalf of family members. All the same, most independent observers of Soviet elections agreed that levels of turnout were indeed extremely high, if not as high as the reported figures. It was thought that in the communist period only around 3 per cent of eligible voters failed to turn out to vote, although the proportion was steadily increasing (Roeder 1989: 474–5).

The transitional elections in the spring of 1989 produced a turnout of 86.9 per cent, less than the figures recorded under communism but nevertheless higher than virtually any other established democracy. Since then turnout has declined, falling substantially to 54.8 per cent in 1993 in the first elections to a newly formed State Duma. The 1993 elections saw considerable administrative pressure to ensure a turnout of at least 50 per cent in order to ensure that the new constitution, which was being put to the vote on the same day, could be confirmed (ratification required a minimum threshold of voters turning out). Independent estimates suggested that turnout, in fact, was unlikely to have exceeded 43 per cent (Rumyantsev 1994: 217). Thereafter turnout recovered, in the 1995 Duma election reaching 64.7 per cent. Figure 6.1 shows that turnout has remained at about that level since, with the exception of 2003, when it dropped to 55.7 per cent. This is a level of turnout which is below that found in the established democracies; in a study of 359 elections in 91 countries between 1971 and 1995, Blais and Dobrzynska (1998: 252) estimated average turnout at 77 per cent. By contrast, the average turnout in Russian Duma and presidential elections since 1991 has been 64 per cent.

Election turnout has been consistently higher in presidential elections than in Duma elections, starting with the June 1991 election which returned Boris Yeltsin with a large majority. In that election almost three in every four voters cast a ballot. However, lower level elections have attracted many fewer voters, and there have also been substantial regional disparities in turnout. In the 1993 Duma election, for example, twelve of the country's 89 republics and regions registered a turnout level below 50 per cent. Turnout was lowest of all in Russia's second city, St Petersburg, at just 44 per cent of the registered electorate. These regional disparities in turnout have been largely replicated in elections conducted since then, although regions with strong ethnic identities have generally displayed higher levels (Marsh, Albert and Warhola 2004: 269–70). Voters in these regions evidently see it as important to maintain strong links with Moscow in order to protect economic benefits and welfare entitlements,

Figure 6.1   *Turnout in Russian elections, 1991–2012*

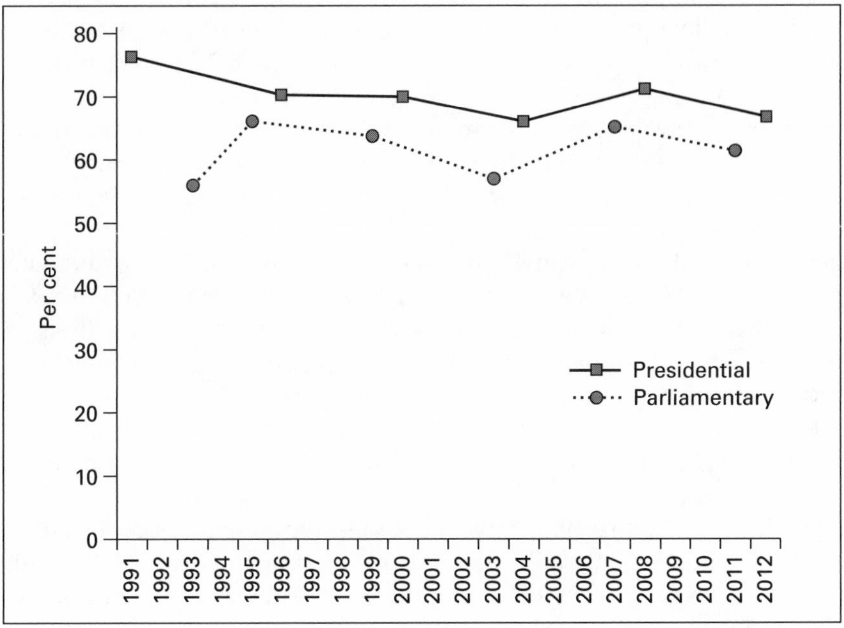

Sources: data from http://www.idea.int; http://www.russiavotes.org/duma/duma_elections_93-03.php.

and local leaderships are no less eager to improve their position by delivering the kind of electoral 'harvest' that the central authorities will have been expecting.

In general, abstention in Russia is driven by the factors that are also found in the advanced democracies (for an overview, see Blais 2007). Russian non-voters are more likely to be from lower socio-economic backgrounds, to be aged under 30, and to exhibit relatively low levels of political interest (Colton 2000: 40; Wyman *et al.* 1995: 597; White and McAllister 2007). A particular factor that is associated with election turnout is social relationships and networks, such as membership of social and voluntary organizations, and those who engage more with others are more likely to exhibit high levels of social as well as political participation. These memberships have also been found to be important in Russia (Colton 2000: 42; White and McAllister 2008), but their political consequences in Russia have been limited because of the endemic weakness of civil society (Evans 2006). Aside from trade unions and membership of the Communist Party of the Soviet Union (CPSU) and its related groups, civic associations were largely non-existent during the communist period (Howard 2003).

In the established democracies, most instances of electoral abstention are attributable to casual or random factors, such as being unable to attend a polling place due to travel commitments or illness. Instances of abstention where voters believe their vote will not make a difference, or where voters object to the choices on offer or even to the political system itself, are relatively rare. By contrast, around half or more of non-voters in the major post-communist states abstain for political reasons. In the 2011 Duma election, for example, 35 per cent reported that they were simply unable to attend the polling place; the remaining reasons were associated with some form of disillusionment with politics or weak political efficacy (here and elsewhere evidence will be drawn from a representative national survey conducted for the author and associates by Russian Research, n=1600). Between 1991 and 2006, voters had an additional means of registering their disapproval of politics: the option of voting 'against all' of the candidates or parties on the ballot paper (McAllister and White 2008a). Around one in ten voters exercised this option in the Duma elections.

Electoral participation in Russia has followed the pattern of the established democracies, with declining turnout occurring during the 1990s and stabilizing thereafter. However, overall election turnout is now lower than is found in most of these other countries. The reasons for this low level of electoral participation can be traced to a widespread public sense of disillusionment with politics in general, with the choices that are on offer, and with low levels of political efficacy. A contributing factor is also the weakness of civil society in post-communist Russia. However, one factor that is relatively unimportant in promoting abstention is a sense that elections are unfairly conducted. While there is a consistent minority who believe that elections are unfairly conducted (McAllister and White 2014), just 7 per cent of non-voters in 2011 gave this as a reason for not turning out to vote.

The burden of history

By 1990, there were few Russians alive who had any memory of a life not under communist rule. The political lives and experiences of every Russian had been exclusively acted out within an authoritarian culture, with all that implied for their views of politics and their political behaviour. This is in contrast to the former communist states of Eastern Europe, which came under communist rule immediately after the end of the Second World War in 1945. In these societies, there were citizens alive in 1990 who could recall how democratic politics was conducted in a pre-communist era. It is arguably for this reason that the transition to a competitive political system in Hungary, Czechoslovakia and other eastern European countries has been an easier process than in Russia (Tucker 2006).

Theories of political socialization predict that political attitudes and behaviour are a consequence of childhood events and experiences that leave a life-long imprint on their recipients. Political change can therefore take place only slowly and through a decades-long process of generational replacement, as a generation imbued with certain values and outlooks is replaced by a newer generation holding different views. An alternative theory is that citizens adapt to new institutions, and undergo a process of political re-learning. Research shows the effects of both of these processes in Russia, with evidence of generational differences in political outlooks as well as evidence of re-learning, as citizens adapt to new political processes, norms and values (Mishler and Rose 2007; Rose and Carnaghan 1995).

Figure 6.2 *Generations and nostalgia for communism*

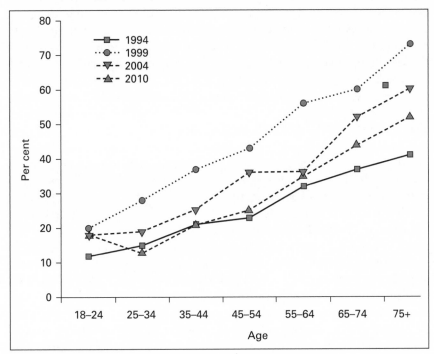

Notes: The question was: 'To what extent do you agree or disagree with the following statements ... it would be better to restore the communist system.' Question wordings differ slightly between surveys.

The burden of history is reflected in the differing political outlooks of the generations, with those who grew up under communist rule displaying different views about the regime compared to those who grew up after the collapse of communism. Using four surveys conducted at approximately five-year intervals, commencing in 1994, Figure 6.2 shows the proportions who wanted a return to communism by age group. All of the surveys show a consistent pattern, with the young being less likely to display nostalgia, as theories of political socialization predict, while older Russians are more likely to want a return to communism. Nostalgia is highest in the 1999 survey and lowest in the 1994 and 2010 surveys. The young show least differences in their views across all four of the surveys; by contrast, there are substantial differences in the patterns among those aged in their 50s or over. This would appear to be the group that is having the most difficulty in adapting to the post-1990 political changes.

Authoritarian regimes transiting to democracy experience particular difficulties in coming to terms with the legacy of the past; these difficulties become more intense the longer the period of authoritarian rule. In the case of Russia, by 1990 the political lives of virtually every single citizen had been experienced exclusively under authoritarian rule. The burden of history weighs on Russian society through the generations, and nostalgia for communism and an idealistic view of the order and predictability that it brought to everyday lives remains salient. However, one clear finding is the strong rejection of communism among the young, which has changed little over the course of the surveys.

Socio-economic status and the vote

Political parties originally emerged during the period of mass democracy in order to represent social cleavages and to address the political demands of various social groups. Explanations of how this process occurred have been dominated by Lipset and Rokkan's 'freezing hypothesis', first advanced in 1967. In their account, contemporary party systems had become 'frozen' around the social cleavages which were dominant when mass suffrage was introduced in the 1920s. Lipset and Rokkan identified four social cleavages – centre–periphery (region), state–church (religion), land–industry (urban–rural), and owner–worker (class) – which they argued had provided the basis for the emergence of European party systems at the turn of the twentieth century. In turn, these cleavages were mediated by electoral institutions, which shaped how political parties chose to compete with one another in this kind of an environment (Bartolini and Mair 1990; Kitschelt *et al.* 1999).

Studies of the translation of social cleavages into the Russian party system have been hampered by the unstable nature of the parties – what Brader and Tucker (2001: 69) describe as 'chaotic, shapeless and lacking in mass partisanship', or what Mair (1997) sees as a 'limited range of alternatives'. Even identifying appropriate parties to analyse can often be problematic (McAllister and White 2007; Whitefield 2002). In addition, three other factors are relevant. First, the political institutions within which the parties operate have often changed, fostering popular suspicion about parties and disrupting political socialization. Second, as the previous section outlined, the character of the old regime has frequently had a major impact on the nature of the new party system (Kitschelt 2001; Linz and Stepan 1996). And third, transition experiences – primarily economic rather than political – may also serve to shape distinctive outlooks that will have political consequences (Whitefield and Evans 1999).

Lipset and Rokkan's 'freezing hypothesis' predicts that parties should emerge to organize party competition around the major social cleavages at the time of democratization. Under communism, Russia displayed both centre–periphery and countryside–industry divisions, but these largely disappeared with the collapse of communism and the absence of any need to unite a widely diverse group of ethnic and regional communities. Owner–worker divisions were also relatively unimportant since in the early post-communist years most employees still worked for the state; it is only in recent years that a significant proportion of the labour force has been employed in the private sector. And while religion has experienced a huge resurgence in the post-communist period, the vast majority of the population are Russian Orthodox; there is no parallel to the Catholic–Protestant or religion–secular divisions which characterized nineteenth-century Europe.

In order to test the importance of some of these divisions in shaping the vote, Table 6.1 examines the support of various groups for the four major parties – United Russia, the Communist Party, A Just Russia, and the Liberal Democrats –that stood and won seats in the 2011 Duma election. As we saw in the previous chapter, United Russia is Vladimir Putin's party, founded in 2001, and is the dominant party, receiving just under half of the votes cast in the 2011 election. The Communist Party (KPRF) is the immediate successor to the CPSU, and with 19.2 percent of the votes in the 2011 election it is the second largest party. A Just Russia attracted 13.2 per cent of the vote in the same election and is a centre-left party in the social democratic tradition. Finally, the Liberal Democratic Party (LDPR) led by Vladimir Zhirinovsky won 11.7 per cent of the vote, and is a nationalist party very much associated with the personality of its outspoken leader.

The results in Table 6.1 show that there are relatively few salient background or socio-economic divisions between the four parties. As

Table 6.1   *Background, socio-economic status and 2011 Duma vote*

	(Mean)	United Russia	KPRF	Just Russia	LDPR
Socialization					
CPSU member (per cent)	(7)	6	12**	4	3
Age (years)	(46.6)	46.7	50.7*	47.2	38.7
Background characteristics					
Ethnic Russian (per cent)	(93)	92	93	95	91
Urban resident (per cent)	(76)	70**	80	82*	76
Gender (per cent male)	(42)	35**	52**	40	53*
Socio-economic status					
University education (per cent)	(23)	21	23	22	22
Living standards (per cent good)	(15)	19**	11*	11	11
Government employee (per cent)	(31)	30	25*	35	31
Religion					
Orthodox religion (per cent)	(87)	89	82*	88	88
Church attender (per cent)	(55)	57	50	57	54

Notes: ** p<0.01, * p<0.05; figures are the percentage voting for each of the four parties in the 2011 election.

expected, former CPSU members and older voters are relatively more numerous among Communist Party supporters, but there are no significant differences among the other three parties. There are some urban–rural differences, with United Russia attracting more support than the other parties from the countryside, and A Just Russia gains more support from urban areas. Socio-economic differences in support for the parties are surprisingly small; United Russia attracts a disproportionate level of support from better-off voters but differences by employment sector are minor, and there are no significant differences in university education or religious affiliation. The only major difference in party support is based on gender, with women being more likely to support United Russia, everything else being equal, and men more likely to support the Communists and the Liberal Democrats; A Just Russia, by contrast, has a gender balance similar to that of the general population.

 There is little evidence, accordingly, that social cleavages matter in structuring the vote for the major parties. What matters is gender, which did not emerge as a social cleavage in the early post-communist years, and is one that is more closely associated with the personalities of the party leaders. It is perhaps notable that the Russian party system has managed to avoid the territorial conflicts that were imprinted on the European party systems of the early twentieth century. It is also surprising that class divisions are not more salient. It suggests that the process of democratic consolidation has proceeded more quickly than a century earlier, which may reflect the rapid dissemination of information via the electronic media that did not exist at the time of the first wave of democracy. This is perhaps one reason why, as Evans and Whitefield (1998) note, the early conflict over communism versus anti-communism was quickly replaced by the more familiar economic conflicts over the role of the market versus the state, albeit in a muted form.

The absence of any strong social cleavages structuring party competition has several implications. First, it implies greater voter volatility than would otherwise be the case, with substantial numbers of citizens changing their vote from one election to the next, since the parties lack firm roots within social groups. Greater volatility will in turn cause greater instability within the party system. However, as Powell and Tucker (2014) note, this is primarily caused by the entry of new parties and the exit of failed parties, rather than by citizens transferring their votes from one election to the next between stable parties. Second, the absence of a social structural base means that other factors are likely to underpin voting behaviour. The next two sections test the hypotheses that performance and personality are rather more closely associated with the various patterns we have so far identified.

Performance and partisanship

If social cleavages do not structure party support, what factors do underpin it? An obvious alternative is voters' evaluations of how the political parties perform. In this model, parties are assessed on their performance while in government and are either rewarded or punished at the next election by voters. These popular evaluations of party performance are at the core of the responsible party government model. In turn, the model assumes that voters are able to assign responsibility for policies to one party – what is often called 'clarity of accountability.' Powell and Whitten (1993) have shown that clarity of accountability is highest in single-party governments in unitary systems and lowest in coalition governments in federal systems, where governing parties find it easy to blame others for policy failures.

Party performance is usually defined in terms of economic performance. Considerable research has shown that voters tend to make either retrospective or prospective judgements about economic performance, and that these judgements are based either on their own ('egocentric') or on a perception of the country's ('sociotropic') economic circumstances (Lewis-Beck and Stegmaier 2007). The balance between these factors –

retrospective versus prospective, and egocentric versus sociotropic – depends on each country's political, social and institutional context. Successive evaluations of party performance, or what Fiorina (1981: 84; see also Gerber and Green, 1998) has called 'a running tally of retrospective evaluations of party promises and performance', creates a stable pattern of partisanship. The origins of mass partisanship in performance rather than in where it is traditionally located, political socialization, is obviously more important in emerging democracies, where the inheritance of partisanship has yet to become established.

Research on the development of partisanship in post-communist societies, and Russia in particular, has come to a variety of conclusions. Early research by Miller and Klobucar (2000) painted an optimistic picture, with a majority of Russian voters identifying with a party. This pattern was refined by Brader and Tucker (2008: 296) who concluded that 'Russians in the mid-1990s were acquiring partisanship in ways largely consistent with the many theories and limited evidence from established democracies.' However, they found less evidence of social groups structuring partisanship, which was confirmed by the results that were reported in the previous section. In general, it seems that transitional factors, particularly related to economic development, play a significant role in the process of party development (Kitschelt *et al.* 1999; Tucker 2006). In virtually all post-communist societies the economic transition has been painful, but societies where the transition has been short and sharp (such as Poland) have tended to move more rapidly on the path to democratization compared to societies (such as Russia) where the transition has been subject to reversals.

Certainly Russia's economic performance since 1990 (as we see in later chapters) has been highly variable. In the years immediately following the collapse of communism, the dismantling of the command economy and the progressive removal of subsidies had a devastating impact on living standards. During the 1990s, per capita GDP declined dramatically, bottoming during the 1998 rouble crisis, which resulted in a devaluation of the currency and a major international loss of confidence in the Russian economy after the government defaulted on its debt. Thereafter the economy grew on the back of increased energy and commodity prices; between 2000 and 2008 the annual growth rate averaged 7 per cent until the global financial crisis in 2008–09. The crisis as such appears to have had little impact on public support for democratization; McAllister and White (2011) explain this by the long history of economic crises in Russia and a tradition of 'getting by' when they do erupt.

At face value, the international economic turmoil since 2008 has had relatively little impact on attitudes towards democracy (McAllister and White 2008b). Figure 6.3 shows that public support for democracy,

Figure 6.3   *Attitudes towards democracy, 2004–2011*

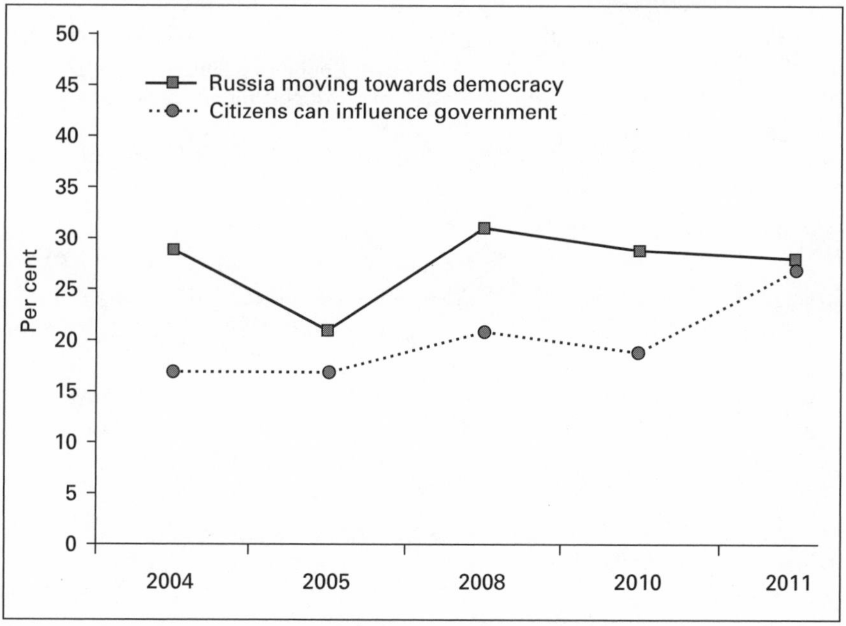

Notes: The questions were: 'In your opinion, the course our country has adopted is character-ized as ... a properly formed democracy ... a country steadily moving towards the establishment of democracy ... a country that is more democratic than it was before ... There was more democ-racy in Soviet times.'; 'To what extent, in your opinion, can people like you have a direct influ-ence on the actions of the central government?'

never high at the best of times, has remained constant at about three in every ten voters since 2008, and feelings of political efficacy have actu-ally increased marginally over the period. However, two events since 2004 do appear to have influenced public opinion. First, the belief that Russia was moving towards democracy declined significantly in 2005, following the street protests that resulted from the decision to convert social benefits into what was regarded as inadequate monetary equiva-lents. By 2008, views about democracy had returned to their pre-2005 levels, and since then around three in ten have taken the view that Russia is moving towards democracy. Second, the protests that followed the contested December 2011 Duma election saw political efficacy increase, from 19 per cent in 2010 to 27 per cent in 2011, as citi-zens saw the protests as having an impact. Nevertheless, the results suggest that economic performance has had relatively little impact on attitudes to democracy.

Feelings of partisanship were higher in the 1990s than in the 2000s. Figure 6.4 shows that nearly half of the electorate felt close to a political

Figure 6.4   *Trends in partisanship, 1999–2011*

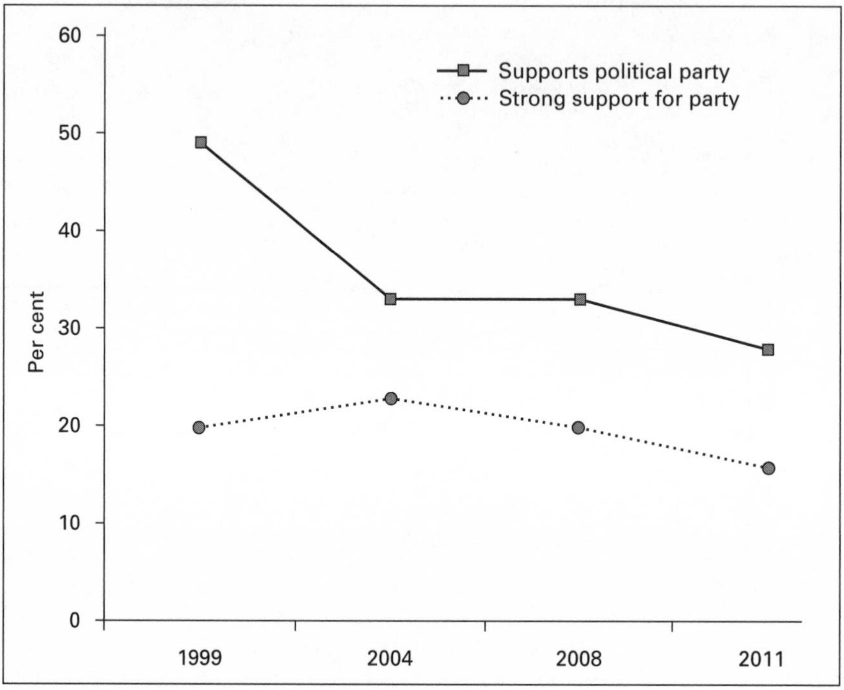

Notes: The 2004-2011questions were: 'Do you support any political party?'; 'To what extent do you support a party with a position closest to your political views?' Wording for the 1999 questions differs slightly.

party in the Duma election of that year. Partisanship has declined at each Duma election since then, with just 28 per cent considering themselves close to a party. At the same time, the strength of attachment has declined at a much slower rate: in 2004, 23 per cent of respondents considered themselves to be very close to a party, and in 2011 the same figure was 16 per cent. While there are variations in question wording between surveys, these results are broadly in line with other research, which shows increasing levels of partisanship in the 1990s and a decline thereafter (Brader and Tucker 2001: 75–6; Brader and Tucker 2008).

The evolution of partisanship in mass electorates is complex, and generally considered to be a process that takes many years, if not generations, before a stable party system is formed with enduring support from voters. The classic theory of Lipset and Rokkan, already mentioned, suggests that the origins of mass partisanship can be located in social cleavages. The evidence presented in the previous section suggested that the main parties, in fact, had only weak links to the Russian social structure. An alternative hypothesis is that party performance underpins partisanship, with voters keeping a 'running tally' of how parties deal with problems, particularly economic ones, and form their political views accordingly. The evidence presented here suggests that this model appeared to be establishing itself in the 1990s, but weakened significantly during the 2000s. Perhaps most tellingly, the global financial crisis appears to have had little impact on regime support, a finding also endorsed by Rose and Mishler (2010). A third explanation for voting behaviour is the attraction of political leaders, and this possibility is examined in the next section.

Political leadership

There is little doubt that elections around the world have become more personalized in recent years, with election campaigns focusing heavily on the personalities, images and activities of the party leaders. The 'personalization of politics', as it has become known, is usually traced to the rise of the electronic media in the 1970s and 1980s, and their insatiable appetite for visual images (Karvonen 2010; McAllister 2007). However, it is too simple to attribute the phenomenon to the media alone: parties also like personalization, since it is easier to get their message across through a personality; voters themselves like it, because it is easier to hold an individual to account than an abstract entity such as a political party; and leaders like it because they can frequently appeal over the heads of their parties to the mass electorate. In short, the personalization of politics suits many of the principal agents and actors within a polity.

While political leaders have always been important in presidential systems, there has been a heightened profile for leaders across both presidential and particularly parliamentary systems. Post-communism is almost an ideal case where highly visible, charismatic political leaders can accrue power based on their personalities. First, the presidential system necessarily focuses attention on a single leader. Moreover, the absence of any clear distinction between the president and the government further directs executive power towards the president (Shevtsova and Eckert 2000). Second, the short history of the Russian presidency is that of a single person exercising wide and often arbitrary powers. The first president, Boris Yeltsin, personally decided to face down his opponents in the Russian parliament, and then imposed his own rules of the game in a new constitution that underpinned his dominant position. The replacement of four prime ministers in 1998–99, and then the choice of Putin as his successor, were entirely personal decisions by Yeltsin.

Yeltsin's successor, Vladimir Putin, took the decision to continue and extend the concentration of executive power in the presidency, as well as to restore the dignity of the office after his predecessor's erratic behaviour. During his first period as president between 2000 and 2008, Putin used his decree powers to centralize political authority in the Kremlin. His period as prime minister between 2008 and 2012, and as president again from 2012, suggest the emergence of a cult of personality to rival anything that had existed under communism (Brown and Shevtsova 2001; Sakwa 2010c; White and McAllister 2008). Putin has gone to considerable lengths, through stage-managed events and carefully crafted media profiles, to nurture the image of a strong leader defending Russian interests at home and abroad. Although he occasionally faltered – his response to the sinking of the 'Kursk' submarine was widely regarded as belated and callous ('It sank', he told the Larry King show on American television, without any obvious sign of remorse) – the overall image that the public saw was strongly positive, especially when compared to Yeltsin's dissolute image during his last years in office.

Figure 6.5   *Approval of Putin and Medvedev, 1999–2013*

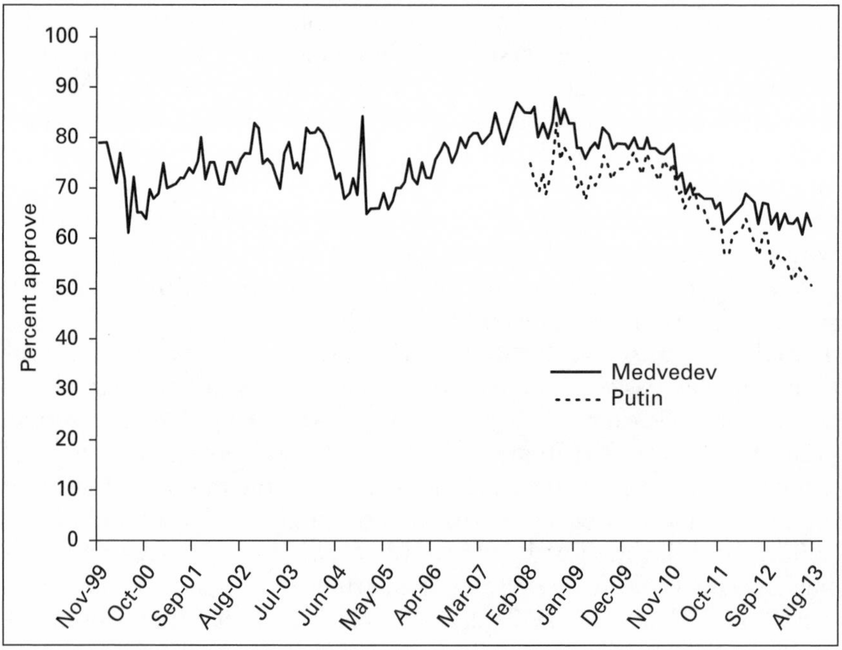

Notes: The question was: 'On the whole do you approve or disapprove of the performance of ....?'

Source: Levada surveys, http://www.russiavotes.org/president/presidency_performance.php.

By any standards, Putin has been highly popular with voters. Figure 6.5 shows that his approval rating has never dropped below 61 per cent, and for most of the period since 1999 it was considerably higher. For example, between November 2003 and March 2004 Putin's approval rating never dropped below 80 per cent, an exceptional level of popular approval for the leader of any major country. There are two short periods when Putin's approval dropped below trend. First, in early 2005 when it declined as a consequence of the monetization of welfare benefits, which resulted in a reduction in the standard of living of those dependent on them. The second period followed the December 2011 Duma election, when there were widespread allegations of vote rigging, resulting in public protests in many of the major cities. Many voters placed the responsibility for the contested election directly on Putin. By contrast, the popularity of Dmitri Medvedev, president from 2008 to 2012 and prime minister since 2012, has consistently trailed Putin's, especially in the period since the contested December 2011 election.

Putin's popularity among voters has rested very much on his handling of international affairs, and particularly his policies on the war in Chechnya. Figure 6.6 shows that a peak of 83 per cent of voters supported his handling of international affairs, a figure which had declined to 67 per cent by 2011 but was nevertheless easily the most highly rated of the four policy areas. Bringing order to the country was also regarded as a strongly positive feature of his leadership, although his success has been tempered by continuing high levels of corruption, which are generally perceived to be getting worse rather than better. Opinions are more equivocal on Putin's contribution to the strengthening of democracy, as well as his contribution to the improvement of living standards. Nevertheless, Putin's success in increasing Russia's international profile was regarded by voters as a major asset for his leadership. While most voters do not hanker for a return to the Cold War confrontation with the United States, they do want to see greater respect for Russia on the international stage, and Putin has been highly effective in achieving this goal.

Putin's popularity has had a major impact on the vote for United Russia, the party that was created as a vehicle for his leadership. The 'Putin phenomenon' has weak roots within Russian society but is very strongly related to economic prosperity, which in turn is associated with the Putin presidency. This is rather different from a 'charismatic' leadership, in which supporters are committed to the personality of the leader without particular regard to policy outcomes; and rather different from a Western-style parliamentary system, in which support is invested in the procedures by which a leadership is selected and only secondarily in the policies that are pursued or the personal qualities of

Figure 6.6   *Support for Putin's policies, 2005–2011*

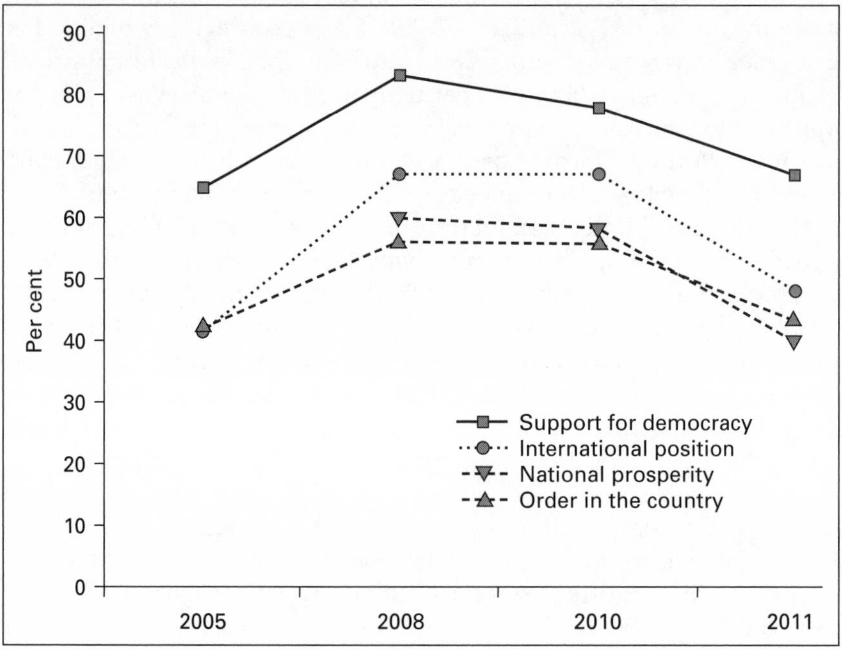

Notes: The question was 'How successful has Putin been in tackling the following problems?'

its individual members. Notwithstanding the cult of personality surrounding Putin, this is a leadership that owes more than anything else to his apparently successful stewardship of the national economy – at least in part a consequence of a rise in the world price of oil that had begun before Putin's accession and already led to a resumption of economic growth.

Conclusion

More than two decades after the collapse of communism, superficially at least Russian democracy appears to be in reasonable health. Electoral participation is moderately high, although lower than is found in the established democracies and very considerably below the levels registered under communism. The party system appears to be consolidating around a small number of parties with a degree of longevity, following a period when there was a multiplicity of parties that emerged and faded away often after just one election. Party policies also broadly correspond to a left–right continuum, with parties on the left espousing greater state intervention in the economy, and parties on the right supporting the free market. And not least, the burden of Russia's authoritarian political past – reflected in nostalgia for communism among older voters – appears to be finally weakening.

Countering this tentatively optimistic view of Russian democracy are at least three factors. First, there have been frequent changes to political institutions, usually for the benefit of the major actors. For example, the Russian parliamentary election law alone was amended 26 times between its adoption in 2005 and the December 2011 election. Such rapid changes in procedures and in the structure of choices – what Mair (1997) has termed 'a closed structure of competition' – make it difficult for voters to form stable patterns of political behaviour. Second, as was demonstrated earlier, voting has shallow roots in social cleavages, which causes volatility in inter-election party support and less predictability in electoral outcomes. The lack of salience for social cleavages has its origins in the endemic weakness of civil society in post-communist Russia, which will take many generations to address. And third, short-term evaluations of economic performance – reflected in support for Putin – appear to be an important driver of voting behaviour.

Voting behaviour in Russia therefore appears to be grounded less in the social group-based model that was apparent in the first wave of European democratization and more in performance evaluations, focused on economic prosperity and channelled especially through political leadership. This is a pattern that is apparent in many third wave democracies, with early examples being Greece, Portugal and Spain (Lisi 2013), but it has also emerged among many of the post-communist countries as well. This presents two dangers. First, the close association between economic performance and political choice in new democracies makes such systems particularly vulnerable when the economy falters, since mass support for democracy is fragile and is often not sufficient to enable the country to ride out a major crisis (Thomassen and van der Kolk 2009). Second, the association of a particular leader with economic performance raises the inevitable problem of engineering a successful leadership transition and the inherent danger that the new leader will perform less well, causing a crisis in the democratic system.

Early accounts of Russian voting behaviour painted a rosy picture, with the emergence of mass partisanship, a consolidating party system, and parties beginning to compete for votes around social cleavages. In the light of Russia's long and deeply authoritarian history, the fact that this model failed to establish itself is understandable. Add to the mix the equivocation among many voters about whether democracy represents what Linz and Stepan (1996) term 'the only game in town', and such an outcome is entirely predictable. The creation of a stable pattern of voting behaviour still remains years away, but it does seem that Russia is on the road to meeting this goal, barring any significant breakdown in the political system.

Chapter 7

Civil Society and Contentious Politics in Russia

GRAEME B. ROBERTSON

The Cathedral of Christ the Saviour is a massive gold-domed building that dominates the skyline of central Moscow. The current structure was built in the 1990s, with lavish financial support from the Moscow city government, to replace the former cathedral, which was demolished and turned into a public swimming pool by the Soviet government. As such, Christ the Saviour is a symbol of the new post-communist Russia constructed over the last 20 years, and in particular, it is an emblem of the return of the Russian Orthodox Church to its former place as a key pillar of the Russian state. Despite its staid appearance, on 21 February 2012 the Cathedral was the site of some unusual politics. Five members of a feminist art collective, performing as a punk band with the provocative name Pussy Riot, entered the cathedral and right in front of the iconostasis performed a song. Though they were quickly stopped by Church officials, that evening a video of the performance was posted on the internet under the title, 'Punk Prayer: Mother of God, Chase Putin Away!'

Far from chasing Putin away, however, this act of political protest in such a symbolic place quickly attracted official attention and the artists in question were arrested and sentenced to two years in prison. Yet despite the severe punishment (they were, in the event, released as a part of a more general amnesty in December 2013), the performance at Christ the Saviour was not that different from many Pussy Riot and related actions that have taken place in Russia in recent years. In fact, since at least 2010, unusual protests have become a staple of the Russian opposition, from cars with little blue children's buckets driving around and holding up traffic, to women kissing surprised policewomen in the Moscow metro, to penises being painted on St Petersburg bridges. Alongside these unusual performances, discontent has also been expressed in thousands of more traditional demonstrations and marches, making demands large and small on authorities across the country.

In this chapter, we will see how and why protest and politics outside formal political institutions have become such an important feature of contemporary Russian politics. In thinking about unconventional or, to use the term social scientists prefer, 'contentious' politics, scholars have in mind a very wide variety of actions in which people come together, often unexpectedly, to make public demands on the state or the political system. These actions range from organizing a vast array of different kinds of protests, to conducting strikes, and to using violence to change the expected order of politics in new and often dramatic ways. As we will see, such acts of contention have played a crucial role in shaping how the contemporary Russian state came into being, how its constitution was written and how its current political institutions operate. We will see too how those institutions have, in turn, shaped the nature and frequency of protest and how contentious politics and more conventional politics are likely to continue to shape each other in the years to come.

Beyond the issue of political protest and contention, in this chapter we will also consider the development of civil society in Russia. Often seen as an indicator of democratic development, civil society and non-governmental organizations typically play an important role in organizing and defending the rights of a broad range of people and groups in society. We will see how the economic collapse that followed the end of communism stifled the nascent civil society in Russia. However, as the economy started to grow again in the 2000s, civil society groups began to flourish across the country. For the most part, this process took place without either help or hindrance from the Russian state. However, as we will see, in recent years the government has intensified efforts to try to make sure that civil society is contained within spaces that do not represent a challenge to the political system.

Political protest and contentious politics in Russian history

Like eskimos and snow, Russians have a lot of words for protest, rebellion and civil unrest. Perhaps this is because, over the centuries of its existence, the political fate of Russia has more often been decided in the streets and fields than in parliaments or elections. A number of such periods in Russian history continue to inform how politicians, journalists and citizens think about politics today. In the 1990s, the favoured historical reference in newspapers and television was to the so-called 'Time of Troubles', which lasted from the death of Tsar Fyodor Ivanovich in 1598 to the establishment of the Romanov dynasty in 1613. The Time of Troubles saw famine, civil war, mass uprisings and foreign occupation; the Russian state that had emerged over the preceding 500 years almost entirely disappeared. Another key period of contention often referenced by Russian politicians and commentators is the Pugachev Rebellion (1773–75), a revolt that took place at a time of foreign war and peasant unrest, which has become a symbol of the cruelty and violence that ensues when order breaks down and the Russian masses become involved in politics. Finally, of course, the tempestuous events of the Russian Revolution of 1917 and the ensuing civil war continue to influence how Russians think about popular participation in politics and its consequences. For conservatives, the Revolution is the clearest illustration of the costs of chaos and disorder. For radicals, the Revolution remains a symbol of the political possibilities of popular participation and of resistance against a corrupt elite.

Far from being of purely historical interest, contention also played a crucial role in creating Russia as the independent federation it is today. Formerly the most populous part of a much larger state, the Soviet Union (USSR), Russia broke off in a huge wave of contention that swept across the USSR. Between 1987 and 1991, nationalist and other protests had severely undermined the political viability of the Soviet state and had brought Soviet Union to the brink of collapse. However, it was an act of contention of a different kind – a failed coup launched by senior Communist officials – that pushed the Soviet state over the edge and led to the emergence of a new independent Russia on 1 January 1992.

Contentious politics and writing the Russian constitution

Although Russia was suddenly independent, the shape of the new country and its political institutions was still to be defined, and action on the streets once again proved decisive. The constitution inherited from the Soviet era was unclear on the powers of the president and the parliament. The result was a stand-off in which president and parliament both claimed to be the legitimate democratic power in the country and where each sought to pursue very different policies.

With no obvious institutional solution in sight, then-President Boris Yeltsin resorted to extraordinary measures. Though he had no constitutional authority to do so, Yeltsin decreed the parliament to be dissolved and called for new elections. The head of Russia's Constitutional Court duly announced that the decree was unconstitutional. The parliament in turn voted for Yeltsin's impeachment and appointed the vice-president in Yeltsin's place. In response, Yeltsin dispatched police units to surround the parliament building. After an 11-day siege, members of parliament and their supporters who had been trapped in the building broke through the police cordon. Along with other supporters, the parliamentarians attempted to seize key government buildings in Moscow, including the main television station, where a gun battle ensued. For some hours the outcome looked in doubt, but finally Yeltsin succeeded in persuading the Russian military leadership to support him and ordered tanks to attack the Russian parliament building. When the siege was over, somewhere between 187 (according to the government) and 1,000 (according to parliamentary supporters) had been killed. Now Yeltsin had a free hand to draw up a constitution that centralized power in his own hands.

Economic crisis, protest and society

Although Yeltsin had effectively established a dominant place for the president in the constitution, many writing at the beginning of the 1990s still expected him to be seriously tested by protest in the streets. After all, they argued, the combination of severe economic challenges that would impoverish millions with new democratic rights and the freedom to protest ought to lead to massive waves of unrest that would destabilize the new political settlement. Despite these challenges, the 1990s was a period in which, paradoxically, intra-institutional politics tended to dominate.

Although Russians did indeed suffer enormous social and economic upheaval, major political upheaval did not follow. It was not that Russians did not take action to address the economic catastrophe that was engulfing much of the country – thousands did, participating in strikes, hunger-strikes, road and railroad blockades and even, in a few extreme cases, public acts of suicide. However, though there were many thousands of protests, these events had little in the way of political consequences. There were many reasons for this. First, the depth of the economic crisis affecting the country meant that Russian workers had little leverage or bargaining power. Stopping working in a situation in which factories were largely at a standstill anyway had little effect. Second, in the 1990s it was extremely difficult to create organizations that could represent workers or put political pressure on the state. The independent civil society organizations that had flourished in the late Soviet period disappeared in the economic crisis and political disappointment of the first years of Russian independence. Moreover, in their place, state-affiliated organizations dominated the field of organizations, and state-sponsored labour unions in particular continued to try to pacify rather than organize workers. Third, and most paradoxically of all, democracy made it more difficult, not less, for workers, pensioners and others to hold the state responsible for their economic situation. Under communism, the state took upon itself direct responsibility for the economic condition of its citizens. When coal miners in 1989 struck over a lack of soap, the head of the Soviet government himself came to negotiate with them. However, in Yeltsin's Russia, the state explicitly downplayed its responsibility for the economy, turning things over, rhetorically at least, to the market. Moreover, electoral democracy meant that legitimate political power derived from the process of winning elections (by fair means or foul), rather than from economic performance, as it had in the Soviet era.

Ethnic and regional politics and contention

In addition to the economic crisis, Russia also faced a major challenge from many of its own ethnic minorities and regions that claimed autonomy from Moscow. Challenges from restive regions and minorities were common and, in many ways, dominated politics in the first half of the 1990s. Most prominent among these were the Volga republics of Tatarstan, Bashkortostan, the vast Siberian region of Sakha and the Caucausus region of Chechnya. However, for the most part, the politics of regional and ethnic autonomy were contained within elite institutions and negotiations between political leaders without large-scale mobilizations on the streets, and Yeltsin and his team were able to buy off the leadership of most regions with a combination of special bilateral treaties and financial transfers.

The major exception to this pattern was the Republic of Chechnya, located in the Caucasus mountains in the south of Russia. In November 1991, the Chechen regional parliament declared Chechnya's independence from Russia. Initially, the Russian government was too concerned with the myriad other problems it faced at the moment of the Soviet collapse to do much more than complain. However, in late 1994 Yeltsin and his team could no longer ignore the existence of a de facto autonomous state within Russia that had become a centre of lawlessness and instability. In December 1994, Yeltsin opted to launch a full-scale military intervention in order to re-establish Russian control. Despite the overwhelming advantage the Russian forces had in terms of numbers and equipment, the Russian military was unable to defeat the Chechen forces and, after a bloody and fruitless conflict, the Russians were forced to accept a peace deal in 1996 that allowed de facto Chechen independence.

However, the uneasy coexistence between Russia and Chechnya was shattered in 1999, when a large group of militants, closely associated with international Islamic fighters, invaded Dagestan, a region of Russia bordering on Chechnya. This provocation came on top of years of cross-border raiding from Chechnya and the kidnapping of dozens of citizens of neighbouring regions. Faced with this escalation, the Russian government launched another full-scale invasion. In contrast to the street fighting of the first war, this time Russian forces rapidly seized control of the main population centres, including the Chechen capital, Grozny. While successful, the Russian assault was also brutal, inflicting thousands of civilian casualties and committing innumerable human rights violations. Facing defeat on the conventional battlefield, Chechen fighters resorted increasingly to attacks on civilian targets outside the borders of Chechnya, the most horrifying of which involved the taking hostage of an entire elementary school in Beslan, North Ossetia, on the first day of classes in September 2004. In the fighting that followed some 350 hostages, many of them young children, were killed. Other atrocities have included hostage-taking in a central Moscow theatre and bombings of apartment buildings, airliners, subway trains, rock concerts, hospitals, trains, and markets. More than a thousand people have been killed in terrorist incidents in Russia since 1991, with some 600 killed in Moscow alone by 2007 (Taylor 2011). Although by 2010 the federal authorities had largely defeated pro-independence Chechen militants and established a Chechen-led regime in power, acts of terrorism and violence have continued, especially in the North Caucasus region, and isolated incidents have also occurred elsewhere in Russia.

Aside from the obviously disastrous impact within Chechnya itself, the conflict has made the task of building a law-bound and democratic state in Russia much harder. Both the fighting in Chechnya and terrorism in the rest of Russia have been used to justify limitations on media freedom and human rights. Civilians and conscripts alike have suffered in the brutality of a civil war. Famous journalists and human rights activists and ordinary men, women and children have been killed, with the finger of blame often pointed at Russian forces. Media freedom has suffered as limits on reporting about the conflict have been justified on grounds of state security. In Chechnya, peace has been restored at the cost of installing a repressive and often violent Chechen regime. In the rest of Russia, fear of terrorism has sometimes led to reprisals against ethnic Chechens and other Caucasians. More generally, Russian citizens have for the most part been willing to support their government in actions that have frequently breached both democratic and human rights norms. In short, the bloody Chechen conflict has made the environment much more difficult for democracy in Russia.

Putin and protest

As awful as the Yeltsin years were for all but a small minority of Russians, by the turn of the millennium the economy had started to bounce back. As the economy began to recover, the opportunities for local organization and participation increased and civil society organizations started to play a small but nonetheless noticeable role in many places in Russia. The government responded to this development by creating new institutions designed to integrate civil society into political and administrative decision-making. The new economic and political context of the Putin years also saw the re-emergence of political protest and the beginnings of a more coherent opposition to the existing political system.

With the wrenching economic crisis of the 1990s over, voluntary organizations and non-governmental organizations (NGOs) began to emerge in different parts of the Russian Federation. Thousands of new organizations were registered and began to participate in local politics and society (Evans *et al.* 2005). The Russian government was aware of this development and took a number of measures to channel this emerging civil society sector in directions that would help the government rather than challenge it. At the federal level a new assembly, known as the Public Chamber, was created to give representatives of non-governmental organizations a voice in public policy. The Public Chamber sat for the first time in 2005 and consists of representatives of civil society chosen by the government, who in turn elect further members. The Chamber is supposed to increase citizen involvement in both legislative and executive action and comment on draft legislation and the implementation of existing law. The Public Chamber also manages a system of competitions for federal funding of NGO projects throughout Russia. In addition to the federal Public Chamber, similar bodies were set up at the regional level across the country.

Opinions have been divided on the role of the Public Chambers in practice. Supporters argue that the Chambers provide a unique voice for the third sector in Russia and give civil society organizations unparalleled influence over policies that affect NGOs directly. These supporters also cite the intervention of the Public Chamber in a number of important cases over the years. Critics, on the other hand, argue that the system is intended to promote only pro-government organizations and to provide incentives for groups to avoid criticism of the government in return for access to funding and positions in the Chamber. What is clear is that the creation of the Public Chambers constitutes recognition on the part of the Russian government that a thriving state in the contemporary world needs a thriving society. However, by creating formal state institutions to which some have access and others do not, the system creates in society an insiders/outsiders divide that may make the development of that thriving society harder rather than easier to achieve.

Alongside the growth in civil society, the Putin years also saw the re-emergence of contention as an important part of Russian politics. The first sign that politics was returning to the streets of Russia came in January 2005. As part of a package of liberal economic reforms, the government introduced a new system whereby benefits in kind – particularly free transportation – that were provided to pensioners, war veterans and others were to be replaced by cash payments. The reforms were highly controversial and protests quickly spread in Moscow, St Petersburg and across much of Russia.

The government responded with a mixture of concessions and repression of activists and the protests gradually petered out. However, the protests represented a turning point. For the first time since Putin had come to power, the government had looked vulnerable to a challenge from the streets. Policies created by the executive and pushed through Russia's sleepy parliament had mobilized tens of thousands of angry citizens and had been partially reversed due to action on the streets. Moreover, the protests had included a broad range of groups from pensioners and liberal human rights activists to nationalist and neo-Bolshevik youth and had impressed upon these diverse groups the possibilities offered by creating a united front. Consequently, in the aftermath of the protests, especially in the biggest cities, Moscow and St Petersburg, meetings to coordinate non-parliamentary opposition activity began for the first time.

The non-system opposition that emerged from these meetings formed from two primary sources – alienated former parliamentary parties and politicians, and supporters of parties and movements at the right and left fringes of Russian politics. The initiative to coordinate was primarily local and so the character of the emergent opposition varied from place to place. In St Petersburg, for example, activists got together to form a united opposition bloc that stretched from liberals supported by businessman and philanthropist George Soros to members of the National Bolshevik Party, whose activists celebrate Stalin. Achieving cooperation across an opposition that spans such an enormously broad spectrum was a difficult task, so activists focused on opportunities where a united front against the incumbent regime could be presented. The G8 summit of major world leaders in St Petersburg in 2006 was a one such event, and though the protesters were kept far from the official meetings, the non-system opposition used the occasion to launch itself politically. Similarly, in Moscow, a parallel organization, 'Other Russia', was created around the time of the G8 summit. Other Russia included an extraordinary array of people and groups. Prominent among the leadership were liberal and former world chess champion Garri Kasparov, former Prime Minister Mikhail Kasyanov, Viktor Anpilov, a Stalinist who had fought on the side of the parliament against Yeltsin in 1993, National Bolshevik Party leader Eduard Limonov and a former head of the neo-liberal Union of Right Forces, Irina Khakamada. Other Russia began a regular series of protests by holding a 'Dissenters' March' in Moscow on 16 December 2006. The march was followed by others the following year in Nizhny Novgorod, St Petersburg and Moscow. In 2009, Limonov and others also began 'Strategy 31', a series of protests held on the 31st day of each month to mark the alleged violation by the authorities of article 31 of the Russian constitution, which guarantees freedom of assembly.

Over the months that followed, the non-system opposition continued to focus on non-parliamentary tactics. Deprived of access to television, activists sought creative ways of attracting attention. Traditional street protests were supplemented with flash mobs and other creative 'happenings' intended to destabilize the authority of the ruling administration. A key feature of the protests is the broad range of issues that have brought people together. Instead of the almost uniformly economic demands of the 1990s, protests now feature a much broader range of demands reflective of a rapidly changing society. Much of the energy behind street protests in Russia since the late 2000s has been driven by economic development and the environmental and distributional challenges that growth tends to generate. Urban building projects are one of the most common causes of protest in recent years as developers seek to make more profitable use of crowded urban space, often violating the rights of former tenants. Similarly, civil rights complaints, and especially problems with the criminal justice system and with corruption, have come to play a bigger role.

Environmentalists have also played a big role in the development of civil society and informal politics. Russia has a tradition of environmental protests, dating back to the Soviet period and efforts to preserve the pristine environment of Lake Baikal in Siberia. In recent years, the environmental movement has continued to focus on Lake Baikal, but has also been involved in a wide range of issues, including protesting against pollution from gas production facilities, environmental destruction resulting from construction projects associated with the 2014 Winter Olympics in Sochi, and exploitation of natural resources in the Arctic. From a political perspective, the most significant environmental protests of recent years took place in 2010, when thousands of activists fought a summer-long campaign involving civil disobedience in an attempt to stop the construction of a major highway through the Khimki Forest, part of the greenbelt on the outskirts of Moscow and home to elk, wild boar and several endangered plant and insect species. By the end of the summer President Medvedev ordered a suspension of construction, marking a rare climbdown on the part of the authorities. Many of the activists involved in the Khimki protests have continued to participate in civil society and local politics.

By contrast, labour unions have played a somewhat marginal role in civil society and politics. Although workers' strikes and independent labour unions played a major role in bringing down the Soviet Union, in the post-communist era the largest unions have generally been co-opted by employers and the state, depriving workers of genuine representatives. Nevertheless, as the economy grew in the 2000s, efforts at independent labour organizing began again to spread across the country, focusing in particular on flourishing industrial and natural resource enterprises, transportation and foreign-owned industrial plants. So far, the government and employers have worked hard to repress the new unions and labour organizing remains a difficult and sometime dangerous task.

The protest cycle of 2011–12

In December 2011, the nascent protest movement in Russia took centre stage in the international news for the first time. On 4 December 2011, elections took place to the lower house of Russia's parliament, the State Duma. Russian and international observers, as we saw in Chapter 4, condemned the elections, citing barriers to candidate registration, ballot-box stuffing and violations in counting the votes. As the results came in that evening, the perception that the elections had been marred by fraud was widespread in opposition circles. The reaction to fraud, however, differed between those who had a place in Russia's divided political system and those who were excluded. Communist Party leader Gennadii Zyuganov, whose party had won the second largest number of seats in the Duma, at first condemned the elections on television. Later, after his party was awarded a number of key committee assignments in the new parliament, Zyuganov changed positions and the Communists duly took up their seats.

By contrast, the non-parliamentary opposition quickly took to the streets. There were demonstrations the same evening. And the day after the elections, Monday 5 December, a few thousand activists protested in Moscow, denouncing the elections as unfair. Since no permit had been granted for the protest, the gathering was technically illegal and police arrested some 300 participants. More than one hundred activists were also arrested at a similar event in St Petersburg. The gathering attracted a number of politicians who had been active in Other Russia, as well as other activists and cultural figures. Finding themselves together, an informal committee was quickly formed to coordinate protests against the elections.

The following day unsanctioned protests continued in the centre of Moscow and a number of protest leaders were arrested. At the same time pro-government supporters rallied in front of the Kremlin and the authorities moved large numbers of police and security officials into the capital. Nevertheless, the number of people willing to participate in protests seemed to be growing rapidly. One opposition group, Solidarity, had a permit for a legal demonstration of 300 people on Saturday, 10 December. However, as the date approached it became clear from social media that many thousands more were intending to participate. As a result, the authorities agreed to a much larger demonstration on an island in the Moscow River, in a place called Bolotnaya (Swamp) Square. On the day, somewhere between 25,000 and 80,000 people participated in a peaceful gathering. Leading cultural figures, authors and rock stars joined the politicians in addressing the crowd. Similar, if much smaller, protests were held in St Petersburg and other cities across Russia.

International and Russian commentators celebrated the protests as a new stage in Russian politics and argued that the event marked the beginning of the end of the Putin regime. Whether this turns out to be correct or not, only time will tell, but it was already clear back in December 2011 that the end of the Putin regime, if it were to happen, would not be coming soon. After all, even if the largest opposition estimates of 80,000 protesters in Moscow were correct, this was still a small number in a city of over 10 million inhabitants, and the events were limited in size compared with the kinds of crowds that had gathered to denounce election fraud in neighbouring countries like Ukraine and Georgia. Moreover, unlike election protests in other countries where protests were sustained over a number of days, it was fully two more weeks, 24 December, before the next large protest event took place, when between 28,000 (the police estimate) and 120,000 (the opposition estimate) people gathered on Prospekt Sakharova in central Moscow. A third mass event took place in Moscow on 4 February 2012, with a march culminating in Bolotnaya Square. Between 40,000 and 160,000 people braved the -20 Celsius temperatures to participate.

Consequently, though the authorities in the Kremlin had initially seemed rattled by the protests, by March the situation seemed very much under control. Vladimir Putin ran for and was duly elected president on 4 March with little challenge either on the streets or at the ballot box. With Putin firmly back in office, the authorities also began to take a tougher stance towards the protesters. A demonstration at Bolotnaya Square on 6 May 2012, the day before Putin's inauguration, took place in the context of a massive police presence. At the rally, scuffling broke out between police and protesters and about 400 protesters were arrested and 80 injured. This was the first significant violence of any of the protest events and was indicative of a more aggressive line being taken by police.

Protest, civil society and politics since 2012

The protest cycle that began in December 2011 seemed to have largely petered out by the summer of 2012. Increasingly, the protesters have sought to institutionalize their movement and create the organizational capacity to sustain an opposition force even as politics moves out of the streets. A key part of this strategy was the institutionalization of a 45-member Coordinating Council (CC) to represent the protesters. In October 2012, 81,000 people participated in self-organized elections to select representatives of the council. This was a novel and highly innovative attempt on the part of a loosely organized street movement to create the capacity for continuity after the peak of protest activity. Nevertheless, in a broader context, though participation in the elections was impressive for a protest movement, it was very small when compared to the Russian electorate as a whole and, like the protests, was highly Moscow-centric. Moreover, the CC, itself divided between liberal, nationalist and leftist lists, looked too cumbersome an instrument to provide real leadership

In the aftermath of the violence on Bolotnaya Square, the Putin administration began tightening the screws on protest and on the street opposition. A series of measures were adopted that significantly increased the legal penalties for participation in protest events that were not licensed by the authorities. Moreover, people who had participated in protests were now targeted for prosecution. During the clashes in Bolotnaya Square itself around 400 people were arrested, but, as had typically been the practice, the authorities released most of them quickly afterwards. However, in a significant departure from the usual practice, over the following weeks and months the police and prosecutors office began rounding up activists in a series of dawn raids. Overall, a group of 20 or so young people were arrested and charged with participation in mass disorders and with using violence against representatives of the state. The accused, in what has become known as the Bolotnoe Affair, face up to ten years in jail on these serious charges. It was hard to miss the political message in these prosecutions. None of those arrested had participated in major violent incidents and none of them was a politically important figure. Instead, the message is aimed at protest sympathizers in the general population and to parents: participating in opposition politics can be very risky. As Anna Zarva, lawyer for one of the accused, PhD chemist Fyodor Bakhov, told the website gazeta.ru, 'a representative of the investigators told me unofficially why they picked specifically these people. Because it includes all strata of society. Let them not think that just because they are students or businessmen they can escape responsibility. They had no business going to demonstrations.'

At the same time as the Bolotnoe Affair was taking place, international attention was focused on the Pussy Riot case with which this chapter began. The purpose of this case seems quite different. The point here was not so much to frighten would-be sympathizers but rather to associate the opposition with, to conservative minds, its most radical and least mainstream elements. It is crucial to remember that Pussy Riot were an obscure group of artists, hardly known outside their circle of friends, until the authorities chose to make an example of them. The decision to prosecute was also a decision to make Pussy Riot the face of the protest movement and to present the movement as being out of step with Russian values. Survey data suggest that this approach worked too. According to Levada Center polling, by September 2012, 84 per cent of Russians had heard of the Pussy Riot case. Moreover, most of them disapproved. Only 5 per cent of people thought the Christ the Saviour events an artistic performance, while 41 per cent thought it an act of simple hooliganism and a further 19 per cent claimed it as a deliberate attack on Orthodoxy and the Church. Indeed, 53 per cent of Russians considered the performance deliberately intended to offend religious Russians, and 78 per cent thought the two-year prison terms handed down to the band either appropriate or insufficient. In the light of such data, the message of solidarity signalled by the administration to conservative Russians, and particularly to the Orthodox Church, seems to have been successful communicated.

Another element in the strategy of the Putin administration has been to try to isolate any emerging leaders among the street opposition. Most of the Other Russia leaders were people with a long history of association with the opposition and so were old news and little feared in the Kremlin. However, the protest cycle of 2011–12 brought forward some new faces that represented more of a challenge to politics as usual in Russia. Amongst the most prominent was Sergei Udaltsov, leader of a group called Left Front. With his allegiance to leftist and even revolutionary positions, Udaltsov is far from the political mainstream in Russia, but he nevertheless represents a challenge to the current system and, in particular, to the comfortable place of the Communist Party within it. Consequently, Udaltsov has faced serious intimidation by the Russian authorities, including frequent periods of detention. In February 2013, he was placed under house arrest in Moscow and charged with having conspired with Georgian agents in a plot to overthrow the Russian president.

Most prominent of all the new oppositionists is the anti-corruption blogger and sometime nationalist rabble-rouser, Alexei Navalny. Navalny has an aggressive, irreverent political style that matches well in competition with the macho image of President Putin. Navalny's most famous contribution to Russian political debate so far has been his relabelling of Russia's ruling United Russia Party as the 'Party of Crooks and Thieves', a label that has stuck and become common currency amongst the opposition. Navalny steadily emerged as the figurehead of the opposition, at least in Moscow. In October 2010, Navalny won 'virtual elections' held online to elect a 'Mayor of Moscow' in protest against the appointment of a long-time Putin associate (Sergei Sobyanin) to that job. Then, in October 2012, he had the biggest support in the election to the opposition Coordinating Council, with 53 per cent those who participated selecting him for the council.

In response to Navalny's rising profile, the authorities launched a series of investigations into Navalny's activities in an attempt to bring down the anti-corruption campaigner with corruption charges of their own. By the summer of 2013, Navalny was the defendant in three different trials, accused of embezzling money from a forestry company, Kirovles, from the Post Office and from a right wing political party, Right Cause. In July 2013, Navalny was convicted in the Kirovles trial and sentenced to five years' imprisonment. Bizarrely enough, the authorities promptly released Navalny pending appeal – an extremely unusual step in Russia – and he returned to Moscow to run in the real elections for Mayor of Moscow in September 2013. After a lively campaign of meeting voters and engaging directly with citizens – he was largely excluded from television during the campaign – Navalny polled a very creditable 27 per cent of the vote, coming close to forcing the winner and incumbent mayor, Sobyanin, into a run-off vote.

More broadly, in the aftermath of the protests, the Kremlin has sought to make life difficult for NGOs that it deems to have been involved in politics. On 13 July 2012, the Duma passed the so-called law on 'foreign agents' that required any NGO engaged in (vaguely defined) 'political' activities and receiving funding from foreign sources to register as 'foreign agents'. The law has been used to target high-profile groups, in particular, the election monitoring organization, Golos, the public opinion polling company, the Levada Center, and the human rights organization, Memorial. However, the pressure has not been limited to groups with an international presence. Smaller local groups including numerous research organizations focusing on women's rights, LGBTQ issues and anti-discrimination in general have also been targeted. By cutting off the flow of funds to NGOs from abroad, Russian organizations are likely to either have to close down or become increasingly dependent on the state for support.

Conclusion

Although the 2011–12 election cycle protests took some observers of Russian politics by surprise, as we have seen in this chapter the organizational and political basis for protest had been a growing for several years. The big effect of the protests is that contention is now on the agenda in Russia politics in a way that it has not been for years. Nevertheless, it is not clear what the role of contention is likely to be in the future. The most plausible answer is that the effect will neither be as large as optimists think nor as limited as pessimists think. It is unlikely that that the current political system in Russia will soon be overthrown in street protests. However, it is also unlikely that Russian politics can return to business as usual as though the protests never happened. Politics in Russia has been undergoing a gradual transformation. The extraordinary turmoil and devastation of the 1990s scarred Russian society and contributed to the construction of a closed, hierarchical political system. This system was designed to minimize contestation and to seal politics off from contention and pressure from below. However, as the economy recovered, Russian society has grown wealthier, better organized and more like societies in countries to Russia's west. At the same time, activists and others excluded from the political system sought to use protests and other forms of politics to gain a voice. The protest cycle of 2011–12 was a watershed moment in this process and a loud wake-up call to the authorities that politics as usual has to change. It is still not clear what direction that change will take. Initially, the Russian authorities have cracked down, increasing the use of repression. However, this is not a sustainable strategy in the longer term, as some in the administration seem to understand. Consequently, there are important forces pushing for a greater liberalization of the political environment to accommodate those who feel excluded from the current system. What balance is struck between liberalization and repression will be a crucial feature to watch in Russian politics in the coming years.

Chapter 8

Russia's Media and Political Communication in the Digital Age

SARAH OATES

According to the international ranking of media freedom by Freedom House, there are only 21 countries in the world that have less media freedom than Russia. That might seem confusing at first, in that Russia would appear to have a high degree of media diversity, particularly with its highly engaged and critical citizens in the online sphere. The puzzle is how Russia has used the media as a weapon against democratization while maintaining this veneer of a diverse and varied media environment. That façade has been sorely tested since late 2011, particularly by the ability of the internet to create political momentum as well as the seeming inability of the Kremlin to control this phenomenon. At issue for this chapter is how long the Russian government can successfully manipulate the media and its audience for its own ends in the digital age.

From a distance, Russia provides a communications paradox in that there is so much information and so little democracy. The economic stability of the Russian media, in particular television, increased steadily as the economy improved under President Vladimir Putin in the first years of the twenty-first century. Yet despite the growth in media companies and their establishment as successful businesses, the last decade has seen a distinct decline in media pluralism and diversity of opinion in Russia. In some ways it might even appear that the contemporary Russian media have more to do with the Soviet media than any Western model. While information sources have diversified and become technically more professional, the idea of the media as 'objective' or 'balanced' has never been widely accepted. All segments of Russian society, from politicians to the public to the journalists themselves, perceive the mass media as political actors rather than watchdogs that can provide a check on political power. Thus, while there is no overt system of top-down state censorship in Russia today, the media are not free to contribute to the democratic process. This is due to an intertwined set of societal factors. These elements include a lack of professional acceptance of the concept of journalistic balance or objectivity; the use of the media as political pawns by leaders; and the public's acceptance of the media as a voice of authority rather than the purveyor of information.

While it might be tempting to dismiss these factors as an echo of the Soviet state or particular features of authoritarianism, the forces that drive the Russian media system are more subtle and complicated. Beneath the appearance of social and political unity behind the Kremlin elite, there are sources of alternative information available to a large sector of the population. In particular, the internet has seen unprecedented growth over the past decade, now rising to reach almost half of the population as 47 per cent of Russians were online by June 2012, according to www.internetworldstats.com. This means that 67 million out of 142.5 million Russian were online at this time. While this is lower than the rates of penetration in countries such as the United Kingdom and the United States, the growth in internet use represents the fastest expansion in Europe between 2000 and 2010 (Oates 2013). While the international organization Freedom House ranks the Russian media as not free, it deems the internet as partly free, highlighting opportunity for media freedom to develop more quickly and deeply in that medium (Freedom on the Net 2013).

The history of the Russian media

Any analysis of the media – or of any other aspect of Russian society – has to be within the context of the Soviet legacy. As discussed in other chapters of this book, Russian politics are heavily influenced by the long period of Soviet rule, which started with the overthrow of the Romanov monarchy in 1917 and ended with the collapse of the Communist Party of the Soviet Union in 1991. The Soviet Union, of which Russia was the largest part, declared itself to be a communist state and was opposed to the idea of Western capitalism. That meant that, in theory, the state was run by the people for the public good. In reality, the Soviet system was run by a small, elite group of leaders who used fear and repression to hold on to power and maintain rule over the masses. A key part of this was media control.

In the Soviet era, the media had a clear model. Its function was to educate the public in the central tenets of the ideology of the ruling Communist Party and to inculcate support for communist ideals. The country was run by the Communist Party (which did not tolerate any other political forces), notionally in the name of the working class, but actually the utopian state of worker self-rule never emerged. Rather, the country was an authoritarian regime that punished dissent with imprisonment or death. Although the severity of repression varied under different Soviet leaders, no opposition to the regime or legitimate free media was tolerated. At the same time, the Soviets worked hard to develop a robust mass media system for propaganda, convinced that it was necessary to instil the values of communism into Soviet citizens. By the end of the Soviet period in 1991, television could reach up to 98 per cent of the vast territory of the country. In contrast, only 40 per cent of Soviet homes had telephones by 1991, according to official statistics (Goskomstat 1996: 165). This shows how the Soviet state emphasized public communication over private contacts.

While the ability to spread propaganda was clearly a priority, ironically it was this vast propaganda machine that accelerated the collapse of the Soviet regime. In 1985, the new Soviet leader Mikhail Gorbachev introduced the policy of *glasnost* or 'transparency' in the media. Gorbachev believed that this greater transparency would help people to understand and correct some of the problems of Soviet society. Yet, this new freedom to criticize minor problems soon led to vocal and public challenges to Soviet power itself. Once public opinion was unleashed, it turned against the Soviet leaders and the Soviet regime ended after an attempted hardline coup collapsed in 1991.

This Soviet past is key to understanding the current Russian media situation because journalistic norms appear to have changed relatively little from those times. From *glasnost* to the creation of the new Russian state, there was enormous variation, discussion and innovation in the mass media. However, the norms present in democratic systems did not emerge. For example, commercial media owners perceived their media outlets as tools for shaping public opinion for their own causes. State-run media outlets were clearly instruments to garner support for leaders, such as first Russian president Boris Yeltsin and Putin as his successor. In both the US and British models, media outlets typically support the general principles and values of the state. Yet in both systems there is a substantial attempt to find objectivity (in the US) or balance (on British television) on the part of journalists. There are many examples of how media in the West fail, but it is generally accepted that the media should serve as an independent force in the service of citizens and/or consumers. In Russia, the media are perceived as political players. As a result, they are in the service of their political or commercial masters. While this is a condition that Russian media, politicians and the public accept as normal, it makes the growth of civil society enormously difficult. The Russian journalist has much in common with the Soviet journalist: he or she understands that the media are there to serve rather than to challenge. At the same time, the Russian audience has much in common with the Soviet audience, in that they understand and accept (to a large degree) that the media present a façade of order (Oates 2006: 44–65).

One key way in which the Russian media has failed as a democratic institution is in its coverage of the elections held since the Soviet collapse. After the adoption of the new Russian constitution in 1993, elections have been held regularly for parliament and the presidency (as well as for many regional and local leaders). It was expected that regular elections would aid in the development of democratic institutions, particularly political parties, and show the Russian public the value of free choice. What happened was rather different, in that from the very first elections for parliament in 1993, the government gave an unfair advantage to parties friendly to the Kremlin's agenda. Although the electoral law technically provides for free and equal time for all parties on state-run television – as well as fair news coverage – political influence has meant unequal treatment for parties that challenge the Kremlin's hegemony. This has been clear from content analysis of news coverage, free time and paid political advertising over several parliamentary and presidential elections (see particularly the reports of the Organization for Security and Cooperation in Europe at www.osce.org/odihr). While this pattern continued over several elections, the degree of apparent unfairness in the 2011 Duma elections sparked widespread protest and media challenges, which will be discussed below.

The Russian media landscape today: one nation, two audiences

The Russian audience, like the Soviet audience before it, are enthusiastic consumers of mass media. According to the Federal Bureau of Government Statistics, there were 8,978 newspapers being published in Russia in 2008, with a total circulation of 8.2 billion. The top three daily newspapers were listed as *Moskovskii komsomolets* (with a daily circulation of 2,040,000), *Komsomolskaya pravda* (640,900) and *Rossiiskaya gazeta* (218,905) (European Stability Initiative 2009: 2). While the first two publications could be described as general interest, *Rossiiskaya gazeta* is published by the Russian government and serves as a paper of official record. Another prominent daily is *Novaya gazeta* (circulation 171,000 in 2008, according to the same source), a publication noted both for having significant staff ownership and being a vocal critic of the Kremlin. A dominant weekly publication is the tabloid *Argumenty i fakty*, which dwarfs other weeklies with a huge circulation of 2.75 million (ibid.: 3).

Russians love television even more than print media. State-run television has dominated the political sphere in Russia, both during the Soviet era and up to the present day. Surveys have consistently identified state-run television as one of the most trusted and authoritative political institutions in the country (Oates 2006). Commercial television enjoys a much lower level of trust, but the best-established commercial station called NTV claims it is available across almost the entire country. While the Russian authorities have found state-run television to be a particularly effective tool at framing and controlling the political sphere, the power of television everywhere is on the wane. Nations around the globe are experiencing a shift in audience from traditional outlets to online news sources. While the adoption and use of the internet vary a great deal among countries, there are global trends that are widely shared. In particular, the adoption has been faster and the use wider among the younger generation. This creates a challenging phenomenon for leaders, many of whom struggle to understand the fundamental change that has taken place in the news environment. Thus, while leaders can fairly readily understand the concept of a new media *distribution* system, fundamental changes in *media ecology* such as crowd-sourcing and horizontal information sharing among trusted circles are not something they intuitively grasp. As a result, elites can be slow to understand the power and authority of new media, ranging from blogs and Facebook pages to YouTube.

While Russian leaders are by no means alone in having to deal with fast and fundamental change in the media system wrought by the internet, they face some particularly powerful challenges. The key issues are very rapid internet adoption in a short time span; a gap between a non-free media and a relatively free online sphere; an online/offline divide that reinforces other social cleavages in a country with a very distinctive Soviet and post-Soviet divide; and a young generation that matches advanced Western countries in its internet use and skill (for a full discussion, see Oates 2013). Indeed, it may be a disturbing thought for the Kremlin that these are all elements that parallel the conditions in Egypt just before the Arab Spring.

What is particularly interesting is that the Russian government itself is clearly aware of the expanding growth of the online audience and has viewed it quite positively (Russian Federal Agency on the Press and Mass Communication 2011). In this government report, Russian authorities compiled a range of data to predict that internet use among those under 40 would reach almost 100 per cent by 2015. In part, this has been fuelled by the ubiquity of mobile phones, which are enormously popular. However, the Russian love of technology and interest in information has also driven this growth. While both the report and analyses on website-tracking companies such as Alexis.com show that Russians are more interested in consumer rather than political issues online (as is true virtually everywhere), at the same time they are engaging with a far greater range of sources outside the control of Russian government.

That is not to say that people are not watching television in Russia. National television was still the most popular media outlet in Russia in 2010, according to a survey of 2,017 Russians (White and McAllister 2010). In the survey, only a handful of people (1.5 per cent) claimed they never watched national television. Three-quarters of the population watched national television routinely, 18 per cent occasionally and about 5 per cent 'seldom'. In the same survey, almost half of the respondents replied that they had never been online and only 23 per cent reported they went online routinely, 16 per cent said they went online sometimes and 14 per cent said they seldom went online. The survey also highlighted generational differences that show the significant shift from television to the internet for younger citizens. While about 82 per cent of those 43 and older reported that they watched television routinely, only 66 per cent of those 29 or younger did the same. That means that the audience for national television shrinks by 20 per cent from one generation to the next. It seems unlikely that their media habits will switch as they age, particularly given the breadth of offerings online. Still, state television has a particularly authoritative news voice. The flagship news programme (*Vremya* or *Time*) on the state-run First Channel far outdistanced the news on commercial NTV (*Segodnya* or *Today*): 78 per cent of the respondents in the 2010 survey claimed they watched *Vremya* compared with 53 per cent who watched *Segodnya*.

State-run news relies on its authoritative voice to shape the news agenda and frame key societal issues (or to virtually ignore some, such as the fighting in Chechnya or endemic bribery at the highest levels). Authoritarian news frames only work if the information is not challenged by other legitimate sources. There is a symbiotic relationship between First Channel and its viewers, as has been shown in earlier work (Oates 2006). Although viewers are aware that much of what they see is either biased or highly selective, they often approve of the coverage in the interest of national pride and stability. Thus, they are not attracted to the idea of objectivity (which they claimed in focus groups is mythical at best and at worst another way that people fool themselves) or even balance. The news should 'lead' and not 'follow': those who are loyal should be rewarded and celebrated with coverage, those who are out of favour should be ignored or vilified through biased coverage. However, this illusion of stability is hard to sustain in the face of competing news frames, as offered by popular internet sources.

Media freedom

It is important to understand the gap that exists in Russia between media diversity and media freedom. While freedom of speech is guaranteed by the 1993 Constitution, this has not served as a foundation for media laws that would support the ability of the mass media to function as a force for democracy or even political plurality. Rather, the law has tended to work against the interests of free speech (Oates 2013). As highlighted elsewhere in this volume, there is a general lack of rule of law in Russia. As such, the government can apply the law selectively in order to limit political opposition. This lack of transparency is particularly apparent in the media sector, in which the Putin administration used financial laws to force a change in ownership of a relatively outspoken media group (Media-Most) in 2001. In addition to problems with central government, media outlets face significant constraints at the local level. Not only can the Russian regions use their own laws to threaten outspoken media, local bureaucrats and officials can bring considerable pressure to bear on local media outlets by threatening to take away state premises, impose fines or taxes or even organize quite selective 'tax inspections' to confiscate material.

In 2002, a law that banned 'extremism' in media coverage was passed as part of a package of anti-terrorism legislation. While many societies are concerned about the role of the media in radicalization, this law in Russia also means that officials can interpret a wide range of government opposition as 'extreme'. Essentially, the media law in Russia is structured and deployed in such a way that it is far better suited as a weapon against journalists than as a bastion of free speech.

The law aside, there are other factors that seriously constrain the ability of journalists to pursue a broad range of creative and politically significant work. It is impossible to ignore the aura of threat and violence that – coupled with the politicized nature of the legal system – makes it very difficult for individuals to engage in meaningful political communication. Put more simply, becoming a journalist who chooses to challenge the government can be a very dangerous profession. Russia has been one of the deadliest countries in the world for journalists, as measured by international groups such as Reporters Without Borders. Part of this is due to ongoing violence in Chechnya, but the violence is not confined to this region.

Violence against Russian journalists and even their murder has been extensively documented. The most high-profile case in recent years was the 2006 assassination of Anna Politkovskaya, who wrote in depth on the Chechen war for the oppositional *Novaya gazeta* newspaper. Politkovskaya was shot dead in the elevator of her apartment building in Moscow as she returned home from shopping. Although her death caused worldwide comment and outrage, President Putin was fairly dismissive of her work, saying she had little influence on political life in Russia. This sort of example is chilling for all journalists. The lack of uproar over Politkovskaya's death in Russia is not surprising, in that the Committee to Protect Journalists has estimated that 56 journalists have been killed in Russia since 1992 (https://cpj.org/killed/europe/russia/).

The reputation of the Russian media abroad

Aside from the international media attention to the murder of Politkovskaya, how are the Russian media perceived on the world stage? The simple response to this would be 'not well'. Despite the diversity and range of media outlets, it is clear that Russian media are failing to provide objective or balanced information to the citizenry. Rather, the media are mostly outlets for political interests, particularly those of the Kremlin. According to non-governmental organization Freedom House, Russia was just below Rwanda and Sudan and ahead of Azerbaijan for 176th place out of 197 countries in the 2012 Freedom of the Press World Rankings.

The US-based organization lists several reasons for this low ranking (Norway and Sweden were tied for first and North Korea and Turkmenistan were tied for last, see www.freedomhouse.org). The Freedom House report on Russia for 2012 painted a grim picture of heightened repression of the media, in particular since Vladimir Putin was re-elected for his third term as Russian president in March 2012. In mid-2012, the president and the parliament approved a 'series of repressive, vaguely worded measures that significantly expanded the array of regulatory tools available to stifle legitimate news reporting on politically embarrassing issues and limit of the work of non-governmental organisations (NGOs) on media matters' (Freedom of the Press 2013). This was in keeping with a general crackdown on protest behaviour, which included increased fines for participation at 'unsanctioned' rallies as well as the requirement for NGOs with foreign funding to register as 'foreign agents' with the Justice Ministry. In 2012, the US Agency for International Development (USAID) was expelled from Russia, signalling a new low in Russian–American relations.

Overall, there were a number of measures that contributed to more restrictions against freedom of the media, including charges against a number of government critics as well as new government powers to shut down websites. At the same time, according to the Freedom House report, there were more than two dozen documentaries praising Putin in the weeks before the March 2012 presidential elections. The Freedom House report also reported on ongoing violence against journalists, including the murder of Kazbek Gekkiyev, a local anchor for a state broadcaster, who was killed in Nalchik in the North Caucasus after death threats from Muslim separatist fighters. While Gekkiyev's death highlights threats from separatist violence in southern Russia, journalists are also threatened by the state itself. In particular, Russian journalists faced police violence and arrest during post-election protests in 2011, according to the Freedom House report.

While the 2012 Freedom House report on internet freedom in Russia noted that the internet still remained freer than the traditional mass media in Russia, the demonstrations in 2012 were linked with more action against the online sphere than in previous times. The problems included denial-of-service attacks against websites that challenged the government, action against individual bloggers such as Navalny as well as a growing level of ownership of online sites by pro-government allies, according to the 2012 report (Freedom on the Net 2012). Although the repression is targeted at a handful of individuals, this serves as a clear warning for all those who engage online as well as encouraging self-censorship. Nonetheless, the Freedom on the Net report for 2012 labelled the post-election period in 2011 as an 'important period of awakening for the Russian digital civil society … citizens and netizen activism ultimately led the government to concede a few demi-measures to pacify the protest movement, including the installation of electoral web cams … and the liberalization of political party regulations'. On the other hand, the activism certainly focused the government's attention in a more concentrated way on the need to control internet activism.

By the following year, Freedom House had become more pessimistic about freedom online in Russia (and elsewhere), finding evidence that the Russian government was taking more direct action against free speech online (Freedom on the Net 2013). In particular, the report noted that the number of websites classified as 'extremist material' and blocked by the Ministry of Justice increased by about 60 per cent from January 2012 to February 2013. In July 2012, the Duma passed a law that allows the government to list websites that internet service providers must block. The 2013 Freedom House report found that while this law was allegedly passed to target sites with child pornography or extremist material, the new law has been used to block sites with legitimate content. Worryingly, cases of criminal prosecution for online activities increased almost threefold from 38 in 2011 to 103 in 2012; while this is not a particularly large number overall, the trend suggests that the law is increasingly used as weapon of censorship and repression. In addition, Russian law was amended in July 2012 to re-criminalize defamation in both traditional and online media (Freedom on the Net 2013).

Journalists and self-censorship

Russian journalists routinely practise self-censorship across a range of subjects. This is an area in which there is a strong legacy from the Soviet era, when journalists were obliged to adhere to strong central censorship. The key question about Russian journalists is whether they have the desire to fundamentally change from the Soviet era. It would be understandable if older journalists who acquired their training and professional experience at that time had trouble shifting to different attitudes toward reporting. Worryingly, though, there is evidence that the post-Soviet generation of journalists fail to perceive themselves as political watchdogs or even conduits of political information to the public (Voltmer 2000; Pasti 2005). In almost all commercial and state-funded media outlets, journalists are expected to adhere to the editorial line, which in turn is limited by government pressure and interference. With the lack of an independent court system, there is little legal recourse for media outlets selectively targeted by financial or libel lawsuits. While the unsettled political and economic situation in the early 1990s allowed for a fairly wide variation of opinions, no major sector of the media developed an attempt to provide balanced information of use to citizens. Rather, it was a cacophony of opinionated news that quieted down as political opinions themselves were reduced. It is a spiralling phenomenon – the narrower the political elite, the smaller the range of media outlets. Yet this equilibrium will be challenged by the online sphere.

In what ways has the online sphere challenged the relative narrow public discourse in traditional media outlets in Russia? The internet has enabled online social entrepreneurs, such as Alexei Navalny, to challenge the dominant media frames on key issues such as state corruption. Navalny rose to prominence through his Rospil website (www.rospil.ru), which collected documented evidence on official corruption in Russia. While many internet activists could be seen as localized or elite protests, such as those surrounding the development of a new highway through the Khimki forest near Moscow that was noted in the previous chapter, Rospil's focus on corruption deals with an issue that touches the daily lives of all Russians. This was amplified through the popularity of native web platforms for blogging and networking, such as LiveJournal (www.livejournal.ru) and Vkontakte (www.vkontakte.ru, which means 'in touch' in Russian). Analysts and researchers noted a rise in crowd-sourcing that naturally increased as internet usage spread in Russia (Oates 2013).

The 2011–12 protests and the Russian mass media

Until the end of 2011, there was a reasonable argument to be made that the Russian media was effective at building social consensus despite the corrupt and unfair nature of Russian governance. There was little meaningful protest and what few protest rallies there were had low attendances and virtually no news coverage. While there were no widespread protests, however, there was evidence that people were aggregating interests online and even taking action locally or on targeted issues. This was apparent not only in the ways that Russians responded to widespread forest fires in 2010 by setting up a crowd-sourced map of areas needing help or through online protests about the development of forest lands near Moscow, but more particularly in protests to gain access to social benefits taking place in various parts of Russia. Navalny and other social-activist bloggers had gained significant followings online.

The scale and scope of online protest changed when at first thousands, then tens of thousands of citizens took to the streets to protest against electoral fraud in the December 2011 parliamentary elections. As we have noted in earlier chapters, elections have been heavily manipulated by the Kremlin, not only via the state-dominated media but also through an electoral law that is increasingly aimed at consolidating state-backed parties at the expense of grass-roots opposition. The only general protests had been isolated and small, considered to represent such a minority of Russian citizens that protestors were only rarely arrested or even harassed. Against this backdrop, the rapid and extensive protests about the conduct and results the December 2011 Duma elections caught many observers and analysts off guard. Seven key factors are identifiable as catalysts for these protests: (i) the failure of a state censorship that relied on traditions of self-censorship; (ii) an online sphere that was freer than the traditional mass media; (iii) an explosion in internet use that eroded the dominance of state television; (iv) a lack of understanding about citizen attitudes and the online sphere on the part of elites; (v) crowd-sourcing; (vi) online political networks; and (vii) the role of online social entrepreneurs such as Navalny (Oates 2013).

In the pre-internet age, the Russian state could either censor or bully media outlets into not challenging the state on key issues such as corruption among elites, violence in Chechnya, and skewed elections. The internet, however, made it possible not only to tell people about conflicting information (such as obviously manipulated ballot results) but to show them the data itself (such as on the results page of the Central Elections Commission website, in which many results had curious anomalies in favour of the ruling party – such as the 99 per cent vote for the United Russia party in Chechnya). It was this element of eyewitness evidence, particularly through uploaded videos, that particularly challenged the Russian state's control on information. United Russia won 49 per cent of the vote in 2011, which was not far off the predicted return, but anomalies in returns as well as reports of electoral irregularities were rife.

Some protests began immediately after polling day on December 4. The largest number of arrests (estimated at hundreds) occurred during the early protests, including the detention of Navalny along with other opposition figures. A larger protest was quickly organized for 10 December at Bolotnaya Square in Moscow under the banner of 'For Fair Elections', managing to gain a sanctioned area on which to protest in Moscow. Other protests were planned for around the country, aided by the internet's ability to circumvent the controls on official news channels. Another even larger protest was held on 24 December, with the largest meeting on Sakharov Prospect in Moscow and additional rallies across the country. Although the movement called for new Duma elections, the removal of the chair of the elections commission and an investigation into the falsification in the Duma results, none of these demands was ever met. Another set of protest meetings was organized for 4 February, again at Bolotnaya Square in Moscow and around the country. Pro-Putin demonstrations started to appear as well, with the largest in Moscow on 4 February with a reported 130,000 participants.

A qualitative analysis of coverage of three large protest days during this Russian 'winter of discontent' shows that there were significant differences between state-run television news, commercial television news and in three important online news sources (Oates and Lokot 2013). All three of these key information sources presented different aspects of the protests, although state-run news clung as much as possible to the frame of the protestors as either trivial, relatively small in number and – most significantly – concerned with the implementation of government rules rather than disgusted with the government itself. Both commercial news and the internet framed the protests as something quite different, that is, movements much more critical of the Russian government. In particular, commercial news made an attempt to show the true scope, scale and character of the events. Commercial news *Segodnya* nipped at the heels of the state news *Vremya* coverage, questioning the latter's low estimate of crowds, challenging the state's framing of the pro-Putin marches as engineered, and – most importantly – presenting the 'For Honest Elections' movement as a legitimate political force. This suggests that the media logic in Russia is more complicated than a stable landscape of total control. Although both state and commercial media practise self-censorship, they practise it to different degrees and savvy viewers can pick up on rising political tensions.

An even more important part of the story of the 2011–12 Russian protests is how the internet was able to contribute to much fuller coverage of the events. The internet was able to deliver much more detail, in part due to its structure: unlike the constraints in traditional media outlets, there is almost unlimited space for content. Thus, there was space to show not only the words of the protestors and their leaders, but also to carry a wide range of citizen journalism as well as key logistical information about the events themselves. It was not just quantity but a different quality of coverage that was far less in thrall to the Kremlin. This content could then be discussed, redistributed, repackaged and commented upon by millions of Russians online, which is particularly important in terms of extending social capital beyond the edges of the protest crowds in Moscow and a handful of other Russian cities. Another key point is the relative lack of censorship in the online sphere. Although major websites are subject to scrutiny, pressure and even the occasional shutdown, this is still relatively rare and the Russian internet maintains enough flexibility to make it extremely difficult for the authorities to establish effective 'choke points' under the current system.

Ultimately, the key point is that while state-run news, commercial news and the online sphere are three different realms, the coverage of the Russian winter of discontent shows how there was 'bottom up' influence from the internet on to television. While state-run and even commercial television networks were constrained by the relatively strong controls on the traditional media, the Russian internet was not subject to these controls. Thus, there was a type of a 'trickle-up' media freedom – as the internet reported on the true scale and meaning of the protests for Russians, this liberated commercial television to report in a more realistic and positive manner on the protests in terms of citizen mobilization. As commercial news shifted the frame, the state-run news was forced to adjust its frame as well so as to come close enough to reality to resonate with viewers. Thus, the pressure on reporting truthfully and accurately welled up from internet to the state-run news even in a controlled media system. It is difficult to see how this can be avoided in the future without a significant increase in control of the internet in Russia, suggesting that the Russian state now faces a choice: either to accept the greater engagement of the public in politics, or start controlling the internet more effectively.

Conclusions

The Russian media pose two big questions about media in general. First, how much free media can you have in a state that is not democratic?

Second, how can you say a media system is not free if there is a relatively open exchange of information and ideas online? Russia presents us with this paradox and, as a result, serves as one of the most interesting cases that is currently available in understanding the relationship between media and democracy.

On the one hand, there is the power of the media to inform and mobilize citizens. The media serve as a key component in democratization. It would seem difficult, if not impossible, to prevent citizens from demanding their rights if they are informed of current events by the media. On the other hand, much of the Russian media is more about show than substance. A lack of journalistic professionalism means that many stories are not covered, while some people such as President Putin and the United Russia party receive uncritical or even sycophantic attention. While there is no extensive censorship apparatus as in Soviet times, virtually all Russian journalists practise self-censorship in order to keep their jobs or even avoid violent attacks. By the same token, the audience has low expectations that journalists will serve the common good instead of their political masters. Finally, corruption and a general lack of a rule of law pervade the media sector as they do all of Russian society. The law offers no practical protection for journalists; rather, it more often serves as a way for political elites to control journalists by using tax, libel or even national security laws as a way of silencing critics of the state.

To judge from the increasing actions that have been taken against bloggers and websites, it is clear that the Russian authorities believe the internet can be controlled to a degree by targeting those who are visible dissidents in the online sphere. The problem is that the Russian authorities seem to believe that online dissidence is a cancer that can be cured by selective treatment. In fact, evidence suggests that a wide swathe of Russian citizens is being transformed by information and exchange in the digital world. The evidence for this lies not only in the generational shift away from television and toward internet content, but also in the manifestation of street protests and the broad interest in online content in general. As they log on to discussion groups, to email their friends, to engage in social networking as well as to learn more about their communities, the Russian population is being engaged and politicized 'below the radar' of the Kremlin understanding of politics in their own country.

What does this mean for the future of Russian politics and the media? People may be learning to turn off their self-censorship and starting to question the government in some fundamental ways. As the Russian government continues to think that dissidence is coming from a handful of people, it is missing the signs that some fundamental shifts are occurring within the population in general. This suggests that its current media strategy, both online and offline, is not working. Once the Russian government has lost the information heights, it will find it very difficult to continue ruling in an arbitrary and capricious manner. This would suggest that there will be significant political changes within the relatively near future.

Chapter 9

Assessing the Rule of Law in Russia

KATHRYN HENDLEY

Russia, in recent years, has witnessed a serious of politicized trials in Russia that have left the reputation of law and the courts in tatters. The trial and conviction of campaigner Alexei Navalny on embezzlement charges in 2013 is only the latest in a series of high-profile cases, the outcomes of which were generally thought to be pre-ordained by the Kremlin. It came on the heels of the convictions of the members of a group called Pussy Riot for their anti-Putin stunt in a Moscow cathedral in 2012, and the fraud conviction of Mikhail Khodorkovsky for tax evasion and fraud in 2005 and the subsequent dismantling of his oil company, Yukos. These cases and others like them have created an image of Russian law as an instrument used by the state to impose its will on dissenters. That is, of course, part of the story, but the focus on the sensational has obscured the role of law in the everyday lives of ordinary Russians. Despite their misgivings about the inability of judges to stand up to the Kremlin, Russians are taking their mundane disputes to the courts in ever-increasing numbers, suggesting that the story of law is more complicated than it might appear at first glance.

This chapter begins with a historical overview of the somewhat peripheral role of law in the Soviet Union and the effort to revitalize it that was begun in the late 1980s under Gorbachev. That institutional transformation continued through the decades that followed and a comparison between the Soviet legal system and that of the present day serves to highlight the many changes that have occurred. The bulk of the chapter is devoted to an evaluation of the extent to which these reforms have moved from good intentions to being implemented in practice. The chapter concludes with some reflections on the prospects for the rule of law in Russia.

The heritage of Soviet law

The Soviet Union is sometimes thought of as a state that was completely outside the rule of law, but at the formal level, at least, it was not. The

USSR had a series of constitutions that, much like constitutions elsewhere, laid out the structure of the government and established a wide range of rights for citizens. It also had a full complement of statutory laws and administrative regulations. Yet this formal structure mostly failed to take account of the role of the Communist Party. In reality, whenever the law proved inconvenient, the party elite were able to bend it to suit their interests. This made law an instrument to be used by the state (in the guise of the party) and stripped law of its predictability. The idea that citizens could use law as a shield to protect themselves from arbitrariness was laughable. The long list of rights included in Soviet-era constitutions (which were more extensive than those available through the US Bill of Rights) turned out to be illusory because their exercise had to be consistent with citizens' duties to the Soviet state. Efforts by political dissidents to defend themselves by citing the constitution were uniformly unsuccessful.

One reason why efforts to realize constitutional rights fell on deaf ears was the composition of the Soviet judicial corps. Judges were elected, but in single-candidate elections that were controlled by the Communist Party. Not surprisingly, a majority of judges were party members; but even those who were not party members toed the line. Judicial terms lasted only five years; gadflies were quickly tossed aside. Likewise other legal professionals knew better than to challenge the system.

Yet law was not entirely irrelevant in the Soviet Union. Though the all encompassing presence of the Communist Party undoubtedly had a chilling effect on the behaviour of all participants in judicial processes, reality dictated that party officials took an active interest in relatively few of these. The vast majority of cases proceeded according to the written law, especially when the issues involved were mundane. The flaw with this sort of dualistic system in which law matters sometimes but not all the time is that predicting when outside influence will swoop in is perilous. As a result, Russians were reluctant to take their disputes to courts, preferring to resolve them informally.

The virtual non-existence of acquittals in Soviet criminal trials is sometimes cited as evidence of the politicization of justice. The explanation is more complicated. After the Second World War, Communist Party officials mounted a campaign to improve the work of the criminal justice system. Acquittals became seen as a failure of effort of all involved. They were a stain on the work records of judges, prosecutors, and police, and tended to stymie their rise in the ranks. As a result, once a criminal case was initiated, the institutional incentives pushed in favour of keeping it going until a conviction was obtained (Solomon 1987). Politics certainly played a role, but they operated at an abstract level that mooted the merits of individual cases.

When Gorbachev, the first law-trained leader of the Soviet Union since Lenin, came to power in 1985, a thorough rethinking of the role of law followed. At the 19th Party Conference in 1988, he advocated the introduction of a 'socialist rule-of-law-based state' (*sotsialisticheskoe pravovoe gosudarstvo*) in which law and not political connections would dictate the outcome of cases. Under his leadership, the Communist Party was stripped of its influence in the judicial selection process, a key prerequisite to building greater independence among judges. This period also witnessed the first, albeit tentative, steps toward judicial review with the creation of the Committee on Constitutional Supervision, which was charged with reviewing the acts of the legislative and executive branches.

The institutional structure of the Russian legal system

Many of the ideas put forward during the Gorbachev years were actualized in the decades that followed. Figure 9.1 presents an organizational chart of the current legal system. The introduction of the Constitutional Court in 1991 institutionalized judicial review. In doing so, Russia followed the example of many of its European neighbours who shared the civil law legal tradition (under which judicial decisions are binding only on the participants, but do not have precedential value for others) by creating a stand-alone court that is empowered to hear challenges to the constitutionality of statutes and administrative regulations from legislators and ordinary citizens. In a decisive break with the Soviet past, its decisions have the force of law and, if they go against the government, can invalidate laws or regulations. On paper, the Constitutional Court gives substance to the proclamation of the 1993 constitution that the judicial branch is equal to the legislative and executive branches (Trochev 2008). A number of regions have created their own constitutional courts, which are charged with maintaining the constitutionality of regional legislation and are not part of a formal hierarchical system.

The early 1990s also witnessed the creation of a hierarchy of courts, known as *arbitrazh* courts, designed to resolve the sorts of commercial disputes that would inevitably arise with the transition from a command economy to a market economy. These courts also handled bankruptcy claims. Over the two decades of their existence, the *arbitrazh* courts have repeatedly revised their procedural rules in an effort to respond to the needs of their constituency.

The vast majority of claims, including criminal prosecutions, divorces and child custody, and labour disputes, continued to be handled by the

Figure 9.1   *Organizational chart of the current legal system*

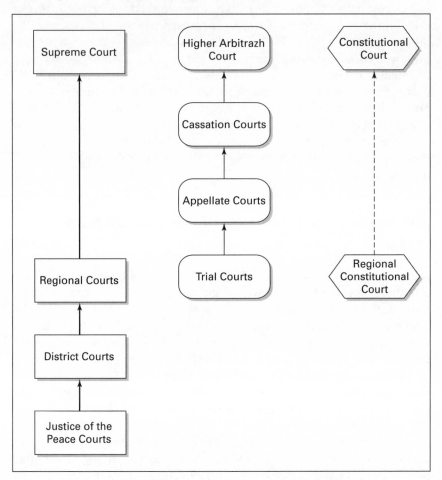

courts of general jurisdiction. The basic structure of these courts was a carry-over from the Soviet period, with trial courts, appellate courts, and a supreme court. An experiment with jury trials for serious crimes, begun in the 1990s, was institutionalized throughout Russia under Putin (Esakov 2012). In an effort to ease the burden on trial judges, justice-of-the-peace courts were authorized in 1998. Over the first decade of the twenty-first century, these courts were introduced across Russia (Hendley 2012a). They handle simple cases, thereby freeing up judges at higher level courts to devote more time to complicated cases.

As Figure 9.1 indicates, each court system has its own distinct hierarchy. This approach, which gives rise to multiple top courts, mirrors what is found in many continental European judicial systems. It can give rise to inconsistencies, when the top courts issue different rulings on similar questions. The top courts managed this problem by meeting periodically and issuing 'guiding explanations' on particularly thorny areas of law that were aimed at smoothing out these differences. In June 2013, Putin proposed combining the top tribunals of the courts of general jurisdiction and the *arbitrazh* courts. Doing so will require amending the 1993 constitution. This process began in late 2013 with the approval of legislation creating a 170-member top court, and is expected to continue throughout 2014 as the amendments are submitted to the regions for approval. The new court will be located in St Petersburg (along with the Constitutional Court). A number of top lawyers and legal commentators have criticized this reform, worrying that the strong reputation for impartiality earned by the Higher *Arbitrazh* Court will be compromised when it is subsumed into the Supreme Court.

Post-Soviet judges are no longer elected. They are now selected through a competitive process in which vacancies are advertised and those interested apply to their local qualification commission (Trochev 2006). The use of such commissions is common throughout continental Europe. Candidates are put through a battery of interviews and tests and, in theory, the most competent candidates prevail. But because the membership of these commissions is dominated by sitting judges, they tend to prefer candidates who have served as judicial clerks rather than practising lawyers. Prosecutors have an inside track for openings on the criminal bench.

The Russian courts have become increasingly transparent in recent years. All courts are required to have websites on which their decisions are published, along with their address and hours of operation. Some courts also post their schedule and provide a calculator that computes filing fees automatically. The quality of the websites varies by region. The *arbitrazh* courts have made a significant investment in their websites, creating a searchable national database. These courts have also begun experimenting with allowing litigants to file lawsuits via email, a practice that is standard in the West.

The Russian legal system in action

There is always a gap between the law on the book and the law in action. In Russia, this gap has sometimes seemed more like a chasm as political realities perverted well-intended institutional reforms. For example, the role of the Constitutional Court has shifted over time. Under Yeltsin, the court heard cases that challenged some of his signature policies, including his conduct of the war in Chechnya. Its decisions tended to avoid direct confrontations with the Kremlin, a common tactic among high courts elsewhere. With the rise of Putin and United Russia, however, dissent among legislators has been effectively quashed. As a result, the Constitutional Court has become more quiescent.

More troubling has been the interference of political elites in the judicial process. Both the Kremlin and regional leaders have repeatedly brought trumped-up criminal charges against their enemies as a form of punishment. This harks back to the Soviet era, when selective prosecution was a favourite way to deal with dissenters. In those days, the law criminalized anti-Soviet behaviour and failed to define its prerequisites clearly, thereby giving maximum discretion to officials. The criminal code was stripped of these sections after the demise of the Soviet Union. Creative officials can always find pretexts to indict their enemies, especially when prosecutors and judges are compliant and willing to accept proffered evidence without question. Much as during the Soviet era, the internal incentives for workers within the criminal justice system is to push cases forward. Though Russia has embraced the principle of adversarialism within the courts, which means that defence lawyers ought to be engaging in independent investigations, this rarely happens. Acquittals continue to be the exception in both politically motivated and ordinary cases. Indeed, in a study of a Krasnoyarsk trial court from the late 1990s, one judge comments: 'There are judges that *take a risk* and render judgments of acquittal, but practically not even one of them is left to stand on appeal, they are reversed ... To acquit *is very scary*' (Pomorski 2001: 457).

Another troubling development is the growing criminalization of failed business transactions (Firestone 2009). When business partners grow disenchanted with one other, rather than accepting their losses and moving on, they often accuse one another of criminal fraud or embezzlement. The accuser assembles documentary evidence which frequently stretches the truth and bribes the police to open a criminal case. His victim languishes in jail waiting for the trial because, despite introducing bail, it is rarely granted. In his absence, the accuser is able to solidify his control over the formerly joint assets. This story has become so familiar that, in 2012, an ombudsman was appointed to protect the rights of entrepreneurs. Though this is a distinctly post-Soviet phenomenon, the remedy of having the legislature grant an amnesty to those victimized is familiar from the past (Pomeranz 2013).

As the descriptions of politicized justice and criminalized business deals suggests, corruption remains a nagging problem within the courts, just as for most Russian institutions. Top judicial officials, including the chairmen of the Russian Supreme Court and the Higher *Arbitrazh* Court, have conceded that bribery persists. The same qualification commissions that select judges are also charged with reviewing complaints of ethical violations. Such charges tend to be difficult to prove.

An even bigger challenge to the integrity of the judicial corps is the deference given to court chairmen at all levels. At every stage in a judge's career, their relationship with the chairman of the court matters. Staying in their good graces is essential to career stability and advancement. Many commentators have criticized the influence of these chairmen as yet another source of dependence (Volkov *et al.* 2012; Solomon 2007; Pomorski 2001). Chairmen have multiple levers of influence. In many courts, they control case assignments and can direct politically sensitive cases to judges who will follow the unwritten rules (Anonymous 2010). Former judges have spoken out about their heavy hand and have argued that a determined chairman can always find a disciplinary pretext to get rid of a judge who refuses to go along. Yet even those who make these allegations concede that not all chairmen take this line. For example, Mariana Lukyanovskaya, a Volgograd *oblast* court judge who handled criminal cases who was removed from the bench in 2009 by a disciplinary review initiated by the chairman of her court, is unforgiving when it comes to that chairman. She says that 'independence is only declaratory. In every case, the judge is dependent on his leadership'. She believes she was pushed out due to her refusal to accept the claims of the police and prosecutors without corroborating evidence. But she emphasizes that this sort of atmosphere had not always prevailed at her court. She quotes the previous chairman, whose mantra was: 'My boss is the law' (*Moi nachalnik – eto zakon*) (Eismont 2012). Thus, despite the common wisdom that chairmen treat their courts as their 'personal fiefdoms' (Anonymous 2010), whether a chairman exerts a positive or negative influence from the point of view of judicial independence depends on their own internal moral compass. Much depends on the character of the chairmen and their attitude towards the sanctity of law.

Russians' expectations of the legal system

All of this might lead one to believe that Russians are distrustful of their courts and unwilling to use them. The reality is more complicated. Survey data confirm that a majority of Russians (60 per cent) are sceptical of the fairness of the courts (Levada Center 2013d). At the same time, they are using them in record numbers, albeit only as a last resort when all other options have been exhausted. This suggests that trust is not necessary for use; litigants can have a variety of motivations for initiating a lawsuit (Hendley 2012b). Over the 15 years from 1995 to 2010, the annual number of cases grew almost five-fold, from 6.2 million to 29.3 million (Rassmotrenie 2013). Given the coercive reputation of the Russian state, it might be assumed that criminal prosecutions account for this increase.

But criminal cases, as a percentage of the total caseload, have actually decreased over time from 17.4 per cent in 1995 to 3.6 per cent in 2010. The number of cases that go through the *arbitrazh* courts is much smaller, but it also grew five-fold between 1995 and 2010, from less than 250,000 in 1995 to 1.2 million in 2010 (Sudebno 2006; Tablitsa 2012).

More surprising is that Russians are generally satisfied with their experiences in the courts. A 2009 survey sponsored by the Moscow office of the American Bar Association (the 'ABA Survey') in which 1,200 individuals from three regions (Nizhnii Novgorod, Rostov on Don, and St Petersburg) were queried about their experiences in the justice-of-the-peace courts, where most cases now originate, shows that litigants were generally satisfied. Over one-third of the respondents to the ABA Survey described their experience as 'successful'. Another 28 per cent said it was successful, but bemoaned the bureaucratic red-tape that was involved (Kriuchkov 2010).

As Tyler (2006) has argued in the US context, litigants can often put aside disappointing outcomes if they are treated fairly. This sense of procedural justice shines through in the data from the ABA Survey. Over 80 per cent believe that justices of the peace (JPs) are well-trained and competent. A plurality of 48 per cent said their judges had been completely independent, while an additional 24 per cent said they had mostly, but not always, acted independently. As to the fairness of the court process, over 70 per cent of respondents were convinced that JPs typically ruled in favour of the side that was stronger from a legal point of view. A similar majority felt that their JPs complied with all procedural norms during their hearing, conducted themselves tactfully, and not only gave both sides an equal opportunity to present their arguments, but also paid close attention to both. This suggests that rumours that judges base their decisions on 'telephone law' (orders from bureaucratic superiors or political elites that determine case outcomes) are less true for mundane disputes than for politicized cases.

One source for litigants' satisfaction with their experience is the speed and modest cost with which the courts conduct their business. Filing fees are deliberately kept low in order to facilitate access. If the petitioner prevails, then the cost of filing the case is shifted to the defendant. A number of categories of cases likely to arise among ordinary Russians, most notably consumer claims, can be pursued at no charge. The procedural code lays out clear deadlines for resolving cases that range from several weeks to several months. Violations of these deadlines rarely exceed 5 per cent. Russian judges' advancement in the system depends on their ability to manage their docket. Those within the judicial management structure have openly acknowledged that quantitative indicators such as delay rates and reversal rates are taken very seriously.

Criminal cases are generally heard in the district or regional courts rather than the JP courts (whose jurisdiction is limited to cases for which the maximum penalty is three years in jail or less). Given that almost all criminal cases result in convictions, it is doubtful that the satisfaction levels are as high as for the JP courts. Criminal defendants are provided with defence counsel at no cost if they are unable to afford lawyers of their own. These lawyers are poorly paid, earning less than the equivalent of twenty dollars for each instance. They tend to be overworked and are not always able to devote a great deal of attention to individual cases. In recent years, a form of plea bargaining has grown commonplace, according to which defendants admits their actions and give up the right to appeal their convictions, although they can appeal their sentence if dissatisfied.

Most cases are of little interest to those not intimately involved; relatively few attract the attention of elites. The politically charged cases that generate headlines in Western newspapers are not featured in the Russian media, and ordinary Russians, for their part, do not follow them closely and are not especially sympathetic towards the defendants. For example, during the same month when Navalny was sentenced, fewer than 5 per cent of those polled in a national survey admitted to following the case carefully, and over 20 per cent did not know who Navalny was (Levada Center 2013b). Along similar lines, when queried about Khodorkovsky, a plurality (38 per cent) were convinced that his conviction had been ordered by the Kremlin, but few (less than 5 per cent) felt any sympathy towards him (Levada Center 2013a). Over time, all the same, support for his early release has grown. In 2007, only 19 per cent favoured it, but by 2012 this had increased to 31 per cent (Levada Center 2012); it eventually took place when a presidential pardon was issued in December 2013. As to Pussy Riot, a majority (56 per cent) felt their sentence had been appropriate (Levada Center 2013c). The release of Khodorkovsky and of the members of Pussy Riot in December 2013 as part of an amnesty intended to commemorate the adoption of the Russian Constitution can be seen as compassionate, but cannot be seen as a reflection of a new-found devotion to the rule of law by the Kremlin. After all, amnesties are by their nature somewhat arbitrary and inconsistent with the principle of due process that is at the heart of the rule of law.

More generally, periodic surveys between 1994 and 2013 reveal that a majority of Russians think that maintaining law and order is more important than protecting human rights (Levada Center 2013e). Along similar lines, Russians tend to place more value on social and economic rights than on civil and political rights. For example, about two-thirds of those surveyed from 1994 to 2010 consistently placed a high value on the right to free education and medical care. By contrast, only 8 per cent saw freedom of speech as critical in 1994, though this percentage had increased to 22 by 2010 (Levada Center 2010). Perhaps this yearning for stability reflects a nostalgia for the Soviet past, which many now remember as a simpler time when jobs were guaranteed, conveniently forgetting the repressive nature of the regime. It may also be a reaction to the chaos of the 1990s in which a small group of Russians became very wealthy and many more Russians saw the social guarantees that they had come to rely on during the Soviet era disappear. Whatever the reasons, Russians remain comfortable with a strong state, even a state that encroaches on their personal liberties. And they seem willing to tolerate censorship and other forms of political repression if the authorities promise social and economic stability.

Some argue that Russians have given up on law. Indeed, when gearing up for his successful 2008 presidential campaign, Dmitri Medvedev famously commented that '[w]ithout exaggeration, Russia is a country of legal nihilism. ... [N]o other European country can boast of such a level of disregard for law' (Polnyi tekst 2008). Such sentiments are not a post-Soviet phenomenon: they have endured through Russia's many political upheavals. Alexander Herzen, a prominent political philosopher of the nineteenth century, wrote: '[w]hatever his station, the Russian evades or violates the law wherever he can do so with impunity; the government does exactly the same thing' (quoted in Huskey 1991). In the present-day context, claims of widespread legal nihilism turn out to be hyperbole. Analysis of survey data shows that, in general, Russians are not significantly more prepared to ignore the law than their counterparts elsewhere. All the same, it does reveal some troubling trends. Those most disillusioned with law are not the elderly who survived the blatantly instrumental use of law by the Communist Party, but those now in their forties and fifties who were victimized by the economic turmoil of the 1990s. Younger generations are also more likely to embrace legal nihilism than their elderly relatives. These demographic realities suggest that legal nihilism may be on the upswing (Hendley 2012c). At present, however, popular disenchantment with the law is not a particular problem.

Prospects for the rule of law in Russia

Where does this leave Russia in terms of the rule of law? Defining what is meant by the rule of law is the first step. At its heart, the concept captures the goal of having a legal system in which all are treated equally and judged by law regardless of their wealth or political connections. Packed within this seemingly simple definition are a myriad of institutional goals, such as independent, accessible and non-corrupt courts, clarity and transparency in the written law, and the availability of due process for all (Fuller 1964). This is the definition that is used in this chapter. Because it focuses mostly on procedural indicators, it is sometimes referred to as a 'thin' definition. Others have argued that the rule of law should actively embrace certain substantive goals, such as a full complement of human rights and guarantees of property rights (for instance Møller and Skaaning 2010). But this sort of 'thick' definition of the rule of law assumes that all countries share the Western commitment to civil and property rights. The failure to distinguish between these two concepts of the rule of law has led to a remarkable lack of clarity in the public debate over how to encourage transition countries to move towards this goal.

Without doubt, the keystone of the rule of law is equal treatment for all. As the foregoing has documented, Russia has a spotty record on this critical issue. Opponents of the Kremlin live with the very real fear that they may be prosecuted on trumped-up charges as a way of discrediting them and their views. Businessmen who toil in obscurity have likewise been subjected to criminal prosecution due to the willingness of the police to accept bribes to open an investigation. The institutional incentives against acquittals have landed many such businessmen in jail for extended periods. The written law has been largely irrelevant in these cases. The spectre of corruption in all state institutions has likewise undermined the power of the law on the books. These realities help explain why Russia is typically seen as being at the lower end of the spectrum in terms of the rule of law.

But if the Russian courts were completely incapable of acting as honest brokers, then few would use them voluntarily. Just the opposite is happening: individuals and companies, in fact, are turning to the courts in ever-increasing numbers. Moreover, as the results of the ABA Survey suggest, they are mostly satisfied with their treatment by the courts. This should not be taken to mean that there is deep societal trust of the courts. Rather it may indicate a grudging willingness to use the courts when efforts to settle break down. In-depth interviews with ordinary Russians have at least convinced this author that they understand when the courts are reliable and when they may be compromised. My respondents were uniformly prepared to take their quarrels with neighbours or local governmental agencies to court, if necessary. But if they stumbled into a dispute with someone of higher status or with a powerful state office, they studiously avoided the courts, fearing that the other side would be able to dictate the outcome through informal extra-legal mechanisms (Hendley 2009).

Russia presents a paradoxical case. The vast majority of cases respect the rule-of-law principle of equality before the law, but a small well-publicized minority do not. In some ways, the Russian legal system is not so different from Western legal systems in which the ability to retain competent lawyers has a profound influence on the chances of victory. In Russia, the currency is less likely to be money and more likely to be political connections, but the impact is the same. Where Russia parts company from its Western counterparts is in the lack of predictability as to when 'telephone law' will trump the law that is set out in statutes, and in its willingness to use criminal prosecutions as a weapon against opponents. These features raise the stakes considerably and help explain why Russia consistently languishes near the bottom of all indexes that purport to measure the rule of law.

Having a legal system that treats everyone equally means little if it is difficult to access. On this criterion, Russia's performance is more impressive. Going to court, in fact, is a relatively quick and inexpensive way to resolve problems. This does not mean that Russians are eager to do so. As in other countries, going to court in Russia is a last resort exercised only when efforts to resolve difficulties informally have failed. Once in court, cases are generally resolved within several months, if not more quickly. The filing fees have deliberately been kept low and the procedural rules are sufficiently straightforward that many litigants in non-criminal cases are able to represent themselves. The weakness of the adversarial system means that parties who oppose one another in court need not emerge as mortal enemies, as is so often the case in purer adversarial systems like those in the US and the UK. In comparison to Western legal systems, the Russian courts are easier for non-legal specialists to access. For the most part, however, the indexes that track levels of the rule of law around the world do not take account of this more positive aspect of the Russian legal system.

Chapter 10

A Federal State?

DARRELL SLIDER

Federalism in Russia has always been a contested concept. Regional elites and liberal politicians at the centre have seen the division of power and decentralization of some policy making as a precondition for effective governance and further democratization of the political system. More traditional Russian political views, including those held by most communists and Russian nationalists, have viewed regional autonomy or a genuine sharing of powers with the regions as first steps toward the disintegration of the country. For many it conjures up memories of the collapse of the Soviet Union, as Soviet republican leaders took power through elections and forced concessions from Mikhail Gorbachev that set in motion the weakening of central power. The ethnic identity of republics has led some Russian nationalists to urge the redrawing of administrative boundaries to eliminate republics, perhaps by restoring the administrative boundaries of the *guberniyas* that existed in the Tsarist era.

When Vladimir Putin became president in the spring of 2000, the first issue he confronted was the relationship between the regions of Russia and the centre (the federal government). Under Yeltsin, Russia for the first time in its history had adopted federalism as a basis for organizing the relationship between the centre and the regions. The historic pattern of governance had always been highly centralized, despite the formal label in Soviet times which designated Russia as the 'Russian Soviet Federated Socialist Republic'. The ethnically driven democratization of the late Gorbachev era was employed not just by the Baltic republics, Georgia, Ukraine and Russia to push for greater autonomy *vis-à-vis* the Soviet Union but within Russia as well. Yeltsin's adoption of a federal model was in part making a virtue out of necessity: the Russian government was too weak and divided to exert control over the provinces, and allowing regions some political and economic autonomy overcame separatist pressures. The only region that was an exception to this was Chechnya, where Yeltsin launched a brutal war in late 1994 in an unsuccessful effort to bring the republic back under Russian control.

Tax revenues under Yeltsin were allocated in ways that helped to buy off regions that were 'most likely to secede'. Some sort of redistribution is essential in a state like Russia, where oil and natural gas are the biggest sources of tax revenue, since only a few, sparsely populated regions account for the bulk of these revenues. Precise data on the relative share of centre/region revenue sharing are impossible to obtain because regions were using non-monetary barter deals to collect taxes from enterprises at this time. Special provisions gave regions such as Tatarstan and Bashkortostan the right to keep resource revenues that normally would go to the centre. Overall, both the federal centre and regions suffered from the lack of revenues due to economic disruption and low resource prices through the 1990s.

Yeltsin's 1993 constitution provided the broad outlines of a division of powers between centre and regions, though much was left to be done through subsequent legislation. At the time the constitution was adopted, there were 89 'subjects of the federation', which included different types of entities which in large part were a legacy of the Soviet-era administrative divisions. Republics (as well as smaller entities such as 'autonomous *oblasts* or regions) had been created to reflect historic homelands of non-Russian ethnicities. By 2014 the number of federal entities had declined to 83, as a result of the mergers of regions that took place during Putin's second term, between 2005 and 2008; the result was that many of the sparsely populated 'autonomous *oblasts*' were absorbed by neighbouring *oblasts*. The most numerous regional administrative entities which contain most of the population are ethnically Russian *oblasts* and larger *krais* or territories (Russians comprise around 81 per cent of the total population), along with two cities that have federal status – Moscow and St Petersburg. From the beginning of the Yeltsin period, the realities of the distribution of political power and the role of nationalism among several key non-Russian ethnic groups meant that the Russian model of federalism was 'asymmetric': some regions were given more powers than others. Yeltsin famously urged ethnic republics to 'take as much sovereignty as they could swallow'. Bilateral treaties and agreements were negotiated separately with regions, sometimes with provisions that took the form of secret protocols.

Initially Yeltsin appointed governors of regions. Popular elections of republican presidents and later of *oblast* governors at first took place without central approval, but by 1995 Yeltsin had accepted the principle of elected regional leaders. Konitzer (2005) makes the case that the elections held between 1995 and 2001 saw real contestation; on average there were three viable candidates competing for the top regional post. Konitzer also argues that voters often rewarded or punished sitting governors based on the economic performance of their regions. Voters often elected candidates whom the Kremlin opposed. 'Red governors' from the Communist Party managed to win elections in many of the more conservative regions (by 1999 there were 14 Communist governors), and candidates from other political movements also won in a few cases. New regional legislatures were also elected regularly, starting in 1994. At first, political parties were hardly represented in these bodies, but over time party fractions developed, and assemblies in some regions played an active and independent role in governance.

The constitution provided for an upper house of parliament to represent regional interests, the Federation Council. It consisted of two representatives from each region who were initially elected, but later the top executive and legislative official in each region became 'senators'. In the Yeltsin years, the Federation Council played a major role in the legislative process, and it often vetoed laws that had been submitted to it by the State Duma which were perceived to threaten regional interests. According to Remington (2003), between 1996 and 1999 the Federation Council vetoed approximately 23 per cent of the draft laws submitted to it.

Putin's vertical of power

In Putin's narrative of the 1990s, one which he has retold again and again, the regions became too powerful at the expense of the centre and threatened the continued existence of the Russian state. Putin was himself a regional official, deputy mayor of St Petersburg until 1996, and in 1997–98 held the Kremlin post that oversaw the regions. Once he became president, Putin set about to establish a 'vertical of power' (in Russian, *vertikal vlasti*) that would subordinate regions to the centre in a hierarchical chain of command. Since regional executives – governors or republican presidents – were the key political actors in the regions, he began by creating a system that would allow him to better monitor their performance without depending on information from governors themselves.

One of the very first changes introduced by Putin was a new division of Russia into seven macro-regions – 'federal districts' comprising the Northwest, Central, Southern, Volga, Urals, Siberian, and Far Eastern territories. (In 2011, while Dmitri Medvedev was president, an eighth federal district, the North Caucasus district, was carved out of the Southern district.) A new administrative entity outside the constitutional structure was created to oversee these districts, called 'authorized representatives' of the president (*polpred* in Russian). The calibre and experience of the officials appointed to the post varied greatly, which reflected the fact that presidential priorities differed from region to region. Initially, most of the officials were not political figures or even government bureaucrats. They were drawn from the *siloviki* – that is, senior officials with a military or police background. Perhaps as a reflection of Putin's university degree in law, one of the first assignments he gave to his representatives was to bring regional legislation into line with federal legislation. While the *polpreds* were supposed to oversee regional leaders, they had few powers of their own and no funds to distribute. Their strength lies in their role as Putin's emissaries and their line of communications to the Kremlin. Over time, appointments to the post of *polpred* have become quite varied. In crisis situations, Putin has turned to some of his closest and most trusted associates such as Dmitri Kozak (sent to the Southern district in 2004), Aleksandr Khloponin (sent by Medvedev to the North Caucasus in 2010), and Yuri Trutnev (appointed to the Far East in 2013). Yet in 2012, Putin's first staffing appointment upon returning as president was the Urals *polpred*, Igor Kholmanskikh, a foreman from a Nizhnii Tagil tank factory with no political or administrative experience. Kholmanskikh had come to Putin's attention during a live, televised question and answer session with the president in December 2011, just after massive anti-Putin demonstrations had been held in Moscow. Kholmanskikh offered to bring 'his boys' to Moscow to help subdue the protesters, if the police were not up to the task.

One of the purposes of 'restoring' the vertical of power was to reduce the degree to which Russian regions had asymmetric powers. Yeltsin's bilateral agreements were either phased out or scrapped entirely. This affected most of all ethnic republics such as Tatarstan, Bashkortostan, and the North Caucasus republics. The implicit deal offered by Putin allowed the most popular and powerful regional leaders to remain in office, even if they initially resisted his strategy. More recently, even symbolic aspects of regional autonomy have been targeted – for example, the practice adopted in the early 1990s of calling the heads of republics 'presidents'. By 2013, all, except for Tatarstan, had dispensed with that title and leaders are now called simply the 'head' of a republic. Tatarstan, which is home to part of Russia's largest ethnic minority (Tatars make up about 4 per cent of the total population), retained some elements of its special status in a treaty signed by Putin in 2007, but the new treaty effectively eliminated the special status that Tatarstan had been awarded in its 1994 treaty.

A critical development in the strengthening of the vertical was the decision in late 2004 to end the popular election of regional executives. The pretext for this, as we have noted elsewhere, was the terrorist takeover of a school in Beslan, North Ossetia. The authorities' confusion and disputes over who was in charge at Beslan led Putin to conclude that Russia was not ready for democratic governance at the regional level. Ending elections gave Putin the ability to appoint his own choice as governor, though formally his nominations had to be approved by regional assemblies. Putin was also increasingly able to remove governors who had 'lost his trust', although he rarely exercised this power and many of the Yeltsin-era regional 'heavyweights' continued to run their regions until 2010–11.

Another element of tightened central control was the rise of the ruling party United Russia. Almost all governors were forced to give up any previous party affiliations and join the ruling party. The Kremlin set as its goal a United Russia majority in every regional assembly. As a result of elections held between 2004 and 2010, United Russia went from a majority in 20 regions to a clear majority in 82 of the 83 regional assemblies (all but St Petersburg). In 62 of these regions United Russia held two-thirds or more of the seats, which allowed it to adopt any law without the support of other legislators. The declining popularity of United Russia in the aftermath of the December 2011 elections presented a dilemma for the Kremlin, which still sought to maintain a political monopoly in the regions. Most regions had mixed electoral systems, with at least half chosen by party list and half of the seats chosen by individual races in legislative districts. United Russia always dominated district contests to a much greater extent than proportional party-list voting, and this is what allowed the party to achieve a super-majority in most Russian regions. In late 2013, the Kremlin proposed a new law on regional elections which would reduce the seats allocated by party list to 25 per cent. This appears to be designed to permit a less popular United Russia (or a successor such as the 'All-Russian United Front') to take advantage of its near-monopoly control over local elites in order to preserve majorities in regional assemblies.

The speed with which Putin was able to transform an emerging federal system into a centrally controlled state was remarkable. Why did powerful regional leaders succumb to the new relationship with the centre virtually without a fight? In social science terminology, what regional leaders faced was a collective action dilemma. To stand up to the Kremlin individually would mean political suicide for even the strongest of regional leaders. The Kremlin was rapidly consolidating power – the 1999 Duma elections and subsequent defections to the ruling party (then called Unity) combined with Putin's convincing election victory in 2000 created a new political reality. Meanwhile, Putin was demonstrating at this time how brutally the regime could act to bring a rebellious region under control – he had launched the second Chechen war when serving as prime minister in late 1999.

Part of the explanation for the shift in relative power from regions to the centre was the result of what Putin did to the Federation Council. Putin moved quickly to dismantle the principal mechanism for collective action by the regional elite that had been established in the Yeltsin years.

He transformed the upper house by first removing governors and speakers of regional assemblies as senators. They were replaced with appointees that were technically nominated by the regions (one each from the executive and legislative branches of regional government) but who were actually candidates 'suggested' by the Kremlin. At least one-third had no ties to the region they supposedly represented, and almost all were subject to manipulation by the Kremlin by virtue of the fact that they spent almost all of their time in Moscow. They soon understood that their well-being did not depend on representing their regions, but on maintaining good relations with the Kremlin office tasked with supervising them. As a result, the Federation Council virtually ceased to act as a defender of regions' rights and federal principles. A Federation Council veto of a Kremlin-sponsored law, even if it was designed to undermine the powers of the regions themselves, came to be virtually unthinkable.

Scholars who have sought to explain the rapid change of centre–regional relations have offered alternative explanations. Goode (2011) makes the case that an important reason for regional leaders' compliance with the new order was an implicit bargain that they would be allowed to impose the same hierarchical control over sub-regional political actors such as mayors and city councils. Sharafutdinova (2013), drawing on the experience of the non-ethnic Russian republics that had most aggressively asserted their sovereignty in the 1990s, argues that a radical shift in the political discourse under Putin left regional leaders with little choice. Public statements by leaders of Tatarstan could no longer tout federalism and democracy as a way of defending the republic's special status. Putin had changed the rhetorical frame of reference to one of strengthening the state and overcoming disunity.

There were also powerful economic and budgetary factors that enhanced central control over the regions. Economically, thanks to rising oil prices and the recovery of the Russian economy in the period after the August 1998 default, the centre had access to greater resources with which to fund federal programmes and buy cooperation in the regions. Hanson (2005) has shown that federal revenues as a share of GDP increased dramatically at the same time that Putin was strengthening the vertical. Most regions were not given substantial revenue sources of their own and were therefore increasingly dependent on the Kremlin and the Ministry of Finance for budgetary subventions. In recent years, the budgetary problems of regions have worsened. Election campaign promises by Putin in 2012 required regions to raise wages for state employees in education and health care, but regional budgets were not correspondingly increased. As a result, according to the Russian regional expert Natalya Zubarevich, two-thirds of the regions in 2013 experienced serious budget deficits that have forced a reduction in government spending in other areas, such as infrastructure investment (*Vedomosti*, 24 September 2013).

In a response to demands expressed by opposition demonstrators after the December 2011 State Duma elections, the Kremlin reinstated the popular election of regional leaders. Restrictions on competition and built-in advantages for the sitting governor, though, meant that the change has done little to change the place of governors in the system. Governors, elected or not, serve only if they are acceptable to Putin. They will still be evaluated by the Kremlin, and the process of elections is tightly controlled to prevent 'accidental' candidates from winning. When legislation for the return to elected governors was passed, it included a 'municipal filter' at the candidate registration stage which, when combined with other legal and extra-legal measures, effectively restricted political contestation. The municipal filter requires the signatures of between 5 and 10 per cent of local council members in the region; some regions further stipulated that the total would have to include at least one signature from 75 per cent of the councils. All the candidates favoured by the Kremlin won re-election and usually won by large margins. In October 2012, the first set of gubernatorial elections produced the following winners, all nominated by Putin: Amur (Oleg Kozhemyako), 77 per cent; Belgorod (Yevgenii Savchenko), 78 per cent; Bryansk (Nikolai Demin), 65 per cent; Novgorod (Sergei Mitin), 76 per cent; and Ryazan (Oleg Kovalyev), 64 per cent. In September 2013 the share of the vote taken by Putin's nominees was as follows: Khabarovsk krai (Vyacheslav Shport), 64 per cent; Magadan (Vladimir Pechenyi), 73 per cent; Chukotka (Roman Kopin), 80 per cent; Zabaikal krai (Konstantin Ilkovsky), 72 per cent; Khakasiya (Viktor Zimin), 63 per cent; Vladimir (Svetlana Orlova), 75 per cent; Moscow *oblast* (Andrei Vorobyev), 79 per cent. The only candidate who came close to having to run in a second round was Moscow's Sergei Sobyanin, who won 51 per cent (according to the official results). Viable opposition candidates in several regions were removed from the ballot or prevented from registering; in other cases candidates that the Kremlin wanted in the race were helped to pass registration barriers. Many regions adopted election laws that require all candidates to be nominated by a registered political party, thus precluding self-nomination.

In almost all regions it was precisely the fact that a sitting governor was running that predetermined the outcome. Governors and their subordinates have enormous advantages, which have become known over the years as 'administrative resources', that create an extremely unlevel playing field. Even in the election that was universally judged the most open and honest, Moscow's mayoral election in September 2013, the advantages of incumbency proved decisive. Putin's choice for mayor, Sergei

Sobyanin, tried to increase the legitimacy of his presumed victory by discouraging the typical forms of Russian vote fraud. He also supported steps to keep Aleksei Navalny, the emerging opposition leader, in the race. The municipal filter could have prevented all candidates except Sobyanin from running, since municipal councils were dominated by United Russia. Despite the effort to run a 'clean and honest' election, even in Moscow many aspects of the election were blatantly discriminatory. The two national government television channels which are viewed by the largest number of Muscovites ran repeated and lengthy reports on Sobyanin's 'achievements', including the ceremonial opening of a suspiciously large number of roadways, bridges, and metro stations in the days before the election. The same channels mentioned Navalny on the day he was registered as a candidate in July and then did not mention his name again until after the voting was over on 8 September. Navalny's attempts to purchase advertising spots on major radio stations were denied, apparently after pressure was placed on the stations from the mayor's office. Supporters of Navalny who hung banners for their candidate from their balconies saw city workers descend from the roofs on ropes to cut them down. Debates, without Sobyanin's participation, were limited to local channels with low ratings at inconvenient times of the day. That Navalny was still able to win, according to the official results, over 27 per cent of the vote was testimony to a vigorous campaign conducted mostly through face-to-face meetings with voters and aided by a small army of mostly young volunteers.

To provide an extra margin of control in 'difficult' regions – designed in particular for use in the North Caucasus republics – Putin pushed for a new law at the beginning of 2013 that allows regions to opt out of popular elections for governor. Instead, the regional legislature can select the head of the region, based on the nomination of candidates by Putin. In both Ingushetia and Dagestan in September 2013 the new provision was put to use, and republican legislatures in both regions overwhelmingly supported Putin's favoured nominees.

At the sub-regional level, the main officials are mayors of cities and municipalities. Unlike governors, they have continued to be popularly elected – a fact which potentially leaves them outside the Kremlin's power vertical. The 1993 Russian constitution intended this to be the case, as local government institutions were called 'organs of local self-management'. Notwithstanding the constitution, Putin's Kremlin has pursued multiple strategies over the years to bring mayors back under central control. First, the United Russia party was active in recruiting sitting mayors and played a major role in local elections of both mayors and city councils. As a result, the vast majority of Russian mayors are at least formally members (although this has not precluded conflicts between mayors and regional governors from the same party). Second, in many cities elected mayors have either been replaced or forced to share their powers with 'city managers' who have been chosen directly by city councils. Usually city managers have the power to determine how the local budget is expended. Third, a suspiciously large number of city leaders – particularly those who were political independents or members of opposition parties – have been removed from office on charges of corruption or misallocating city funds. In 2013, two of the most spectacular removals of Russian officials from their posts were the arrests (shown widely on Russian television) of the mayors of Makhachkala (the capital of Dagestan) and Yaroslavl. Both mayors were viewed as threats to the power of regional leaders who had close ties to the Kremlin, and were arrested by federal law enforcement agencies and immediately transferred to pre-trial detention facilities in Moscow. Finally, financial centralization has hit cities especially hard, and cities and municipalities became increasingly dependent on allocations from regional budgets and federal agencies.

There is little doubt that governors in the Putin era have continued to exercise considerable discretionary powers, and the post of governor is still highly desired among the Russian administrative elite. There have been a number of cases in recent years of federal ministers who have been appointed governors, and this is not viewed as a demotion. Among those 'promoted' to governorships have been Aleksei Gordeev, from Minister of Agriculture to Voronezh *oblast*, Sergei Shoigu, from Minister of Emergencies to Moscow *oblast* (though soon he was brought back into government as Minister of Defence), and Viktor Basargin from Minister for Regional Development to Perm krai. Fewer have taken the opposite career trajectory, from governor to federal minister.

Interactions between governors and the president

Direct personal interaction between governors and Putin, and Medvedev when he was president, is one key indicator of the relationship between these institutions and how it has changed over time. These meetings took place in a variety of settings. Many occurred in the course of visits to the regions by Putin or Medvedev, during which the president and governor would meet alone for discussions. In late summer, both Putin and Medvedev followed a practice of inviting governors to meet with them at the summer presidential residence in Sochi. The pattern of meetings shows several changes over time. Initially, Putin was reluctant to spend his time meeting with governors or republic presidents. In his first full year as president, Putin went a full nine months (from February to November

2000) without meeting a single regional leader face-to-face. This appears to have been part of a strategy to preclude regional lobbying as he tightened central control. After Putin had more or less established the terms of the 'vertical', meetings with governors became more frequent from 2001 to 2004. There was another major increase in the number of meetings between 2004 and 2005. This marked the beginning of presidential appointments of governors and a change in their status to component parts of the 'power vertical'. Henceforth, there was a much clearer dependent relationship between governors and the president. The second change in the frequency of these meetings took place between 2009 and 2010, during Medvedev's presidency. This was a time of intensive personnel changes among governors, as the long-serving veterans of the Yeltsin era were forced out. The increased frequency of individual meetings ensured that virtually all of the (by now) 83 governors would meet with the president at least once every two years. Putin's return to the presidency in 2012 corresponded with the return of elections for governors, and while the number of these contacts continued to be higher than during Putin's first term, they began to return to the norm he had established in the mid-2000s. When Putin nominated an appointed governor for election, this meant the governor had to formally resign his or her post. The now 'temporarily acting' governor would meet once or twice with Putin in advance of polling day. This was a fairly transparent attempt to influence the outcome of the elections by demonstrating Putin's personal support.

Meetings with governors came to be routinely scheduled in order to conduct a periodic evaluation of performance. Face-to-face encounters provided an opportunity for governors to report on their regions, and sometimes they were subjected to an uncomfortable grilling when confronted by contrary evidence that the president had obtained from his own sources. In July 2012, for instance, at a meeting with Belgorod governor Yevgenii Savchenko, Putin tried including in these meetings several representatives of various local interests – in this case, a school principal, an entrepreneur, a hospital director, and the chairman of the region's 'youth government' who was also an entrepreneur. The point appeared to be to go beyond the normal recitation of statistics about regional performance in various sectors and hear testimony from the citizens of a region. The usefulness of this practice immediately came into question, given the obvious role of governors in selecting who would be invited to attend. One of the entrepreneurs, the owner of a coffee shop, had only positive things to say about the business environment in Belgorod and helpfully volunteered that 'no one has come to me with an inspection for the purpose of getting a bribe'; he had to be coaxed by the governor to 'name at least one problem'. The hospital director argued for more federal support for regional health care, to which Putin replied 'Did Yevgenii Stepanovich [the governor] coach you to say that?' The principal of the rural school talked about her pay increase and new computer technology that had been installed at her school. After several attempts to repeat this experiment, the practice of inviting other guests from the regions was discontinued by 2013.

Despite the fact that regional leaders have very little time with the president, the issues discussed – at least in the part of the meetings that is made public – are usually drawn from recent initiatives or promises made by the Kremlin. A significant portion of the interaction could be categorized as an attempt to verify policy implementation: for example, Putin would ask why was Kurgan region not yet paying teachers at a rate equal to or higher than the average pay in the region (as Putin had promised would happen)? Much of the discussion is centred on regional performance on economic and social indicators. Over time, the Kremlin developed a supposedly objective system for evaluating the performance of appointed governors. Soon it took on the appearance of micro-management. The first list of indicators, issued in 2007, included 43 criteria. By the end of the Medvedev presidency, the number of indicators had reached 460, with 260 'basic' and 200 'supplementary' indicators. A system of bonuses from the budget, amounting to an extra billion roubles per year to some regions beginning in 2008, was tied to the evaluation of regional governments' effectiveness.

In August 2012, Putin signed a decree changing the basis for evaluating governors, which greatly simplified the system. It reduced the indicators to 11, and governors were required to present reports based on the previous year's performance to the government by 1 April of each year. Changes in regional leaders are virtually never connected to regional evaluations, whether of 460 or 11 criteria. The formal list is supplemented with an informal list that is constantly being revised as new problems emerge. At the end of 2012, for example, in the context of controversies over adoption procedures, governors were tasked with monitoring adoptions and the development of regional sport complexes in their regions. Many of the indicators listed are outside the ability of governors to influence in any significant way. Demographic factors such as the size of the population and the death rate, for example, are less dependent on policy or policy implementation than on trends that were set years earlier. The birth rate is heavily dependent on the number of women of child-bearing age, and there is no means at this stage of overcoming the massive drop in the birth rate of the 1990s. Economic conditions, such as regional unemployment, are similarly dependent on the state of the overall economy. The climate for small business and outside investment is a function not just of regional policies but the policies of federal ministries that are implemented by federal agencies in the regions. Businesses large and small are subject to tax audits, visits by police, fire and health inspections, and federal migration service raids.

For those indicators over which governors can have an impact, the process sometimes encourages a perverse manipulation of the outcomes. When regions are judged on the basis of test scores on the university entrance examinations (the Unified State Examination, or YeGE), the desire to help students get better scores than they deserve – by cheating – is shared by not just students and their parents but also by teachers, principals, city education officials, regional education ministers, and governors themselves. A similar set of incentives helps explain the temptation to commit vote fraud in national and regional elections, which it turns out are also often overseen by the school teachers who serve on precinct election commissions. One major unlisted indicator is the ability of governors to deliver votes for national presidential or Duma elections. The largest wave of resignations in recent years came in the aftermath of the December 2011 Duma elections, mostly in regions where United Russia received a share of the vote that was lower than the national average, and just before the new law on electing governors came into force. The message to regional officials is clear: failure to use their control over regional election commissions to squeeze out a higher vote for United Russia or for Putin could cost them their jobs. Reuter and Robertson (2012) have made the case that election results in the regions are the best predictor of whether or not a governor is removed or reappointed, and this factor is far more important to Russia's authoritarian leadership than 'good governance' as measured in economic performance.

The only expressly political factor in the indicators is the approval rating of regional government, an indicator measured through public opinion surveys. Ideally, the resumption of popular elections for governors should make this indicator superfluous. But that would presume fair elections, taking place among an informed electorate and, most critically, the presence of genuine competition and at least one effective opposition party. For virtually every region, none of these conditions is in place, and governors work actively to preserve this political status quo. In this respect, the authoritarian political system established by Putin at the national level has been recapitulated at the regional level.

Group meetings with the complete contingent of regional leaders were also an important forum for Putin to hear views from the regions while announcing the goals and priorities that he had himself established. Particularly important were meetings with the State Council (Gossovet), an institution formed in 2000 with the purpose of providing a regular forum for discussions – led by Putin personally – on major issues of policy. In July 2012, the membership of the State Council was expanded to include the speakers of both houses of parliament and the heads of the party fractions in the Duma. The group meets quarterly, sometimes in one of the regions, to consider topics such as improving the attractiveness of regions for investors (December 2012) or the quality of housing-related services (May 2013). Several months prior to the session, a working group is normally formed, headed by a governor, which prepares reports and recommendations. Several months after the session, Putin typically issues a set of detailed instructions to the Council of Ministers or particular agencies on preparing reports or draft laws, with deadlines for completion. A working body called the presidium is formed by choosing one regional leader from each of federal districts and then rotating the membership every six months. The presidium meets separately with the president four times a year and has an agenda that is different from that of the State Council. The State Council and its presidium allow for input by governors on important policy questions, but everything is advisory in nature and must pass through the presidential administration. No one who has observed a meeting of the State Council would be under the illusion that governors are treated as the political equals of the president. On several notable occasions Putin has scolded members for poorly preparing for the session or for not paying attention (talking among themselves or sending tweets, for example). In one widely reported exchange, Valerii Shantsev, long-time governor of the important industrial region of Nizhnii Novgorod, was warned by Putin to 'never interrupt me again' during a State Council session in May 2013.

Federal agencies in the regions and the problem of decentralization

The concept of a 'power vertical' is misleading in that it implies that there is one channel from top to bottom, from the Kremlin to the regions. The reality is that there are many dozens of channels, with each federal ministry and agency overseeing its own chain of command. Since 2000, hyper-centralization has produced an explosion in the numbers of regionally based officials of federal agencies. There are now roughly 2.5 times as many federal administrative employees in the regions as there are regional government employees. These federal officials in the regions are paid by, and report to, their headquarters in Moscow. They are not subordinate to regional officials, and yet the activities of these federal agencies in the regions greatly affect how regions are actually governed.

It is not unusual in federal systems for there to be such national-level agencies (the FBI, for example, in the United States) with offices in the regions. This reflects the division of powers and responsibilities that defines federalism. As the system has developed under Putin, however, the number of these agencies and the scope of their activities is far from normal. Federal agencies include not just law enforcement (the prosecutor's office, the Ministry of Internal Affairs (police), the FSB, the drug enforcement agency and the Investigative Committee) and tax inspectors. A partial list would include the anti-monopoly agency, the office for registering property, the youth affairs agency, conservation officials, the migration service, technical standards enforcers, emergency services and fire inspectors, the federal roads agency, and many more.

The same complexity applies to the allocation of budget revenues from the centre to the regions. The actual practice of the Russian financial redistribution to the regions is typically not through regional governments, but through regional branches of federal ministries and agencies. In theory this gives the central government more control over how monies from the centre are spent. In practice distribution of much of this money is highly non-transparent. Rather than formula-based allocations (say, based on population or economic conditions) funds are distributed in response to behind the scenes lobbying. A large part of agency directed funding takes the form of various subsidies and subventions, including funding to support federal programmes in the regions. As a simplification measure the Minister of Finance in March 2013 proposed consolidating budget transfers (subsidies) from the current 90 (!) to 42, which would then correspond to the number of state programmes designated for the regions.

The pattern of numerous vertical channels of control and finance creates massive monitoring and coordination problems, which contributes to corruption and misallocation of resources. An obvious solution would be to roll back the excessive centralization of the Putin years and give more decision-making authority to regional leaders. During the Medvedev presidency, in June 2011, two of Russia's most important regional administrators, Dmitri Kozak and Aleksandr Khloponin, were assigned to head working groups to prepare proposals for decentralization of administration and finance. They reported their conclusions at a meeting of the State Council in December 2011. Kozak, a long-time Putin aide and former *polpred* for the North Caucasus, presented the most radical proposal: He called for a reorganization that would transfer to regions over 100 functions currently carried out by federal agencies. Over 220,000 federal employees in the regions, around 38 per cent of the total, would be reassigned to new regional agencies. Governors would also have greater say over who should head the federal agencies that remained in the region. Khloponin, also a former Putin aide and the current *polpred* in the North Caucasus, proposed budgetary reforms that would replace the multiple funding streams with a single subvention or block grant to the region, so that governors could make their own choices about how to allocate the money. He also proposed increasing incentives for innovation and development by allowing regions to keep more of the taxes generated by these activities. As one might expect, governors were enthusiastic in their support of these proposals, while federal ministers found them 'problematic'. Minister of Finance Anton Siluanov, for instance, warned that regional inequality would sky-rocket, while macro-economic stability would be undermined. Putin, still prime minister at the time, raised doubts that his budgetary priorities (for the military, security agencies and pensions) could be satisfied under the new scheme. He also doubted that 'national standards' could be maintained if regions took over federal functions (the State Council session transcript from 26 December 2011 is at president.kremlin.ru/news/ 14139).

Once Vladimir Putin returned to the presidency, there was a noticeable shift in tone. Very few new powers, it became clear, would be given to the regions, and the process would take place slowly to monitor any negative impact. At a second State Council meeting on this question in July 2012, Putin emphasized the accountability of governors if they did not effectively carry out any transferred responsibilities, thus setting the stage for dismissing even elected governors if federal ministers complained about their performance. At a December 2012 meeting with regional legislators Putin admitted that he was bored with the whole process of redistributing powers: 'It all comes down to one thing – to the interests of specific agencies, unfortunately. As soon as you begin to talk about something being transferred to the regional level, this and this and this, immediately arises a whole mass of arguments from federal agencies on why it would be wrong to do so' (see president.kremlin.ru/news/17125). While Putin has promised some decentralization, it was clear that his heart is still with federal ministers. As one Russian scholar with close Kremlin ties, Yevgenii Minchenko, put it, 'The federal authorities, having announced a process of decentralization, really don't want to give money to the regions' (quoted in *Kommersant-vlast'*, 9 July 2012).

To summarize, it is difficult to describe Russia today as a federal state, since so many of the elements that constitute federalism have been deliberately undermined by Putin's Kremlin. Regional politics has been, in effect, depoliticized by predetermining the outcome of elections or eliminating them altogether. Putin has frequently stated that the ideal governor is not a politician, but an effective manager. Institutions that are supposed to represent regional interests at the centre have been weakened or destroyed. New institutions such as the State Council seem designed to control and channel the efforts of regional leaders, rather than seek their input. The division of powers and budgetary resources has become both highly centralized and yet compartmentalized, making coordination within a region nearly impossible.

Chapter 11

Managing the Economy

PHILIP HANSON

The management of the Russian economy is becoming more difficult. Russia's GDP growth, in common with that of other emerging economies, slowed in 2012–13. It had been in the range of 4–5 per cent per annum in 2010–11. In 2012 the rate of growth dipped to 3.4 per cent. At the time of writing the outcome for 2013 was not known, but it is likely to be of the order of 1.6 per cent. There is talk in Moscow of 'stagnation', and considerable concern about the near future. For an emerging economy that was growing at 7 per cent a year before the financial crisis this is a challenge, even in a world of slower growth.

So far as GDP growth is concerned, Russia has ceased to perform better than the rest of the world. In 2013–16 the consensus of independent forecasters, compiled by Moscow's Higher School of Economics in October 2013, is that the Russian economy will be growing more slowly than the global economy as a whole (as projected by the IMF); see Figure 11.1.

Policy-makers, accordingly, face a challenge that is different from that which they encountered in the first phase of the global crisis, in 2008–09. On that occasion the falling oil price was the immediate source of trouble for Russia (even though it was not the whole story), and that price moved back up again in less than a year. Russia remains heavily dependent, financially, on the export of oil, gas and metals but this time something different is going on. In 2012–13, oil prices fluctuated moderately around a historically high nominal level. Yet Russia, a supposedly emerging economy, has begun to grow more slowly than the world as a whole. For good reason, the choices to be made in economic policy and reform are under intense scrutiny.

Meanwhile, for reasons that go beyond the recent slowdown, Russian economic policy-making has become more contentious. In 2006, a senior Russian economist remarked to me that disagreements on economic policy within the leadership 'are mainly technical these days – that's an improvement'. The making of economic policy in Russia, he implied, was no longer the outcome of head-on collisions of radically opposed points of view.

Figure 11.1   *Russia and the world: GDP growth 2007–12 actual and
2013–16 projected (% change year on year)*

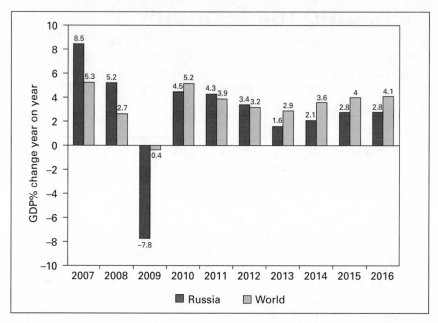

Sources: Rosstat (Russia 2007–12 actual); HSE 2013, p. 4 (Russia consensus forecast
2013–16); IMF World Economic Outlook database October 2013 (World 2007–12 actual and
2013–16 projected).

At the time, this was a fair comment. Since late 2011, however, things
have changed. The change came in September 2011, when Aleksei Kudrin
resigned as Minister of Finance. Here was a former long-serving and
internationally admired finance minister, known to be a personal friend of
Vladimir Putin, who was arguing publicly, not just for more prudent fiscal
policies and a curbing of military spending, but for radical institutional
reform: in particular, moves towards an independent judiciary and real
competition in politics (see, for instance, KGI 2012, and other statements
by the Committee of Civil Initiatives, formed by Kudrin). It was one thing
for academic economists and other members of the intelligentsia to voice
such ideas; another thing for a prominent insider to do so.

The limits of the politically possible have become more blurred at the
conservative end of the scale, as well. Another sign of changing and uncertain times in economic policy-making was the appointment (by a presidential edict of 27 July 2012) of Sergei Glazyev as an economic advisor to
President Putin. Glazyev, a leftish nationalist, was at the opposite end of
the policy spectrum from Kudrin and certainly not in the mould of other
members of the economic-policy elite. In January 2013, he delivered a

radical report on economic strategy that was strongly statist and very much at odds with the conventional wisdom (see http://www.glazev.ru/). Another sign of uncertain times was the airing by the chairman of the Duma's economic policy committee of an exotic idea: a return to 'State Corporation Russia', a state-led, vertically integrated national business, drawing on the 'best of the experience of the Soviet Union' (Sergeev 2013).

Policy uncertainty, in other words, has increased. The underlying frictions, not unknown elsewhere, between the upholders of fiscal and monetary discipline, on the one hand, and spending lobbies, on the other, and between free marketers and statists, have been there all along. But it is now less clear how far policy might go in either direction. It remains the case that the main state bodies concerned directly with the making of economic policy – the Ministries of Finance and of Economic Development, the Central Bank and some parts of the Presidential Administration – are managed by people generally categorized as liberal. But these people do not decide economic policies or institutional reforms unilaterally. Other players are also involved.

In this chapter I shall sketch, first, the economic heritage of the Yeltsin years, then the major developments that have changed the economic environment in which Russia's policy-makers operate, and then the more important shifts observable in the main domains of Russian economic policy under Putin and Medvedev: macro-economic management in the boom period and then in the crisis and after; next, micro-economic policies in the sense, primarily, of regulatory and institutional change, where the approach has shifted back and forth both in the boom and in the crisis. The main conclusion is that, so far, constraints imposed by the Russian political and social order hamper a response to the current economic slowdown: external circumstances are indeed unhelpful, but domestic impediments to investment, innovation and competition are also substantial. Those impediments arise from the way in which the political regime maintains itself.

The changing environment of Russian economic policy

The Yeltsin inheritance

From 1989 up to 1996 recorded Russian output fell heavily. Signs of recovery in 1997 were eclipsed by the severe financial crisis of summer 1998, when Russia effectively reneged on a large part of its foreign debt and the exchange rate of the rouble fell fast from around six to the US dollar to 24. The overall fall in measured output (GDP) between 1989 and 1998, of about 45 per cent, summed up for some the failure of 'shock ther-apy' as a route from state socialism to a market capitalist economy. Others questioned whether the very idea of a transition or transformation to capitalism was a desirable aim in the first place.

Yet amidst the inflation and impoverishment that marked Russia's 'transition recession', it turned out that the decontrol of prices, the priva-tization of state companies and the opportunity to set up new firms had achieved something. There was a population of firms that could and did expand supply when profits provided an incentive to do so. The steep devaluation of the rouble, pricing many imports out of the market, prompted a revival of domestic production. Soon after, in 1999, interna-tional oil prices began to rise. The growth that came to be associated with Putin's first two presidential terms (2000–08) began before he had taken office.

The boom years, 1999–2008

The oil price did not rise continuously, but it rose most of the time between 1998 and 2008. The price of Urals oil (the key price for Russia) went from as low as $10/barrel in 1998 to over $130/barrel in July 2008. This was a period when most of the world economy was also growing, most of the time. Russia benefited from its own rising export revenues mainly from oil, gas and metals (about four-fifths of the nation's merchandise exports, and equivalent to almost a quarter of GDP). This meant that Russia's terms of trade were strengthening. In other words, a fixed unit of Russian exports could buy more and more imports. Export revenues were swelling the country's state, corporate and personal incomes, and raising demand – which in turn stimulated domestic production. It also stimulated demand for imports, but export earnings were rising so fast that Russia maintained a large trade surplus.

Consequently, personal real incomes rose more rapidly even than GDP. This was sustainable as long as the terms of trade went on improving. Household consumption led Russian growth. Investment also grew, but not so fast that the share of gross fixed investment in GDP rose much above a modest 22 per cent – far below the investment rate in China and India, though not very different from the rate in Brazil. This was a happy state of affairs for Russia. Prosperity was manifestly increasing. Poverty, as officially measured, affected a diminishing share of the population. Unemployment was declining. Inflation was, with some interruptions, tending to slow; consumer price inflation dipped below 10 per cent in 2006. On the whole, as Figure 11.2 illustrates, the improvement was substantial.

Figure 11.2   *Russia: declining poverty and (mostly) declining inflation, 2000–12 (year-on-year % change in the consumer price index to year-end, and annual % of population in poverty)*

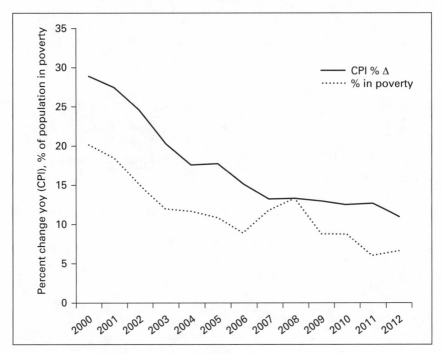

Sources: IMF World Economic Outlook database; Rosstat.

The oil price remained critical. Figure 11.3 puts fluctuations in the Urals oil price alongside changes in Russian GDP in recent years. Clearly the relationship was not a tight one and of course the amplitude of fluctuations in the oil price greatly exceeds those in GDP. But the period of rapid growth comes to an end in 2008–09 for both variables. What follows the acute phase of the crisis is less clear, as we shall see.

The crisis and after

The global financial crisis hit Russia a little later than many other countries, in mid-to-late 2008. So far as annual GDP growth numbers are concerned, it shows up in a slowdown in 2008 and a remarkable fall of 7.8 per cent year-on-year (yoy) in 2009. This was, notoriously, the steepest fall experienced by any G20 nation. It was, it is true, less than the declines experienced in several smaller countries, such as the Baltic states, but declining output was not at this time the experience of other large

Figure 11.3   *Russia: GDP and Urals oil price, 2006-13 (year-on-year % changes, quarterly data)*

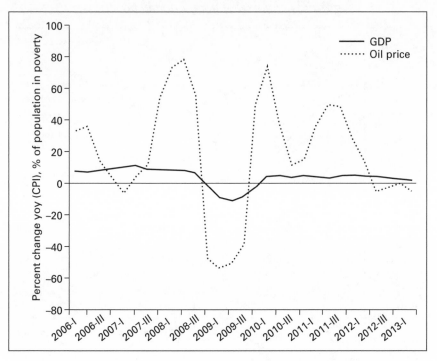

Sources: data from Rosstat and Central Bank of Russia.

emerging economies or major hydrocarbon exporters (except for Kuwait). It was an event that was not easily accounted for, as we shall see when we discuss the implications for policy.

Growth resumed in the first quarter of 2010. Russia's recovery was both faster and more clearly marked than that of Europe, which soon slipped back into difficulties, and even when compared with the United States, where the turnaround was slow and accompanied, for a long time, by little in the way of revived employment. However, the Russian recovery did not extend as far as a return to anything close to the 1999–2008 rate of growth. Instead of the earlier average annual growth rate of about 7 per cent, Russian GDP increased between early 2010 and mid-2012 at somewhat over 4 per cent a year. Then it slowed quite markedly, as Table 11.1 shows. Consumption, previously the main demand-side driver of growth, began to decelerate, albeit from a respectable rate.

The period from 2008 onwards, accordingly, poses a number of questions about the workings of the contemporary Russian economy. Why did Russia react so dramatically to the 2008–09 global crisis in comparison

Table 11.1   *The recent Russian slowdown: year-on-year % changes in GDP and retail sales, 2009–13 (annual and quarterly data)*

	GDP	Retail sales
2009	--7.8	-5.1
2010	4.5	6.4
2011	4.3	7.0
2012	3.4	5.9
2012–I	4.9	7.6
2012–II	4.0	7.0
2012–III	2.9	4.8
2012–IV	2.3	4.5
2013–I	1.6	4.0
2013–II	1.2	3.5

Source: data from Rosstat (www.gks.ru).

with other large emerging economies and other oil exporters? Why did the recovery not return Russia to the growth rate of its pre-crisis boom period? Is the further slowdown from mid-2012 merely a brief pause or is it the start of a new period of stagnation? What is the respective weight of internal and external factors in the country's recent slower growth? We shall get to some provisional answers to these questions later.

Two developments will play major roles for some time to come: the economic stagnation (if not worse) of Europe, the destination of a half of Russian exports; and the decline in the available Russian workforce as the number of young labour-force entrants plummets. The official projection of the population of working age, shown in Table 11.2, displays a clear fall. This estimate includes projected net immigration. The fall in numbers of new young labour-force entrants, apart from reducing the absolute size of the workforce and raising the ratio of dependants to those in work, has two likely side-effects. It reduces the geographical and occupational mobility of the workforce, and it probably reduces the rate at which that workforce improves its skills. Both of these effects mean a slower growth of productivity. Neither of these developments can be blamed on Russian economic policies. However, the policy-makers have to cope with them.

An analysis of all the reasons for the slowdown in Russian economic growth is important as a guide to policy, but the degree of analytical consensus is small, whether in Moscow or among observers more generally. Liberal critics of the Putinist social order highlight domestic impediments to growth, and the weakness of institutions (courts and law enforcement especially) in particular. For them, Russia's rapid growth of 1999–2008 was above all the product of a global commodity boom that

Table 11.2   *Projected working-age (15–72) population of Russia,*
2011–20 (millions)

2011	87.5
2012	86.6
2013	85.6
2014	84.7
2015	83.6
2016	82.5
2017	81.5
2018	80.5
2019	79.7
2020	79.0

Note: these figures show the middle of three projections, all of which show a decline; projected net immigration is included.

Source: data from Rosstat (www.gks.ru).

allowed Russia to grow without the fundamental reform that is needed for healthy long-run development. Others, reasonably enough, point to the malign effects of a prolonged global crisis. Many go further and either implicitly or explicitly absolve Russia's rulers of any responsibility for the slowdown. The advocates of a strong state speak of the diversification of Russian economic activity and 'modernization' as projects in which the state could and should play a leading role.

Before examining these larger, quasi-philosophical debates, however, we review the main lines of economic policy in the Putin era (which is taken here to include the Medvedev presidency of 2008–12).

Economic policies and policy-making, 2000–13

Macro-economic management: (A) during the boom, 2000–08

In the face of a large and rising inflow of petro-dollars, fiscal policy was mostly prudent. The Ministry of Finance, headed until September 2011 by Aleksei Kudrin, sought to hold down spending, build up reserves against a rainy day and 'sterilize' the inflow of funds – in other words, to limit its impact on the domestic flow of income and spending – in order to contain and gradually subdue inflation. With up to half of federal–budget revenue (the exact proportion varies from year to year) stemming from oil and gas extraction taxes and oil and gas export duties, it was important not to let spending simply follow the rising oil price. That price, after all, could also come down.

Meanwhile monetary policy, in the hands of the Central Bank of Russia (CBR) under Sergei Ignatiev gave priority to managing the exchange rate, slowing the change in the nominal value of the rouble while allowing it to rise in real terms (adjusting for inflation in Russia and its trade partners) against the euro and the dollar.

These two policies coexisted somewhat uneasily. Containing the rise of the real exchange rate required the emission of roubles to buy up foreign currency, making the control of inflation more difficult. However, there was a logic to this exchange-rate targeting: a rapid strengthening of the rouble would have undermined the competitiveness of domestic production in short order. As it was, the benefits to domestic producers of the huge 1998 devaluation were eroded, but this happened more slowly than would have been the case in the absence of the policy.

Aleksei Kudrin, as Finance Minister from 2000 to 2011, presided over budgetary policies that were aimed at reducing inflation and boosting confidence in the rouble. He was the ultimate club treasurer who resists all new spending. For much of the time he succeeded. The federal budget was in substantial surplus in 2000–07. The uptick in inflation in 2007–08 (see Figure 11.1) reflects a short period when spending pressures temporarily overcame Kudrin's resistance. With parliamentary elections due in December 2007 and presidential elections the following spring, spending pressures prevailed. The 2005 budget was in surplus to the extent of 7.7 per cent of GDP with an average Urals oil price that year of $50/barrel. In 2008, with an oil price averaging $94.7/barrel, the surplus had shrunk to 4.1 per cent of GDP (data from Sberbank Investment Research, July 2013). This was still a surplus unachievable in developed Western countries, but it allowed a lot more spending. For much of the time, however, Kudrin's cautious approach prevailed

Fiscal prudence was emphasized with the establishment in 2004 of the Reserve Fund. It was built up from state oil and gas revenues (in practice from the mineral extraction tax plus oil and later also gas export duties). In 2008, the fund was split into the Reserve Fund and the National Prosperity Fund (FNB in its Russian acronym). The rationales of the two funds were distinct. The Reserve Fund was developed as a safety net for the budget in the event of a sustained fall in oil prices. Accordingly, it was invested in safe but low-yield foreign securities. The FNB was initially intended to be a sovereign wealth fund, designed as a store of wealth for future generations. Sovereign wealth funds are usually kept at arm's length from the domestic economy and invested long-term in foreign assets, chiefly equities; this was originally the plan for the FNB. It was the Ministry of Finance's aim to build up the Reserve Fund to 10 per cent of GDP and only thereafter allocate oil and gas windfall funds to the financing of infrastructure. The FNB was not to be touched in the short term.

The onset of the global crisis forced some changes in these plans, but the prudent policies of the boom period unquestionably helped Russia when the crisis hit. These policies, associated with Kudrin, must have had at least the acquiescence, and most likely the active support, of President Vladimir Putin. It is a plausible conjecture that in 2007–08 that support was, for electoral reasons, temporarily withheld. In the longer run, however, Putin's concern for social and political stability and his dislike of foreign debt seem to have led him to favour sound public finances.

Macro-economic management (B): the global crisis and after

The fall in Russian activity in 2008–09, as we noted above, was unusually steep for a large emerging economy and for an oil exporter. Other major oil exporters typically encountered a slowdown in 2009, despite the fact that the oil and gas sector in most of them is a larger share of GDP than it is in Russia. For example, GDP growth in Saudi Arabia slowed to 1.8 per cent; and in Norway there was a modest downturn of 1.4 per cent (IMF World Economic Outlook Database, April 2013).

So why was the effect in Russia, where oil and gas account for a smaller share of GDP than they do in Saudi Arabia, so severe? Economic activity in Russia appears to be unusually sensitive to bad news about the oil price. One possibility is that confidence in the Russian business environment is especially fragile, and the oil price is seen as a guide to a particularly variable country risk. Funds flow out of Russia when the oil price falls, to an extent not seen in other oil-exporting nations. (For further discussion see Hanson 2009.)

Whatever the factors behind this steep fall may have been, the Russian public finances were in good shape to cushion it. The federal budget balance in 2009 was a deficit of 5.9 per cent of GDP. Much of the financing of this deficit came from the Reserve Fund and – contrary to its original purpose – the FNB, and very little from state borrowing.

The swing in the budget from surplus to deficit was partly due to the working of 'automatic stabilizers': the effect of a downturn in lowering tax and other state revenues and of raising spending on items like unemployment benefit. But it can be calculated that the net discretionary stimulus delivered by the budget, in the form of deliberately reduced tax rates and targeted anti-crisis spending was about 2.8 per cent of GDP (Hanson 2009: 28). This was by international standards quite a large stimulus package, yet it left Russia still with minuscule foreign public debt: less than 4 per cent of GDP at the end of the year.

Individual anti-crisis measures were open to criticism. Large firms with good political connections were favoured. Interest-rate subsidies distorted the market. Barriers erected to car imports were a form of protectionism. Several private banks were taken over by (stronger) state banks. However, most countries' responses to the global financial crisis were vulnerable to similar charges. The point to be made here is that an earlier emphasis on sound public finances enabled Russia to emerge from the acute phase of the global crisis with no significant burden of public debt, and in general without the handicaps that have been so conspicuous in the developed world since 2008.

One consequence of a slow recovery after 2009 was that tensions between advocates of big public spending and advocates of fiscal prudence became more marked. The room for compromise was narrowed. On top of that came the next electoral cycle: 2011–12. Major spending promises were made, chiefly by Vladimir Putin. Pensioners and state employees received substantial rises in income through policy decisions of 2009–11. This explains the absence of any spike in poverty rates in the crisis (see Figure 11.2). In 2011, the leadership pledged a very large expansion of military re-equipping and technological upgrading: 20 trillion roubles' spending in 2013–20, which works out at about 4 per cent of GDP during the period at 2013 prices and levels of real GDP (for manoeuvrings over this spending see Tovkaylo 2013).

The struggles over priorities have been intense. The military, along with military industry, have been pitted against the Ministry of Finance and indirectly against the lobbies for healthcare and education spending. Alongside these contests there has been a debate over the design and implementation of 'budget rules', intended to determine total federal budget spending. There had been hopes that the combat on this and other matters of economic policy might be resolved by the adoption of an overall strategy. It was decided soon after the recovery began that the country's long-term economic strategy to 2020, promulgated in 2008, should be reviewed. Too much had changed since the happy days of 7 per cent growth, and the framework for policy needed reconsideration. A large taskforce of economists, headed by Vladimir Mau, the rector of the Academy of the National Economy and Public Administration, and Yaroslav Kuzminov, rector of the Higher School of Economics, beavered away and produced a compendium of recommendations (*Promezhutochniy* 2011 was the interim draft).

These recommendations were soon pushed aside, except for the general idea of a budget rule to cap the extent to which the federal budget could depend on revenues from oil and gas, and to preserve the stabilization funds. The chances of its being implemented in future are uncertain. However, as Kudrin has observed, investors (both Russian and foreign) want to see a budget rule implemented to reassure them of the country's future financial stability. This struggle continues. In the budget plans for 2014–16 the share of GDP allocated to healthcare and education has been cut and that of defence and security increased. Attempts by the Ministry of Finance to have some of the military budget postponed have been blocked (Tovkaylo 2013). Meanwhile revenue of the consolidated budget (federal plus regional plus local, amounting in recent years to around 38 per cent of GDP) has been falling short of plan as the economy grows more slowly than expected and VAT and profits tax revenue have stagnated (http://www.kommersant.ru/doc/2239895, accessed 24 July 2013).

Infrastructure spending is another sore point. Should it be expanded to stimulate a flagging economy? Or should it be trimmed for the sake of building up a fiscal reserve against an even rainier day? The questions are particularly sensitive because public investment costs are known to include a good deal of illicit siphoning-off of funds by contractors and other interested parties. Indeed the prospect of this siphoning-off is one of the incentives to lobby for public projects in the first place. The spending lobbies appear, as of early 2014, to have won the day. Commitments given by President Putin now require expenditure in 2014–16 amounting to 1.3 trillion roubles (about $40 billion at mid-2013 exchange rates) on a high-speed rail line from Moscow to Kazan, the development of the Russian Far East and preparations for the 2018 football world championship. This will be funded in part from the FNB, which is contrary to its original purpose.

In other words, as the economic situation has grown more worrying, the sound-money advocates have lost ground. This is not for want of trying on the part of Kudrin's successor as Minister of Finance, Anton Siluanov. He may lack the international prestige and close links with Putin that helped his predecessor, but Siluanov has defended the sound-money position eloquently and persistently. It may be wondered whether, in the same conditions, Kudrin himself could have done any better. Many of the issues that arise in Russian budgetary politics are familiar elsewhere: the struggle between spending lobbies and proponents of sound money is perennial and universal. One feature of the Russian fiscal environment, however, is not so widely shared. Russia is a major hydrocarbon exporter, and oil-exporting nations have to make very special efforts not to be fiscally comfortable. Figure 11.4 illustrates this.

One long-term difficulty facing macro-economic policy in Russia is that it may be losing some of that oil-induced budgetary cushion. As yields decline in the established oil and gas fields in West Siberia, there is a move to develop major new fields offshore and in East Siberia. The reserves are there but the costs of exploiting them are much higher than those that have obtained in West Siberia. Already a range of tax exemptions is in place to encourage this development. Shale oil in West Siberia may provide one way of alleviating this difficulty (Gustafson 2012), but there is a long-term danger that Russia's oil-and-gas tax base will be narrowed.

Figure 11.4 *Russia and selected oil-exporting and other nations, 2011:
budget balances and government debt as % GDP*

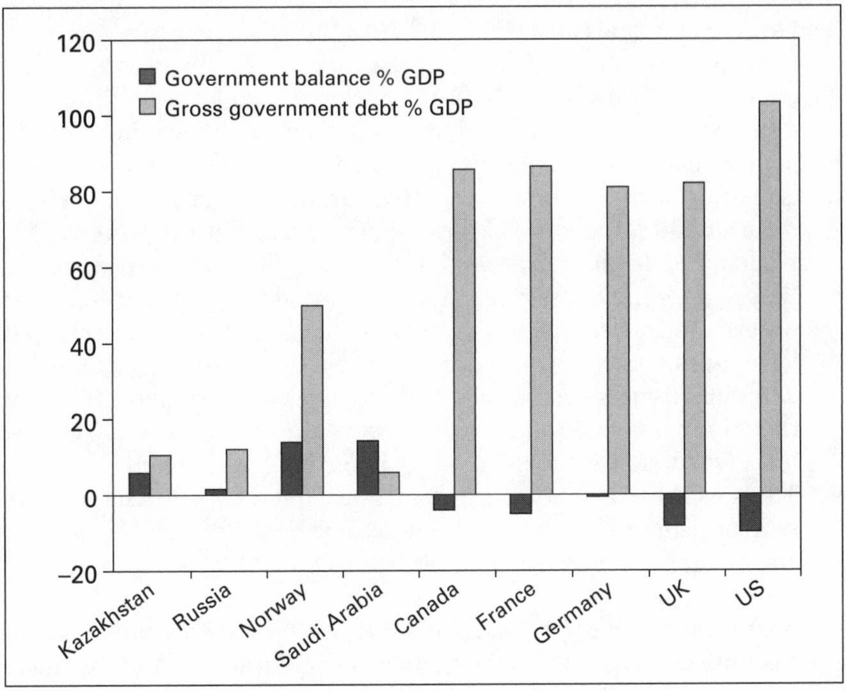

Legend:
- Government balance % GDP
- Gross government debt % GDP

Categories: Kazakhstan, Russia, Norway, Saudi Arabia, Canada, France, Germany, UK, US

Source: data from IMF World Economic Outlook database.

Micro-economic policies: market reform versus sistema

Alongside the struggle between big spenders and proponents of sound
money, the other long-running battle in the making of Russian economic
policy is between liberals and statists. This is not primarily about the scale
of state ownership within the economy, although that is relevant. It is
chiefly about the strength of informal, state-linked networks in deciding
how businesses operate in Russia, particularly, though not exclusively, in
the sectors which generate very large streams of revenue: oil, gas and
metals. This informal governance is part of a wider set of arrangements,
extending beyond the running of the economy, that Alena Ledeneva
(2013) has called called '*sistema*'.

Informal governance, a weak rule of law and a close interweaving of
state power and wealth are far from unique to Russia. They are however
rather unusual in a country that the World Bank now classifies as 'high
income'. It is above all the establishment of a rule of law, constraining the
actions of the political elite, that liberal critics have in mind when they

talk of Russia still requiring 'radical' or even 'systemic' reform. Reform discussion in Russia is often conducted in terms of 'improving the business environment'. Certain features of that business environment will help to convey what is at stake:

- Most privately owned large firms are closely held by one main owner or a small group, through holding companies based offshore.
- The population of small firms, including unincorporated sole traders, is modest; small business accounts for around 21 per cent of employment in 2009, less than half the share in most European countries (source and details in Hanson 2012: 25).
- Illegal grabbing of assets by competitors aided by law enforcement officials and (often) the courts is not uncommon; this is often achieved by manipulation of the criminal code. Reportedly, in 2008–13, 240,000 business people were convicted under 'economic' articles of the criminal code (a limited amnesty was announced in 2013: see http://www.gazeta.ru/business/2013/06/21/5389277.shtml).
- There has been a net outflow of private capital from Russia in every year since the collapse of the USSR except 2005 (when gross flows in and out approximately balanced), 2006 and 2007.

These are some of the symptoms of a difficult business world, in which political protection matters, property rights are insecure and the likely consequence is that less is invested in Russia than would otherwise be the case and competition between firms is hampered. The World Economic Forum, in its assessment of global competitiveness ranks Russia 133rd out of 144 countries on 'property rights', 124th on 'intensity of local competition' and 117th on 'availability of financial services'. It is only fair to add that Russia ranks high on such indicators as macro-economic environment, enrolment in higher education and broadband internet subscriptions: Russia is indeed in many respects a very modern country. But the institutional arrangements that condition the world of business are distinctly unhelpful. This is what the friction between economic liberals and economic statists is about.

The shifting patterns of market reform and 'manual control'

Between 2000 and 2003, the Putin leadership introduced a number of measures that were of a liberal, pro-market kind: a flat rate of personal income tax (which had been pioneered in Estonia); 'de-bureaucratization' measures to reduce state interference in small business; business-friendly amendments to the labour code, and the establishment of a market for land. The direction of change was clear. These measures were not accompanied by political liberalization, but on the separability of economic and political liberalization opinions were divided.

Then in 2003 came the arrest of Mikhail Khodorkovsky, the boss of what was then the country's largest oil company, Yukos. The Yukos affair developed slowly, but one result was the acquisition of most of Yukos's assets by the state company, Rosneft. In the period between the arrest of Khodorkovsky and the onset of the global crisis the state expanded its direct role in the economy in other directions as well: another leading private oil company, Sibneft, was taken over by Gazprom; state corporations were created to run the shipbuilding and aerospace industries and a hotch-potch of other defence-related entities: the United Ship-building Corporation, the United Aircraft-building Corporation and Russian Technologies (Rostekhnologii), respectively. Rosstekhnologii brought together a particularly wide range of assets, from run-down state design bureaux to the privatized and thriving titanium giant VSMPO-Avisma. (On the pressures used to acquire VSMPO-Avisma from its reluctant owners see Finn 2006.)

This amounted to a turn towards interventionism, or what Russian liberals call 'manual control' (*ruchnoe upravlenie*). Remarkably, however, it was accompanied by one major exercise in liberalization: the 'unbundling' and partial privatization of the electricity industry, under the leadership of Anatolii Chubais. Putin, again, either acquiesced in or more likely protected this isolated exercise in liberalization.

Therefore the turn to manual control was not an across-the-board change. It was however associated with some new formal restrictions being placed on inward foreign direct investment. These took the form of a law 'On procedures for making foreign investments in Russian commercial entities of strategic importance to the security of the Russian Federation', which came into effect in May 2008 (PBN 2007, 2008). This set default ceilings, subject to possible exceptions after case-by-case review, on the share that a foreign company could take in Russian firms in 39 narrowly defined lines of activity (overwhelmingly defence-related) plus major broadcasters and telecoms companies. There were similar restrictions in the natural-resource sector. The ceilings have not been rigidly applied. Quite a few exceptions have been negotiated and previous arrangements (such as BP's 50 per cent stake in TNK-BP) were allowed to stand. In some cases the role of foreign investors even increased. The Finmeccanica aerospace subsidiary Alenia went ahead with its joint venture with Sukhoi, developing the Sukhoi Superjet 100 medium-haul airliner, and Boeing was able to develop its joint venture in titanium processing with VSMPO-Avisma. Pragmatism prevails, subject to a characteristic bias in favour of control.

In the acute phase of the crisis, from late 2008 to the end of 2009, the role of the state tended to increase anyway. This was hardly surprising. It happened everywhere. In the Russian case a number of weak banks were taken over by stronger banks, which in practice meant state banks such as Sberbank and VTB, and some big companies which were over-borrowed were bailed out.

The message went out that mass redundancies were to be avoided. Here the highly adjustable Russian wage system (Gimpel'son and Kapelyushnikov 2008) helped: earnings could be, and were, cut substantially but employment fell relatively little. Particular concern was expressed about the fate of 'mono-towns' in which one or two employers accounted for most of the available jobs. This was no minor problem, for many such settlements had been built up in Soviet times, often geographically isolated, and now linked to declining lines of production. State assistance was provided, and the mono-towns limped on. (For an analysis of the Russian reform process that places this legacy at the heart of the problem see Gaddy and Ickes 2013.)

As the recovery proceeded after 2009, other items came on to the agenda. The underlying issue was the growth rate. External conditions were manifestly less favourable than between 1999 and 2008. Oil prices might not go on rising, export markets might be weak for some time, external credit was less abundant, the workforce was expected to fall, but surely Russia could do better than 4 per cent annual growth? In early 2013 the question was revised: surely Russia could do better than 2 per cent growth? On 31 January 2013, Putin repeated his call for the government to find ways to get the economy growing at a minimum of 5 per cent per annum; earlier he had spoken of 5–6 per cent (Netreba and Butrin 2013).

Acceleration was thought to require something referred to as 'modernization'. During the Medvedev presidency (2008–12) there had been much talk of modernization and reform, mostly emanating from Medvedev. Medvedev's latter-day version was most vividly expressed in his 'Russia, Forward!' blog posting of September 2009 (*Rossiiskaya gazeta*, 11 September 2009: 1, 3). It implied that Russia's modernization needed to extend to some degree of social liberalization and some strengthening of the rule of law. Putin's version was more narrowly technological.

For liberal economists, modernization was above all a strengthening of the rule of law. This they saw as fundamental to improving the business environment and strengthening competition, investment and innovation, for reasons outlined above. The role of Kudrin, as a liberal insider or former insider, offering radical views, added a new dimension to policy debates. Since resigning as deputy prime minister and minister of finance, he had criticized the criminal case brought against Aleksei Navalny and asserted that political competition was a necessary part of the setting for a well-functioning economy.

Might he or might he not come back to high office, perhaps as prime minister? In May 2013 he said that he was not willing to serve as a 'technical prime minister' implementing 'alien policies', and that there were 'some contradictions' between him and the political leadership (www.newsru.com/russia/20may2013/kudrin.html).

So the struggle between economic liberals and statists continued, if anything in a more intense phase than before. Meanwhile there were in 2012–13 events and policy developments that had a bearing on that struggle: in particular, Russia's accession to the World Trade Organization (WTO) in summer 2012, a continuing series of policy disagreements over the state pension system and a scaling back of privatization plans for 2014–16. WTO accession had taken 18 years of negotiation, longer than any other WTO entrant. The Russian accession represents a liberal opportunity. Moscow's trade practices are now officially open to international scrutiny. It has formal obligations about levels and forms of import protection, state support for Russian firms and openness to inward foreign direct investment that it must in principle fulfil. It has been estimated that some long-run benefit should accrue to the Russian economy, chiefly through greater openness to foreign investment in the services sector. The best estimates of the gains, however, are modest and they rest on there being supporting liberalization of the domestic economy. (For more on this see Connolly and Hanson 2012.)

The reform of the state pension system has pitted the Ministry of Finance and the Ministry of Economic Development (together, for once) against the 'social bloc' of the government. Russia continues to have a male retirement age of 60, a female retirement age of 55, a fairly high ratio of average pension to average wage (40 per cent in 2010), a rising ratio of retirement age to total population and, as an almost unavoidable consequence, an increasingly under-financed state pension fund, drawing heavily on the federal budget instead of being self-supporting. Broadly speaking, the economic liberals engaged in the policy-making process want to see the pension age raised, the preservation of the 'funded' pillar of the pension system (where pension contributions for an individual fund that individual's pension) and the pension fund's drain on the federal budget radically reduced. Their opponents are nervous about the potential political costs of raising the pension age and requiring larger employer contributions. This particular division over policy is one that could be closely matched in many other countries (Oxford Analytica 2012).

In the summer of 2011, during the Medvedev presidency, and apparently with strong support from Medvedev himself, a rather bold new privatization plan was launched. Russia has had a series of three-year privatization programmes, so the process is in principle continuous. These programmes are marked by, (a) a substantial component of small state entities of little consequence, and (b) large and consistent under-fulfilment. The 2011 proposals were comparatively radical. In particular, they would have taken VTB, the country's second largest bank, entirely private and left the state no longer a majority stakeholder – though with a golden share conveying certain veto powers.

Objections came from the statists, and especially from those who have been called 'state oligarchs': the bosses of large state entities from which they derive power and wealth without formal ownership. One argument widely used was that it was not a good time to sell; the prices obtainable would fall short of what could be obtained in better times. Thus the statists deployed a market argument, which was countered by a liberal refrain to the effect that this was no adequate reason for not preparing these assets for sale in a long-term programme; postponement was not ruled out. The revised programme of 2013 can be seen as a victory for the statists. They included Igor Sechin, formerly a deputy prime minister and now the boss of Rosneft. Under his leadership Rosneft, in late 2012, had bought TNK-BP for around $52 billion (Swint 2012), an amount closely similar, at the mid-2013 exchange rate, to the planned privatization yield for 2014 of 180 billion roubles (Sigal 2013). The difference is that the 180 billion roubles will not materialise.

Conclusions

In the Putin era (2000 onwards) the Russian economy has performed quite well in comparison with the developed West. Part of this performance has been down to the good luck of being a commodity exporter during a commodity boom (1999 to mid-2008). Part of it has been attributable to the rising productivity accompanying the catching-up process that could be expected of an (initially) middle-income country capable of absorbing technology from abroad, with an extra boost coming from the substitution of more productive activities for the often value-subtracting production structure bequeathed by socialist central planning.

Part, however, can reasonably be attributed to policy: prudent macro-economic policies enabled the nation to cope with a large and rising inflow of petro-dollars. Those policies provided a cushion that supported Russia through the acute phase of the global financial crisis.

The micro-economic side of policy has been less successful. Radical reform may or may not be achieved at some stage, but so far it has been neglected when the going was good, up to mid-2008. Now, when the going is not so good, its absence can be felt. The effect of institutional change should not be over-confidently assessed, but there must be a good chance that if Russia can make its way to independent courts, the rule of law and reasonably well-protected property rights, many of the present barriers to market entry and exit will be reduced. It is reasonable to expect in these conditions that the share of investment in GDP will be pushed up, including investment in product and process innovation.

Meanwhile talk of 'modernization', even in the limited sense of more rapid 'catching up' in technology and productivity, cannot readily be turned into reality. The lack of Russian technological dynamism is reflected, for instance, in figures for the growth of international patent filings in comparison with a number of other large emerging economies. The level of Russia's patent filings is respectable in light of the country's population size and income level. But that level, like so much else in Russia today, reflects the Soviet heritage. There is not very much being built on that particular heritage, either in fundamental science or (with a few exceptions) in technology. It is the lack of rapid growth in measurable invention (shared with Brazil) that is striking.

Pekka Sutela (2012: 1) is surely right that Russia is in many ways a 'statistically normal' country. The chances, however, of its doing much better than that – of its productivity levels catching up with the faltering but much higher levels of the developed West – seem to rest, not only on the continuation of sound macro-economic economic policy but on something that is politically even more demanding: radical institutional reform.

Chapter 12

Society and Social Divisions in Russia

SVETLANA STEPHENSON

Since the collapse of the Soviet Union, Russian society has grown increasingly unequal. In Soviet times, the state attempted to eliminate significant inequalities by administrative means. Since 1992, marketization and competitive capitalism have led to a growing differentiation between social groups and between regions of Russia. This chapter addresses the social divisions that have developed between rich and poor; men and women; the residents of areas which have now become part of the global economy and those who live in depressed backward regions; successful and 'failed' consumers (Bauman 1992); and between people included in social networks and patrimonial structures and those excluded from the opportunity of formal and informal support. It will also address the difficulties and challenges faced by civil society organizations and the voluntary sector in Russia today, particularly in the area of welfare, and emerging prospects for new forms of civic solidarity.

In 1992 the Russian government embarked on a programme of market reforms that included the liberalization of prices, large-scale privatization and withdrawal of the state from the distributive sphere. These reforms led to a massive rise in income inequality, the emergence of a wealthy class of oligarchs, and the large-scale impoverishment of workers in many sectors of the economy. Declines in incomes, mass dismissals, and the late (or non) payment of wages and pensions all contributed to an unprecedented decline in living standards. Although the available estimates about the number of poor in Russia are problematic, most of them show a sharp increase in poverty during the 1990s. The figures which appeared in the Soviet literature of the mid-1970s and the 1980s suggest that the officially designated poor (or *maloobespechennye*) constituted about 15–20 per cent of the Soviet population (Silverman and Yanowitch 2000: 38). In 1998, after the collapse of the currency, the World Bank estimated the percentage of poor in the Russian population as 49 per cent.

Psychosocial stress, associated with rises in poverty and marginaliza-tion, mortality (particularly among working-age men), and poor health and low fertility rates created a demographic crisis unprecedented in peacetime. Since 1993 the number of deaths has exceeded the number of births by 11.2 million, with population losses amounting to some 700,000 per year. By 2002, life expectancy for men had sunk to around 60 years (from 68 in 1990) and, according to the World Bank report, by 2010 this had only recovered to 63.

Rise in inequalities

In the 2000s, after the rouble devaluation of 1998, and with economic recovery supported by high energy prices, Russia experienced renewed economic growth and rise of prosperity. Between 1999 and 2008, as the catastrophic economic collapse and decline in living standards of the 1990s were becoming things of the past, the country experienced an impressive 7–8 per cent annual growth before it was hit by global economic crisis. By the mid-2000s poverty levels had gone down (and are currently estimated at 12–15 per cent), and a significant part of the coun-try's population had reached levels of material well-being never seen in Russia throughout its history. But the gains were highly uneven. Throughout the 2000s, income inequality was on the rise, with the incomes of the richest strata increasing faster than those of everybody else (see Table 12.1). Overall inequality in Russia reached similar levels to those of the United States, overtaking most other post-communist coun-tries. By 2008, around 50 per cent of incomes in both countries went to the richest 20 per cent of the population and 3–5 per cent went to the poorest quintile (Remington 2011: 265).

Inter-regional differences also widened. Some regions, endowed with natural and human resources, became beneficiaries of the Russian entry into the global economy, while others, dependent on obsolete technolo-gies and heavily subsidized by the central government, lagged behind. The diversity of Russia's regions in relation to their average incomes is about twice as great as in the United States, and close to that of China, India, and Brazil. Particularly striking is the difference between Moscow and St Petersburg and the rest of the country. The former have become part of the global economy, with more diverse labour markets and more highly paid jobs. While in Russia as a whole average GNI per capita in PPP terms in 2011 was $14,651, in Moscow it reached $47,000 (and $22,000 in St Petersburg), which is comparable with the figures for developed Western countries. The residents of these two cities also have the highest levels of educational attainment, with 50 per cent of Moscow residents and 44 per

Table 12.1   *Living standards in the 1990s–2000s*
(% changes, year-on-year)

	1990	1995	2000	2005	2006	2007	2008	2009	2010	2011
Real money incomes index (1995=100)		100	88	152	172	193	198	204	215	218
Inequality: decile ratio	4	13.5	14	15	16	17	17	17	17	16
Gini coefficient % below subsistence		0.387	0.395	0.409	0.415	0.422	0.421	0.421	0.421	0.417
Pensions (in real terms)		25	29	18	15	13	13	13	12	13
(1995=100)		100	76	129	136	142	168	186	251	254
As % of subsistence	237	101	76	98	100	102	115	127	165	163

Sources: adapted from *Rossiiskii statisticheskii yezhegodnik*, 2001: 171, *Rossiiskii statisticheskii yezhegodnik*, 2012: 177, 186, 191.

cent of the residents of St Petersburg having a completed tertiary education (Zubarevich 2012: 140).

Gender inequalities have also been significant. While declining from 99 per cent of those of working age at the end of the Soviet period to about 80 per cent in 2001, female participation in the labour market has remained very high. At the same time there has been a significant reduction in the availability of affordable child care and a reduction in labour market protection for women. According to United Nations data, in 2009 the gender pay gap (that is, the difference in average monthly earnings between men and women) stood at 32.1 per cent. The international rating of gender equality by the World Economic Forum puts Russia in 61st place in terms of gender equality in 2012 (between Laos and Brazil). While the Russian government has not seen gender equality as a matter of serious policy concern, from the mid-2000s population decline began to be seen as a serious threat to national security and economic development. In response, the government developed a range of pro-natalist policies. In 2006, they increased birth grants, family allowances, subsidies for pre-school care and municipal child care services. Legislation was passed to extend maternity leave to a maximum of 18 months, with retention of 40 per cent of wages. 'Maternity capital' was introduced for women who gave birth to a second child. This took the form of a one-off payment of 250,000 roubles (about $8710) indexed for inflation – a significant sum for the majority of Russian women. These measures have helped women to reconcile work and family roles (Cook 2011). In 2013, as President

Putin announced in his address to the Federal Assembly, Russia experienced a modest population growth for the first time since the start of the market economy. Pro-natalist policies have also had a coercive dimension, with access limited to abortions on demand. The Russian Duma is currently considering a ban on public funding for abortions unless termination takes place on medical grounds, or in cases of rape.

New consumerism and social distinctions

With the country emerging from the economic and social shocks of the 1990s, it was not just the rich elite but also the educated urban middle class who became the major beneficiaries of newly found prosperity. While there are many definitions of the middle class, in the Russian context education and cultural capital are often seen as its most important attributes. Taking these and other criteria (such as occupational status, income and material possessions) into account, by various estimates towards the end of the 2000s the Russian middle class comprised between one fifth and one third of the total population, reaching up to 50 per cent of the residents of large cities.

As in other advanced Western societies, consumption began to play a major part in the lives of the Russian middle classes. This has been associated with a significant change in the cultural outlook of educated groups. For members of the intelligentsia in pre-revolutionary Russia and in the Soviet Union, even talking about money – let alone displaying wealth – was seen as vulgar or plainly amoral. For an educated Soviet person, the proudest display of 'wealth' was to have bookshelves full of prized literary tomes. The modest levels of income of the Russian intelligentsia were compensated for by the high prestige of belonging to an educated and *kulturnyi* (cultured) stratum. The values of *kulturnost* (culturedness) can be traced to the second half on the nineteenth century, when Russian professional groups (teachers, doctors, engineers and others) were striving to establish their distinctiveness – both from the masses and aristocracy – through 'inner' nobility, taste, cultural refinement, politeness and rejection of crass materialism. In the Soviet period *kulturnost* was promoted by the communist leadership as part of the country's modernization drive, and the wider 'project' to educate and civilize former peasants and residents of the Soviet periphery.

For urban residents, a two or three-room apartment, a dacha outside the city and a Lada car represented the desired living standard. The Soviet consumer culture was one of mending and repair, handing things down to friends and kin, barter and hoarding rather than conspicuous consumption. These coping strategies were a response to modest standards of living and chronic shortages, but also an expression of one's elevated cultural status, implying a disdain for material things. When in the 1990s, 'New Russians', the rising class of wealthy entrepreneurs, arrived on the social scene, the reaction to them by an impoverished but culturally worthy intelligentsia was generally negative. As trade and commerce were occupations regarded as improper and degrading by most Russians in the Soviet era, many businessmen continued (for a while) to be seen as 'speculators' and outright criminals. But the New Russians were in fact a mixed group. They included people who had participated in the underground informal economy in the Soviet Union and who made a fortune in the early 1990s. Some of these underground Soviet businessmen (for example, Vladimir Gusinsky and Roman Abramovich) went on to become media and business tycoons. Other wealthy businessmen and women started their new careers as Soviet researchers and scientists. Many former Party and Komsomol apparatchiks successfully converted their Soviet-era political capital into business assets. Members of organized crime groups were also recruited into the new business activity. The New Russians who came from this sector seemed to influence the whole image of this group.

Representing the descent of society into the realm of unbridled greed, New Russians became symbols of the unfamiliar and frightening capitalist epoch. They also became figures of ridicule for members of the intelligentsia, in what was largely a defensive reaction for people who were losing the social prestige associated with education and fearful of descending into abject poverty. The New Russians were denied positive status on cultural grounds, and on the basis of their presumed lack of taste, demonstrated in a predilection for flashy clothes and their alleged inability to string two words together. All this quickly became a subject of numerous jokes, as well as feeding into television series and popular songs. At the same time the lives of the Soviet intelligentsia were full of hardship. Together with millions of Russians, educated urban residents in the 1990s turned to subsistence agriculture. Planting vegetables, mainly potatoes, on plots of land in suburban areas transformed from being hobby and pastime activities into the main subsistence mechanism (Clarke 2002). Other than consuming home-grown food, the impoverished *byudzhetniki* (public sector workers) were regular customers of street kiosks and wholesale markets, having no money or means of access to up-market shops or Western-style supermarkets. Families cut back severely their spending on going out and social entertaining. They spent their vacations at home or at their dacha. Theatre trips, cinema, concerts, magazines were barely affordable for many families.

In the 1990s, attitudes to consumption represented a complex mixture of saving, self-denial, and reliance for consumption on friends and family rather than the market. Strong suspicion of the foreign goods that were now appearing in Russia (and which were frequently believed to be of substandard quality) necessitated constant vigilance and the ability to make sense of unfamiliar labels, establish provenance (with only American and European produce given a cautious approval), and generally be on guard against companies and traders who were likely to take advantage of inexperienced Russian consumers.

In the 2000s, all this started to change. Over this decade, the share of spending on leisure and culture in middle-class budgets increased six times (Belanovsky *et al.* 2012: 56). Shopping in supermarkets, enjoying new consumer experiences in shopping malls (or increasingly via the internet), as well as holidays abroad soon became the order of the day, particularly for the middle-class residents of major cities. As elsewhere in the late modern world, consumption began to be seen as representing individual choice and serving to express one's identity (Beck 1992; Beck and Beck-Gernsheim 2002; Giddens 1991). In a situation in which class identities were still in flux, and people were looking for positional goods to express their new standing in society, consumption became an important instrument of social and cultural distinction. Expensive items were no longer associated with the vulgar *nouveaux riches*, the criminal (or criminalized) New Russians. They became testaments to one's taste and affluence. For diverse groups of Russians, visions of the good life became associated with participation in the global capitalist market place. Research shows a widespread belief among Russians that, despite all the problems associated with the new social and economic order, building a Western-type market economy was the only possible way forward for the country that was likely to lead to prosperity for themselves and their children. Even those occupational groups whose income and prestige seems to have declined since Soviet days and who hardly participated in the feast of consumption (for example, nurses or teachers) expressed the belief that material respectability and consumer knowledge were valid signifiers of a person's social worth (Patico 2008; Rivkin-Fish 2009).

The 2000s became a decade of *glamur* (glamour). *Glamur* can be seen as a representation of easy, unproblematic, romanticized affluence and beauty. 'The imagery of criminal (or criminalized) money-making has given way to a spectacle of legitimate and unfettered money-spending, as well as the consumption of high style and fashion' (Mesropova 2009: 94). The glamorous images of lifestyles of the wealthy glossed over the complex realities of life as it actually was. A facile spectacle of material accumulation, as well as public celebration of belonging to affluent and privileged social circles, were transmitted by television programmes, movies, adverts, new glossy magazines, and bestsellers such as the novels by Oksana Robski, depicting the new generation of rich Russian women whose main achievement was not professional success (something that used to be celebrated in the Soviet era) but the ability to bag an oligarch. Dominant representations of the rich show them as paragons of success and respectability. Many commentators noticed that *glamur* was officially promoted as a way to mould an apolitical public, enthralled by the vision of spectacular consumption. Indeed, in the 2000s, the decade of Putin's 'stability', opinion polls revealed an apathetic public, alienated from political life and having little idea about the future, but also demonstrating general contentment with the way things were (Levinson 2009).

A striking example of the cult of money and celebrity can be found in the transformation of VDNKh – the 'Exhibition of the Achievements of the National Economy' in Moscow. Built in the 1930s, the exhibition was intended to symbolize the promise of the then new socialist regime. Pavilions around the large site hosted opulent displays of the finest Soviet agricultural and industrial produce. Its golden fountains and beautiful buildings were designed to present a dream landscape in a country where for most people the daily reality was very different, characterized by poverty, queues for scarce goods and, at the height of Stalin's terror, fear of arrest. Nevertheless, the exhibition was very popular and drew visitors from all over the Soviet Union. Following the collapse of the Soviet Union VDNKh experienced its own form of market transformation. Soviet exhibits were removed and replaced in the pavilions by a plethora of small businesses and traders, selling everything from cheap Chinese electronics to Turkish leather bags and pirate CDs. What was once VDNKh's flagship central pavilion, a majestic 100m tall Stalinist building whose spire is topped by a golden star and sheaves of wheat, now hosts a museum of gifts presented to Leonid Yakubovich, the presenter of the highly popular TV programme 'The Field of Fortune'. The programme's format closely resembles 'Wheel of Fortune' but with its own very Russian slant. Participants bring gifts for Yakubovich, which they give him in the studio before playing the game. Some of these gifts are later transferred to the VDNKh museum. They include homemade souvenirs: amateur paintings, models of cars and boats, and hunting trophies. But most gifts take the form of representations of Yakubovich himself: bottles of vodka, little wooden figurines, portraits and souvenir plates all carry his image. It could be said that the pavilion has been transformed into a place of pagan worship, a shrine to the new god of money – and money that is not earned but magically delivered by this deity, inhabiting the new Olympian heights of television.

Social divisions, the welfare state and pathologization of the poor

As consumption became an increasingly important part of life, new divisions emerged between the more affluent and educated groups of the population who turned to the new private sector in education, healthcare and personal services, and those people who remained dependent on a deteriorating public welfare system. In the 1990s, the Soviet welfare system was liberalized in accordance with the prescriptions of the World Bank and the International Monetary Fund. From being the responsibility of central state and socialist companies in Soviet times, many welfare services now became the responsibility of regional and municipal authorities. With fiscal federalism redistributing the lion's share of taxes to the federal centre, the regions were left with a serious lack of resources to spend on social protection and social security. Wide-ranging privatization and deregulation, combined with a weak taxing capacity, meant that public services (particularly in the poorer regions) became fragmentary and inadequate. As a result, private social expenditure began to dominate over public expenditure, and significant sections of society found themselves excluded from access to welfare.

Access to public goods and services (such as pre-school and higher education, health and social care) meanwhile became increasingly based on the ability to pay. More affluent groups became the key consumers of privatized services, while being reluctant to consume low-quality public services. Public provision was deliberately or spontaneously privatized. Professionals working in public institutions frequently demanded additional informal payments from their clients. In healthcare, for example, research conducted by the ROMIR centre in 2012 found that 65 per cent of Russians paid for medical services and 20 per cent of patients made informal payments to doctors. Indeed, liberalization and the increasing role of the market have not led to a reduction in informality, and resource-rich groups have a considerable advantage over the resource-poor. The former enjoy better access to networks that allow them to access good hospitals and to get their offspring into a good school or university (as well as helping them to find good jobs). According to one recent poll, among the middle classes only 40 per cent 'do not have connections that would allow them to solve all of the above problems', while among the rest of the population this figure rises to around 65 per cent (Belanovsky *et al.* 2012: 33).

While work-based identity and solidarity is weak, the key divisions in the Russian society are increasingly manifested in the field of consumption, between people who satisfy their needs privately and those who are dependent on the state. These divisions often translate into different political preferences and orientations – just as they tend to do in the West (Saunders 1986), with those who consume privately expressing a preference for a smaller state and greater individual freedoms while those who consume publicly preferring better public provision and a greater degree of redistribution.

As in Western countries, neoliberal discourse in Russia reinforces divisions between the have and have-nots by stigmatizing the poor as lacking the ability to be self-reliant and entrepreneurial, and manifesting cultural incompetence as consumers. In this discourse the urban middle classes, whose representatives sometimes also refer to themselves as members of a 'creative class' seen as the principal producer of ideas, information, and technology (Florida 2002) are constructed as superior to 'dependents' upon the state. Embracing inequality of outcomes, associating morality with self-determination and consumer choice, middle-class people have been asserting their own social and cultural distinction as well as compensating for the perceived privations that educated classes had experienced in an egalitarian Soviet society (Rivkin-Fish 2009) .

Analysts have also noted the pathologization of members of the post-Soviet working class, who – in contrast to their Soviet predecessors (who were seen as heroic builders of a future communist society) – are often perceived as culturally inadequate, backward and threatening. Internet blogs and public commentary by Moscow intellectuals are full of scathing references to Putin's voters and supporters, who are often given derogatory names of *bydlo* (cattle) or *anchousy* (anchovies). Representations of the so-called *gopniks,* low-class young men, widely regarded as unable and unwilling to conform to the norms of 'civilized' conduct on the public sphere, are based on these stigmatizing stereotypes. They are seen as conservative, ignorant and dangerously prone to violence (Stephenson 2012; Walker 2012). Other groups –such as benefit claimants, single parents or homeless people – are commonly pathologized in social welfare discourse and practices. In 'expert' pronouncements they tend to be presented as exhibiting orientations towards dependency, lack of a work ethic, predilection towards alcoholism and other 'underclass' characteristics, well-known from similar Western discourses on the undeserving poor (Iarskaya-Smirnova and Romanov 2012; Stephenson 2006).

The figure of a homeless person, for example, has become almost normalized as part of the urban landscape. For some commentators, street homeless people form a familiar background to the relatively stable and prosperous lives of the urban middle classes. The predominant representation of homelessness in the mass media is linked to the figure of a *bomzh* (a person without fixed abode), with discussion focusing on negative aspects of the person's appearance and behaviour (being dirty, looking drunk, and so on). The root causes of homelessness are very rarely addressed, and the suggested policies often address the consequences, rather than the causes of homelessness. In a process which Polish anthropologist Michal Buchowski, following Edward Said, has described as an 'orientalization' of the mind, people began to see members of certain social groups (such as domestic migrants, immigrants and unemployed) as the 'Other'. 'Otherness is dissected from an exotic context and brought home, thus displaced primitives can be found on our doorstep' (Buchowski 2006: 476). These 'losers' of post-communist transition are seen to have the wrong moral qualities; they are unable to fit into the new dynamic and productive capitalist order. Buchowski stresses that 'Creation of the inferior categories of people, an intellectual process that shares its logic with orientalizing modes of thought, legitimizes political practices, sanctions discrimination and possibly exploitation' (ibid.)

Social networks and patrimonial structures

Social divisions in Russia can only be properly understood in the context of a system in which individual social positions are embedded in traditional structures of reciprocity, favour and dependency. Although informal networks and structures can work effectively to support the well-being and interests of its members, ultimately they are destructive for wider social cohesion and social trust. For people in insecure and precarious positions, personal dependencies on their employers and patrons can lead to further vulnerability and exploitation. An example of the risks inherent in a system of occupational favours and dependencies can be seen in the social practices of the contemporary art community in Moscow, whose members are united in networks that cut across hierarchical positions, and where the better established artists, critics or curators in Moscow help their less fortunate colleagues (often people with few resources, coming from provincial areas) with work or accommodation. In return, the latter often provide low-cost or even free services, and end up in precarious, insecure employment (Chekhonadskikh 2012). Analysing flexibility and precariousness in the Russian service sector, Clement points out that flexible labour in Russia tends to be regulated by informal rules and agreements, where the rights and responsibilities of workers are not contractually fixed. 'In Russian enterprises the bosses follow the legacy of Soviet rules of conduct: "I give you permission [to work flexibly], remember my kindness"' (Clement 2007: 94).

At the governance level informal structures have been variously described as 'anti-modern networks', 'clans' or 'corporatist organizations'. Max Weber's concept of patrimonialism can also be usefully applied to this system of relations. Weber developed the concept of patrimonialism as a tool to explore systems of political authority based on kinship ties, patron–client relations and informal rules and regulations. The archetype for this power is a large traditional household. In patrimonial systems power operates on the basis of arbitrary discretion, material dependence and the personal loyalty of members of the extended quasi-kinship network (Weber 1978).

Patrimonial principles have been shown to operate in the Russian governance system alongside modern bureaucratic systems of authority. Russia demonstrates an intertwining of official hierarchies of modern state power and informal networks (see for instance Kryshtanovskaya and White 2011; Ledeneva 2013). Networks of favour and exchange always played a key role in Soviet society, and despite growing individualism, continue to be highly important for post-Soviet citizens. As Ledeneva demonstrates, 'Networks on the top operate on familiar principles of informality that impose certain norms of reciprocity and informal constraints on people in official positions: blurred boundaries between friendship and the use of friendship; helping a friends at the expense of public/corporate resources or access; recruitment into networks according to a particular logic – it could be loyalty, dependence or transgression/compromised recruit – rather than the logic of competition and professionalism' (Ledeneva 2009: 269).

Patrimonial orientations, coupled with a lack of traditions of occupational solidarity and civic activism, explain a lack of labour activism and the passive position of trade unions in collective bargaining and defence of rights. Although there are some exceptions, trade unions can generally be seen as a part of a patrimonial system rather than agents of labour cohesion and solidarity. The Federation of Independent Trade Unions (FNPR), the main trade union organization, has been largely absent from active protest (and indeed participated in the suppression of independent protest) and allied themselves with Putin's United Russia Party and the Putin–Medvedev government. Research shows that Russian employees rarely identify themselves as part of an occupational group that has collective interests and rights. Large trade union organizations have shown themselves to be reluctant to challenge employers or formulate alternatives to existing social policy, instead primarily occupying themselves with the organization of workers' leisure and cultivating informal sociability. In many instances employers fight together with the workers for concessions from the authorities. A system in which employees and managers form personalized relationships and dependencies has prevailed over the traditional model in which the trade union's role focuses on the self-organization of labour and employment rights. This has also contributed to high wage differentials among workers in the same enterprise. Trade unions tend to engage in social partnership rather than adversarial practices; young people do not find the unions attractive and avoid participating in their activities (Salmenniemi 2008).

Nevertheless, new trends have also been emerging since the mid-2000s, with industrial protest starting to show more traditional patterns of strikes and labour–management bargaining. Research by the Higher School of Economics, conducted in 2010, has revealed signs of new thinking in industrial relations, with emerging stronger demands, leadership and a readiness for active bargaining, particularly in large companies in profitable sectors that are integrated into the global economy (Vinogradova *et al.* 2012).

Exclusionary processes

Increasing prosperity for those people able to take advantage of Russia's economic growth and entry into the global market came together with new exclusionary processes. The deliberate dismantling of institutional welfare and the rise of informal, casualized and precarious employment left many people struggling to find sustainable livelihoods. In a society which, far from providing equal access to opportunities to self-directing individuals (as envisioned by liberal reformers), is enmeshed in corrupt, self-serving or inaccessible networks, people who lack access to these networks find themselves in a spiral of exclusion. But being poor undermines people's social capital and erodes their connections with informal support systems (Manning and Tikhonova 2004). Family and kinship networks, which facilitate the exchange of information and connections, are still vital for finding stable jobs. For residents of economically depressed areas, success in their attempts to migrate to other regions or find better employment are predicated on having such personal connections and ties, and this seriously limits the opportunities for people (including young people) in terms of geographical and social mobility.

Social exclusion did exist in the Soviet Union but it had different causes and manifestations. Soviet modernity – similarly to Western modernity – was associated with attempts to 'order' society and purge those groups that were deemed redundant to the modernist project. The Soviet welfare state operated a system of differentiation and distinction, whereby only productive categories of citizenry were given full social rights, while others were persecuted and segregated. Under Lenin and Stalin, the state conducted policies of exclusion and marginalization of various groups that did not fit into the official social structure such as rich peasants (*kulaks)* and the so-called 'former people' – aristocrats, Tsarist army officers and police and the clergy (Fitzpatrick 2005). Later on, the Soviet Union pursued the policies of widespread institutionalization and isolation of

204 Society and Social Divisions in Russia

orphans and disabled people, criminalization of homosexuals, segrega-
tion and incarceration of alcoholics and vagrants. At the same time, inclu-
sivist structures of modernity (Bauman 2000) offered stable opportunities
for working-class employment.

The Soviet economy operated in conditions of mainly administratively
controlled labour mobility and a regulated job market. Informal
economic activity did exist, but even it was normally connected to the
operation (sometimes in the form of additional underground production)
of the enterprise, collective farm or scientific institution. Nearly full
employment, strict administrative control, tight local communities organized around enterprises and collectivistic ethics all precluded social and
economic disaffiliation on any large scale.

The crisis of the Soviet industrial regime of production, and growing
social divisions, have led to new exclusionary processes. Marginalization
and informalization, alongside continuing Soviet-era restrictions on freedom of movement in the form of residency permits, have resulted in the
progressive exclusion of significant segments of the population from the
distributive institutions of mainstream society: the labour and housing
markets, access to education, public healthcare, social benefits and
pensions. Social groups that are particularly vulnerable to social exclusion include families with many children, single parents, migrants, the
elderly, unskilled workers and unemployed.

In the 1990s, Russia received significant flows of Russophones who
were fleeing from discrimination and economic collapse in the newly
independent republics. Several waves of migration resulted from conflict
and war in the Caucasus and Central Asia. These processes coincided
with the return of previously deported peoples and labour migration to
Russia from – in particular – Ukraine, Moldova, Belarus, Armenia,
Azerbaijan, Georgia and Tajikistan. At the same time Russia became a
part of the global migration system as a final, or transit, destination for
hundreds of thousands of migrants from the 'far abroad', including
refugees, undocumented migrants and temporary economic migrants
from Asia, Africa and the Middle East and such countries as Afghanistan,
Pakistan, China and Vietnam. Altogether, according to the 2002 census,
about eleven million people arrived in Russia between 1989 and 2002.

Immigration flows have declined significantly in the 2000s. Especially
pronounced was the fall in the numbers of ethnic Russians. At the same
time, the numbers of temporary labour migrants (both legal and illegal)
have risen, reaching, according to some estimates, around 4 million
people. The majority of immigrants came from the member countries of
the Commonwealth of Independent States (CIS). There has also been
considerable internal labour migration within Russia, particularly from
the republics of the North Caucasus (which are subjects of the Russian

Federation). Hostility to ethnic migrants has become a widespread phenomenon. The Russian public demonstrates especially negative attitudes towards migrants from the North Caucasus and the republics of Transcaucasia and Central Asia. According to the Levada Center (conducted on a representative sample of the Russian population in 2013) the slogan 'Russia for the Russians' was supported by 66 per cent of those interviewed (Sokolov 2013). An ethnic pogrom in Kondopoga in 2006, a Russian nationalist demonstration in Manezh square in Moscow in 2010, and an ethnic pogrom in the Moscow district of Biryulevo in 2013 were all provoked by the perceived inability of the law-enforcement bodies to protect Russians from crime committed by migrants from the North Caucasus. At the same time ethnic nationals from the Caucasus and Central Asia are routinely subjected to xenophobic violence, often carried out by groups of youths.

The atmosphere of intolerance is exacerbated by the activities of the law-enforcement agencies, which conduct 'special operations' and 'campaigns' against migrants. These operations usually involve checking the documents of 'foreign-looking' people, accompanied by extortion and racial abuse. Labour migrants (the so-called *gastarbaitery*) are often employed without official contracts, and are prone to extreme exploitation and abuse. Since 2002, every immigrant needs to have a migration card and a work permit in order to get employment. In practice, though, most immigrant workers (from 70 per cent to 90 per cent, according to different estimates) are employed illegally. They tend to work in construction and the service sector, where employees are often paid in cash at the end of the working day. Employers may refuse to pay, sometimes justifying this by citing unsatisfactory work, sometimes without any justification. They may also take away documents, effectively denying them any opportunity to leave their jobs or go back home.

Homelessness is a stark manifestation of social exclusion, particularly when it takes the form of street homelessness. Despite the efforts of the government to collect data on the Russian homeless population during the population censuses of 2002 and 2010, there is no reliable information on the total numbers of homeless people and their profiles. Available data collected by NGOs and social researchers shows that the causes of homelessness, as elsewhere in the world, represent a combination of family conflicts, loss of connection to home through long absence or incarceration. The privatization of housing in Russia has led to many people (often vulnerable old people or alcoholics) being cheated or forced out of their housing by criminals. Also, according to the 2005 Housing Code, people can be evicted from their dwellings for a number of reasons, including non-payment of rent and antisocial behaviour. In Russian conditions, the crucial factor in street homelessness is often a loss of supportive ties within informal social networks (Hojdestrand 2009; Stephenson 2006).

The main problem preventing the reintegration of homeless people remains the Russian system of registration at the place of residence. This system links most rights of citizenship (including employment, health-care, rights to social security, voting and even marriage) to registration. People lacking passports with a residency stamp effectively become non-citizens. Some cities (including Moscow and St Petersburg) have provi-sions allowing local authorities to give housing to those ex-prisoners who have lost their municipal accommodation as a result of incarceration. There is a system of social hotels and shelters (with a stay limited to six months). But these facilities only accept Russian citizens who can prove a local connection. A homeless person needs to prove his or her past resi-dency status in the area in order to gain access to these facilities (this requirement is only relaxed in extremely harsh winters). Although many Russian and international NGOs provide help to homeless people, they can very rarely offer them some form of accommodation (and even then it is temporary accommodation for limited categories of homeless people such as ex-convicts or Big-Issue type magazine sellers).With the increas-ing privatization of urban space in Russia, cities are tightening the noose on homeless people. They are progressively denied access to communal and residential spaces, and local authorities try to contain them in degraded facilities of institutional care (often outside the city borders).

The problem of 'social orphans' has also become a matter of serious national and international concern, and was brought into the limelight with the prohibition by law in 2012 of the adoption of Russian children by US citizens and attempts by the Russian government to facilitate domestic adoption. According to official statistics, at the end of 2012 there were 650,000 'orphans' in Russia. The majority of these children have one or both parents living but are deprived of parental rights. Although attempts are made to develop a system of social work with trou-bled families, the state's response to the problem is increasingly associated with the removal of children from the family and the termination of parental rights, with a subsequent 'guardianship' by relatives or the insti-tutionalization of children in state homes. Adoption and foster care remain the least frequent options (Schmidt 2012).

Children from troubled families often join the ranks of child runaways, who live and/or work on the streets. Current displays of youth dislocation – runaway children sleeping on underground pipes, teenagers begging or washing cars, young girls soliciting sex, groups of youngsters roaming the streets in school hours – were all previously absent from the Russian urban landscape, except in times of war and social catastrophe. Research shows that the parents of these children tend to occupy the lowest positions on the social scale and to be in insecure and low-paid employment. Poverty and insecure employment encourage family disruption, and can result in explosive and erratic parent–children interaction or be associated with child neglect and abuse. On the streets, children survive by begging, episodic stealing and doing odd jobs. Some attempt to join informal and criminal communities where they hope to find better protection, but where instead they find greater risk and exploitation. Some join the structures of organized prostitution. Other young people (for example teenage boys who have had direct contact with adult criminals in the past or had a spell in under-age detention) attempt to join street criminal gangs and develop connections with adult criminal groups (Stephenson 2008). Although local authorities are developing systems of outreach work (often in cooperation with NGOs), the main response has been to take children off the street and either place them back with their parents, or send them to children's homes.

Social divisions and civil society: towards new civic solidarity?

While the middle classes have better access to market-based goods and the economic and social capital that allows them to get access to better healthcare, education and jobs, low-income groups have been using the voluntary sector for assistance. The Russian voluntary sector only emerged in the late 1980s and early 1990s following decades of state monopoly. However, this sector (particularly when it comes to organizations working in the area of welfare) has been criticized for its detachment from the policy-making process and for being the preserve of the educated classes. Among the suggested explanations for the failures of the voluntary sector are widespread political apathy and opportunistic double standards, as well as an acceptance by the public of state paternalism. Some analysts speak about a capture of civil society by middle-class professionals, who have been disproportionately represented in voluntary sector organizations, and who have sought to appropriate it and turn it into the preserve of educated experts and specialists. Voluntary organizations in the welfare arena rarely involve their clients in helping themselves or assist in their self-organization. The public is generally vaguely aware about the sector, and does not widely participate in its activities or support it by donations.

The policy of successive Russian governments under Putin and Medvedev has been to include voluntary sector organizations (mainly those working in the area of welfare) into state-led corporatist arrangements, while suppressing independent organizations (predominantly those in the area of human rights). In an attempt by the state to establish further control over the sector, 2006 legislation – widely known as the 'NGO Law' – obliged each organization to present extensive documentation to the controlling authorities regarding its founders, staff, activities and finances, and report all foreign funding. Perceptions within the Kremlin that the so-called 'colour' revolutions were organized and funded by international NGOs and agencies, and that similar influences affected the 2011/12 anti-government protests, gave rise to a series of repressive pieces of legislation, designed to control and 'license' civil society organizations. In July 2012, the Russian parliament passed new amendments to the 2006 Law, according to which NGOs with foreign funding had to declare themselves 'foreign agents' and were required to report every quarter. This has made the activities of NGOs receiving foreign funding practically impossible.

In another development, in December 2012, in response to the passing by the US Congress of a "Sergei Magnitsky Act', the Russian parliament passed a law commonly known as the 'Anti-Magnitsky Law'. Among other provisions, this law prohibited NGOs that participated in political activity on Russian territory from receiving donations from American citizens or organizations, or from having American citizens on their staff. With a dearth of domestic funding sources, independent NGOs found themselves in an extremely difficult situation. Although the government provides grants and subsidies (mostly via the Public Chamber), they are predominantly given to those NGOs that provide social services in partnership with state organizations. Visits to NGOs across Russia by 'inspectors' from the state prosecution service, demanding documentation on all their staff and activities, have been interpreted as an attempt to further undermine the morale and capacity of the voluntary sector.

Recently, however, new developments have emerged within Russian civil society, which can be seen as a revival of independent public activism. It reflects people's need for communal life, for participation in social networks built on trust and solidarity rather than imposed group loyalty and exploitation. Increasingly, rather than joining professional NGOs, people form independent activist networks and groups of volunteers. New civic initiatives organized around both political and non-political projects are coming to life. Despite the defeat of the 2011/12 protest movement, new forms of civic self-organization are taking hold. The informal protests in the 1990s–2000s (by pensioners, home owners, residents of ecological disaster areas and others) have often been seen as expressing concrete interests and everyday experiences, with participants having little engagement with larger political issues (Evans 2012). But while addressing concrete issues, civic activists and volunteers are increasingly challenging the state's ability to solve acute societal problems – in the spheres of housing and infrastructure, healthcare and protection of the environment, and the corruption and brutality of the police.

These developments have been facilitated by the proliferation of internet-based social networks. As we saw in Chapter 8, recent years have shown a rapid increase of the numbers of internet users in Russia. According to the Public Opinion Foundation (FOM), by winter 2013 around 55 per cent of Russians used the internet (up from 10 per cent in 2004). Gradually social networks emerged as the nodes around which new communities could be formed. While throughout the 2000s, members of the intelligentsia were forming a web-based civil society as an alternative for people displaced from public life, a kind of web-based samizdat, by 2010 they had become instruments of political communication and mobilization. A number of political and non-political movements were formed. The 'Blue buckets' movement emerged in protest against a practice where vehicles equipped with blue lights (*migalki*) routinely flouted road rules and made ordinary drivers wait for hours in traffic jams while official motorcades rushed through. Activists began to draw attention to this practice in an imaginative way by installing blue buckets (in lieu of *migalki*) on the roofs of their cars. Armed with video cameras, they have recorded and then publicized cases of traffic violations and fatal accidents caused by officials and heads of corporations.

The volunteering movement also began to play an important role in public life. The Liza Alert community, for instance, organizes searches for missing persons (often children, old people or mentally ill people) in urban areas and in forests. Another example of voluntary activism is a movement to protect the Khimki forest on the outskirts of Moscow from a plan to build a motorway through its territory. From the start this movement, led by Evgeniya Chirikova, involved local residents who sought remedies for specific issue that directly affected them and their families. Eventually it began to attract activists concerned about destruction of environment and lack of accountability and democratic control over the making of public policy and those responsible for it.

In July 2012, volunteers were the first on the scene to provide help to the victims of flooding in the town of Krymsk in Krasnodar region. The authorities failed to warn residents about the coming flood. As a result of the disaster, 172 people died and 34,000 people were affected. Hundreds of volunteers united to help Krymsk residents, by collecting and distributing food, medicines and clothes and helping with rebuilding the houses. Another new feature of public mobilization is a movement to build a network of independent citizen-observers at the elections. By April 2013, volunteers were registered in 10 per cent of the country's electoral districts. According to the Public Opinion Foundation (FOM), 36 per cent of respondents in a 2012 survey of ten Russian cities were prepared to work in a public organization, association or group of activists of this kind.

The era of *glamur* associated with the 2000s has now ended, as has a decade of stability under Putin. There is a desire for social change, although different groups of population show different concerns and aspirations. The inability of the educated middle classes, unhappy with the political dominance of bureaucracy and an absence of civil and political freedoms and rights, to connect with a wider population more concerned about their livelihoods and lack of social protection, has been blamed for the weakness of opposition to the Putin regime. But if traditional Russian concerns with *proizvol* (unaccountability and lawlessness of the authorities) are linked with a new civic consciousness and desire to breach rather than reinforce social divisions, this may form an effective political platform for change.

Chapter 13

Foreign Policy

MARGOT LIGHT

In the first few years after Russia became independent, its foreign policy tended to be incoherent. This reduced its effectiveness, limited its influence, and confused Russian citizens and their international partners. Incoherence is not uncommon in the foreign policies of new states and, in many ways, Russia was a new state and the 1993 Constitution was very different from the constitution in operation when it became independent. Not surprisingly, therefore, Russia had the problems all new states have of setting up foreign policy institutions, establishing how they should relate to one another and deciding what goals the state should pursue in its relations with the outside world.

It is also not unusual for the foreign policy of a country that has lost an empire to be unpredictable. It was unclear that Russia *had* lost an empire, but there was general agreement that Russia had lost its identity when the USSR disintegrated. There was also confusion about Russia's status in the international political system. Attempts to establish Russia's identity and status affected the coherence of foreign policy, and so did the numerous concepts and doctrines adopted by the government to define its foreign, military and security policies.

By 1996, although discordant voices could still be heard, the contours of a more predictable foreign policy had been established. In Vladimir Putin's first presidential term, predictability and pragmatism characterized Russia's foreign policy. However, in his second term, he adopted a more forceful approach, and since then assertiveness has characterized Russian foreign policy.

The first section of this chapter argues that the initial incoherence of Russian foreign policy can be explained by the domestic context – the structure and processes of decision-making and the establishment of a new identity. The following two sections explore Russia's policy, first towards the other Soviet successor states (Russian policy-makers initially referred to them as the 'near abroad'), and then towards the 'far abroad' (other foreign states). They illustrate how initial incoherence was replaced by a more stable and then a more assertive foreign policy. The

211

chapter concludes with a brief consideration of how Russian foreign policy is likely to develop in the next few years.

The domestic context of Russian foreign policy

The initial incoherence of Russian foreign policy was caused by the structural features and processes of decision-making and exacerbated by confusion about Russia's identity and its role in the world.

Foreign policy decision-making: structures and processes

Foreign policy coherence requires a well-organized and widely accepted division of responsibility with clear channels of communication between institutions and individuals. When the USSR disintegrated, the division of responsibility between government institutions in Russia was unclear and often contentious, and there were no established channels of communication.

The 1993 Constitution gave the president predominance in foreign policy. He is responsible for determining the framework of policy, representing Russia abroad, appointing diplomats and Security Council members, and conducting international negotiations. He heads the Security Council, which is responsible for assessing the challenges and threats Russia faces. The Ministry of Foreign Affairs (MFA) is responsible for the conduct of foreign relations. Both houses of parliament must ratify international treaties, and the Duma has the right to scrutinize foreign policy, while the Federation Council has jurisdiction over the use of Russian troops abroad. However, the constitution does not clarify how authority is divided between the government and the president, and it encourages a proliferation of administrative structures serving the president. In 1995, there were legislative changes to make the power ministers, including the MFA and the Ministry of Defence (MoD), directly subordinate to the president.

The incoherence of Russian policy in the 1990s was exacerbated by the president's personality and management style. President Yeltsin's aides and advisers often made statements on his behalf without coordinating them with the MFA, while he himself often made impromptu policy announcements, taking his own staff and his interlocutors by surprise. Moreover, MFA and MoD statements sometimes contradicted official policy. Yeltsin frequently reprimanded his ministers, including the foreign minister, in public. This undermined the foreign minister's status, making him less credible abroad, and it weakened the MFA's authority.

Box 13.1 Russian foreign ministers, 1990 to date		
Appointed by	*Name*	*Dates of appointment*
President Yeltsin	Andrei Kozyrev	June 1990 (as foreign minister of RSFSR) to January 1996
	Yevgenii Primakov	January 1996 to September 1998, when he was appointed Prime Minister
	Igor Ivanov	September 1998 to March 2004
President Putin	Sergei Lavrov	March 2004 to May 2008
President Medvedev	Sergei Lavrov	May 2008 to May 2012
President Putin	Sergei Lavrov	May 2012 to present

When Yevgenii Primakov replaced Andrei Kozyrev as foreign minister in 1996, the status of the MFA rose (a list of foreign ministers over the whole period is provided in Box 13.1). Moreover, the structural problems began to improve; the relationship between the various ministries with foreign policy interests was gradually sorted out, cooperation between different branches of state improved, and channels of communication became established and accepted. Nevertheless, complaints continued to be heard that policy was poorly coordinated and in 2011 President Dmitri Medvedev found it necessary to issue an Executive Order reiterating that the Foreign Ministry was responsible for coordinating Russian foreign policy (President of Russia 2011).

In the 1990s, domestic political conflict aggravated the incoherence of Russian foreign policy. Foreign policy became an arena in which wider political struggles took place and parliamentary deputies frequently used foreign policy in their conflict with the president, for example, by adopting resolutions that appeared to contradict Russia's official foreign policy, or by postponing ratifying treaties.

President Putin's management and foreign policy style was very different. Although he was a more overt nationalist (he calls it patriotism) and even more insistent about Russia's great power credentials, he recognized the relationship between the economy and international power. Moreover, he was aware that the inconsistencies in Russian foreign policy harmed Russia's national interests. Putin set about centralizing power and reasserting the authority of the federal government. His policies made the Duma more subservient to the presidency and the conflict between the

Box 13.2   The Russian foreign policy decision-making process

President's office	Government	Legislature
President	Prime Minister	State Duma Committee for International Affairs
President's Aide for Foreign Policy and International Relations	Ministry of Foreign Affairs	State Duma Committee for Defence
President's Aide for Issues of the Development of Relations with the European Union	Ministry of Defence	State Duma Committee for Security
Presidential Directorate on Foreign Policy	Ministry of Economics and Trade	State Duma Committee for CIS Affairs and relations with Compatriots
Security Council	Federal Security Service (FSB)	Federation Council Foreign Affairs Committee
Presidential Commission for Military Technology Cooperation of the Russian Federation with Foreign States	Foreign Intelligence Service	Federation Council Committee on Defence and Security
State Council	Various coordinating committees	Federation Council Committee on the Commonwealth of Independent States

legislature and the executive came to an end. By 2004, United Russia, a party loyal to the presidency, dominated the Duma and presided over the chairmanship of all its committees, including those that deal with foreign affairs. Although the Duma and its committees continue to be involved in the foreign policy-making process and so, to a lesser extent, does the Federation Council, both invariably support the president's policy. The MFA remains responsible for the conduct of Russia's foreign policy, but during Putin's second presidential term particularly, it was the president and his apparatus who decided what the policy should be (see Box 13.2; for a full discussion see White in Allison, Light and White 2006: 21–44).

Both the 2008 and 2013 Foreign Policy Concepts set out who is responsible for what aspect of foreign policy. They specify that the Security Council assesses the challenges and threats Russia faces, the president directs foreign policy and represents Russia on the international stage, while the Federal Assembly provides legislative support, and the government implements Russia's foreign policy and is responsible for coordinating the foreign policy activities of other executive bodies (President of Russia 2008, Ministry of Foreign Affairs 2013).

Although the 2008 Foreign Policy Concept did not mention a function for the prime minister in Russian foreign policy, Putin retained a prominent foreign policy role when he was prime minister during Medvedev's presidency, appointing an independent foreign policy division to serve the cabinet and prime minister (*Itar-Tass Daily*, 31 May 2008).

Identity and concepts

In addition to the structural, personal and political factors that caused confusion, there was also uncertainty about Russia's identity. Most Russians found it difficult to accept that some areas of the USSR were no longer part of Russia. In part this was simply a question of nostalgia, but there was also genuine confusion about Russia's role in the world. The establishment of new, independent states separating Russia from the rest of Europe revived an old debate: was Russia part of Europe, or had the loss of empire turned it into an Asian or Eurasian power?

There was also a question of Russia's status in the international system. Russia had inherited the Soviet Union's international treaty obligations, its seat on the United Nations Security Council (UNSC) and its diplomatic institutions and nuclear capabilities. In many respects, therefore, Russia inherited its international status. But it had few of the traditional attributes of power: its economy was close to collapse, it did not have an extensive sphere of influence, and although still vast, it was far smaller than the USSR. Russia was clearly not a superpower; indeed, it was questionable whether it was a great power. Yet to ordinary people as well as politicians, it was unthinkable that Russia could be anything less than this. The insistence that Russia should be regarded as a great power became an important theme in foreign policy statements and discussions and it remains an important driver of foreign policy. In the 1990s, however, the mismatch between the self-perception of great power status and the reality of Russia's declining power contributed to the incoherence of foreign policy.

Many intellectuals believed that Russia's identity could be established by defining its foreign policy principles. They demanded that the government should provide a framework for its foreign policy. By April 1993, when the first Foreign Policy Concept was adopted, a broad consensus had been reached about Russia's status and its foreign policy priorities. The concept asserted a prominent international role for Russia, particularly in the 'near abroad', and revealed considerable suspicion of Western intentions towards Russia. The first Military Doctrine, published in October 1993, adopted a harsher stance about Russia's national interests than the Foreign Policy Concept.

The view of Russia's place in the world expressed in these documents did not reduce Russian foreign policy incoherence. First, foreign policy statements made by various politicians and officials did not reflect the contents of either document. Second, there seemed to be little relationship between the priorities set out in the documents and the practice of Russian policy. A series of subsequent official doctrines and concepts compounded the confusion. A National Security Strategy was adopted in December 1997, for example, only to be replaced by a new one in January 2000 which, in turn, was replaced in 2009. A new Military Doctrine and a new Foreign Policy Concept were adopted in June 2000. The Foreign Policy Concept was replaced in 2008 and again in 2013, while a new Military Doctrine was adopted in 2011. There are also Concepts for Scientific and Technical Cooperation (2000) and Border Cooperation (2001), a Maritime Doctrine (2004), and a Strategy for Policy towards members of the Commonwealth of Independent States (2005) (texts of the various concepts may be consulted at the Ministry of Foreign Affairs and Security Council websites www.mid.ru and www.scrf.gov.ru). The later documents were responses to perceived changes in Russia's internal and external environment, but what alarmed Russia's foreign partners was that they indicated a significant hardening of Russian foreign policy. The feature of the 2000 National Security Concept that aroused most anxiety outside Russia was that it envisaged looser conditions under which Russia might resort to nuclear weapons. For Russians themselves, the most important feature of the 2000 National Security Concept and Military Doctrines was that they envisaged the use of military force inside the country, retroactively legitimizing army action in Chechnya.

Western policy-makers were confused. They could understand the external factors that made Russians feel more vulnerable, although they disagreed that they represented a threat to Russian security. But the new documents defined domestic problems (such as the critical state of the economy, crime and the absence of a rule-based state) as far more threatening to Russian security than external factors. These domestic threats had nothing to do with foreign countries, so Western policy-makers could not understand why they required a more assertive foreign policy stance.

Ironically, by 2008, Russia was actively pursuing a more assertive foreign policy, yet the 2008 and 2013 foreign policies are more benign than previous concepts. They list a series of general threats to world order, for example, but do not specify particular threats. They also maintain that Russia has become strong enough to pursue an independent foreign policy, as well as to resolve regional and international problems. The 2013 Concept calls for the use of 'soft power' to increase Russia's international influence (Ministry of Foreign Affairs 2013).

According to the 2000 Foreign Policy Concept, Russian foreign policy is based on consistency and predictability and on mutually advantageous pragmatism. Pragmatism has remained a recurring theme of the foreign policy statements of Putin and his government. The 2013 Foreign Policy Concept reiterates that 'Russia's foreign policy is transparent, predictable and pragmatic' (Ministry of Foreign Affairs 2013: II, 25). Another international political principle frequently extolled by Russian officials is non-interference in the domestic affairs of other states. It is mentioned six times in the 2013 Concept, which is particularly critical of 'military interventions and other forms of interference.... carried out on the pretext of implementing the concept of "responsibility to protect"' (ibid.: III, 31).

It was clear, however, that the considerable clout that Russia acquired from its vast energy resources as energy prices rose changed the definition of what was considered pragmatic (in the sense of achievable). The tone of official foreign policy statements sharpened and they were frequently perceived to be assertive rather than pragmatic. In a speech at a security conference in Munich in February 2007 that resonated throughout the West, for example, Putin insisted that Russia, 'a country with a history that spans more than a thousand years,' would pursue an independent foreign policy, and he appeared to threaten that Russia might re-arm itself with intermediate-range nuclear missiles (abolished by an historic Soviet–American treaty in 1987) in response to US plans to deploy anti-ballistic missiles. Similarly, after the Georgian conflict in 2008, President Medvedev promised to protect the lives and dignity of Russian citizens *'wherever they [were]'*, and asserted that there were regions in which Russia had 'privileged interests' (*Rossiiskaya gazeta*, 1 September 2008: 1; emphasis added).

Russian policy towards the 'near abroad'

The mismatch between what policy-makers said and what they did has been particularly striking with regard to Russia's relations with its immediate neighbours. Strengthening relations with the countries of the Commonwealth of Independent States (CIS) has always been proclaimed a priority, 'the most important part of the Russian Federation's foreign policy' (President of Russia 2007). The 2013 Foreign Policy Concept, like all its predecessors, emphasizes the importance of 'strengthening of the

CIS as a basis for enhancing regional interaction' (Ministry of Foreign Affairs 2013). In practice, however, little multilateral integration has been achieved, and Russia's bilateral relations with its neighbours have frequently been tense, culminating in a short-lived war with Georgia in 2008 and then a hostile confrontation with Ukraine in 2014, after Crimea voted to become part of the Russian Federation and its eastern and predominantly Russian-speaking regions began to assert their independence.

Russia and multilateral relations in the CIS

By 1993, the CIS consisted of all the successor states except the Baltic republics. However, Ukraine has never ratified the agreement, while in 1995 Turkmenistan declared itself only an associate member and Georgia left the organization in August 2008. The CIS has an elaborate institutional structure to further inter-state cooperation and integration, and to develop and strengthen 'relations of friendship, good neighbourliness, inter-ethnic accord, trust and mutual understanding and cooperation' between its members (Preamble, Charter of the Commonwealth of Independent States, 1993). However, few of these aims have been realized.

One reason why the CIS has had limited success in integrating its members is that it does not have supranational powers. Not only does it operate on the basis of consensus; it also permits any member to opt out of a decision to which it objects. A second reason is that in size and in military and economic power, Russia is by far the largest member. Consequently, even the most enthusiastic participants fear Russian hegemony. A third reason is that the variable pace at which the successor states have reformed their economies makes integration very difficult. The main obstruction, however, has been Russian ambivalence. Although Russian policy-makers frequently support integration verbally, they have done little to promote it.

A succession of vehicles for integration has been created, starting with an Economic Union in 1993 (Ukraine became an associate member in 1994), a Free Trade Area in 1994 (ratified by all members except Russia), and a Belarus–Kazakhstan–Russia Customs Union in 1995 that was renamed the Free Trade Zone in 1996. It became the Eurasian Economic Community (EurAsEc) in 2000, with Belarus, Kazakhstan, Kyrgyzstan, Russia and Tajikistan as full members (Uzbekistan joined in 2005), with Moldova, Ukraine and Armenia obtaining observer status in 2002–3. Until 2010, none of these vehicles resulted in a functioning free-trade regime or customs union, however, primarily because of Russia's insistence on a long list of exclusions and quotas.

Russia has been more enthusiastic about the collective defence of the CIS. A Collective Security Treaty was signed in Tashkent in 1992 by Russia, Belarus, and Armenia (Moldova, Ukraine and Turkmenistan acceded in 1993, but effectively seceded when the Treaty was renewed in 1999). Five of the six signatories agreed to establish joint peacekeeping forces; in effect, however, CIS peacekeeping forces are primarily Russian, raising the suspicion in the CIS and more widely that Russia has neo-imperialist intentions. A treaty providing for the collective defence of the Commonwealth's external borders was concluded in May 1995, but Azerbaijan, Moldova, Turkmenistan, Ukraine and Uzbekistan did not accede to it, nor did they join the treaty establishing a common air defence system in February 1996 (by 1998, however, Turkmenistan, Ukraine and Uzbekistan had joined the latter).

The existence of a number of parallel multilateral regional organizations suggests that Russian policy-makers are not alone in being ambivalent about the CIS. The Central Asian states, for example, are members of the Central Asian Cooperation Organization (Russia joined in 2004; in 2005 the member states decided to merge CACO with EurAsEc), of the Economic Cooperation Organization (Azerbaijan is also a member) and also, with the exception of Turkmenistan, of the Shanghai Cooperation Organization (SCO, which includes Russia and the People's Republic of China). There is also an Organization of Black Sea Economic Cooperation, consisting of the littoral states, as well as Armenia and Azerbaijan. In 1997, the four countries that have been most resistant to closer CIS integration, Azerbaijan, Georgia, Moldova and Ukraine (joined between 1999 and 2005 by Uzbekistan), established GUAM as a counterweight to Russia's perceived hegemonic ambitions in the post-Soviet space.

President Putin reduced the gap between Russia's rhetoric about integration and its policy. On his initiative, for example, the six original Tashkent Treaty members formed a rapid reaction force in May 2001, primarily to deal with incursions into Central Asia by Islamic militants. The CIS (minus Turkmenistan) also established an Anti-Terrorist Centre in Bishkek in September that year. In 2001 Kyrgyzstan, Tajikistan and Uzbekistan granted the USA and its allies access to their bases for the 'war on terrorism' in Afghanistan (Uzbekistan cancelled the agreement in 2005), raising the prospect that Russia would no longer exercise sole influence in Central Asia. However, in November 2003 Russia opened an air force base at Kant in Kyrgyzstan, just a few kilometres from the Ganci air base (at Manas international airport) of the US-led coalition forces. Moreover, in 2002 the Tashkent Treaty was upgraded to the Collective Security Treaty Organization (Uzbekistan suspended its membership in 2012), which regularly conducts military exercises in which a number of members participate.

In September 2003, again in response to a Russian proposal, the presidents of Russia, Belarus, Ukraine and Kazakhstan agreed to form a Single Economic Space, which was envisaged as progressing in three stages, from a free-trade regime to a customs union, and finally to a Single Economic Space in 2007 with freedom of movement for services, capital and workforce (CIS Countries Legislation Database 2003). It took until 2007, however, for the first agreements to be signed on creating the customs union between Russia, Belarus and Kazakhstan by 2010 (*RIA Novosti* 25 January 2005). Although Russian analysts predicted that 'operation CIS' would be a major objective of Putin's second term (Trenin 2004), progress was not much faster than it had been in the previous decade. But in October 2011, Putin launched a new integration effort, publishing plans for the creation of a Eurasian Union by 2015 (Putin 2011). A Single Economic Space would be launched on 1 January 2012, followed by the establishment of a Eurasian Economic Commission on 1 July 2012. So far, only Russia, Belarus and Kazakhstan are members of the Single Economic Space, but Kyrgyzstan has applied to join it. Considerable pressure – unsuccessful so far – has been applied to Ukraine to follow suit.

While there has been more progress within the customs union and the Single Economic Space than in previous integration efforts, most observers agree that the evolution towards a fully fledged Eurasian Union is likely to be very difficult (Dragneva and Wolczuk 2012).

Russia and internal and inter-state conflicts in the CIS

When the USSR disintegrated in 1991, three violent conflicts were already taking place in the South Caucasus, and three more soon erupted in Tajikistan, Georgia and Moldova. Russia became involved both in peacekeeping and in attempting to mediate between the conflicting parties, laying it open to accusations of using or instigating the conflicts to further its own neo-imperialist goals.

There was no controversy about the role of Russian border and army troops in Tajikistan. By 1997, the Russian government had helped to mediate a peace agreement. Following an Islamist insurgency in 1999 that initially targeted Kyrgyzstan (Uzbekistan was the ultimate goal), there was little pressure on Russia from the Central Asian governments to withdraw its troops.

Russia was directly involved in the conflict that erupted when the Moldovan region of Transdniestria declared its independence from Moldova in 1992. Soldiers from the Russian 14th Army stationed in the area were accused of fighting with the separatists. When a cease-fire was agreed in June 1992, Russian troops were entrusted with keeping the peace. Protracted negotiations have failed to resolve the issue of

Transdniestria's future status. In 2004, the Organisation for Security and Cooperation in Europe (OSCE) proposed a federative solution, but Transdniestria insisted on a confederation. Negotiations resumed in 2011, so far without producing a result acceptable to all. A constant bone of contention between Russia and the West is the failure of Russia to fulfil an undertaking made to the OSCE in 1999 to withdraw its troops and military equipment from Transdniestria (Wolff 2012)

The conflicts in the South Caucasus, over the right of minorities to self-determination, erupted when the central governments reduced the degree of autonomy the disputed areas had enjoyed under the Soviet constitution. In Nagorno-Karabakh, a predominantly Armenian enclave within Azerbaijan, the conflict escalated into a war between Armenia and Azerbaijan during which Armenia annexed the Azerbaijani territory that had previously separated Nagorno-Karabakh from Armenia itself. Although there has been a cease-fire since 1994, regular negotiations by the 'Minsk Group' of the OSCE (which includes Russia) have not resolved the conflict (Pashaeva 2012).

There were three separate conflicts in Georgia. The first, essentially a struggle for political power, began before the USSR disintegrated and ended when Eduard Shevardnadze, the former Soviet Minister of Foreign Affairs, returned to become President of Georgia in March 1992. The other two were secessionist conflicts between the central Georgian government and Abkhazia and South Ossetia. Under CIS auspices and with some UN cooperation, Russia intervened directly in the conflict between Georgia and the Autonomous Republic of Abkhazia, sending peacekeeping forces in September 1993 after Georgian troops (and the ethnic Georgian population of Abkhazia) had been evicted from Abkhazia and the Georgian state appeared on the brink of collapse. In South Ossetia, after two years of sporadic fighting, a cease-fire was agreed, policed by Georgian, Russian and South Ossetian troops. Attempts to mediate a resolution to the conflicts between Georgia and the two secessionist areas constantly failed because, as in Nagorno-Karabakh, a mutually acceptable compromise on the future status of the two areas could not be found.

Russia's bilateral relations with the successor states

Russia has been more active in advancing its bilateral relations in the near abroad than in promoting multilateral integration within the CIS. Given the dependence of many of the former Soviet states on Russian energy, achieving economic influence has proved a more cost-effective way of fulfilling Russia's economic and political aims than investing in multilateral integration. In the 1990s, Russia tended to use its energy resources as 'soft power', subsidizing the price CIS states paid for their oil and gas (Hill 2006). During Putin's presidency, however, Russia has raised energy prices, often with little warning, and has turned off the taps when its customers have refused to agree to the new price or have failed to settle their energy debts. Although the Russians have insisted that price rises are based entirely on commercial criteria (and, indeed, close allies such as Belarus and Armenia have also been charged higher prices), many in the CIS and the outside world accuse Russia of using energy as a coercive instrument of foreign policy (Sherr 2013).

Russia's closest relationship in the near abroad has been with Belarus. In 1996, the two presidents declared that Russia and Belarus would establish a Community of Sovereign Republics. A year later the Community was converted into a Union of Sovereign Republics and in 1999 a confederal Russian–Belarusian union state was proclaimed. However, since Belarus has adopted few economic and political reforms, there has been little real progress in creating the union state. In the past decade, there have been intermittent serious disputes between the two countries about energy prices and supplies. Nevertheless, the 2013 Foreign Policy Concept pledges Russia to 'increase interaction with Belarus within the Union State to extend integration processes in all areas' (Ministry of Foreign Affairs 2013).

Russia's most difficult bilateral relations have been with the Baltic states and, more recently, with Georgia and Ukraine. The Russian government complains regularly about the infringement of the human rights of the very large Russian minorities in Latvia (34 per cent) and Estonia (30 per cent). Since their accession to NATO and the EU, the Russian government has been convinced that the former East European socialist states and the Baltic states have turned the two organizations against Russia.

Russia's relations with Ukraine and Georgia have never been easy, but they became far more difficult after the two states experienced 'colour revolutions' in 2003 and 2004. In the early years, the most contentious issue in the Russian–Ukrainian relationship was the division of the Black Sea fleet and the location and status of naval bases in Crimea for the Russian fleet. The problem was resolved in May 1997 when a 20-year lease was signed (extended in 2010 until 2042). Other difficulties remained, however, including heavy debts incurred by Ukraine to Russia for its energy supplies. After the 2004 'Orange Revolution', President Viktor Yushchenko adopted a firmly pro-European foreign policy, aimed at early membership for Ukraine of both NATO and the EU. The Russian government is strongly opposed to any further NATO expansion and Ukraine's 'European choice' remains a bone of contention. Although President Viktor Yanukovich (ousted in early 2014) was less hostile to Russia, relations remained difficult. In particular, Moscow wants Ukraine to join the customs union and the future Eurasian Union rather than signing an Association Agreement with the EU, and wishes at all costs to retain its naval base at Sebastopol (Lukyanov 2013).

Georgia and Russia have been in intermittent dispute about the presence of Russian peacekeepers in Abkhazia and South Ossetia, the difficulty of returning Georgian refugees to Abkhazia, and Russia's delay in implementing an undertaking given at the OSCE Summit in 1999 that it would withdraw from its remaining military bases in Georgia. The Russian government also accuses Georgia of harbouring Chechen terrorists in the Pankisi Gorge region. In 2002, the US sent military advisers to train Georgian forces to conduct anti-terrorist operations, arousing the perception in Moscow that in the South Caucasus, as in Central Asia, Russia would no longer exercise uncontested influence.

In the absence of a political agreement, South Ossetia and Abkhazia operated as quasi-independent states. Russia gave them political and economic support, while officially supporting Georgia's territorial integrity. When Mikhail Saakashvili became president of Georgia in January 2004, he pledged that he would restore Georgia's territorial integrity. He also announced Georgia's intention of seeking NATO membership. Relations between Russia and Georgia deteriorated. In September 2006, four Russian military officers were arrested and accused of spying for Russia; Russia applied severe economic sanctions on Georgia in response. Throughout 2007 and 2008 there were repeated clashes between peacekeepers in Abkhazia and South Ossetia and Georgian troops. By June 2008 they were occurring daily, and each side declared that the other was about to launch a war. On 7 August, Georgia launched an attack on South Ossetia which appeared initially to take Russia by surprise (neither Putin nor Medvedev was in Moscow). Within a few days, however, Russian troops had driven the Georgians out of South Ossetia, launched air attacks on targets in Georgia, sent troops and armour into Abkhazia and occupied a 'buffer zone' in the area between Georgia and the two separatist areas (Allison 2008). The EU brokered a cease-fire agreement on 16 August, but Russia almost immediately reneged on its terms. After a further agreement with the EU, Russia began to withdraw its troops from Georgia at the beginning of September in return for a Georgian pledge not to use force against Abkhazia. By that time, however, Russia had formally recognized the independence of South Ossetia and Abkhazia and Georgia had withdrawn from the CIS.

Russia's conflict with Georgia affected Russian–CIS relations, alarming those members that have large ethnic minorities and real or potential secessionist problems and once again renewing the fear of Russian hegemony in the post-Soviet space. It also had repercussions on Russia's relations with the West.

Russian policy towards the 'far abroad'

After an initial euphorically pro-Western policy, Russian leaders, disappointed that their orientation to the West did not bring the expected benefits, began to revive relations with some former Soviet allies. At the same time, Western countries turned their attention to relations with the other successor states, arousing anxiety in Moscow that they would make inroads into an area which Russians regarded as their own sphere of influence. Although political and economic cooperation continued, a number of contentious issues created tension between Russia and the United States and Europe. These tensions became far more severe in Putin's second presidential term and, despite attempts by Presidents Obama and Medvedev to reset US–Russian relations, Russia's relations with the West remain uneasy.

Sources of tension: NATO expansion and arms control

The issue of NATO expansion has been a persistent irritant in Russian–Western relations. Perceived as a threat to Russian security, the establishment of a NATO-Russia Permanent Joint Council (PJC) in May 1997 was intended to alleviate Russian anxiety. However, since NATO announced an 'open door' policy to membership in 1999, at the same time as admitting the Czech Republic, Hungary and Poland into the alliance, Russian apprehension increased. NATO also adopted a new strategic doctrine in 1999, which envisaged military operations in non-NATO countries. Since NATO had already launched an attack on Serbia, Russians perceived the doctrine as a direct threat to Russian security.

Following the terrorist attacks on the World Trade Center and the Pentagon on 11 September 2001, Russian–NATO relations improved. In May 2002, the NATO–Russia Council (NRC) replaced the PJC. Russia and the 19 NATO member countries in the NRC have equal voices on issues such as combating international terrorism, peacekeeping, civil emergency planning, defence modernization and preventing the proliferation of weapons of mass destruction. However, NATO expansion continued; notwithstanding Russian objections, the Baltic states joined in May 2004, together with Slovakia, Slovenia, Bulgaria and Romania. At the same time, Ukraine and Georgia began to petition for membership. The Russian leadership reiterates constantly that Georgian and Ukrainian membership of NATO is unacceptable.

Apart from NATO enlargement, arms control has also been a source of friction between Russia and the West. Russian–US relations began with a flourish, when the second Strategic Arms Reduction Treaty (START) was signed in January 1993. It envisaged each side reducing its nuclear arsenals to 3,500 warheads, as well as a 50 per cent reduction in US submarine-launched nuclear warheads and the elimination of all multiple warheads and of Russia's heavy land-based intercontinental missiles. In December 2001, in response to President Bush's announcement that the USA was unilaterally withdrawing from the 1972 Anti-Ballistic Missile (ABM) Treaty, President Putin announced that Russia was withdrawing from START. Nevertheless, a new US–Russian strategic arms limitation treaty was concluded in May 2002, limiting each side to a nuclear arsenal of 1,700–2,200 warheads. It was superseded in April 2010 when Presidents Obama and Medvedev signed a new START treaty limiting each side to 1,550 nuclear warheads and bombs and 700 delivery systems.

The ABM treaty limited Russia and the United States to one anti-missile system each. The US wanted to modify or abrogate it so as to develop a national or ballistic missile defence (NMD or BMD) system. Believing (as did many European governments) that the ABM treaty was the foundation of the strategic deterrence that had kept the world safe from nuclear war, the Russian government was adamantly opposed, arguing that the deployment of even a limited US NMD system would undermine Russian deterrent capabilities (Pikayev 2000). Despite their protests, President Bush abrogated the ABM treaty in 2001 and began negotiations to deploy elements of a NMD system in Eastern Europe (a radar system in the Czech Republic and ten interceptors in Poland). President Putin threatened that if the deployment went ahead, Russia would be forced 'to retarget [its] missiles against the sites that represent a threat' (Putin 2008). In 2009 Obama changed US deployment plans and offered to cooperate with Russia on creating a global BMD system. However, US and Russian definitions of cooperation are very different and there has been little progress. As a result, missile defence remains a bone of contention.

The 1990 Conventional Forces in Europe (CFE) treaty also fell victim to increasing tension in Russian–Western relations. When the USSR disintegrated, the conventional forces permitted it by the CFE agreement had to be divided between the European successor states. By then, however, the Russian government believed that the forces it was permitted on its southern flank were inadequate to deal with the security threats arising from the conflicts on its periphery. After initial reluctance, NATO member agreed to renegotiate the treaty and a new CFE agreement was adopted at the OSCE Istanbul summit in November 1999. Russia ratified the treaty in 2000, but NATO members refused to ratify it until Russia had fulfilled a commitment made at the summit to withdraw all its forces from bases in Georgia and Moldova. President Putin threatened a moratorium on Russia's observance of the treaty unless all NATO members ratified it. When they failed to do so, Russia suspended its commitment to the treaty (*Itar-Tass*, 12 December 2007).

Political and economic relations

The decision to expand NATO and the abrogation of the ABM treaty convinced many Russians that the US wanted to undermine Russian security. The US was also blamed for the hardships Russia's economic reform produced (American advisers had played a prominent role in designing it) in the 1990s and the corruption that accompanied it. Other issues began to affect Russian–US relations, for example, US objections to Russian arms and civil nuclear sales, Russian opposition to US policy in the Balkans and towards Iraq. Russians became increasingly bitter about the 'unipolarity' that they believed the United States wanted to impose upon the international system.

Well before the US and its allies acquired bases in Central Asia for the 'war on terrorism', Caspian Sea energy resources and the route by which they reached world markets had become a contentious issue in Russian foreign policy. Russia controlled the pipelines through which the resources were exported and the Russian government was determined both to ensure that it had a major share of the resources and to retain the leverage that controlling the pipelines gave it over the other former Soviet littoral states. The multinational oil companies involved in extracting the resources were equally determined to diversify transport routes. The other littoral states wanted to reduce Russia's leverage, while surrounding countries like Georgia were keen to provide lucrative transit facilities. A legal framework was agreed in 1999 for the construction of a pipeline from Baku, in Azerbaijan, via Tbilisi, in Georgia, to the Turkish Mediterranean terminal at Ceyhan. Since then, Russia has made a concerted effort to re-establish its dominance over energy transport by investing in pipelines such as Nord Stream, Blue Stream and South Stream to deliver gas to Europe and to world markets.

Initially, Russians had far more benign perceptions of Europe than of the US, and Russian–European multilateral and bilateral relations were not affected by NATO expansion or the CFE difficulties. Like NATO, the European Union (EU) also planned to enlarge. It tried to ensure that Russia was not sidelined by enlargement, concluding a Partnership and Cooperation Agreement (PCA) with the Russian Federation in June 1994 which aimed to develop closer political links, foster trade and investment, and support economic and political reform. The EU was already a major aid donor to Russia and when the ten-year PCA came into force in December 1997, it created a dense network of institutions and political consultations between the EU and Russia, including regular six-monthly EU–Russia summits. In 2005, Russia and the EU agreed four 'roadmaps', setting out the steps that they would take to reach 'common spaces' in the fields of economics, Justice and Home Affairs, External Security, and research, education and culture (European Union External Action 2005). The EU is extremely important to Russian foreign trade: in 2010, 47 per cent of Russia's external trade was with its member countries (White and Feklyunina 2014: Table 3.4).

As enlargement approached, however, a number of difficulties arose in Russian–EU relations. Russians became increasingly apprehensive about the effects of the Schengen visa regime on cross-border movement between Russia and the accession countries and, particularly, between Kaliningrad, which would become an exclave in the EU, and the rest of the Russia. In 2006, during a Ukrainian–Russian gas dispute, the supply of Russian gas to Europe was disrupted. As a result, EU members became alarmed by their increasing dependence on Russian energy (by then, the EU imported more than a quarter of its energy from Russia) and called for energy supplies to be diversified. A second Ukrainian–Russian gas dispute in January 2009 left a dozen European countries with major gas shortages for a fortnight. The 1,200 km-long North European Gas Pipeline (Nord Stream), which began operating in 2011, bypasses the transit states and decreases the vulnerability of the EU's gas supplies.

A series of difficulties in Russia's bilateral relations with the newer EU member states delayed the negotiation of a new agreement to replace the PCA when it expired at the end of 2007 and confirmed the Russian belief that the former socialist members of the EU have turned the organization against Russia. Nevertheless, the PCA has been renewed annually, negotiations on a new agreement have continued and, in the meanwhile, Russia and the EU concluded a Partnership for Modernization in 2010, involving the EU in contributing to President Medvedev's programme to modernize Russia (there is a full discussion in White and Feklyunina 2014).

Russian policy-makers developed good bilateral relations with individual European states (in particular, Germany, France and Italy) and they also began to revive relations with former Soviet partners such as Cuba, North Korea, Iraq and India. They established good relations with Iran. Border disputes with the People's Republic of China were settled, and Sino-Russian trade relations expanded. In 2005, Russia and China held joint military exercises for the first time and there have also been regular joint SCO military exercises (Lo 2008). Russia and China have cooperated closely within the UNSC, opposing resolutions that, in the view of their leaders, call for interference in the domestic affairs of sovereign states. Further afield, Russia has established good relations with Venezuela. The 2013 Foreign Policy Concept policy refers to this diversification of relations as Russia's 'multi-vector policy', another aspect of which is Russia's enthusiastic participation in various multilateral organizations and forums such as the G20, the BRICS (Brazil, Russia, India, China and the Republic of South Africa) and APEC.

President Putin's foreign policy certainly fulfilled one of his primary aims, which was to raise Russia's international stature. Having achieved a long-standing Russian ambition – Russian membership of the G7 (an annual meeting of the leaders of the major industrial democracies to deal with major economic and political issues), which turned it into the G8 – he served as chairman of the G8 in 2006 (and will serve again in 2014). For him and for many Russians, this reflected international recognition of Russia's great power status. However, by the time his second term as president had come to an end, Russia's increasingly assertive rhetoric, and the many disputes with the US, NATO and the EU, had caused analysts in both Russia and abroad to wonder whether a new Cold War had begun.

Prior to the presidential election in March 2008, there were predictions that President Medvedev would pursue a less confrontational policy than his predecessor. In fact there was a change in tone, but the substance of Medvedev's policy was no different from Putin's. True, he embraced the 'reset' proposed by the Obama administration with alacrity and he and President Obama reached agreement on a new START treaty in 2010 in record time. But he also proposed the creation of a new all-European security pact – an old proposal that has been mooted at regular intervals since the 1950s – although he can scarcely have expected that the West would agree to disband NATO in favour of a wider pact (*RIA Novosti* 5 June 2008). Moreover, as president, it was Medvedev who ordered the Russian army to respond to Georgia's attack on South Ossetia, and who became the main target of external criticism for Russia's disproportionate use of force, failure to adhere to cease-fire terms to which they themselves had agreed and the decision to recognize the independence of South Ossetia and Abkhazia. He continued to put pressure on Ukraine and Georgia to dissuade them from their NATO aspirations. To the alarm of Russia's neighbours and the outside world, Medvedev declared after the Georgian war that protecting Russians abroad was a foreign policy priority and that there were 'regions in which Russia has privileged interests' (Medvedev 2008). In short, most observers agree that from 2008 to 2012 Russian foreign policy was 'Dmitry Medvedev's in form, but Putin's in essence' (Trenin 2013a).

Russia and the Arab Spring

When the street protests began in the Middle East at the end of 2010, Russians were convinced at first (as they had been about the 'colour revolutions') that they were instigated by the West. Nevertheless, to reflect the spirit of cooperation embodied in the reset in US–Russian relations, Russia supported the UN resolution imposing a ban on arms sales to Iran in 2010 and suspended the delivery of S-300 missile defence systems to Iran. Russia also supported the UN arms embargo imposed on Libya in February 2011 and abstained from voting on resolution 1973 in March, thus tacitly agreeing to the imposition of a no-fly zone over Libya. However, the way in which the no-fly zone was implemented infuriated Russians. They believed Western countries had duped them into accepting regime change, since the coalition (in effect, NATO) that enforced the no-fly zone helped to bring about the fall of Qaddafi.

Determined to prevent a similar forcible regime change in Syria, Russia vetoed UN resolutions against President Bashar al-Assad, calling instead for a political settlement and demanding that both sides observe a cease-fire. Although Russia acted in concert with China, Western officials aimed their public condemnation at Russia, although their own publics were clearly opposed to intervention. Russia's relations with the US, the UK and France deteriorated badly. Apart from objecting to externally imposed regime change, Russia wants to retain its military base at Tartus. Although of little strategic use, it has high symbolic value, demonstrating Russia's presence in the Mediterranean (Malashenko 2013). Russia is also anxious about the growing influence of extreme Islamist elements among the rebels.

Moscow will probably lose financially when Assad falls – in 2010 alone, Syria concluded arms contracts with Russian firms worth US$15 billion and there are also valuable energy contracts. A new Syrian government will probably do what the new Libyan government has done, reneging on $10 billion worth of contracts that Russia had concluded with Qaddafi. Russia had already lost heavily, when the US and its allies attacked Iraq in March 2003. First, all hopes of receiving repayment of the $8 billion Iraqi Soviet-era debt had to be abandoned. Second, the ten-year programme for the Development of Trade, Economic, Industrial and Scientific–Technical Cooperation that Russia had negotiated with Iraq said to be worth $40 billion came to an abrupt end.

For a long time, Moscow's stance on Syria appeared simply to demonstrate Russia's weakness. Impervious to Russian appeals to moderate his policy, Assad used increasingly sophisticated weapons in what had turned into a civil war. However, when chemical weapons were used against civilians and a US military strike seemed imminent, Putin scored a diplomatic coup. On 9 September 2013, he proposed that Syria should surrender its chemical weapons to an international commission headed by the United Nations, so that they could be removed and destroyed. Assad quickly agreed. So far, the deal appears to be on track. It has not, of course, brought the civil war to an end, but the spirit of cooperation it has engendered has renewed hopes that a negotiated settlement may be possible (Trenin 2013b).

Future prospects

During the presidential campaign at the beginning of 2012, Putin published a newspaper article on foreign policy (Putin 2012). He had published his plans for a Eurasian Union a year earlier (Putin 2011). In this article, he discusses Russia's relations with the rest of the world. For the most part, it is filled with familiar complaints: he deplores NATO expansion and plans to deploy NMD in Europe; objects to attempts, particularly by the USA, to engage in 'political engineering' in areas of traditional importance to Russia; censures military interference under the pretext of humanitarian intervention and the use of force against sovereign countries without the approval of the UNSC. A large section is devoted to his view of the Syrian conflict and the Arab Spring more generally. Interestingly, he depicts China's rising economic power not as a threat but as a challenge to Russia, offering the potential for cooperation. He welcomes China's increasing international status, since Beijing shares Moscow's world vision. He is less sanguine about Russia and the EU and the USA and calls for an 'economization' of relations.

In retrospect, the aspect of Putin's article that he translated into action most quickly was his criticism of the 'privatization' of human rights, the use of 'illegal instruments of soft power' and the activities of foreign-funded 'pseudo-NGOs' that try to destabilize other countries (Putin 2012). Although 'pseudo-NGOs' are discussed in the context of the Arab Spring, Putin was clearly reacting to the street protests that had erupted in Russia after the 2011 parliamentary elections. He set about dealing with potential foreign influences on Russia's domestic politics as soon as he was elected president, initiating a series of laws and measures that clamp down severely on opposition leaders, on NGOs, and on Russian civil society more broadly. This has led to criticism by the EU and the American administration. However, since the global economic crisis, Putin no longer considers the West a model to be followed, so aligning with Western values is no longer necessary.

In fact, Western criticism of Russia's domestic politics has been tempered by problems with civil liberties at home and the need to cooperate on issues such as the war in Syria and the withdrawal from Afghanistan in 2014. So just as pragmatism is claimed to be the basis of Russian foreign policy, it is likely that pragmatism will dictate Western policy towards Russia. The evidence of the agreement on disposing of Syria's chemical weapons suggests if pragmatism means allowing Russia to be part of the solution rather than making it the problem, cooperation on issues of mutual concern will be possible, even if there are continuing frictions in Russia's relations with the outside world.

Chapter 14

The Military, Security and Politics

JENNIFER G. MATHERS

In the period since Vladimir Putin first became president, Russia's political leaders have presented Russian security as dependent on the creation of a strong state, and one of the main symbols of the strength of the Russian state is the armed forces. However, Russia has not yet managed to develop a military that is effective, affordable and acceptable to society. These are challenges faced by every state, but they are complicated in Russia's case by the chaotic circumstances in which its armed forces were created. Uncertainties about the role that the army should play in politics, society and ensuring the security of the state were mirrored by doubts about Russia's identity and its role in the international community. Although the first Putin presidency provided answers to some of these questions, the Russian armed forces continued to face serious problems throughout the Medvedev–Putin 'tandem', and the course of Russia's defence and security policy after Putin's return to the presidency is by no means clear.

The Russian military in the twenty-first century

The Russian military has enjoyed increased funding and a higher profile since 2000 than it did during the 1990s, but has not solved the problems that it inherited from the Soviet period. In spite of many attempts at reform, Russia still has a military that is unable to provide an effective response to the security challenges posed by low-level conflicts and which few of its young people are willing to join. The most serious and sustained efforts at reshaping the Russian armed forces to meet the demands of the post-Cold War period came during Anatolii Serdyukov's tenure as Minister of Defence (2007–12). It remains unclear whether his replacement Sergei Shoigu is willing to risk his popularity with the officer corps to continue on the path of serious reform and whether the very high level of defence spending authorized by Putin since his return to the Kremlin in 2012 will succeed in creating a military fit for the needs of the twenty-first century.

Size and structure

Russia has a large standing army and the stated intention of maintaining such a force in the foreseeable future. An estimated 845,000 troops are under the control of the Ministry of Defence, including ground, navy and air forces equipped with both conventional and nuclear weapons and anti-aircraft and anti-missile defences. The Russian military is organized into the following commands: Army; Military Air Forces; Navy; Strategic Deterrent Forces (including submarines, strategic missile forces, long-range aviation command and radar); and Space Forces (responsible for missile defence and military spacecraft). The heads of each of these commands report to the Minister of Defence, who in turn reports to the Russian president as Commander-in-Chief. The Minister of Defence has a number of deputy ministers, each with an area of responsibility, such as armaments, logistics and accommodation. There are also two first deputy ministers, one of whom is the Chief of the General Staff, who oversees operational and administrative functions such as mobilization, military intelligence and communications.

In addition to the armed forces under the command of the Ministry of Defence, which are the principal focus of this chapter and which are generally regarded as 'the military', Russia has a number of other forces. These increase the number of personnel serving under arms by nearly a further half a million: the Federal Border Guard Service (160,000 soldiers directly subordinate to the president); Interior Troops (170,000 soldiers controlled by the Ministry of the Interior or MVD); the Federal Security Service or FSB (4,000 troops); the Federal Protection Service (10,000–30,000 troops including the Presidential Guard); the Federal Agency for Special Construction (50,000 troops); and the Federal Communications and Information Agency (55,000 troops) (IISS 2013: 235). While each of these agencies has its own responsibilities, such as counter-intelligence against organized crime and terrorism (FSB) or dealing with violent disorder in the Russian Federation (MVD), the missions of the security services complement and sometimes overlap with the responsibilities of the Ministry of Defence. This can be seen in the conflict in Chechnya, which was initially fought by Ministry of Defence troops but gradually augmented by forces controlled by the MVD, which was later given overall responsibility for the operation.

The Russian military has undergone a great deal of turmoil since it was created in the spring of 1992. Although Russia was the largest of the Soviet successor states, it did not receive a commensurate share of the Soviet armed forces. Other newly independent states asserted their claims to virtually everything located within the borders of their territories and as a result Russia lost control of some key military installations, such as large radar stations in the Baltic states and Ukraine and the Baikonur missile and space complex in Kazakhstan, while inheriting many under-strength units located in remote parts of their own country. A distribution was eventually agreed that gave Russia approximately half of the military equipment that had formerly been owned by the Soviet Union (Miller 2004: 5–7) and approximately 2 million of the estimated 3.4 million Soviet military personnel (IISS 1991: 36; IISS 1993: 99).

During the first decade after the formation of the Russian military, discussions about the future of the armed forces degenerated into bureaucratic infighting and personality clashes and effectively prevented any significant action from being taken. President Boris Yeltsin failed to provide the military with leadership on the issue of reform and many of the most energetic and forward-looking young officers left the armed forces to seek opportunities in the new market economy. Most of the officers who remained occupied themselves with preparing for a large-scale war with NATO and spent years attempting to recreate the Soviet armed forces on a slightly smaller scale (Barany 2007).

Putin recognized the need to improve the combat readiness of the armed forces from an early stage in his leadership, and during his first two terms as president took steps to tackle some of the most pressing problems in the military, such as delays in the payment of wages. The frequency and amount of training increased significantly, especially for highly skilled specialists such as pilots. As will be discussed below, the level of state funding for the armed forces and the defence industry increased, and a new generation of weapons systems began to enter service. Putin also showed greater decisiveness than his predecessor in dealing with infighting within the Defence Ministry, in particular removing the conservative Chief of the General Staff Anatolii Kvashnin, who had been a significant obstacle in the path of serious military reform (Herspring 2006: 523–4).

Reform of the armed forces progressed most rapidly, however, during Dmitri Medvedev's presidency, when the Ministry of Defence was led by Anatolii Serdyukov. Serdyukov was appointed Defence Minister in 2007 for his financial acumen, gained during his time in the tax service, in order to bring order to the military's finances and tackle corruption. Following Russia's less than impressive performance in the conflict against Georgia in August 2008, his brief was expanded to include military reform. Serdyukov thoroughly shook up the officer corps, cutting its size by over 200,000, reshaping its structure and cutting the number of military educational institutions. He also introduced measures to improve training and particularly the training of non-commissioned officers (a serious gap in the command structure) and streamlined the formerly bloated 203 under-staffed divisions into 80, better-staffed, brigades (Herspring 2013: 262–71).

Serdyukov's reforms laid the foundations for a more efficient and better-trained military but they came to an end with his dismissal in November 2012 amid allegations of corruption and his replacement by Minister of Emergencies Sergei Shoigu. While Shoigu has expressed his intention to continue to modernize and improve the armed forces, he has reversed some of Serdyukov's most unpopular policies and has given little indication of how he intends to transform the Russian military into a force which is prepared to meet the diverse and rapidly changing challenges of the twenty-first century.

Recruitment, retention and morale

The Russian armed forces have yet to recover from the crisis in recruitment that began in the late 1980s. During the Gorbachev period, the system of conscription began to break down as large numbers of young men evaded compulsory military service. As a result of *glasnost*, the Soviet media began to publicize serious problems in the armed forces which made families reluctant to entrust their sons to its care. At the same time, the nationalist movements that swept through many of the Soviet republics made military service in the armed forces particularly unappealing for young men from these nations. By 1991, less than a quarter of the conscript quotas were being met in republics such as Lithuania, Armenia and Georgia (IISS 1991: 34).

Rather than encouraging their teenage sons to carry out their patriotic duty, increasing numbers of parents began to help their children to avoid conscription. Many turned for help to their local Committee of Soldiers' Mothers (CSM), a network of civil society organizations which seek to protect the human rights of soldiers and to provide material and moral support for their families. In addition to high-profile actions taken at the national level, such as lobbying for changes in legislation on alternative forms of service for conscientious objectors and opposing Russia's war in Chechnya, CSM organizations provide practical advice on legal ways to avoid conscription (Eichler 2012: 88–107). Such advice is widely sought-after and very effective. According to (then) Minister of Defence Pavel Grachev, in 1992 some 75–80 per cent of the young men in Russia who were eligible for military service actually evaded conscription (Dawisha and Parrott 1994: 243). Two decades later, demographic trends and public health issues have overtaken draft-dodging as the most serious impediments to Russia achieving the million-man army demanded by the country's top political and military leaders. The collapse in the Russian birth rate between the late *perestroika* period and the end of the 1990s means a reduction of 50 per cent in the numbers of young men coming to adulthood, a trend that is not due to improve until the 2020s (IISS 2013:

200). Furthermore, the poor state of health of many of Russia's young men makes them ineligible for military service. As a direct result the Ministry of Defence has halved its targets for the number of young men to be conscripted in five consecutive draft periods since late 2011 ('Russian Army Improves Quality of Combat Training' 2012).

In the early 1990s, a form of voluntary military service (known as contract service) was introduced to supplement conscription. In spite of the manifest failures of conscription, the decision to introduce even an element of voluntary service was controversial among many senior Russian officers. The older generation of Russian military leaders believed that universal (male) service in the armed forces was the best way to instil civic values into the nation's youth, as well as providing trained reserves that could be mobilized quickly in a national emergency. Support for the continuation of conscription is also linked to the argument that Russia needed a mass army rather than a smaller, professional force in order to meet current and future security threats. Although there has been a gradual acceptance among officers of the need for a sizable volunteer contingent, the Ministry of Defence has been slow to recognize the need to offer competitive salaries, reasonable living conditions and an attractive career path in order to attract the calibre of recruits the armed forces both wants and needs. Accordingly, few of the country's most intelligent, able and physically fit young men choose to serve in the armed forces; those who do tend to be the ones who struggle to find or keep a civilian job as well as young men from the countryside and those with lower socio-economic status, for whom military service is seen as offering an opportunity for advancement (Eichler 2012: 71).

Women make up a considerable proportion of those who offer themselves as contract soldiers. Although it would appear that encouraging women to join the armed forces could help to alleviate its staffing shortages, the Ministry of Defence is very ambivalent about women's military service. Women's presence in the ranks was accepted during the Second World War, when millions of women served in the Soviet armed forces. Once the emergency was over and the war was won, the women were quickly demobilized. Since 1945, conscription has only been applied to men, and while women were allowed to volunteer even before the introduction of contract service, only a tiny number ever did so. Women tend to serve in a very narrow range of military positions, chiefly in areas such as administration and medicine, and few are able to advance very far up the career ladder due to restrictions on the length of time they can serve and on opportunities for advanced training. Women soldiers themselves tend to regard military service as a means of solving short-term economic problems rather than as a possible career. Many of Russia's women soldiers are the wives or daughters of officers who live in remote areas where there are few other opportunities for paid employment. Contract service offers the chance of an additional income for the family until the main breadwinner gets a promotion, is transferred or leaves the military altogether (Mathers 2006). The number of women contract soldiers has declined significantly in recent years, down from about 100,000 in the first decade after the introduction of contract service to about 45,000 in 2013. This decline may be due, at least in part, to the significant reduction in the number of officers resulting from Serdyukov's reforms. In the spring of 2013, the Duma began to consider a draft bill that would introduce a form of 'voluntary conscription' for young women, but it is not clear that this measure would reverse the downward trend in the number of women volunteering for military service.

The persistence of poor living conditions for soldiers and officers is another reason for the continued crisis in recruitment. Throughout the 1990s, it was normal for soldiers to wait for months to receive their pay, and often by the time they were paid, the spending power of their wage packets had been diminished by rapid inflation. Under Vladimir Putin, the problem of delayed wage payments was finally addressed. Officers' salaries also increased during Putin's first presidency, but they nevertheless failed to keep pace with salaries in the civilian economy. Housing, especially for officers with families, continues to be difficult to obtain and inadequate even where available. According to a study published in 2012, the overwhelming majority of officers reported that a military career did not provide appropriate living standards for their families (Obraztsov 2012: 516). Living conditions for conscripted soldiers are not only uncomfortable but can also be life-threatening, as they are often subjected to abuse by officers and fellow soldiers alike. The failure of the Ministry of Defence to stamp out this practice, known as *dedovshchina,* is a major reason for the continued crisis in recruitment.

Dedovshchina is translated into English as 'bullying', but that term does not fully convey the extent and horror of this systematic abuse of conscripts. *Dedovshchina* is derived from the Russian word *ded* or grandfather, and refers to the power that the most senior conscripts (or grandfathers) exercise over the newest group of soldiers to enter their unit. There are many well-documented cases of young conscripts suffering savage beatings, sometimes requiring hospitalization, surgery and the amputation of limbs (Arnold 2007). Soldiers have been beaten to death by their fellows as punishment for some transgression while others are willing literally to do anything to escape the relentless abuse and torture, including risking lengthy prison sentences by deserting their units or even committing suicide (Colin Lebedev 2006: 66–70; Webber and Zilberman 2006: 169–75).

The Ministry of Defence has been forced to acknowledge the existence of *dedovshchina* as a result of pressure from elements of the media and from the Committee of Soldiers' Mothers, although senior military figures continue to dispute the extent and significance of the phenomenon. There is debate among observers of the Russian armed forces about whether the Defence Ministry is unwilling or unable to address this serious problem. Some have argued that *dedovshchina* is tolerated and even encouraged in some units as a method of controlling the raw conscripts under the command of overstretched officers. Others suggest that it reflects a fundamental callousness towards the individual on the part of a large and impersonal bureaucracy, while still others see it as an indictment of the Russian military and its claims to effectiveness and combat readiness. If the Ministry of Defence cannot even control what happens to its own troops within its own barracks, what hope does it have of providing an effective fighting force to defend and protect Russia's territory and its citizens?

Defence budgets and military spending

After a brief period of relative openness during the late Gorbachev and early Yeltsin years, which coincided with a downturn in the fortunes of the military and the defence industry, secrecy in relation to the amount of state funding devoted to defence has been reinstated, and this trend shows no signs of being reversed. During Putin's second term as president, the number of items that were classified (not available to the public) increased and included procurement and research and development (IISS 2008: 209). Restrictions on the information that can be released about the state defence budget do more than make it difficult for outsiders to calculate how much Russia is spending: they place significant obstacles in the path of Russian citizens, journalists, civil society groups and even Duma deputies who wish to scrutinize policy decisions and to hold to account the Ministry of Defence and other beneficiaries of the state defence budget. Many Duma deputies are reportedly unwilling to undergo the security clearance required to gain access to the details of the defence budget because they fear it would impose onerous restrictions on their own actions, such as limits on meeting foreigners and travel abroad (Cooper 2006: 143). These rules have discouraged them from sitting on the Duma's Defence Committee, with the result that the Committee is dominated by former members of the armed forces. This in turn reduces the range of defence expertise in the Duma as well as limiting *de facto* civilian oversight of a key element of Russian policy.

The figures that are available for the Russian defence budget are estimates, but it is possible nevertheless to discern the impact of changing economic conditions and policy decisions on defence spending. During the 1990s, Russia allocated more than 5 per cent (and perhaps as much as 7–8 per cent) of its gross domestic product to defence. While this is a very high proportion of GDP for a country to devote to its military budget, it needs to be seen in the context of the condition of the Russian economy during that decade, which was characterized by slow growth rates and high inflation. The result was a sharp decline in defence spending, which dropped by an estimated 45 per cent in the first half of the 1990s (IISS 1996: 107). The first presidency of Vladimir Putin, by contrast, coincided with a substantial rise in the growth of the Russian economy, fuelled by the export of Russian oil and gas at high international prices. The defence sector was one of the major beneficiaries of Russia's new prosperity, and although the proportion of GDP allocated to defence during Putin's presidency was lower than in the 1990s (approximately 2.5–2.8 per cent between 2000 and 2008), the rise in the gross domestic product, the slowing of inflation and the reduction in the size of the Russian armed forces (from 2 million in the early 1990s to just over 1 million in 2008) meant that there was significantly more money in the military budget to go around (IISS 2008: 210).

By the end of Putin's second term as president, the Russian armed forces were beginning to see the benefits of this investment. The long-awaited *Topol-M* intercontinental ballistic missiles began to enter service in 2006. The *Topol-M* is designed to carry up to six warheads and is intended to replace Russia's ageing, Soviet-built nuclear missile arsenal. The submarine-launched version of the missile, the *Bulava*, began testing in 2007 (IISS 2008: 206–7), while the first of the new *Borei*-class submarines, which carry the *Bulava* missiles, entered service in 2013.

Russia's defence sector has seen a sustained increase in its funding beginning in June 2006, when a major arms procurement programme involving an estimated US$190 billion of additional investment was announced for the period 2007–15. This programme was intended to provide an across-the-board conventional and nuclear build-up, including tanks and armoured vehicles, aircraft, ships and air defence complexes (Bjelakovic 2008: 527–35). The State Armaments Programme 2011–20, signed by then-President Dmitri Medvedev in 2010, dedicated another US$610 billion to defence procurement (IISS 2013: 199). At the start of his second presidency, Putin made it clear that modernizing the military and providing it with the most up-to-date weapons and equipment was a crucial part of his strategy to strengthen Russia and improve its standing in the world. The priority assigned to defence and the armed forces is clear: while the 2014 budget calls for increases in defence spending from 15.7 per cent to 17.8 per cent of the budget, funding for domestic and social programmes is set to stagnate or decline (Bowen 2013).

But while the defence budget has grown since 2000 and looks set to continue to expand, there are grave doubts that Russia's defence industry will be able to provide the quality of new equipment expected of it. The sector struggles to deliver new systems on time and still exhibits the Soviet-era tendency to make incremental improvements to existing systems rather than taking technological leaps ahead. The ability of the defence industry to provide the modern weapons needed by the military is, ironically, also undermined by widespread corruption within the Ministry of Defence itself. Corrupt practices in the armed forces range from the actions of opportunistic individuals, such as senior officers making use of soldiers as unpaid labour, to organized fraud and embezzlement on a large scale. As a result, the amount of money that actually reaches the defence sector is significantly less than the sums authorized.

The military and politics

The military's relationship to politics in Russia is a complex one that has gone through a number of distinct stages. During the Soviet period, the armed forces were co-opted supporters of the *status quo*. In the 1990s, large numbers of officers entered electoral politics and attempted to challenge the regime, chiefly over the issue of defence spending, although the military proved to be unsuccessful as an interest group and had to wait for the election of a new president and a dramatic improvement in the country's economy to enjoy more generous funding. The reconciliation between the military and the state which began during Putin's first presidency was accompanied by the appointment of the *siloviki* – those with a background in the armed forces or security services – to many important positions in Russian politics. This phenomenon prompted many observers to express concerns about the growing power of the military (see particularly Kryshtanovskaya and White 2003), although there are reasons to question the coherence of this group and their effectiveness in promoting shared values or policy preferences.

The military as a political actor

A feature of Russian politics is the presence of former members of the 'force structures' (the military and security services), whether in elected or appointed positions. In some respects this is a contemporary version of an old phenomenon. It was common for representatives of the military and security forces to serve at senior levels in politics during the Soviet period, although this nearly always took place under carefully controlled conditions. Successive Soviet political leaderships sought to guard against any tendency towards 'Bonapartism' (the pursuit of political power by military officers) and to ensure the loyalty of the military by co-opting the officer corps into the political elite, providing the armed forces with generous resources and permitting them a certain degree of autonomy. Most officers were members of the Communist Party, while representatives of the armed forces were visible at the most senior levels of political life through their presence in such bodies as the USSR Supreme Soviet and the Communist Party's Central Committee.

The relationship between the military and civilian authority began to change from active partnership to something more adversarial during the late Gorbachev period, when military personnel were encouraged to use their compulsory political education sessions to debate current political issues. Groups of like-minded officers organized officers' assemblies to articulate and publicize their political views and some individuals sought elected office. Forty-four officers were elected to the Russian Congress of People's Deputies in 1990 (Barany 2008: 587), while two senior officers stood as Russian vice-presidential candidates in the 1991 election.

Throughout the 1990s, serving and former Russian military officers participated in politics in large numbers, with some being elected to political office at the national and regional levels. Few of these candidates sought to address the wider social, economic and political problems facing Russia and instead appeared to be motivated by the desire to create a lobby group on behalf of the Ministry of Defence. This was clearly related to the fact that the armed forces were relatively unsuccessful in the struggle for state funding during Boris Yeltsin's presidency. There was a strong view among senior Russian military officials that the needs of the Defence Ministry were not being met by the politicians and that the only way to remedy this situation was for members of the armed forces to occupy positions of political power. This view was articulated during the campaign for the 1995 Duma election, in which the Minister of Defence called on members of the armed forces to stand for election in order to create this kind of military lobby. But while 123 officers were chosen as official Ministry of Defence candidates and another 40 stood as candidates for various political parties in 1995, only 22 'military candidates' were elected to the Duma, and only two of those had been put forward by the Defence Ministry (Thomas 1996: 536). There has not been a concerted attempted by the military to fill large numbers of elected positions since that time, although a steady trickle of serving and retired officers has continued to enter the Duma and several prominent former officers have been elected as governors of Russian regions. Alexander Rutskoi, for example, was governor of Kursk region from 1996 to 2000. Alexander Lebed (who stood as a candidate in the 1996 Russian presidential election) served as governor of Krasnoyarsk from 1998 until his death in a helicopter crash in 2002, while Boris Gromov was governor of Moscow region from 2000 to 2012.

During the 1990s, the armed forces also began to be viewed by candidates for political office as an important constituency. Political parties and their aspiring Duma deputies actively courted 'the military vote', and parties would often place one or two high-profile officers near the top of their party lists. There is little evidence, however, that members of the armed forces voted as a distinct bloc. On the contrary, the fact that so many different political parties were able to attract military officers as candidates demonstrates the failure of the military to organize around a single political position or party.

Several wider political trends have had a significant impact on the nature of the military's participation in politics since 2000. The consolidation of political parties, the greater degree of party discipline and the fact that most of the parties represented in the Duma now support rather than oppose the policies of the government means that there are far fewer opportunities for individual military officers to enter parliament as challengers to the *status quo*. Changes in the way that regional governors are chosen, from direct election to presidential nomination of candidates for approval by regional legislatures, has also reduced the potential for figures of this kind to oppose the central authorities. These structural changes mean that electoral politics no longer provides an opportunity for disgruntled officers to build support for their own political positions.

Putin's first presidency also marked a major shift in the relationship between the political leadership and the armed forces. From the very beginning of his campaign for president in 2000 Putin stressed the importance of the military to the future of Russia in his speeches and made high-profile gestures of support for the armed forces, such as visiting troops in Chechnya soon after he was appointed acting president at the end of 1999. As President, Putin continued to express his support for the military and to declare that attention must be paid to pressing defence and security issues, frequently speaking of Russia's return to its proper position in the international community as a great power and of the importance of building a strong Russia based on a strong military. Perhaps most importantly, Putin's pro-military rhetoric was matched by a substantial increase in spending which reassured them that at last Russia had a leader who could be trusted to look after the defence of the nation. This combination of symbolic and practical support for the armed forces continued during Medvedev's presidency and has, if anything, been strengthened since Putin returned to the Kremlin in 2012.

The military and security forces, taken as a whole, clearly have a presence in Russian politics. Not least, they occupy a range of elected and appointed political positions. But they do not necessarily act together in support of common goals, and in those cases where they do have shared political aims (such as increasing defence spending), the military have been remarkably unsuccessful in achieving them without the support of the president. Rather than viewing the military as a powerful institutional actor that exercises undue influence over the political leadership, the evidence of the military's involvement in Russian politics so far suggests that its fortunes are highly dependent on the goodwill and priorities of the political leadership.

Civilian control of the armed forces

Concerns about the extent of control which Russia's political leaders exercise over the armed forces tend to focus on extreme scenarios involving the complete or near-total loss of control. In the 1990s, there was much speculation about when, rather than if, the military would take political control. But while conditions of economic, political and social turmoil have indeed been the catalyst for military takeovers in other countries, in Russia the armed forces lacked the confidence, coherence and leadership to attempt a seizure of power of this kind. The only instance of direct military involvement in a political dispute took place during Boris Yeltsin's confrontation with parliamentary rebels in October 1993, but on that occasion the armed forces supported the elected civilian leadership. The emphasis on such extreme possibilities has tended to distract attention from more subtle although no less important factors that determine the nature of the relationship between Russia's civilian and military authorities.

A serious obstacle to effective civilian control of the military and security forces in Russia is the reliance on highly personalized relationships between the leaders of these organizations and the president. This has created a tendency to equate civilian control with the loyalty of the force structures to the president, which has led to the neglect of other forms of civilian control that would enable greater accountability of the military and security services to society. One such form of accountability relates to parliamentary and public scrutiny of the defence budget, which, as discussed above, is very limited.

Another measure that could lead to greater institutionalization of civilian control of the military is the introduction of civilians at senior levels of the Ministry of Defence. The presence of senior civilians in the institution could be a mechanism for challenging established ways of thinking and patterns of behaviour as well as providing agents for greater accountability and civilian oversight. Some steps have been taken in this direction, although the pace of change has been slow and the results have been mixed. Former First Deputy Minister of Defence Andrei Kokoshin advised Gorbachev and helped to shape his radical approaches to security and defence issues. Kokoshin was first deputy minister from 1992 to 1997 and was responsible for liaising between the Ministry of Defence, the defence industry and the Duma, but his impact on the activities and the working culture of the Ministry was minimal. Kokoshin's responsibilities were, in effect, duplicated by other officials within the institution and he found himself having to function with reductions in both influence and staff (the latter an important indicator of the power and status of a senior official). Deputy Minister of Defence Lyubov Kudelina was appointed by Vladimir Putin in September 2007 and given the responsibility for improving accounting and financial controls within the Ministry. But while Kudelina – a civilian and a woman – appeared at first to be a radical choice, she demonstrated an enthusiasm for maintaining and extending the secrecy surrounding the military budget that exceeded even that of her uniformed colleagues. Far from increasing the level of external scrutiny and accountability of the Ministry of Defence, she became one of the strongest supporters of the *status quo* (Betz 2004: 103–5).

The experiences of Kokoshin and Kudelina suggest that civilians, even when appointed to very senior positions, are not necessarily effective as agents of change within the Ministry of Defence. The tenure of Anatolii Serdyukov as Defence Minister lends further support to this conclusion. Serdyukov was arguably Russia's first genuinely civilian Minister of Defence as his immediate predecessor, Sergei Ivanov, had a background in the Foreign Intelligence Service which diminished his claims to civilian status. Serdyukov was an outsider appointed to bring about dramatic change in the armed forces, but the substance and style of his reforms were deeply resented by many officers, who used his civilian status and lack of experience in the military to cast doubt on his ability to develop effective and workable policies. Serdyukov's unpopularity within the military and the absence of a significant base of support in the Defence Ministry made him personally dependent upon the patronage of the president. In November 2012, just six months after Putin's return to the presidency, that patronage was evidently withdrawn when Serdyukov (as we have already noted) was abruptly replaced by the former Emergencies Minister, Sergei Shoigu. Civilian leadership of the Russian military appears to be a fragile plant with shallow roots, subject to the whims of political patronage and the post holder's ability to create his or her own client/patron networks within the institution.

The militarization of state and society

Since Putin's first presidency, the military and security services have gained a higher profile in Russia through symbolic measures such as presidential rhetoric as well as the appointment of *siloviki* to important official positions and policy decisions such as the increase in defence spending and the introduction of military training in secondary schools. The combination of these measures has caused some observers to warn that the Russian state and society are undergoing a process of militarization – in other words, that the armed forces and its values and priorities are encroaching on and being accepted into everyday life. The responses from Russian society to these developments have been mixed and suggest that militarization is a complex process that has achieved, at most, only partial success in Russia.

The introduction of military–patriotic education in schools is perhaps the most blatant attempt by the Russian state to bring the military into everyday life. The problems of recruitment and retention of personnel in the armed forces are often blamed by Russian military officials on the rise in social problems among young soldiers that are, in turn, attributed to a malaise in Russian society at large. The remedy in the eyes of many senior military officers is the reintroduction of some form of basic military training in schools. This was a feature of secondary education during much of the Soviet period but had been allowed to lapse after the collapse of the USSR. Such a programme of training would, it is suggested, improve physical fitness and instil a sense of moral purpose and patriotism in young people, together with an appreciation of the work of the armed forces and an eagerness to serve.

While still acting President, Vladimir Putin introduced such a course of study, 'Foundations of Military Service', as part of a broader programme of 'Patriotic Education of the Citizens of the Russian Federation'. The military training element was initially an optional subject but it met with a great deal of resistance on the part of both parents and teachers and as a result few schools actually offered the course. It was then made compulsory in 2003, but even this step did not ensure that the programme of patriotic education achieved its aims. Although military training is a formal part of secondary education in Russia, those with personal experience of the course report that it is not taught effectively or taken seriously by the pupils (Webber and Zilberman 2006: 179–80, 186–7).

The evidence of public opinion polls, however, lends some support to the argument that Russia has indeed become a more militarized society. According to monthly polls conducted by the Russian Public Opinion Research Centre (VCIOM) in 2007, between 41 and 46 per cent of Russians surveyed expressed approval of the army. This compared favourably with a number of other institutions such as law enforcement agencies, political parties and the judiciary, although the media were rated more highly (VCIOM 2007). By 2013, the percentage of Russians expressing approval for the armed forces had risen to 58 per cent, with only the media and the Russian Orthodox Church being rated more highly (VCIOM 2013). There has also been an upward trend in the proportions of those Russians surveyed who say they would want to see a close relative serve in the armed forces – from 19 per cent in 2000 to 36 per cent in 2011 (Zorkaya 2012: 138).

These surveys indicate that many Russians have an attachment to the idea of the military, perhaps linked to its role as a symbol of a strong Russian state. There is a discrepancy between these expressions of support and the unwillingness of young men to join the army and of parents to entrust their sons to its care. Similarly, approval of the armed forces was not sufficient to persuade millions of parents and teachers to devote valuable time during the school day to military training when they were given the choice and, once made compulsory, the subject has not proved popular. The survey data cited above, however, suggests an increasing tendency among Russians to regard the military as a less dangerous place, although there is still a large gap between the generalized approval of the army as an institution and the more personal response of individuals to the prospect of surrendering a son to it. In other words, while the Russian state exerts pressures on society towards greater acceptance of the military and its values in everyday life, the response of society has been more complex than simple acceptance or rejection.

Conclusion

The armed forces occupy a central place in the plans articulated by several successive Russian presidents – and by Vladimir Putin in particular – to ensure that Russia is regarded as a strong state and is treated with respect in the international community. Enormous attention and resources have been focused on the defence sector since 2000 to reverse the neglect that it suffered during the 1990s and to realize the vision of the Russian military as a disciplined and effective force, equipped with the latest technology and capable of responding appropriately to the security challenges facing Russia. While there has been progress towards creating a reformed and more efficient military, Russia's armed forces continue to struggle with deep-seated problems, many of which are the result of pervasive institutional cultures and practices – such as the extent of corruption and the acceptance of the brutal treatment of conscripts known as *dedovshchina*.

Ultimately, however, the greatest security challenge Russia faces lies in aligning the instruments it has for dealing with security threats to the threats themselves. There is a danger that Russia's focus on building up its defence sector – allocating large and growing sums to its defence budget, acquiring more and more advanced weapons, maintaining a million-man army – will prove doubly counter-productive. Russia's military build-up is interpreted by many in the West as a threatening move and may contribute to an arms race mentality. At the same time, a large, standing army which is top-heavy with tanks, nuclear weapons and a fleet of big ships and submarines is not ideally suited to the type of small-scale conflicts and counter-terrorist operations that Russia is likely to face in the foreseeable future.

Chapter 15

Trajectories of Russian Politics: An Interpretation

VLADIMIR GEL'MAN

Since the Soviet collapse in December 1991, Russia has moved from communist rule to what will be regarded in this chapter as a new form of authoritarian regime, dubbed 'competitive' or 'electoral' authoritarianism. Regimes of this type proliferated around the world after the end of the Cold War not only due to a changing international environment but also because of the key role of elections as the main element of their domestic political legitimacy. These regimes incorporate multi-candidate and multi-party elections that are meaningful, and stand in contrast to 'classical' versions of authoritarian regimes (including communist ones), which are known for their non-competitive 'elections without choice'. Under 'competitive' or 'electoral' authoritarianism, and in contrast to electoral democracies, elections are marked by an uneven playing field, based on formal and informal rules that construct prohibitively high barriers to participation, sharply unequal access for the various competitors to financial and media resources, abuses of power by the state apparatus for the sake of maximizing incumbent votes, and multiple instances of electoral fraud. These basic 'rules of the game' greatly contributed to other multiple deficiencies of contemporary Russian politics, outlined in previous chapters of this volume, such as weak and impotent political parties, heavily censored or self-censored media, rubber-stamping legislatures at the national and sub-national levels, subordinated and heavily biased courts, the arbitrary use of the economic powers of the state, and endemic corruption.

The tendencies of Russia's post-communist regime changes towards a new authoritarianism could be best illustrated while looking at the annual ratings of political rights and civic freedoms reported by Freedom House – a New York-based organization that has produced such reports since the 1970s based on data obtained from various agencies as well as expert evaluations, and which have secured wide if not universal acceptance. According to its scale, the country rated as 1 in both rankings (such as

Table 15.1   *Political rights and civil liberties in Russia
and its neighbouring states, 1992–2012*

Country	1992	1997	2002	2007	2012
Russia	3.5 (PF)	3.5 (PF)	5.0 (PF)	5.5 (NF)	5.5 (NF)
Ukraine	3.0 (PF)	3.5 (PF)	4.0 (PF)	2.5 (F)	3.5 (PF)
Georgia	4.5 (PF)	3.5 (PF)	4.0 (PF)	4.0 (PF)	3.0 (PF)
Lithuania	2.5 (F)	1.5 (F)	1.5 (F)	1.0 (F)	1.0 (F)
Poland	2.0 (F)	1.5 (F)	1.5 (F)	1.0 (F)	1.0 (F)
Kazakhstan	5.0 (PF)	5.5 (NF)	5.5 (NF)	5.5 (NF)	5.5 (NF)
Finland	1.0 (F)	1.0 (F)	1.0 (F)	1.0 (F)	1.0 (F)
North Korea	7.0 (NF)	7.0 (NF)	7.0 (NF)	7.0 (NF)	7.0 (NF)

Source: data from www.freedomhouse.org (indices constructed as an average of annual ratings of political rights and civil liberties). F = free country, PF = partly free country, NF = non-free country.

Finland), is a near-ideal example of democracy, while a country rated as 7 in each of the rankings (such as North Korea or pre-1987 Soviet Union) is among the world's most repressive autocratic regimes. As one can see from Table 15.1, after the end of communist rule, Russia demonstrated a mixed record over the 1990s; but by the 2000s it had degraded to the category of 'non-free' countries (that is, autocracies) and by the end of 2012 its distance from democratic standards (a 5.5 average on both Freedom House scales) was similar to that of Jordan or Angola. Meanwhile, many of the former communist states of Eastern Europe gradually raised their performance to the category of 'free' (democratic) countries; and among the republics of the former Soviet Union, the state of political rights and civic freedoms in Moldova, Ukraine, Georgia and Armenia was more positive than it was in Russia.

Beyond observing this (rather gloomy) picture, we have to discuss why a new authoritarian regime emerged and became entrenched in Russia, what are its major features *vis-à-vis* other non-democratic regimes in other parts of the globe as well as in Russian history, and what kind of evolutionary trajectory we might expect in the foreseeable future. This chapter seeks answers to these questions.

Explaining Russian politics: optimism, pessimism, and realism

To a certain degree, the various scholarly approaches to analysis of Russian politics may be divided into 'pessimists', 'optimists' and 'realists', as this distinction was understood in a late-Soviet joke. In the 1970s and

1980s, Soviet citizens sometimes argued that optimists were learning English (due to their expectation of a war with the United States), pessimists were learning Chinese (and thus preparing to go to war with China), and realists were learning how to use a Kalashnikov so as to be ready for a war with any enemy. In essence, this joke has not lost its relevance. As for scholars, one might consider similar divisions among various groups of specialists, who are very different in terms of their assessments of the Russian political regime and its major features as well as in their explanations of the trajectory of post-Soviet political development and their outlook for the future. 'Pessimists' see Russia's authoritarian trends as a logical outcome of chronic inherited diseases that are embedded in Russian history and culture, and cannot be reversed in one way or another. 'Optimists', on the other hand, considered post-Soviet authoritarianism as a by-product of the protracted growing pains that emerged in the wake of the collapse of the Soviet system and its complex transformation; their focus is the prospects for economic growth in Russia, whose social consequences are expected to bring about the demise of authoritarianism. Finally, 'realists' analysed the impact of special interests on the process of regime changes and institution building. Their outlook on the future of Russia's authoritarianism is rather sceptical, due to the fact that Russia's rulers are seeking maximization of their own power and do not want to lose it. They are lacking incentives for democratization, and deliberatively pervert the 'rules of the game' in a way that holds back and distorts the trajectories of political, economic, and social development that would otherwise take place..

The key assumption of the 'pessimists' is based upon the undoubted fact that Russia has the strong legacy of a non-democratic past, and has faced an essential continuity in its mode of government throughout its entire history. This kind of path-dependency is akin to a genetically transmitted disease that cannot be healed in the foreseeable future. According to this view, not only do Russia's rulers tend to replicate autocratic patterns of politics with a lack of respect for human rights and the rule of law, but also Russian citizens tend to deny many civic and political freedoms for the sake of economic well-being and the preservation of political order. Some experts argued that these popular attitudes and beliefs lie at the heart of Russia's political culture because of the peculiar impact of the Soviet and/or pre-Soviet legacy. Indeed to judge from numerous sources, including survey data, one might even suggest that Russia is incompatible with democracy. This determinist statement, however, is less than convincing if we place Russia within a wider perspective. Over the last two decades, numerous countries with a previous lack of democratic experience (ranging from Mexico to Mongolia) have made substantial progress towards democracy, and there is no reason to consider

Russia incapable of following the same pattern. Also, despite the fact that Russian citizens are not among the most consistent supporters of many democratic ideas, they are not great advocates of autocracy, either. Thus, the chances for changes of Russian political values and attitudes are not hopeless, in the medium term at least.

The argument of 'optimists' is focused on the very fact that by international standards Russia is just an average country with an intermediate level of socio-economic development and perhaps one should not expect that it could made a democratic breakthrough just twenty years after the end of communism. According to this view, recent political trends are somewhat similar to a post-traumatic syndrome, which could be cured over time. Yet the market economy in Russia is well-established now, and economic growth between 1999 and 2008 was very impressive. Given the well-known assumption that well-to-do nations tend to be more democratic, one might expect that the economic development in the not-so-distant future will inevitably contribute to democratization in Russia because of the increasing democratic demands of an emerging middle class. Also, there are some expectations about the positive influence of international linkages and globalization as agencies of the gradual evolution of Russia towards democracy. The problem, however, is that democracy has not always emerged as a side-effect of economic advancement and well-being. This is particularly true for a number of oil-reliant countries due to the negative political effects of the so-called 'resource curse'. And even if one could agree with this line of reasoning, the experience of various countries tells us that democracy did not emerge by default and its making often took some decades and required major efforts by political actors and the society at large.

Finally, 'realists' pointed out that if democracy is a political system where leaders lose power because of electoral defeats, it is hardly surprising that most politicians around the world do whatever they can to avoid such an undesirable outcome – although many of them are unable to do so. In mature democracies, major 'rules of the game' protected the mechanisms for a transfer of power through the ballot box. But in some newly emerged regimes (including post-communist ones) political leaders were able to craft biased sets of rules which were intended to prevent them losing power in this way. Russia's rulers, especially in the 2000s, were very successful in maximizing their control over the key levers of power and establishing an effective informal ruling coalition based around personalist networks. Since then, the authoritarian regime in Russia has sustained itself over time, so it is hard to expect a major breakdown unless the ruling coalition collapses or is reshuffled due to exogenous shocks or a rebellion by ordinary citizens. This explanation seems oversimplified – to some extent it is reminiscent of Hollywood movies with their picturing of characters as 'good guys' or 'bad guys' (even though, contrary to film scripts, there are no expectations of an inevitably happy end). In fact, Russia's political actors (as well as their counterparts in other countries) by definition are neither good nor bad guys: their behaviour usually depends on numerous domestic and international factors that are difficult to predict.

As one can see, all three viewpoints are not mutually exclusive but rather supplementary to each other, and some experts combine elements of each of them in their analysis of Russia's political regime. But what about the genesis of Russian authoritarianism and the mechanisms of maintenance of political order: how were they built and reproduced in a post-communist environment?

Out of the frying pan into the fire

Leo Tolstoy started his novel *Anna Karenina* with the famous words: 'happy families are all alike, every unhappy family is unhappy in its own way'. To follow him, one can similarly note that at least in terms of basic political institutions democracies are all alike, whereas virtually every authoritarian regime has attempted (successfully or not) to build its own set of institutions which are intended to keep its rulers powerful, and its rivals and the wider society powerless. This is particularly true of the authoritarian regimes that came into existence in a post-communist environment. While Uzbekistan, Kazakhstan or Turkmenistan after the Soviet collapse quickly converted one-party rule into personalist dictatorships that have lasted more than two decades without any sign of democratization, the rulers of Georgia, Ukraine, and Kyrgyzstan lost their powers after the wave of 'colour revolutions' in 2003–05. As for Russia, its trajectory from a communist one-party regime to post-communist authoritarianism was more complicated.

The period of the 1990s was marked by severe elite conflicts which were resolved as a series of zero-sum games. In 1991, Russia's popularly elected president, Boris Yeltsin, eliminated the power of his arch-rival Mikhail Gorbachev in the wake of collapse of the Soviet Union. In 1993, Yeltsin dissolved the Russian parliament and imposed a new constitution, which granted the president a wide discretion of virtually unlimited power. But these victories did not make him an unconstrained dictator: given the weakness of the Russian state, a protracted economic recession, and the low level of the regime's public support, none of the actors was able to achieve fully fledged dominance. Yeltsin was faced with major constraints imposed by other actors, such as the Russian parliament, regional elites and business leaders, but given their fragmentation and the lack of cooperation, enjoyed wide scope for manoeuvring, which helped him to win the highly contested 1996 presidential election and survive the major economic crisis of 1998. Yeltsin was unable to stay in power until the end of his second term and it is no wonder that the 'war of the Yeltsin Succession' in 1999 became a decisive moment in the establishment of a new and authoritarian regime. Since Yeltsin could not automatically transfer power to a loyal successor (as Heydar Aliyev, for instance, had been able to do in Azerbaijan), the leadership succession crisis provoked the threat of major political conflicts, but the Kremlin achieved a major victory over the rebellious factions of the elite. The skyrocketing rise in the popularity of Yeltsin's chosen successor, Vladimir Putin, against the background of the beginning of post-crisis economic growth and the Kremlin's control of the media, which ensured its prevalence in the 'information wars', contributed to this outcome.

The new ruling group led by Putin, after its takeover of the political leadership in 2000, had to respond to the political challenges of the previous decade. In the 2000s, strengthening the state against a background of unprecedented economic growth, Vladimir Putin and his entourage established firm control over key political and economic resources and enjoyed wide popularity among the ordinary people. Putin's correction of the mistakes of the new authoritarianism over the 2000s would be worth an A+ in the College for Dictators. The major lessons the Kremlin learned from the experience of the post-communist elite conflicts of the 1990s, and from the subsequent wave of 'colour revolutions' in the other post-Soviet states, were that political monopoly could not be sustained over time just by default. It was strengthened by the adoption of political and institutional instruments that prevented alternative coordination by elites and citizens at large, and increased entry barriers to the political market. Those measures were complemented by heavy pressure on already weak organizational entities such as oppositional parties, independent media and NGOs that might otherwise have served as providers of this alternative coordination and decreased the costs of political participation. Almost all of these organizations were faced with the tough choice between co-optation into the regime as its loyal junior subordinates and the marginal status of a hopeless 'niche' opposition.

Meanwhile, political institutions were effectively adjusted and fine-tuned for the purposes of the ruling group. In particular, elections served as a means of the legitimization of political order, and they allowed the ruling group to adopt various policies in different arenas irrespective of the preferences of voters. They also helped to rotate Russia's elites without a competition for votes, due to the very fact that winners of future elections were appointed well before the voting had taken place (such as in 2008, when Vladimir Putin picked his *pro tempore* successor, Dmitri Medvedev, who met no resistance from other candidates as well as from the voters). Yet the 'return substitution', when Medvedev in 2011 stepped down and paved the way for a new Putin presidency, contributed to large-scale public discontent, when for the first-ever time since the Soviet collapse the previously passive and inept Russians were deeply involved in political protests. The wave of unrest against unfair elections shook the capital cities of the country, but in terms of power and government the political status quo remained largely unchallenged. To summarize, an authoritarian regime in Russia is consolidated at the moment, and no major signs of its decline have yet been observed.

Making autocracy work: foundations and pillars

As Adam Przeworski noted, 'Authoritarian equilibrium rests mainly on lies, fear, or economic prosperity' (Przeworski 1991: 58). All these three pillars played an important role in the case of Russia's authoritarianism, even though probably in reverse order. Certainly, in the 2010s the living standards of most of the Russian people are much higher than in the 'good old' Soviet times, let alone the turbulent period of the 'roaring 1990s'. The consumption boom, especially in the large cities, was visible; unemployment was incredibly low; and the benefits from the export of hydrocarbons were enough for the Kremlin to buy the loyalty of its subjects. Yet many Russian citizens endorsed an authoritarian regime only as long as it provided them with material well-being and not because of a mass belief in its legitimacy as such. Even the deep but short-term recession during the global economic crisis of 2008–09 did not lead to a damaging decline in mass support for the regime as such, even though it provoked some changes in mass political demands.

A relative economic prosperity also allowed Russia's rulers to rely on 'carrots' rather than 'sticks' as the major tools of their dominance and to avoid systematic repression. On the contrary, the regime granted its subjects (at least on paper) a wide array of individual and some civic freedoms, although it severely constrained their political rights. Repression of the regime's opponents was certainly limited: the list of political prisoners in Russia that was compiled after the protest rallies in February 2012 in Moscow included only 39 names, a remarkably low number by comparison with other authoritarian regimes. The risk of facing major losses due to unsanctioned political activism was not so high, until 2012 when the Kremlin launched a campaign of 'tightening the screws' against its rivals. But in a broader sense, the fear of excessively high costs of political disequilibration among various social groups (especially after the painful experience of post-communist transformation) greatly contributed to the preservation of the *status quo*. Fears of losses and risk aversion contributed to the fact that even for those Russians who complained about the current authoritarian regime, its continuity looked like a lesser evil *vis-à-vis* any other possible alternatives.

Finally, the third pillar of authoritarian equilibrium – lies – became one of the most visible elements of the Russian regime. Thanks to monopoly control over the major information channels, the Kremlin had ample opportunities for manipulative propaganda, relying upon a wide range of techniques. A noisy and unwanted independent media milieu was driven into the ghetto of the internet and some other outlets; beyond these narrow circles the Kremlin and its loyalists enjoyed a fully fledged dominance over the political agenda. A monopoly information supply was matched by a low level of demand for alternative information sources among many Russians. Until 2011–12, an unsurprisingly large proportion of survey respondents evaluated elections in Russia as 'fair' despite widespread fraud and manipulations. However, as Abraham Lincoln put it, 'one can fool some of the people all of the time, and all of the people some of the time, but cannot fool all of the people all of the time', and lies became less effective with the spread of the internet, especially during the wave of political protests of 2011–12 in Russia and its aftermath.

As the experience of many failures of authoritarian regimes, ranging from 'colour revolutions' to the 'Arab spring' suggests, a power monopoly cannot last long just by default. On the contrary, Russia's rulers have had to invest tremendous efforts into regime consolidation in order to ensure its sustainability over time. For this purpose, they rely upon three major sources, which provided the institutional basis for the regime, namely: (1) super-presidentialism; (2) sub-national authoritarianism; and (3) a dominant party.

Super-presidentialism as a model of the separation of powers assumes weak checks and balances on the presidential executive and wide latitude of discretion for a popularly elected political leader of this kind. The zero-sum nature of presidential elections dramatically increased the cost of a loss to the incumbent. Therefore, super-presidentialism creates additional incentives for rulers to hold on to power at any cost, but also poses new challenges. They are faced with the temptation of eliminating electoral competition as such and turning into a 'classical' authoritarian regime (like in Kazakhstan under Nazarbayev) and with the risk of undermining political order in the case of leadership succession due to an almost inevitable reconfiguration of patronage ties, which maintains the loyalty of elites (this is actually what happened in Ukraine and Georgia before the 'colour revolutions'). It was no wonder that Putin aimed to force various segments of Russia's elites to accept unequivocal submission and to achieve the long-term loyalty of all stakeholders. This goal was achieved by the co-optation of sub-national political machines, controlled by regional governors and city mayors, under the Kremlin's control, and reformatting of the party system into a tightly managed hierarchy under the dominance of the pro-Kremlin party United Russia. Key institutional changes, such as the elimination of popular elections of regional chief executives and the reframing of electoral and party legislation, played a major role in this process.

The pivotal role of sub-national leadership in maintaining an authoritarian regime is undeniable, especially due to its electoral nature: the Kremlin's need for provincial votes could be satisfied only by powerful local bosses who were able to control electoral processes in their respective areas. However, given the decentralization of the Russian polity in the 1990s, this task has been implemented on an ad hoc basis by informal bargaining between the Kremlin and sub-national leaders. After 2004, as part of a wider policy of recentralization, regional chief executives became de facto appointed from Moscow, the Kremlin agreed to the power monopoly of regional leaders if they brought the required quantity of votes with them and demonstrated their ability to control local politics for the sake of the preservation of the regime itself. A new informal contract with sub-national leaders, which was based on the principle of 'a regional/local power monopoly in exchange for the "correct" voting results', became a major element of centre–regional relations in Russia. Even though, in 2012, gubernatorial elections were nominally restored, this institutional framework has not changed much in practice.

Also, the Kremlin succeeded in establishing a tightly controlled party system, which was essential for maintaining the regime in the national and sub-national electoral and parliamentary arenas. As comparative experience suggests, party-based autocracies are usually more stable and longer-lived than personalist or military dictatorships. In fact, UR became a major Kremlin tool, which allowed the ruling group to acquire an unchallenged monopoly in both parliamentary and electoral politics. This monopoly had been reached after a series of institutional changes that are discussed in earlier chapters, including toughening the rules on the registration of political parties, raising the threshold for parliamentary elections, shifting from a mixed to a proportional electoral system for State Duma elections, and the like. After getting monopoly status, UR became the only available choice for all meaningful national and sub-national political actors. Still, several other parties were present on the periphery of the Russian electoral arena without presenting a serious danger to the regime, decreasing the risk of the rise of a disloyal 'anti-systemic' opposition, and to a certain extent also supporting the regime. But the overall impact of parties (including UR) on politics and policy-making remained rather limited. Unlike in communist regimes, when the ruling party exercised its control through the state machinery, in post-communist Russia the state apparatus used party politics as an effective instrument of its control over the political process. However, with the relaxation of the registration rules for political parties in 2012 the dominance of UR over the party landscape became more questionable.

Russia's authoritarian regime successfully adopted some political and institutional arrangements that are typical for democracies – such as a parliament, elections, and political parties – but emasculated their substance. To what extent will these features of Russia's authoritarianism persist into the future?

The problem of the institutional trap

As one can see, the current political regime in Russia has relied on a complex web of interrelated and informal 'rules of the game', which formed a sort of institutional 'core'. These rules are: (1) a unilateral monopoly in the hands of the country's leader over the adoption of key political decisions; (2) a taboo on open electoral competition among elites given elections that are themselves unfree and unfair; and (3) the de facto hierarchical subordination of regional and local authorities to the central government (the 'power vertical').

These rules are clearly imperfect, indeed they are inherently inefficient given extremely high levels of corruption, hidden but quite determined competition for rent access and resource redistribution among organized interests, and the ruling group's inability to conduct reforms that might prejudice the equilibrium that presently obtains, which also explains the ineffective attempts at Russia's authoritarian modernization. Nevertheless, these rules have persisted over time.

At first sight, the growing demand for change among various segments of Russian society, given the regime's claim to the supply of the previous 'stability', poses the threat of the rise of political tensions and increases the risks of regime change. However, the attractiveness of the existing regime is not the only reason for maintaining political equilibrium. The alternatives to the *status quo* may look even more unattractive or unrealistic; and more importantly, the costs of transition from the existing political order to something else may seem prohibitively high. The business community fears a new property redistribution, while the employees of state-dependent enterprises are afraid of structural reforms and unemployment; the 'systemic' opposition, which remains loyal to the regime, believes that regime change will significantly reduce its influence, and the like. In short, many actors and ordinary people see political continuity as a lesser evil as compared with major regime change. As long as the costs of a *status quo* equilibrium do not exceed its current benefits for the ruling group and society at large, this equilibrium will be endorsed by the major actors: they have little incentive to challenge it. Thus, the institutional trap – a stable but socially ineffective equilibrium that almost no one wants to break – becomes rooted in Russian politics. This equilibrium may well prove self-enforced – not only due to the weakness of the actors that are capable of challenging the regime, but also because of the inertia created by the 'rules of the game' themselves. The longer the current *status quo* is maintained, the greater the costs of overthrowing it.

As the regime and the 'stability' it offers endure over time, Russia ends up in a 'vicious cycle'; the longer the *status quo* persists, the smaller are the chances of successfully overcoming this 'institutional trap'. Indeed, the current political equilibrium effectively creates incentives for the ruling group to preserve the *status quo* at any cost as a goal in itself; at the same time, the notorious inefficiency of governance narrows the time horizons for major actors, making them sacrifice long-term goals for the sake of short-term gains here and now. Moreover, as the current Russian leadership learned from Gorbachev's *perestroika* experience, actors that launch political liberalization run the risk of losing power.

Is Russia's exit from the 'institutional trap' possible? Can Russia reject inefficient electoral authoritarianism and establish new, more stable and successful 'rules of the game'? As the experience of various countries suggests, exits from 'institutional traps' often result from the impact of exogenous shocks – wars, ethnic conflicts, revolutions, or economic crises. However, predicting such developments is an impossible task *a priori*. Therefore, let us attempt to avoid further discussion of exogenous shocks and their possible impacts; instead, we will focus on the role of internal political factors on the continuity and/or change of the Russian political regime and consider some alternative paths of the evolution of Russian political regime, such as:

- the preservation and further decay of the current political regime;
- increasing authoritarian tendencies as a result of the ruling group's reaction to the challenges to its dominance (the 'iron fist' mechanism);
- a sudden collapse of the current regime in certain circumstances (not necessarily those caused by powerful external shocks);
- a gradual and, most probably, inconsistent creeping democratization of the political regime under societal pressure.

In fact, the regime's trajectory may represent a combination of some of these scenarios and alternations of their various elements. We will try looking at each of these scenarios in order to understand their potential constraints and risks.

'Institutional decay': towards a new stagnation?

Provided the environment in which the political regime operates does not significantly change in the foreseeable future, given roughly the same constellation of key actors with their rent-seeking capabilities, and assuming that pressure on the regime from the protest movement is reduced to the level it had reached before late 2011, one should not expect that the ruling group will be likely to revise the 'rules of the game' and change the institutional 'core' of the regime. An inertia-based scenario that preserves current political institutions with some insignificant changes looks more desirable than either democratization or a shift towards a repressive authoritarianism.

However, maintaining an inefficient political equilibrium cannot occur by default; it will require substantial effort on the part of the ruling group. Besides the skilful of use of 'carrots' and 'sticks', the authorities will most certainly be obliged to resort to targeted and strictly limited repression in relation to their opponents; they will have to adopt 'divide and rule' tactics towards the moderate opposition and correct both the formal and informal rules of the game in order to consolidate the institutional 'core' of the political regime rather than simply preserve it in its current form. A crackdown on some protest activities, increasing fines and sanctions for violations of rules of meetings and rallies, the return of criminal prosecution for defamation and a number of other intimidatory actions were accompanied by the partial liberalization of party registration procedures and a return to the popular election of regional chief executives. But the partial revision of the rules of the game was intended to entrench and reinforce the *status quo*, in a new form.

A path to 'institutional decay' that involves further regime consolidation and rearrangements will not be able to resolve the problems of the current political order in Russia, but will most probably exacerbate them. In this case one should expect a further deterioration of principal–agent problems in centre–regional relations as well as an increase in corruption and deepening conflicts over rent redistribution among organized interests. The 'decay' will also lead to sharp increases in the costs of maintaining the political equilibrium due to the rising payoffs which the authorities will have to offer to political and economic rent-seekers for their loyalty.

And what about the society at large? The demand for changes can be satisfied to a certain extent through some concessions on second-order issues through the effective co-optation of some moderate opponents, and through the relatively successful resolution of certain issues, or in some instances it may simply remain at the level of latent discontent and local 'rebellions', which do not pose a major threats to the rulers. Without cumulative and relatively prolonged societal pressure on the regime, 'institutional decay' may last until the cost of maintaining the *status quo* becomes prohibitively high or until the current generation of Russian leaders simply become extinct, akin to the generation of the Soviet leaders of the Brezhnev period.

Although the 'decay' scenario should be presently be treated as a baseline, there are two important constraints to its implementation. First, in order to maintain the political equilibrium, the ruling group will require a constant and substantial rent inflow that will support the loyalty of all the important actors and of the society at large. Second, the regime's manipulative strategy may become less efficient over time. Thus, attempts to preserve the *status quo* through 'institutional decay' are not necessarily bound to be successful.

'Iron fist': a dictator's solution

An alternative scenario of Russian political development assumes that the ruling group will face an increase in actual and potential challenges to its domination, which may take a vast variety of forms. Protest activism might grow in scope and scale and taking new, possibly violent forms. Risks of 'rebellions' by some of the regime's current loyalists might increase, and the potential of their co-optation and/or use of other tools of maintaining loyalty might be exhausted. The experiences of some other authoritarian regimes in different parts of the world suggest that under such circumstances their leaders tend to pick up a 'stick' and use it in a robust manner. Although this strategy rarely proves to be successful in the long term (especially if the regimes do not enjoy mass support and the protests increase), in the short term such reaction to crises may postpone their negative consequences for the regime. Thus, in order to maintain their domination, the Russian authorities might possibly opt for an 'iron fist' response, which would mean that they would have to partially or completely dismantle the democratic façade and replace it by openly authoritarian rule while still retaining the regime's institutional 'core'.

It is hard to predict the Kremlin's steps along this path; they might involve an expansion in the discretion of law enforcement agencies and the security services and further restrictions on individual rights and liberties, more far-reaching attacks on independent media and the internet, greater pressure on NGOs and so forth. The possible design of new 'rules of the game', as well as the scale and scope of any repression, depends upon perceptions of threats of challenges and associated risks by the ruling group rather than upon the actual danger of these challenges and risks. 'Tightening the screws' will allow the authorities to cope with some of the symptoms of regime pathologies but by no means improve government performance. On the contrary, one might expect the turn towards an 'iron fist' would lead to a sharp increase in the cost of maintaining the political equilibrium due to the rise in the payoffs that would have to be made to the coercive apparatus to reward its loyalty. The risk of becoming a hostage to the coercive apparatus is a problem for any repressive regime, and in the case of Russia, the law enforcement agencies and security services do not enjoy much public support. However, one should not assume that the turn towards an 'iron fist' scenario would necessarily provoke political disequilibrium, even if the increase in repression posed a threat to a large number of previously loyal actors or other dissidents.

Also, there are some risks for the ruling group if it opts for an 'iron fist' authoritarian turn. First, international experience suggests that authoritarian regimes that initially refrain from repression quite rarely become far more repressive. Using a 'stick' is quite a difficult task after a long and successful distribution of 'carrots'. Second, the international consequences of a turn towards repressive authoritarianism would most probably be negative, in circumstances in which international legitimacy is of the utmost importance to the elites. Finally, repressive authoritarianism might open the door to conflicts within the ruling group and reveal the poor performance of the coercive apparatus. The unsuccessful use of repression might even bring about the collapse of the authoritarian regime, as happened after the August 1991 coup in the Soviet Union. Given the unpredictable consequences of such developments, an 'iron fist' might prove to be one of the possible causes of regime collapse and far from a 'dictator's solution'.

Regime collapse: a horrible end v. endless horror?

At first glance, political regime collapse appears unlikely in contemporary Russia. Such a collapse would imply the regime's sudden and relatively rapid breakdown as a result of mass protests or other internal conflicts accompanied by a virtually complete turnover of the ruling elite and a total rejection of the previous rules of the game. Such a scenario is hindered by the conspicuous absence of a 'revolutionary situation' in Russia, at least as of the present. The scale of anti-system mobilization and the potential of the opposition are clearly insufficient to overthrow the regime; at the same time, the degree of consolidation of the ruling group and their allies is still quite high. Moreover, even the emergence of a revolutionary situation does not necessarily lead to the revolutionary outcome of a political process. But quite frequently, such developments result in a spontaneous, sometimes even mostly accidental, constellation of events at a given 'critical juncture' in history. Thus, one cannot completely exclude the possibility of the regime's collapse, especially given the ever-increasing difficulty of maintaining political equilibrium.

A horrible end is sometimes better than endless horror, as conventional wisdom goes. However, this notion is questionable when it comes to the collapse of political regimes. Both the experience of the 1917 collapse of the Russian monarchy and the 1991 collapse of the Soviet Union led to the replacement of one authoritarian regime by another, which might become even more repressive. If after the collapse of the current authoritarian regime, Vladimir Putin is simply replaced by a new authoritarian leader, it would probably not bring about the country's democratization but would rather signal a regime change from bad to worse.

Yet it is also plausible that Russia may successfully capitalize on the chance of democratization if and when such a chance appears in the aftermath of regime collapse. However, such a situation will hardly emerge by default and be followed by successful democratization without a special effort by political actors and the society at large; thus, relying on such a scenario is as reasonable as relying on a winning lottery ticket. The risks of a sudden political collapse of the Russian regime are quite high, while its positive consequences are not so obvious.

'Creeping democratization': opportunities and risks?

'Creeping democratization' is a complex, incremental and sometimes quite lengthy process of transition from authoritarianism to democracy through a series of strategic interactions of the ruling group and the opposition, who adjust their strategies in response to each other's respective moves. Ruling groups may agree to a partial regime liberalization under pressure from the opposition, and then – given increasing pressure and the regime's inability to eliminate liberalization – accept an extension of the scope for political participation, which, in turn, may lead to deepening divisions within the ruling group and an increasing role for the opposition within the political process. Further developments may involve different options, among which are a compromise between the reform-minded section of the ruling group and the moderate section of the opposition (an 'elite settlement', like the one that was achieved by Polish round-table talks in 1989), as well as the ruling group's initial steps towards regime democratization, which allows it to maintain power through competitive elections (like in South Korea in 1987). The process may even develop into a series of electoral competitions with a playing field that becomes more even over time, guaranteeing a peaceful transfer of power to the opposition (as in Mexico in 1997–2000). Such trajectories resulted in democratization 'success stories' in some countries, and there is no reason to rule them out in case of Russia. Bearing these prospects in mind, one may consider the 2011–12 protests as the first (necessary yet insufficient) step towards the country's 'creeping democratization'.

The challenge to the authoritarian regime may arise from below only if various social groups and political actors are able to consolidate and mobilize a large number of their supporters on the basis of a negative consensus against the status quo. The experience of 'creeping democratization' in a number of countries suggests that in order to reach their goal, regime opponents require the cooperation of a number of segments of the opposition and the mutual support of their potential allies. The various segments of the opposition would have to seek the support of different cross-sections of the citizens; they would also have to refrain from publicly attacking one another to accomplish their principal goal; in addition, they would have to demonstrate their ability to reach tacit compromises and their willingness to be ideologically flexible.

Besides the opportunity they provide for different forms of mass protest activism, elections serve as an important element capable of undermining the current authoritarian equilibrium. The nomination of opposition-backed candidates and party lists, and even the support of 'anyone but' regime nominees, might deal the Kremlin a most serious blow. If regional and local elections prompted a cascade of 'stunning' effects, one might expect that in the run-up to the 2016 parliamentary and 2018 presidential elections, the ruling group would be forced to opt for far more swift and serious regime liberalization by changing the formal and informal rules of the elections, thus opening political opportunities for the opposition. If these trends spread across space and time, then national elections would become a key challenge to the preservation of the *status quo*, especially under highly uncertain conditions.

Of course, turning away from democratization to other forms of authoritarianism are as likely as the kind of 'success story' we have just set out: 'creeping democratization' often turns out to be inconsistent and may involve numerous false starts. Moreover, successful democratization does not simply happen by default as the authoritarian regime is overthrown.

Concluding remarks: Russia will be free

The collapse of communist rule and the breakup of the Soviet Union occurred at a time in which many observers took it for granted that a worldwide process of transition to democracy would also affect the post-Soviet states, which were doomed to become democratic more or less by default. These naïve expectations proved to be wrong. What was being considered as the emergence of a new post-Soviet democracy in Russia over twenty years ago has actually turned into the rise of a new post-Soviet authoritarianism.

However, the failure of Russia's first post-communist democratization attempt after 1991 by no means indicates that democracy is doomed to fail, and that a second democratization attempt – if and when it takes place – will inevitably result in a new turn towards authoritarianism, or, say, a vicious cycle of conflicts, crises, and violence (although these possibilities cannot be ruled out). All the same, after two decades of authoritarian regime building, the ruling group was able to shut the 'window of opportunity' for democratization. However, the situation in Russia is gradually changing over time as a result of learning effects from the recent past and also due to the effects of generational changes. The trial-and-error political experience of the post-Soviet period was not in vain: now, the country is probably better prepared for a deliberate and consistent transition to democracy than it was in the early 1990s, despite the fact that the political conditions for such a transition are less favourable today than they were immediately after the end of communist rule. The public demand for changes will likely grow over time, and this trend offers some hope that Russia will not repeat the same flight from freedom that happened in the 1990s and especially in the 2000s. Therefore, the main slogan of opposition rallies – 'Russia will be free!' – may be perceived not just as a call for action but also as a key item on Russia's political agenda for the foreseeable future. Russia will indeed become a free country. The question is, exactly when and how this will happen, as well as what will be the costs of Russia's path to freedom.

Guide to Further Reading

The listing that follows suggests a number of items that students and others may find useful to consult on the themes that are covered by each chapter of this book. Current developments in Russian politics are regularly covered in several academic journals including *Europe-Asia Studies* (ten issues annually), *East European Politics* (formerly the *Journal of Communist Studies and Transition Politics*, quarterly), *Post-Soviet Affairs* (quarterly), *Communist and Post-Communist Studies* (quarterly), and *Problems of Post-Communism* (six issues annually). Legal and constitutional issues across the post-communist countries generally are given particular attention in the *Review of Socialist Law* (quarterly). The *Current Digest of the Russian [formerly Post-Soviet] Press* (weekly, also available online) is a well-organized digest of translations from newspapers and journals. Other electronic sources are considered in the final section.

Chapter 1 Politics in Russia

There are a number of good overviews of the Soviet system. These include Gooding (2001), Keep (1996), Kenez (1999), Malia (1994), Marples (2010), Sakwa (1998, 2010), Sandle (1997), Service (2005), Suny (1998) and Westwood (2002). The Gorbachev period is covered by Aron (2012), Brown (1996, 2007), by Gorbachev himself (1987), Sakwa (1990) and White (1994). Arnason (1993) provides a fine analysis of the overall failure of the Soviet system, while Cox's edited book (1998) presents debates about the academic study of the fall. More detailed analyses can be found in Kotkin (2001), Kotz and Weir (1997) and an overview in White (2000). General analyses of contemporary Russian politics can be found in Bacon and Wyman (2010), Brown (2001), Dutkiewicz and Trenin (2011), Lane (2002), Ledeneva (2013), Lynch (2011), McFaul, Petrov and Ryabov (2004), Remington (2004) Ross (2004), Sakwa (2008a), Treisman (2011), Wegren (2013) and White (2011). Fine biographies of Yeltsin are provided by Aron (2000) and Colton (2008), and his leadership is compared with Gorbachev's by Breslauer (2002), while the Putin period is analysed by Herspring (2003), Judah (2013) and Sakwa (2008b, 2011), with his own views presented in Putin (2000).

Chapter 2 The Hegemonic Executive

Current information on the institutions, personalities, and politics of the Russian presidency, federal executive, and political system is most readily found on the internet, with many valuable sites in Russia offering their information in English. Especially notable are the official internet site of the

264

Russian presidency (http://eng.kremlin.ru/) and Russian government (http://government.ru/en/). Russian news sites with up to date discussions include the news agency, RIA Novosti (http://en.rian.ru/), Russia's leading English-language newspaper, *The Moscow Times* (http://www. themoscow-times.com/), and the government-funded news channel, Russia Today (http://rt.com/). Especially useful Western sites include the compendium news website, Russian News Online (http://russiannewsonline.com/), and the daily listserv of Russian news, Johnson's Russia List (http://www.russialist.org/). Survey data, including barometers of public approval levels of Russian politicians and institutions, are to be found at the Levada Centre (http://www. levada.ru/eng/) and VTsIOM (http:// www.wciom.com/).

For contrasting discussions of the Putin presidency, policy programme and legacy, see Åslund and Kuchins (2009), Karppinen (2006), Mendras (2012), Sakwa (2011), Shevtsova (2007), Trenin (2007), Wegren (2013), and Willerton (2007). Roberts' book on United Russia is definitive (2011). Among the various texts on Putin, Hill and Gaddy (2013), Hutchins with Korobko (2012), Lynch (2011), and Solovyov (2008, in Russian) set out alternative viewpoints. For a discussion of the dynamics of presidential popularity, see Rose, Mishler, and Munro (2011). For those fluent in Russian, Zenkovich (2006) provides detailed coverage of the Putin regime, while Gill and Young (2012) provide an encyclopaedic overview of the institutions and politics of the Putin era. For a discussion of Soviet period institutions and policies, see Hough and Fainsod (1979).

Chapter 3 Parliamentary Politics in Russia

The Russian Constitution of 1993 is available in a number of convenient editions, and may be consulted electronically at a number of locations; an easily followed English language version is available at www.bucknell. edu/russian/const/constitit.html (note that this and other online and printed versions may not always incorporate amendments, especially the extension of the parliamentary and presidential terms in December 2008). On representative institutions since the late Soviet period see Fish (2005), McFaul (2001) and Remington (2001), and on the contemporary Duma and Federation Council see Chaisty (2006), Haspel *et al.* (2006), Remington (2006), Troxel (2003), and Smith and Remington (2001). Reuter and Remington (2009) deal with relations between the Duma and United Russia.

Chapter 4 The Electoral Process

The development of the late Soviet and electoral system is considered in White, Rose and McAllister (1997), and the more recent period in White *et al.* (2012). The reports on recent Russian elections by the OSCE are available at http://www.osce.org/odihr/elections/russia. Election monitoring has its own literature, including Kelley (2012). Myagkov *et al.* (2009) is an excellent econometric analysis of electoral fraud that reads like a detective novel. The December 2011 elections and popular responses are considered in a special issue of *Problems of Post-Communism*. The Central Electoral Commission's website may be consulted at www.cikrf.ru; much of its material is available in English. Full sets of results of recent elections may be consulted in two handbooks: Rose and Munro (2009) and Nohlen and Stöver (2010).

Chapter 5 Russia's Political Parties and their Substitutes

For analysis of the overall evolution of Russia's parties through Putin, see Gel'man (2005) and Hale (2006). Comprehensive discussions of Russia's parties in individual election cycles can be found for 1993 in White, Rose and McAllister (1997) and Colton and Hough (1998), for 1995–96 in Colton (2000) and Belin and Orttung (1997), for 1999–2000 in Colton and McFaul (2003), Hesli and Reisinger (2003), and Rose and Munro (2002), and for 2003–04 in Hale (2006). On parties during the late Soviet period and in Russia before the 1993 Duma election, see Fish (1995) and McFaul and Markov (1993). On the rise of United Russia, see Colton and McFaul (2000), Hale (2004a), Smyth, Wilkening, and Urasova (2007), and Roberts (2011). For analysis of the CPRF's origins, see Urban and Solovei (1997). The fate of Russia's liberal parties is discussed in Hale (2004b) and Kullberg and Zimmerman (1999). The virtual parties are explained in Wilson (2005). Smyth (2006) supplies a discussion of Russian party organization, and Hanson (2003) examines the role of ideology in Russian parties. McFaul (2001) treats the origins of Russia's election system and its effects on parties. Parties in the legislature are examined by Remington (2001).

Chapter 6 Voting Behaviour

Useful overviews of Russian voting behaviour and more general public attitudes to politics can be found in Colton (2000), Brader and Tucker (2001, 2008), and Rose, Mishler and Munro (2011). White and McAllister (2007, 2008) examine the main aspects of electoral participation, and place it in a broader comparative context. Early studies of the impact of age and generation on political outlooks include Rose and Carnaghan (1995), with a more detailed analysis in Mishler and Rose (2007). Voting behaviour and its relationship to social groups, including the development of the party system, is examined in depth in Brader and Tucker (2001) and in Kitschelt (2001), while partisanship and its consequences are covered in Brader and Tucker (2008) and McAllister and White (2007). Overviews of Putin as a political leader can be found in Sakwa (2010c) and the electoral implications of Putin's leadership are examined in White and McAllister (2008).

Chapter 7 Civil Society and Contentious Politics in Russia

On protest and contention in the USSR see Viola (2002) and Kozlov (2002). For the role of protest in the collapse of the USSR, Beissinger (2002) is essential reading. Those interested in civil society in the Gorbachev era should see Brovkin (1990). On the difficulties of organizing in the 1990s, read Ashwin (1999). On the first Chechen war Lieven (1998) makes interesting reading. For a moving journalistic account of the Beslan hostage-taking see Phillips (2007). On the evolution of civil society see Evans *et al.* (2005) and for protest politics in Russia over the last decade see Robertson (2011). For an assessment of the importance of the election protest cycle in 2011–12, see the special edition of *Problems of Post-Communism* (2013).

Chapter 8 Russia's Media and Political Communication in the Digital Age

For a discussion of how news is produced in the post-Soviet environment, see Koltsova (2006). For more details about the internet, state power and citizen activism in Russia, see Oates (2013). For reports on media freedom, see Freedom House for both general reports on media and specific country reports on the Russian internet in its Freedom on the Net series (www.freedomhouse.org). If you are interested in the role of the media in countries such as Russia in general, see Voltmer (2013). For a lively account of media transitions from the Soviet era to the Russian regime, see Mickiewicz (1999). If you are interested in how journalists struggle for media freedom, see the international organizations Reporters Without Borders at http://en.rsf.org and Committee to Protect Journalists at cpj.org.

Chapter 9 Assessing the Rule of Law in Russia

For a comprehensive overview of the Russian law and legal system, see Maggs, Burnham, and Danilenko (2012). See Henderson (2011) and Sharlet (1992) on the constitution. For an assessment of ongoing legal reform, see Kahn (2008), Solomon (2007), and Kurkchiyan (2003). For more information on the Russian courts, see Solomon and Fogelsong (2000) on the courts of general jurisdiction; Hendley (2012a) on the justice-of-the-peace courts; Trochev (2008) on the constitutional court; Hendley (2004) on the *arbitrazh* courts; Trochev (2006) on selecting judges; and Esakov (2012) on jury trials. For more on criminal justice, see Favarel-Garrigues (2011), Firestone (2009), Pomorski (2001), and Solomon (1987). On Russians' attitudes towards law, see Hendley (2012c, 2009) and Ledeneva (2008).

Chapter 10 A Federal State?

A good compilation of papers on federalism and regional issues by leading scholars is Ross and Campbell (2009). For a detailed analysis of the important factors behind Russia's wars to retain control over Chechnya, see Hughes (2007). A novel study of regional issues based on political 'boundary issues' is Goode (2011).

Chapter 11 Managing the Economy

Economic developments and policies in Russia, as elsewhere, change rapidly. One good way of keeping abreast of events is to read the *BOFIT Weekly*, put out by the Bank of Finland Institute for Economies in Transition, accessible without charge at www.bof.fi. The institute's working papers, accessible through the same site, are also useful, though more technical. Underlying issues do not change so rapidly, but they do take ever-shifting forms, so that it is generally worthwhile to read the more recent overviews and monographs. Of these, two are outstanding: Sutela (2012) and Gaddy and Ickes (2013). On the critically important oil industry, Gustafson (2012) is authoritative and also highly readable. For understanding the wider socio-political system in which Russia's economic institutions are embedded, Ledeneva (2013) is strongly recommended.

Chapter 12 Society and Social Divisions in Russia

On the social structure of Russian society, including social class, gender and generation, see Salmenniemi (2012). Many of the aspects of social inequalities in Russia are discussed in White (2011), chapter 5. On Russian welfare reforms see Cook (2007). On how Russians have navigated social change see Shevchenko (2009). The changing destinies of working class men are discussed in Walker (2010). On informal relations and social networks in the Russian society see Ledeneva (2006). For the analysis of the welfare state, the voluntary sector and grassroots activism see Jäppinen *et al.* (2011). For historical and contemporary analysis of homelessness and social exclusion in Russia see Stephenson (2006).

Chapter 13 Foreign Policy

General accounts of Russian foreign policy under Putin may be found in Mankoff (2011), Kanet (2010) and Tsygankov (2013). On foreign policy decision-making, see White in Allison *et al.* (2006). Trenin (2013a) considers what Putin's foreign policy will be in the near future. On Russian policy towards the near abroad, see Nygren (2008) and Donaldson in Gill and Young (2012). Allison (2008) analyses the Georgian war, while Eurasian Economic Commission (www.eurasiancommission.org) has a timeline and useful data about the proposed Eurasian Union and various previous integration efforts. Russia's relations with the far abroad are covered by Thorun (2009). Saivetz looks particularly at US–Russian relations (in Gill and Young 2011), while Engelbrekt and Bertil Nygren (2010) and White and Feklyunina (2014) concentrate on Europe. Lo (2008), Menon (2009) and Rozman (in Gill and Young 2011) examine Sino-Russian relations. Malashenko (2013) offers a useful analysis of Russia and the Arab Spring.

Chapter 14 The Military, Security and Politics

For discussions of the condition and readiness of the Russian military, see Miller and Trenin (2004), Herspring (2006 and 2013) and Barany (2007). Webber and Mathers (2006), Betz (2004), Eichler (2012) and Barany (2008) focus on the links between the armed forces, society and politics. See Daucé and Sieca-Kozlowski (2006) and Webber and Zilberman (2006) on *dedovshchina*. Bukkvoll (2008) provides in-depth discussion of corruption in the military. Cooper (2006) considers many aspects of the defence economy, including secrecy and access to information about the defence budget. For discussions of the phenomenon of Putin and the *siloviki*, see Kryshtanovskaya and White (2003) and Renz (2006).

Chapter 15 Trajectories of Russian Politics

A wide range of assessments of current developments and trajectories of Russian politics can be found in the annual reports of numerous international NGOs, such as Human Rights Watch (www.hrw.org), Amnesty International (www.thereport.amnesty.org) and especially Freedom House (www.freedomhouse.org). Varieties of authoritarianism are discussed in Ezrow and Frantz (2011); comparative analyses of 'competitive' or 'electoral' authoritarian regimes may be found in Levitsky and Way (2010) and Schedler (2013). A historical and cultural determinist account of Russian politics is presented by Pipes (2004), while Shleifer and Treisman (2004) offered a more optimistic view of post-Soviet changes. Hale (2005), Way (2005) and Gel'man (2008) examine trajectories of regime changes in Russia *vis-à-vis* other post-Soviet countries. Fish (2005) focuses on the impact of presidentialism on authoritarian trends in Russian politics, while Gel'man and Ross (2010) and Golosov (2011) dealt with the crucial role of its sub-national dimension. On scenarios of Russia's political developments and discussions about prospects for the future, see Lipman and Petrov (2011, 2013).

Electronic resources may most conveniently be consulted through one of the gateways that provide a specialist service. Particularly comprehensive and well maintained is REESWeb, hosted by the University of Pittsburgh; its services include an annotated link list, a full-text search engine and a central announcement and calendar system (www.ucis.pitt.edu/reesweb). The Library of Congress maintains a 'Portals to the World: Russia' at www.loc.gov/rr/international/european/russia/ru.html. Guides to electronic resources are maintained by several other libraries, including the British Library in London ('Guide to Slavonic and East European Internet Resources' at www.bl.uk), the School of Slavonic and East European Studies in London ('Directory of Internet Resources on Central and Eastern Europe and Russia' at www.ssees.ac.uk), and the Bodleian Library at Oxford University ('Guide to Slavonic & East European E-resources' at www.bodley.ox.ac.uk). An inter-university network maintains 'Intute', which provides a comprehensive and (above all) annotated selection of more than two hundred websites from and about the region at www.intute.ac.uk/socialsciences/cgi-bin/browse.pl?id=120952).

For current events, the Radio Free Europe/Radio Liberty Newsline from 1995 to 2008 may be consulted at www.rferl.org/archive/en-newsline/latest/683/683.html, and English-language versions of its broadcast coverage may be found at www.rferl.org. A very useful ongoing collection of journalistic writings on Russian politics and society is Johnson's Russia List (website and e-mail newsletter, by subscription, at www.cdi.org/russia/johnson/default.cfm). For the Russian government's perspective on current developments, in English, see for instance RIA Novosti (www.en.rian.ru), and Russia Profile (www.russiaprofile.org). The Voice of Russia broadcasts in English (www.ruvr.com), and so does the television channel Russia Today (www.russiatoday.com). The *Moscow Times* (www.moscowtimes.ru) and *St Petersburg Times* (www.sptimes.ru) are lively and independent; they are available on subscription, but current issues may normally be consulted on their websites without charge.

References

Aldrich, John H. (1995), *Why Parties?* Chicago: University of Chicago Press.

Allison, Roy (2008), 'Russia Resurgent? Moscow's Campaign to "Coerce Georgia to Peace"', *International Affairs*, vol. 84, no. 6, pp. 1145–71.

Allison, Roy, Margot Light and Stephen White (2006), *Putin's Russia and the Enlarged Europe*. Oxford: Blackwell for the Royal Institute of International Affairs.

Andrews, Josephine T. (2002), *When Majorities Fail: The Russian Parliament, 1990–1993*. Cambridge: Cambridge University Press.

Anonymous (2010), 'Repressivno-truslivoe pravosudie', *Novaya advokatskaya gazeta* (July). Available at http://www.advgazeta.ru/ arch/72/442.

Arnason, Johann P. (1993), *The Future that Failed: Origins and Destinies of the Soviet Model*. London: Routledge.

Arnold, Chloe (2007), 'Conscript's Prostitution Claims Shed Light on Hazing', *Radio Free Europe/Radio Liberty Report*, 20 March, http://rfe.rferl.org/featuresarticle/2007/03/09d16e9f-0374-4ca2-84f6-88b9b6f2d0e1.html.

Aron, Leon (2000), *Boris Yeltsin: A Revolutionary Life*. London: HarperCollins.

Aron, Leon (2012), *Roads to the Temple: Truth, Memory, Ideas, and Ideals in the Making of the Russian Revolution, 1987–1991*. New Haven and London: Yale University Press.

Ashwin, Sarah (1999), *Russian Workers: The Anatomy of Patience*. Manchester: Manchester University Press.

Åslund, Anders, and Andrew Kuchins (2009), *The Russia Balance Sheet*. Washington, DC: Peterson Institute for International Economics.

Bacon, Edwin and Bettina Renz with Julian Cooper (2006), *Securitising Russia: The Domestic Politics of Putin*. Manchester and New York: Manchester University Press.

Bacon, Edwin and Matthew Wyman (2010), *Contemporary Russia*, 2nd edn. Basingstoke: Palgrave Macmillan.

Barany, Zoltan (2007), *Democratic Breakdown and the Decline of the Russian Military*. Princeton, NJ: Princeton University Press

Barany, Zoltan (2008), 'Civil–Military Relations and Institutional Decay: Explaining Russian Military Politics', *Europe-Asia Studies*, vol. 60, no. 4, pp. 581–604.

Barnes, Andrew (2001), 'Property, Power, and the Presidency: Ownership Policy Reform and Russian Executive–Legislative Relations, 1990–1999,' *Communist and Post-Communist Studies*, vol. 34, no. 1, pp. 39–61.

Bartolini, Stefano and Peter Mair (1990), *Identity, Competition, and Electoral Availability: The Stabilisation of European Electorates 1885–1985*. Cambridge: Cambridge University Press.

Bauman, Zygmunt (1992), *Intimations of Postmodernity*. London: Routledge

Bauman, Zygmunt (2000), *Liquid Modernity*. Cambridge: Polity Press.

Beck, Ulrich (1992), *Risk Society: Towards a New Modernity*. London: Sage.

Beck, Ulrich and Beck-Gernsheim, Elizabeth (2002), *Individualization: Institutionalised Individualism and its Social and Political Consequences*. London: Sage.

Beissinger, Mark R. (2002), *Nationalist Mobilization and the Collapse of the Soviet State*. Cambridge: Cambridge University Press.

Belanovsky, Sergei, *et al.* (2012), 'Socio-economic change and political transformation in Russia. November 2011', in Brian Anderson, Rebecca Baldridge, and Mikhail Dmitriev (eds), *Russian State and Society in Political Crisis*. Moscow: Center for Strategic Research, The Russian Presidential Academy of National Economy and Public Administration.

Belin, Laura and Robert Orttung (1997), *The Russian Parliamentary Elections of 1995: The Battle for the Duma*. Armonk, NY: M.E. Sharpe.

Betz, David J. (2004), *Civil–Military Relations in Russia and Eastern Europe*. London and New York: RoutledgeCurzon.

Bjelakovic, Nebojsa (2008), 'Russian Military Procurement: Putin's Impact on Decision-Making and Budgeting', *Journal of Slavic Military Studies*, vol. 21, no. 3, pp. 527–42.

Blais, Andre (2000), *To Vote Or Not To Vote? The Merits and Limits of Rational Choice*. Pittsburgh, PA: University of Pittsburgh Press.

Blais, Andre (2007), 'Turnout in Elections,' in Russell J. Dalton and Hans-Dieter Klingeman (eds), *The Oxford Handbook of Political Behavior*. Oxford: Oxford University Press.

Blais, Andre and Agnes Dobrzynska (1998), 'Turnout in Electoral Democracies,' *European Journal of Political Research,* vol. 33, no.2, pp. 239–61.

Bogoslovskaya, Yelizaveta, Ella Polyakova and Yelena Vilenskaya (2001), 'The Soldiers' Mothers of St Petersburg: A Human Rights Movement in Russia', in Stephen J. Cimbala (ed.), *The Russian Military into the Twenty-First Century*. London: Frank Cass.

Bowen, Andrew (2013), 'Military Modernization and Power Projection', *The Interpreter*, 10 October, available at http://www.interpretermag.com/military-modernizatsiia-and-power-projection/.

Brader, Ted and Joshua A. Tucker (2001), 'The Emergence of Mass Partisanship in Russia, 1993–1996,' *American Journal of Political Science,* no. 45, no.1, pp. 69–83.

Brader, Ted and Joshua A. Tucker (2008), 'Pathways to Partisanship: Evidence from Russia', *Post-Soviet Affairs,* no. 24, no. 3, pp. 263–300.

Breslauer, George W. (2002), *Gorbachev and Yeltsin as Leaders*. Cambridge: Cambridge University Press.

Brovkin, Vladimir (1990), 'Revolution from Below: Informal Political Associations in Russia 1988–89', *Europe-Asia Studies*, vol. 42, no.2, pp. 233–57.

Brown, Archie (1996), *The Gorbachev Factor*. Oxford: Oxford University Press.

Brown, Archie (ed.) (2001), *Contemporary Russian Politics: A Reader*. Oxford: Oxford University Press.

Brown, Archie (2007), *Seven Years that Changed the World: Perestroika in Perspective*. Oxford, Oxford University Press.

Brown, Archie and Lilia Shevtsova (eds) (2001), *Gorbachev, Yeltsin, and Putin: Political Leadership in Russia's Transition*. Washington, DC: Carnegie Endowment.

Buchowski, Micha? (2006), 'The Specter of Orientalism in Europe: From Exotic Other to Stigmatized Brother', *Anthropological Quarterly*, vol. 79, no 3, pp. 463–82.

Bukkvoll, Tor (2008), 'Their Hands in the Till: Scale and Causes of Russian Military Corruption', *Armed Forces and Society*, vol. 34, no. 2, pp. 259–75.

Bunce, Valerie J. (1995), 'Should Transitologists be Grounded?', *Slavic Review*, vol. 54, no. 1, pp. 111–27.

Buzin, A. Yu. and A. Ye. Lyubarev (2008), *Prestuplenie bez nakazaniya: Administrativnye tekhnologii federal'nykh vyborov 2007–2008 godov*. Moscow: Nikkolo M.

Carothers, Thomas (2002), 'The End of the Transition Paradigm', *Journal of Democracy*, vol. 13, no. 1 (January), pp. 5–21.

Chaisty, Paul (2006), *Legislative Politics and Economic Power in Russia*. New York: Palgrave Macmillan.

Charter of the Commonwealth of Independent States (1993), *Rossiiskaya gazeta*, 12 February, p. 6.

Chekhonadskikh, Maria (2012), 'Trudnosti perevoda: prekaritet v teorii i na praktike', *Khudozhestvennii zhurnal*, available at http://xz.gif.ru/numbers/79-80/chekhonadskih/.

CIS Countries Legislation Database, Agreement on forming a Single Economic Space (2003), http://cis-legislation.com/document.fwx?rgn=4879.

CIS (2011), *Zayavlenie missii nablyudatelei ot SNG po rezul'tatam nablyudeniya za podgotovkoi i provedeniem vyborov deputatov Gosudarstvennoi Dumy Federal'nogo Sobraniya Rossiiskoi Federatsii shestogo sozyva*, at http://www.cis.minsk.by/news.php?id=435.

Clarke, Simon (2002), *Making Ends meet in Contemporary Russia: Secondary Employment, Subsidiary Agriculture and Social Networks*. Cheltenham: Edward Elgar.

Clement, Carine (2007), 'Fleksibil'nost' po-rossiiski: ocherk o novykh formakh truda i podchineniya v sfere uslug', *Sotsiologicheskii zhurnal*, no. 4, pp. 74–96.

Cohen, Stephen F. (2004), 'Was the Soviet System Reformable?', *Slavic Review*, vol. 63, no. 3 (Fall), pp. 459–88.

Colin Lebedev, Anna (2006), 'The Test of Reality: Understanding Families' Tolerance Regarding Mistreatment of Conscripts in the Russian Army', in Françoise Daucé and Elisabeth Sieca-Kozkowski (eds), *Dedovshchina in* the Post-Soviet Military: Hazing of Russian Army Conscripts in a Comparative Perspective.* Stuttgart: ibidem-Verlag.

Colton, Timothy J. (2000), *Transitional Citizens: Voters and What Influences Them in the New Russia.* Cambridge, MA: Harvard University Press.

Colton, Timothy J. (2008), *Yeltsin: A Life.* New York: Basic Books.

Colton, Timothy J. and Henry E. Hale (2014), 'Putin's Uneasy Return and Hybrid Regime Stability: The 2012 Russian Election Studies Survey', *Problems of Post-Communism,* vol. 61, no. 2 (March/April), pp. 3–22.

Colton, Timothy J. and Jerry F. Hough (eds) (1998), *Growing Pains: Russian Democracy and the Election of 1993.* Washington, DC: Brookings.

Colton, Timothy J. and Michael McFaul (2000), 'Reinventing Russia's Party of Power: "Unity" and the 1999 Duma Election', *Post-Soviet Affairs,* vol. 16, pp. 201–24.

Colton, Timothy J. and Michael McFaul (2003), *Popular Choice and Managed Democracy: The Russian Elections of 1999 and 2000.* Washington, DC: Brookings Institution.

Connolly, Richard, and Philip Hanson (2012), 'Russia's Accession to the World Trade Organization: Commitments, Processes, and Prospects', *Eurasian Geography and Economics,* vol. 53, no. 4, pp. 479–501.

Cook, Linda J. (2007), *Postcommunist Welfare States: Reform Politics in Russia and Eastern Europe.* Ithaca, NY: Cornell University Press.

Cook, Linda J. (2011), 'Russia's Welfare Regime: The Shift toward Statism', in Maija Jäppinen, Meri Kulmala, and Aino Saarinen (eds), *Gazing at Welfare, Gender and Agency in Post-Socialist Countries.* Newcastle: Cambridge Scholars, pp. 14–37.

Cooper, Julian (2006), 'Society–Military Relations in Russia: The Economic Dimension', in *Military and Society in Post-Soviet Russia,* edited by Stephen L. Webber and Jennifer G. Mathers. Manchester and New York: Manchester University Press.

Cox, Gary W. (1997), *Making Votes Count.* Cambridge: Cambridge University Press.

Cox, Michael, (ed.) (1998), *Rethinking Soviet Collapse: Sovietology, the Death of Communism and the New Russia.* London: Cassell Academic.

Daucé, Françoise and Elisabeth Sieca-Kozlowski, (eds) (2006), *Dedovshchina in the Post-Soviet Military: Hazing of Russian Army Conscripts in a Comparative Perspective.* Stuttgart: ibidem-Verlag.

Dawisha, Karen and Bruce Parrott (1994), *Russia and the New States of Eurasia: The Politics of Upheaval.* Cambridge and New York: Cambridge University Press.

Dragneva, Rilka and Kataryna Wolczuk (2012), 'Russia, the Eurasian Customs Union and the EU: Cooperation, Stagnation or Rivalry?', *Chatham House Briefing Paper,* Russia and Eurasia Programme.

Dutkiewicz, Piotr and Dmitry Trenin, (eds) (2011), *Russia: The Challenges of Transformation.* New York: New York University Press.

Eichler, Maya (2012), *Militarizing Men: Gender, Conscription and War in Post-Soviet Russia.* Stanford: Stanford University Press.

Eismont, Mariya (2012), 'My dolzhny verit' ne dokazatel'stvam, a silovikam na slovo', *PublicPost*, May 25, available at http://www.publicpost.ru/theme/id/1495/my_dolzhny_verit_ne_dokazatelstvam_a_silovikam_na_slovo/.

Engelbrekt, Kjell. and Bertil Nygren, (eds) (2010), *Russia and Europe: Building Bridges, Digging Trenches*. London: Routledge.

Erikson, Robert S., Michael MacKuen and James A. Stimson (2002), *The Macro Polity*. New York: Cambridge University Press.

Esakov, Gennady (2012), 'The Russian Criminal Jury: Recent Developments, Practice, and Current Problems', *American Journal of Comparative Law*, vol. 60, no. 3, pp. 665–702.

Eurasian Economic Commission (2013), *Eurasian Economic Integration: Facts and Figures*. At http://www.eurasiancommission.org/ru/Documents/broshura26Body_ENGL_final2013_2.pdf, accessed 21 October 2013.

European Institute for the Media (1994), *The Russian Parliamentary Elections: Monitoring of the Election Coverage of the Russian Mass Media*. Düsseldorf, Germany: European Institute for the Media, available online at http://www.media-politics.com/eimreports.htm.

European Institute for the Media (February 1996), *Monitoring the Media Coverage of the 1995 Russian Parliamentary*. Düsseldorf, Germany: European Institute for the Media, available online at http://www.media-politics.com/eimreports.htm.

European Institute for the Media (September 1996), *Monitoring the Media Coverage of the 1996 Russian Presidential Elections*. Düsseldorf, Germany: European Institute for the Media, available online at http://www.media-politics.com/eimreports.htm.

European Institute for the Media (March 2000), *Monitoring the Media Coverage of the December 1999 Parliamentary Elections in Russia*. Düsseldorf, Germany: European Institute for the Media, available online at http://www.media-politics.com/eimreports.htm.

European Institute for the Media (August 2000), *Monitoring the Media Coverage of the March 2000 Presidential Elections in Russia*. Düsseldorf, Germany: European Institute for the Media, available online at http://www.media-politics.com/eimreports.htm.

European Stability Initiative (2009), *ESI Manual: The Russian Debate on the South Caucasus: Who is Who?/Part 1: Russian Print Media*. Available online at http://www.esiweb.org/pdf/esi_-_russia_manual_-_part_1_-_print_media.pdf.

European Union External Action (2005), EU-Russia Common Spaces, http://eeas.europa.eu/russia/common_spaces/index_en.htm.

Evans, Alfred B. (2006), 'Civil Society in the Soviet Union,' in Alfred B. Evans, Laura A. Henry and Lisa McIntosh Sundstrom (eds) (2005).

Evans, Alfred B. (2012), 'Protests and Civil Society in Russia: The Struggle for the Khimki Forest', *Communist and Post-Communist Studies*, vol. 45, no. 3-4, pp. 233–42.

Evans Alfred B., Jr., Laura A. Henry and Lisa McIntosh Sundstrom (eds)

(2005), *Russian Civil Society: A Critical Assessment*. Armonk, NY: M. E. Sharpe.

Evans, Geoffrey and Stephen Whitefield (1998), 'The Evolution of the Left and Right in Post-Soviet Russia', *Europe-Asia Studies,* vol. 50, pp. 1023–42.

Ezrow, Natasha M. and Erica Frantz (2011), *Dictators and Dictatorships: Understanding Authoritarian Regimes and Their Leaders*. New York: Continuum.

Favarel-Garrigues, Gilles (2011), *Policing Economic Crime in Russia: From Soviet Planned Economy to Privatisation*. New York: Columbia University Press.

Finn, Peter (2006), 'Kremlin Inc. Widening Control over Industry', *Washington Post*, 19 November.

Fiorina, Morris P. (1981), *Retrospective Voting in American National Elections*. New Haven, CT: Yale University Press.

Firestone, Thomas (2009), 'Armed Injustice: Abuse of the Law and Complex Crime in Post-Soviet Russia', *Denver Journal of International Law & Policy*, vol. 38, no. 4, pp. 555–80.

Fish, M. Steven (1995), *Democracy from Scratch*. Princeton, NJ: Princeton University Press.

Fish, M. Steven (2001), 'Conclusion: Democracy and Russian Politics', in Zoltan Barany and Robert G. Moser (eds), *Russian Politics: Challenges of Democratization*. Cambridge: Cambridge University Press, pp. 215–51.

Fish, M. Steven (2005), *Democracy Derailed in Russia: The Failure of Open Politics*. Cambridge and New York: Cambridge University Press.

Fitzpatrick, Sheila (2005), *Tear Off the Masks!: Identity and Imposture in Twentieth-Century Russia*. Princeton, NJ: Princeton University Press.

Florida, Richard L. (2002), *The Rise of the Creative Class: and How It's Transforming Work, Leisure, Community and Everyday Life*. New York: Basic Books.

Fortescue, Stephen (2006), *Russia's Oil Barons and Metal Magnates: Oligarchs and the State in Transition*. Basingstoke: Palgrave Macmillan.

Franklin, Mark N. (2004), *Voter Turnout and the Dynamics of Electoral Competition in Established Democracies Since 1945*. Cambridge: Cambridge University Press.

Freedom on the Net (2012), *Freedom on the Net 2012: A Global Assessment of Internet and Digital Media*. New York: Freedom House, available online at http://www.freedomhouse.org/report-types/freedom-net.

Freedom on the Net (2013), 'Russia'. In *Freedom on the Net 2013*. New York: Freedom House, available online at http://www.freedomhouse.org/report-types/freedom-net.

Freedom of the Press (2013), *Freedom of the Press 2013: Middle East Volatility Amid Global Decline*. New York: Freedom House, available online at http://www.freedomhouse.org/report/freedom-press/freedom-press-2013.

Fuller, Lon L. (1964), *The Morality of Law*, revised edn. New Haven: Yale University Press.

Gaddy, Clifford G., and Barry W. Ickes (2013), *Bear Traps on Russia's Road to Modernization*, Abingdon and New York: Routledge.

Gel'man, Vladimir (2005), 'Political Opposition in Russia: A Dying Species?', *Post-Soviet Affairs*, vol. 21, no. 3, pp. 226–46.

Gel'man, Vladimir (2008), 'Out of the Frying Pan, Into the Fire? Post-Soviet Regime Changes in Comparative Perspective', *International Political Science Review*, vol. 29, no. 2, pp. 157–80.

Gel'man, Vladimir and Cameron Ross, (eds) (2010), *The Politics of Sub-National Authoritarianism in Russia*. Aldershot: Ashgate.

Gerber, Alan and Donald P. Green (1998), 'Rational Learning and Partisan Attitudes,' *American Journal of Political Science*, vol. 42, pp. 794–818.

Gessen, Martha (2012), *The Man without a Face: The Unlikely Rise of Vladimir Putin*. London: Granta.

Giddens, Anthony (1991), *Modernity and Self-Identity*. Cambridge: Polity.

Gill, Graeme, and James Young (eds) (2012) *Routledge Handbook of Russian Politics and Society*, Abingdon: Routledge.

Gimpel'son, V. E., and R. I. Kapelyushnikov (eds) (2008), *Zarabotnaya plata v Rossii. Evolyutsiya i differentsiatsiya*. Moscow: Higher School of Economics.

Golosov, Grigorii V. (2011), 'Regional Roots of Electoral Authoritarianism in Russia,' *Europe-Asia Studies*, vol. 63, no. 4, pp. 623–39.

Golosov, Grigorii V. (2012), 'The 2012 Political Reform in Russia: The Interplay of Liberalizing Concessions and Authoritarian Corrections,' *Problems of Post-Communism*, vol. 59, no. 6, November–December, pp. 3–14.

Goskomstat (1996), *Rossiiskii statisticheskii yezhegodnik*. Moscow: Logos.

Goode, J. Paul (2011), *The Decline of Regionalism in Putin's Russia: Boundary Issues*. London and New York: Routledge.

Gooding, John (2001), *Socialism in Russia: Lenin and His Legacy, 1890–1991*. Basingstoke: Palgrave Macmillan.

Gorbachev, Mikhail (1987), *Perestroika: New Thinking for Our Country and the World*. London: Collins.

Gosudarstvennaia Duma: Stenogramma zasedanii (2003), *Byulleten' no. 78* (526), 21 February. Moscow: Izdanie Gosudarstvennoi Dumy.

Gudkov, L. D. *et al.* (2012) *Rossiiskie parlamentskie vybory: elektoral'nyi protsess pri avtoritarnom rezhime*. Moscow: Levada Centre, at http://www.levada.ru/books/rossiiskie-parlamentskie-vybory-2011-goda.

Gustafson, Thane (2012), *The Wheel of Fortune. The Struggle for Oil and Power in Russia*. Cambridge, MA: The Belknap Press.

Hahn, Gordon M. (2002), *Russia's Revolution from Above, 1985-2000: Reform, Transition, and Revolution in the Fall of the Soviet Communist Regime*. New Brunswick, NJ: Transaction Publishers.

Hale, Henry E. (2004a), 'The Origins of United Russia and the Putin Presidency: The Role of Contingency in Party-System Development', *Demokratizatsiya: The Journal of Post-Soviet Democratization*, vol. 12, no. 2, pp. 169–94.

Hale, Henry E. (2004b), 'Yabloko and the Challenge of Building a Liberal Party in Russia,' *Europe-Asia Studies*, vol. 56, no. 7, pp. 993–1020.

Hale, Henry E. (2005), 'Regime Cycles: Democracy, Autocracy, and Revolution in Post-Soviet Eurasia,' *World Politics*, vol. 58, no. 1, pp. 133–65.

Hale, Henry E. (2006), *Why Not Parties in Russia? Democracy, Federalism, and the State.* Cambridge: Cambridge University Press.

Hale, Henry E. (2011), 'The Putin Machine Sputters: First Impressions of Russia's 2011 Duma Election', *Russian Analytical Digest*, no.106, 21 December, pp. 2–5.

Hale, Henry E., and Timothy J. Colton, (2013), 'What Makes Dominant Parties Dominant in Hybrid Regimes? The Surprising Importance of Ideas in the Case of United Russia', unpublished paper.

Hale, Henry E., Michael McFaul and Timothy Colton (2004), 'Putin and the "Delegative Democracy" Trap: Evidence from Russia's 2003–04 Elections', *Post-Soviet Affairs*, vol. 20, no. 4 (October–December), pp.285–319.

Hanson, Philip (2005), 'Federalism with a Russian Face: Regional Inequality and Regional Budgets in Russia', in P. Reddaway and R. Orttung (eds), *The Dynamics of Russian Politics.* Washington, DC: US Institute of Peace Press, pp. 295–318.

Hanson, Philip (2009), 'Russia to 2020,' *Finmeccanica Occasional Paper*, www.chathamhouse.org.uk/publications/papers/view/-/id/802.

Hanson, Philip (2012), 'The Russian Economy and its Prospects,' in Hanson, James Nixey, Lilia Shevtsova and Andrew Wood, *Putin Again. Implications for Russia and the West.* London: Chatham House.

Hanson, Stephen E. (2003), 'Instrumental Democracy: The End of Ideology and the Decline of Russian Political Parties', in Vicki L. Hesli and William M. Reisinger (eds) *The 1999-2000 Elections in Russia: Their Impact and Legacy.* Cambridge: Cambridge University Press.

Haspel, Moshe, Thomas F. Remington and Steven S. Smith (2006), 'Lawmaking and Decree Making in the Russian Federation: Time, Space, and Rules in Russian National Policymaking,' *Post-Soviet Affairs*, vol. 22, no. 3, pp. 249–75.

Henderson, Jane (2011), *The Constitution of the Russian Federation: A Contextual Analysis.* Oxford: Hart Publishing.

Hendley, Kathryn (2004), 'Business Litigation in the Transition: A Portrait of Debt Collection in Russia', *Law & Society Review*, vol. 31, no. 1, pp. 305–47.

Hendley, Kathryn (2009), '"Telephone Law" and the "Rule of Law": The Russian Case', *Hague Journal on the Rule of Law*, vol. 1, no. 2, pp. 241–69.

Hendley, Kathryn (2012a), 'Assessing the Role of Justice-of-the-Peace Courts in the Russian Judicial System', *Review of Central and East European Law*, vol. 37, no. 4, pp. 373–93.

Hendley, Kathryn (2012b), 'The Puzzling Non-Consequences of Societal

Distrust of Courts: Explaining the Use of Russian Courts', *Cornell International Law Journal*, vol. 45, no. 3, pp. 517–67.

Hendley, Kathryn (2012c), 'Who Are the Legal Nihilists in Russia?' *Post-Soviet Affairs*, vol. 28, no. 2 (April–June), pp. 149–86.

Hermet, Guy, Richard Rose and Alain Rouquié, (eds) (1978), *Elections Without Choice*. London: Macmillan.

Herspring, Dale R. (ed.) (2003), *Putin's Russia: Past Imperfect, Future Uncertain*. Oxford: Rowman & Littlefield.

Herspring, Dale R. (2006), 'Undermining Combat Readiness in the Russian Military 1992–2005', *Armed Forces and Society*, vol. 32, no. 4, pp. 513–31.

Herspring, Dale R. (2013), *Civil-Military Relations and Shared Responsibility: A Four-Nation Study*. Baltimore, MD: Johns Hopkins University Press.

Hesli, Vicki L. and William M. Reisinger, (eds) (2003), *The 1999–2000 Elections in Russia: Their Impact and Legacy*. Cambridge: Cambridge University Press.

Hill, Fiona (2006), 'Moscow Discovers Soft Power', *Current History, vol.* 105, no. 693 (October), pp. 341–7.

Hill, Fiona, and Clifford G. Gaddy (2013), *Mr. Putin: Operative in the Kremlin*. Washington, DC: Brookings.

Hojdestrand, Tova (2009), *Needed by Nobody: Homelessness and Humanness in Post-Socialist Russia*. Ithaca, NY: Cornell University Press.

Hough, Jerry F. (1998), 'Institutional Rules and Party Formation', in Timothy J. Colton and Hough (eds), *Growing Pains: Russian Democracy and the Election of 1993*. Washington: Brookings, pp. 37–73.

Hough, Jerry F., and Merle Fainsod (1979), *How the Soviet Union Is Governed*. Cambridge, MA: Harvard University Press.

Howard, Marc Morjé (2003), *The Weakness of Civil Society in Post-Communist Europe*. Cambridge: Cambridge University Press.

HSE (2013), Higher School of Economics, *Novyi KGB (Kommentarii o gosudarstve i biznese)*, 19 October –1 November.

Hughes, James (2007), *Chechnya: From Nationalism to Jihad*. Philadelphia: University of Pennsylvania Press.

Huntington, Samuel P. (1968), *Political Order in Changing Societies*. New Haven: Yale University Press.

Huntington, Samuel P. (1991), *The Third Wave: Democratization in the Late Twentieth Century*. Norman: University of Oklahoma Press.

Huskey, Eugene (1991), 'A Framework for the Analysis of Soviet Law', *Russian Review*, vol. 50, no. 1, pp. 53–70.

Hutchins, Chris, with Alexander Korobko (2012), *Putin*. Leicester: Troubador Publishing Ltd.

Iarskaia-Smirnova, Elena and Pavel Romanov (2012), 'Doing Class in Social Welfare Discourses: "Unfortunate Families" in Russia', in Suvi Salmenniemi (ed.), *Rethinking Class in Russia*. Farnham: Ashgate, pp. 85–106.

International Institute for Strategic Studies (IISS) (1991), *The Military Balance 1991–1992*. London: Brassey's for the IISS.

International Institute for Strategic Studies (IISS) (1993), *The Military Balance 1993–1994*. London: Brassey's for the IISS.

International Institute for Strategic Studies (IISS) (1996), *The Military Balance 1996–1997*. Oxford: Oxford University Press for the IISS.

International Institute for Strategic Studies (IISS) (2008), *The Military Balance 2008*. London: Routledge for the IISS.

International Institute for Strategic Studies (IISS) (2013), *The Military Balance 2013*. London: Routledge for the IISS.

Ivanchenko, A. V. and A. Ye. Lyubarev (2007), *Rossiiskie vybory ot perestroiki do suverennoi demokratii*, 2nd edn. Moscow: Aspekt Press.

Jäppinen, Maija, Meri Kulmala and Aino Saarinen (2011), *Gazing at Welfare, Gender and Agency in Post-socialist Countries*. Newcastle upon Tyne: Cambridge Scholars.

Judah, Ben (2013), *Fragile Empire: How Russia Fell In and Out of Love with Vladimir Putin*. New Haven and London: Yale University Press.

Kahn, Jeffrey (2008), 'Vladimir Putin and the Rule of Law in Russia', *Georgia Journal of International and Comparative Law*, vol. 36, no. 5, pp. 511–57.

Kanet, Roger E., (ed.) (2010), *Russian Foreign Policy in the 21st Century*. Basingstoke: Palgrave Macmillan.

Karppinen, Antti (2006), *The Hammer, Sickle, and Star: Following the Idea of Russia*. Helsinki: Kikimora Publications.

Karvonen, Lauri (2010), *The Personalisation of Politics: A Study of Parliamentary Democracies*. Colchester: ECPR Press.

Keep, John L. H. (1996), *Last of the Empires: A History of the Soviet Union, 1945–1991*. Oxford: Oxford University Press.

Kelley, Judith (2012), *Monitoring Democracy: When International Election Observation Works, and Why it Often Fails*. Princeton, NJ: Princeton University Press.

Kenez, Peter (1999), *A History of the Soviet Union from the Beginning to the End*. Cambridge: Cambridge University Press.

KGI (2012), 'Zayavlenie komiteta grazhdanskikh initsiativ', 17 October, http://komitetgi.ru/news/news/251/.

Kharat'yan, Kirill (2013), 'Zachem Gosudarstvennaia Duma prinimaet stol'ko zakonov,' *Vedomosti*, 2 July.

Kitschelt, Herbert (2001), 'Divergent Paths of Postcommunist Democracies,' in Larry Diamond and Richard Gunther (eds), *Political Parties and Democracy*. Baltimore, MD: Johns Hopkins University Press.

Kitschelt, Herbert, Zdenka Mansfeldova, Radoslaw Markowski, and Gabor Toka (1999), *Post-Communist Party Systems: Competition, Representation, and Inter-Party Cooperation*. New York: Cambridge University Press.

Koltsova, Olessia (2006), *News Media and Power in Russia*. London: Routledge.

Konitzer, Andrew (2005), *Voting for Russia's Governors*. Washington, DC: Woodrow Wilson Center Press.

Kotkin, Stephen (2001), *Armageddon Averted: The Soviet Collapse 1970–2000*. Oxford: Oxford University Press.

Kotz, David and Fred Weir (1997), *Revolution from Above: The Demise of the Soviet System*. London: Routledge.

Kozlov, Vladimir (2002), *Mass Uprisings in the USSR: Protest and Rebellion in the Post-Stalin Years*. Armonk, NY: M. E. Sharpe.

Kriger, Il–ya (2008), 'V sostoyanii izbirkomy', *Novaya gazeta*, no. 14, 28 February, pp. 7–9.

Kriuchkov, Sergei (2010), *Otnoshenie grazhdan k mirovym sudam*. Moscow: Amerikanskaya assotsiatsiya iuristov.

Kryshtanovskaya, Olga and White, Stephen (2003), 'Putin's Militocracy', *Post-Soviet Affairs*, vol. 19, no. 4, pp. 289–306.

Kryshtanovskaya, Olga and White, Stephen (2011), 'The formation of Russia's network directorate', in Vadim Kononenko and Arkadii Moshes (eds), *Russia as a Network State: What Works in Russia When State Institutions Do Not?* Basingstoke and New York: Palgrave Macmillan, pp. 19–38.

Kullberg, Judith S. and Zimmerman, William (1999), 'Liberal Elites, Socialist Masses, and Problems of Russian Democracy', *World Politics*, vol. 51, no. 3, pp. 323–58.

Kurkchiyan, Marina (2003), 'The Illegitimacy of Law in Post-Soviet Societies', in Denis J. Galligan and Marina Kurkchiyan (eds), *Law and Informal Practices: The Post-Communist Experience*. Oxford: Oxford University Press.

Lane, David (ed.) (2002), *The Legacy of State Socialism and the Future of Transformation*. Oxford: Rowman & Littlefield.

Ledeneva, Alena V. (2006), *How Russia Really Works: The Informal Practices That Shaped Post-Soviet Politics and Business*. Ithaca, NY: Cornell University Press.

Ledeneva, Alena V. (2008), 'Telephone Justice in Russia', *Post-Soviet Affairs*, vol. 24, no. 4 (October–December), pp. 324–50.

Ledeneva, Alena V. (2009), 'From Russia with *Blat*: Can informal networks help modernize Russia?', *Social Research*, vol. 76, no. 1, pp. 257–88.

Ledeneva, Alena V. (2013), *Can Russia Modernize? Sistema, Power Networks and Informal Governance*. Cambridge and New York: Cambridge University Press.

Levada Center (2010), 'Kakie iz prav cheloveka, po Vashemu mneniyu, naibolee vazhny?', available at http://www.levada.ru/archive/prava-cheloveka/kakie-iz-prav-cheloveka-po-vashemu-mneniyu-naibolee-vazhny-otvety-ranzhirova.

Levada Center (2012), 'Okolo treti rossiyan – za docrochnoe osvobozhdenie Mikhaila Khodorkovskogo', available at http://www.levada.ru/25-10-2012/okolo-treti-rossiyan-za-dosrochnoe-osvobozhdenie-mikhaila-khodorkovskogo.

Levada Center (2013a), 'Obshchestvennoe mnenie o Khodokovskom', available at http://www.levada.ru/25-06-2013/obshchestvennoe-mnenie-o-khodorkovskom.

Levada Center (2013b), 'Pervoe vpechatlenie rossiyan ot prigovora po delu

Kirovlesa', available at http://www.levada.ru/26-07-2013/pervoe-vpechatlenie-rossiyan-ot-prigovora-po-delu-kirovlesa.

Levada Center (2013c), 'Rossiyane o Pussy Riot i tserkvi', available at http://www.levada.ru/20-05-2013/rossiyane-o-pussy-riot-i-tserkvi.

Levada Center (2013d), 'Rossiyane o sude prisyazhnykh', available at http://www.levada.ru/31-07-2013/rossiyane-o-sude-prisyazhnykh.

Levada Center (2013e), 'Politicheskie vzglyady rossiyan'. Available at http://www.levada.ru/29-07-2013/politicheskie-vzglyady-rossiyan.

Levinson, Alexei (2009), 'Proshloe – ne navsegda', *Neprikosnovennii Zapas*, no. 64, no. 2.

Levitsky, Steven and Lucan Way (2010), *Competitive Authoritarianism: Hybrid Regimes after the Cold War*. Cambridge and New York: Cambridge University Press.

Levy, Clifford J. (2008), 'Kremlin Rules. Putin's Iron Grip on Russia Suffocates his Opponents', *New York Times*, 24 February, pp. 1–14.

Lewis-Beck, Michael S. and Stegmaier, Mary (2007), 'Economic Models of Voting,' in Russell J. Dalton and Hans-Dieter Klingemann (eds), *The Oxford Handbook of Political Behavior*. Oxford: Oxford University Press.

Lieven, Anatole (1998), *Chechnya: Tombstone of Russian Power*. New Haven: Yale University Press.

Linz, Juan J. and Alfred Stepan (1996), *Problems of Democratic Transition and Consolidation: Southern Europe, South America, and Post-Communist Europe*. Baltimore, MD: Johns Hopkins University Press.

Lipman, Maria and Petrov, Nikolay, (eds) (2011), *Russia in 2020: Scenarios for the Future*. Washington, DC: Carnegie Endowment for International Peace.

Lipman, Maria and Petrov, Nikolay (eds) (2013), *Russia 2025: Scenarios for the Russian Future*. London and New York: Palgrave Macmillan.

Lipset, Seymour Martin, and Stein Rokkan (1967), 'Introduction,' in Seymour Martin Lipset and Stein Rokkan (eds), *Party Systems and Voter Alignments*. New York: Free Press.

Lisi, Marco (2013), 'The Sources of Mass Partisanship in Newer Democracies: Social Identities or Performance Evaluations? Southern Europe in Comparative Perspective,' *International Political Science Review*, published online 19 August.

Lo, Bobo (2008), *Axis of Convenience: Moscow, Beijing, and the New Geopolitics*. London: RIIA, and Washington, DC: Brookings Institution.

Lukyanov, Fyodor (2013), 'Uncertain World: Russia and Ukraine on the Verge of a Decisive Choice', *RIA Novosti*, 22 August, http://en.ria.ru/columnists/20130822/182911246/Uncertain-World-Russia-and-Ukraine-on-the-Verge-of-a-Decisive.html, accessed 15 October.

Lynch, Allen C. (2011), *Vladimir Putin and Russian Statecraft*. Washington, DC: Potomac Books.

Lyubarev, Arkady (2012), 'An Evaluation of the Results of the Duma Elections,' *Russian Analytical Digest*, no. 108, February 6, pp. 2–5.

Maggs, Peter B., Burnham, William, and Danilenko, Gennady (2012), *Law and Legal System of the Russian Federation*, 5th edn, Huntington, NY: Juris Publishing.

Mair, Peter (1997), *Party System Change. Approaches and Interpretations*. Oxford: Clarendon Press.

Malashenko, Alexey (2013), *Russia and the Arab Spring*. Carnegie Moscow Center.

Malia, Martin (1994), *The Soviet Tragedy: A History of Socialism in Russia, 1917–1991*. New York: Free Press.

Mankoff, Jeffrey (2011), *Russian Foreign Policy: The Return of Great Power Politics*. 2nd edn, Lanham, MD: Rowman & Littlefield.

Manning, Nick and Tikhonova, Nataliya E. (2004), 'Russia in Context', in Nick Manning and Nataliya E. Tikhonova (eds), *Poverty and Social Exclusion in the New Russia*. Aldershot: Ashgate, pp. 1–36.

Marples, David R. (2010), *Russia in the Twentieth Century*. Harlow: Pearson Longman.

Marsh, Christopher, Helen Albert and James W. Warhola (2004), 'The Political Geography of Russia's 2004 Presidential Election', *Eurasian Geography and Economics*, vol. 45, pp. 262–79.

Mathers, Jennifer G. (2006), 'Women, Society and the Military: Women Soldiers in Post-Soviet Russia', in Stephen L. Webber and Jennifer G. Mathers (eds), *Military and Society in Post-Soviet Russia*. Manchester and New York: Manchester University Press.

McAllister, Ian (2007), 'The Personalization of Politics,' in Russell J. Dalton and Hans-Dieter Klingemann (eds), *The Oxford Handbook of Political Behavior*. Oxford: Oxford University Press.

McAllister, Ian and Stephen White (2007), 'Political Parties and Democratic Consolidation in Postcommunist Societies,' *Party Politics*, no. 13, pp. 197–216.

McAllister, Ian and Stephen White (2008a), 'Voting "Against All" in Postcommunist Russia', *Europe-Asia Studies,* vol. 60, no. 1 (January), pp. 67–87.

McAllister, Ian and Stephen White (2008b), '"It's the Economy, Comrade!" Parties and Voters in the 2007 Russian Duma Election', *Europe-Asia Studies*, vol. 60, no.1, pp. 931–57.

McAllister, Ian and Stephen White (2011), 'Democratization in Russia and the Global Financial Crisis', *Journal of Communist Studies and Transition Politics*, vol. 27, pp. 476–95.

McAllister, Ian and Stephen White (2014), 'Electoral Integrity and Support for Democracy in Belarus, Russia and Ukraine', *Journal of Elections, Parties and Public Opinion*, DOI: 10.1080/17457289.2014.911744.

McFaul, Michael (2001), *Russia's Unfinished Revolution: Political Change from Gorbachev to Putin*. Ithaca, NY: Cornell University Press.

McFaul, Michael and Markov, Sergei (eds) (1993), *The Troubled Birth of Russian Democracy: Parties, Personalities, and Programs*. Stanford: Hoover Institution Press.

McFaul, Michael, Nikolai Petrov and Andrei Ryabov (2004), *Between Dictatorship and Democracy: Russian Post-Communist Political Reform.* Washington, DC: Carnegie Endowment for International Peace.

Medvedev, Dmitri (2008), *Interview given to Television Channels Channel One, Rossiya and NTV,* available at http://president.kremlin.ru/eng/speeches/2008/08/31/1850_type82912type82916_206003.shtml, emphasis added, accessed 10 October 2013.

Medvedev, Dmitrii (2009) 'Rossiya, vpered!', *Rossiiskaya gazeta,* 11 September, pp. 1, 3.

Mendras, Marie (2012), *Russian Politics: The Paradox of a Weak State.* New York: Columbia University Press.

Menon, Rajan (2009), 'The Limits of Chinese-Russian Partnership', *Survival,* vol. 51, no. 3, pp. 99–130.

Mesropova, Olga (2009), 'The "Discreet Charm of the Russian Bourgeoisie": Oksana Robski and Glamour in Russian Popular Literature', *Russian Review,* January, pp. 89–101.

Mickiewicz, Ellen (1999), *Changing Channels: Television and the Struggle for Power in Russia,* 2nd edn. Durham, NC: Duke University Press.

Miller, Arthur H. and Thomas F. Klobucar (2000), 'The Development of Party Identification in Post-Soviet Societies,' *American Journal of Political Science,* vol. 44, no. 4, pp. 667–86.

Miller, Steven E. (2004), 'Moscow's Military Power: Russia's Search for Security in an Age of Transition', in Steven E. Miller and Dmitri Trenin (eds), *The Russian Military: Power and Policy.* Cambridge, MA: The American Academy of Arts and Sciences.

Miller, Steven E. and Dmitri Trenin (2004), *The Russian Military: Power and Policy.* Cambridge, MA: The American Academy of Arts and Sciences.

Ministry of Foreign Affairs of the Russian Federation (2013), 'Concept of the Foreign Policy of the Russian Federation', *Nezavisimaya gazeta,* 4 March, pp. 9, 11–13 (in Russian).

Ministry of Justice of the Russian Federation (2013) 'Spisok zaregistrirovannykh politicheskikh partii,' http://minjust.ru/ru/nko/gosreg/partii/spisok, accessed 9 November.

Mishler, William and Richard Rose (2007), 'Generation, Age, and Time: The Dynamics of Political Learning during Russia's Transformation', *American Journal of Political Science,* vol. 51, no. 4, pp. 822–34.

Møller, Jørgen, and Svend-Erik Skaaning (2010), 'Systematizing Thin and Thick Conceptions of the Rule of Law'. Available at http://papers.ssrn.com/sol3/papers.cfm?abstract_id=1643367.

Morar', Natalia (2007), 'Chernaya kassa Kremlya', *The New Times,* 10 December, pp. 18–22.

Myagkov, Mikhail, Peter C. Ordeshook, and Dmitri Shakin (2009), *The Forensics of Election Fraud: Russia and Ukraine.* Cambridge: Cambridge University Press.

Netreba, Petr, and Dmitrii Butrin (2013), 'Pravitel'stvo ustoyalo na osnovnykh napravleniyakh', *Kommersant,* 1 February.

Nohlen, Dieter and Philip Stöver (eds) (2010), *Elections in Europe: A Data Handbook*. Baden-Baden: Nomos.

North, Douglass (1990), *Institutions, Institutional Changes and Economic Performance*. Cambridge: Cambridge University Press.

Nygren, Bertil (2008), *The Rebuilding of Greater Russia: Putin's Foreign Policy Towards the CIS Countries*. London: Routledge.

O'Donnell, Guillermo and Schmitter, Philippe C. (1986), *Transitions from Authoritarian Rule: Tentative Conclusions about Uncertain Democracies*. Baltimore: Johns Hopkins University Press.

Oates, Sarah (2006), *Television, Democracy and Elections in Russia*. London: Routledge.

Oates, Sarah (2013), *Revolution Stalled: The Political Limits of the Internet in Post-Soviet Russia*. New York: Oxford University Press.

Oates, Sarah and Laura Roselle Helvey (1997), 'Russian Television's Mixed Messages: Parties, Candidates and Control on Vremya, 1995-1996', paper presented at the American Political Science Association Annual Meeting, Washington, DC.

Oates, Sarah and Tetyana Lokot (2013), 'Twilight of the Gods?: How the Internet Challenged Russian Television News Frames in the Winter Protests of 2011-12', Paper presented at the International Association for Media and Communication Research Annual Conference. Dublin, Ireland (June).

Oates, Sarah and Laura Roselle (2000), 'Russian Elections and TV News: Comparison of Campaign News on State-Controlled and Commercial Television Channels', *The Harvard International Journal of Press/Politics*, vol. 5, March, pp. 30–51.

Oates, Sarah, Lynda Lee Kaid and Mike Berry (2009), *Terrorism, Elections, and Democracy: Political Campaigns in the United States, Great Britain, and Russia*. New York: Palgrave Macmillan.

Obraztsov, Igor V. (2012), 'The Russian Military Elite in the Era of Putin', *Armed Forces and Society*, vol. 38, no. 3, pp. 513–18.

O'Donnell, Guillermo (1993) 'On the State, Democratization and Some Conceptual Problems (A Latin American View with Glances at Some Postcommunist Countries)', *World Development*, vol. 21, no. 8, pp. 1355–69.

O'Donnell, G., Schmitter, P. and Whitehead, L. (eds) (1986) *Transitions from Authoritarian Rule*. Baltimore, MD: Johns Hopkins University Press: vol. 1, *Southern Europe*; vol. 2, *Latin America*; vol. 3, *Comparative Perspectives*; vol. 4, *Tentative Conclusions about Uncertain Democracies*.

Organization for Security and Co-operation in Europe/Office for Democratic Institutions and Human Rights (OSCE/ODIHR) (January 2004), *Russian Federation Elections to the State Duma 7 December 2003 OSCE/ODIHR Election Observation Mission Report*. Warsaw: Office for Democratic Institutions and Human Rights.

Organization for Security and Co-operation in Europe/Office for Democratic Institutions and Human Rights (OSCE/ODIHR) (June 2004), *Russian Federation Presidential Elections 14 June 2004 OSCE/ODIHR Election*

Observation Mission Report. Warsaw: Office for Democratic Institutions and Human Rights.

OSCE (2000a), *Russian Federation. 19 December 1999. Elections to the State Duma. Final Report* (Warsaw: OSCE/ODIHR), at www.osce.org/odihr/elections/russia/16293.

OSCE (2000b), *Russian Federation. Presidential Election 26 March 2000. Final Report* (Warsaw: OSCE/ODIHR), at http://www.osce.org/odihr/elections/russia/16275.

OSCE (2012), *Russian Federation. Elections to the State Duma 4 December 2011. OSCE/ODIHR Election Observation Mission. Final Report* (Warsaw, 12 January), at http://www.osce.org/odihr/elections/86959.

Oxford Analytica (2012), 'Russian Government Struggles to Reform Pension System,' 26 November, available at www.oxan.ru.

Pashaeva, Gulshen (2012), 'In Search of Reciprocal Compromises', *Russia in Global Affairs*, 26 March, http://eng.globalaffairs.ru/print/number/In-Search-of-Reciprocal-Compromises-15509, accessed 10 October 2013.

Pasti, Svetlana (2005), 'Two Generations of Contemporary Russian Journalists', *European Journal of Communication*, vol. 20, no. 1, pp. 89–115.

Patico, Jennifer (2008), *Consumption and Social Change in a Post-Soviet Middle Class*. Washington, DC: Woodrow Wilson Center Press.

PBN (2007, 2008), The PBN Company, *Policy Matters*.

Phillips, Timothy (2007), *Beslan: The Tragedy of School No. 1*. Granta.

Pikayev, Alexander A. (2000), 'Moscow's Matrix', *Washington Quarterly*, vol. 23, no. 3, pp. 187–94.

Pipes, Richard (2004), 'Flight from Freedom: What Russians Think and Want', *Foreign Affairs*, vol. 83, no. 3, pp. 9–15.

'Polnyi tekst vystypleniya Dmitriya Medvedeva na II Grazhdanskom forume v Moskve 22 yanvarya 2008 goda' (2008), *Rossiiskaya gazeta*, available at http://www.rg.ru/2008/01/24/tekst.html.

Pomeranz, William E. (2013), 'How Russia Puts Business Behind Bars', available at http://blogs.reuters.com/great-debate/2013/07/05/how-russia-puts-business-behind-bars/.

Pomorski, Stanislaw (2001), 'Justice in Siberia: A Case Study of a Lower Criminal Court in the City of Krasnoyarsk', *Communist and Post-Communist Studies*, vol. 34, no. 4, pp. 447–78.

Powell, Eleanor Neff and Joshua A. Tucker (2014), 'Revisiting Electoral Volatility in Post-Communist Countries: New Data, New Results and New Approaches', *British Journal of Political Science*, vol. 44, no. 1 (January), pp. 123–47.

Powell, G. Bingham and Guy Whitten (1993), 'A Cross-National Analysis of Economic Voting: Taking Account of the Political Context', *American Journal of Political Science,* vol. 37, pp. 391–414.

President of Russia (2006), Annual Address to the Federal Assembly. Available at http://archive.kremlin.ru/eng/speeches/2006/05/10/1823_type70029type82912_105566.shtml.

President of Russia (2008), 'Kontseptsiya vneshnei politiki Rossiiskoi Federatsii', *Mezhdunarodnaya zhizn'*, no. 8–9, pp. 211–39.

President of Russia (2011), Executive order on the Foreign Ministry's coordinating role in conducting a uniform foreign policy, http://eng.kremlin.ru/acts/3045, accessed 7 October 2013.

Problems of Post-Communism, vol. 60, no. 2, March–April 2013.

Promezhutochniy (2011), *Promezhutochniy doklad o rezul'tatakh ekspertnoi raboty po aktual'nym problemam sotsial'no-ekonomicheskoi strategii Rossii na period do 2020 goda*, accessed 19 August 2011 from http://kommersant.ru/content/pics/doc/doc1753934.pdf.

Przeworski, Adam (1991), *Democracy and the Market: Political and Economic Reforms in Eastern Europe and Latin America*. Cambridge and New York: Cambridge University Press.

Putin, Vladimir (2000), *First Person: An Astonishingly Frank Self-Portrait by Russia's President Vladimir Putin*, with Nataliya Gevorkyan, Natalya Timakova, and Andrei Kolesnikov, translated by Catherine A. Fitzpatrick. London: Hutchinson.

Putin, Vladimir (2004), 'Vladimir Putin vystupil po voprosam gosudarstvennogo upravleniya i ukrepleniya sistemy bezopasnosti strany', *Rossiiskaya gazeta*, 13 September, pp. 1, 3.

Putin, Vladimir (2007), Address at the Munich Conference on Security, *Rossiiskaya gazeta*, 12 February, pp. 1–2.

Putin, Vladimir (2008), Transcript of Annual Big Press Conference, February 14, 2008, http://archive.kremlin.ru/eng/speeches/2008/02/14/1011_type82915_160266.shtml, accessed 10 October 2013.

Putin, Vladimir. (2011), 'Novyi integratsionnyi proekt dlya Evrazii budushchee, kotoroe rozhdaetsya segodnya', *Izvestiya*, 4 October.

Putin, Vladimir (2012) 'Rossiya i menyayushchiisya mir', *Moskovskie novosti*, 27 February, pp. 1, 4-6.

Rassmotrenie del i materialov po I instantsii sudami obshchei yurisdiktsii za period s 1995 po 2012 gody (2013), available at http://www.cdep.ru/index.php?id=79&item=1627.

Reddaway, Peter and Dmitri Glinski (2001), *The Tragedy of Russia's Reforms: Market Bolshevism against Democracy*. Washington, DC: The United States Institute of Peace Press.

Reddaway, Peter and Orttung, Robert (eds) (2005), *The Dynamics of Russian Politics: Putin's Reform of Federal-Regional Relations*, vol. 2. London, Boulder, and New York: Rowman & Littlefield.

Remington, Thomas F. (2001), *The Russian Parliament: Institutional Evolution in a Transitional Regime*. New Haven: Yale University Press.

Remington, Thomas F. (2003), 'Majorities without Mandates: The Russian Federation Council Since 2000', *Europe-Asia Studies*, vol. 55, no. 5, pp. 667–91.

Remington, Thomas F. (2004), *Politics in Russia*. 3rd edn. London: Pearson Longman.

Remington, Thomas F. (2006a) 'Presidential Support in the Russian State Duma', *Legislative Studies Quarterly*, vol. 31, no. 1, pp. 5–32.

Remington, Thomas F. (2006b), 'The Evolution of Executive-Legislative Relations in Russia since 1993', *Slavic Review*, vol. 59, no. 3, pp. 499–520.

Remington, Thomas F. (2011), *The Politics of Inequality in Russia*. Cambridge: Cambridge University Press.

Remnick, David (1993), *Lenin's Tomb: The Last Days of the Soviet Empire*. London, Viking.

Renz, Bettina (2006), 'Putin's Militocracy? An Alternative Interpretation of Siloviki in Contemporary Russian Politics', *Europe-Asia Studies*, vol. 58, no. 6, pp. 903–24.

Reuter, Ora John and Thomas F. Remington (2009), 'Dominant Party Regimes and the Commitment Problem: The Case of United Russia,' *Comparative Political Studies*, vol. 42, no. 4, pp. 501–26.

Reuter, Oran John and Robertson, Graeme B. (2012), 'Subnational Appointments in Authoritarian Regimes: Evidence from Russian Gubernatorial Appointments,' *Journal of Politics*, vol. 74, no. 4, pp. 1025–37.

Rivkin-Fish, Michele (2009), 'Tracing Landscapes of the Past in Class Subjectivity: Practices of Memory and Distinction in Marketizing Russia', *American Ethnologist*, vol. 36, no. 1, pp. 79–95.

Roberts, Sean (2011), *Putin's United Russia Party*. London: Routledge.

Robertson, Graeme B. (2011), *The Politics of Protest in Hybrid Regimes: Managing Dissent in Post-Communist Russia*. New York, NY: Cambridge University Press.

Roeder, Philip G. (1989), 'Electoral Avoidance in the Soviet Union', *Soviet Studies*, vol. 41, no. 3, pp. 462–83.

Rose, Richard (2012a), *New Russia Barometer XIX: The 2011 Duma Election*. Glasgow: Centre for the Study of Public Policy, University of Strathclyde, SPP 490.

Rose, Richard (2012b), *New Russia Barometer XX: Public Opinion of Vladimir Putin's Return as President*. Glasgow: Centre for the Study of Public Policy, University of Strathclyde, SPP 492.

Rose, Richard and Ellen Carnaghan (1995), 'Generational Effects on Attitudes to Communist Regimes: A Comparative Analysis', *Post-Soviet Affairs*, vol. 11, no.1, pp. 28–56.

Rose, Richard and Neil Munro (2002), *Elections Without Order*. Cambridge: Cambridge University Press.

Rose, Richard and Neil Munro (2009), *Parties and Elections in New European Democracies*. Colchester: ECPR Press.

Rose, Richard and William Mishler (2010), 'The Impact of Macro-Economic Shock on Regime Support in Russia', *Post-Soviet Affairs*, vol. 26, pp. 38–57.

Rose, Richard, William Mishler and Neil Munro (2011), *Popular Support for an Undemocratic Regime: The Changing Views of Russians*. Cambridge: Cambridge University Press.

Ross, Cameron (ed.) (2004), *Russian Politics under Putin*. Manchester: Manchester University Press.

Ross, Cameron and Campbell, Adrian (2009), *Federalism and Local Politics in Russia*. London and New York: Routledge.

Rumyantsev, Oleg (1994), *Osnovy konstitutsionnogo stroya Rossii*. Moscow: Yurist'.

'Russian Army Improves Quality of Combat Training' (2012), RIA Novosti, 6 November. Available at http://en.ria.ru/military_news/20131106/184553496/Russian-Army-Improves-Quality-of-Combat-Training.html.

Russian Federal Agency on the Press and Mass Communication (2011), *Internet v Rossii: Sostoyanie, tendentsii i perspektivy razvitiya*. Moscow: Regional Public Centre for Internet Technology. Available at: http://www.fapmc.ru/magnoliaPublic/rospechat/activities/reports/2011/item6.html

Sakwa, Richard (1990), *Gorbachev and His Reforms, 1985–90*. Hemel Hempstead: Philip Allan.

Sakwa, Richard (1998), *Soviet Politics in Perspective*, 2nd edn. London: Routledge.

Sakwa, Richard (2008a), *Russian Politics and Society*, 4th edn. London and New York: Routledge.

Sakwa, Richard (2008b), *Putin: Russia's Choice*, 2nd edn. London, Routledge.

Sakwa, Richard (2010a), 'The Dual State in Russia', *Post-Soviet Affairs*, vol. 26, no. 3, July–September, pp. 185–206.

Sakwa, Richard (2010b), *Communism in Russia: An Interpretative Essay*. Basingstoke: Palgrave Macmillan.

Sakwa, Richard (2010c), 'Putin's Leadership,' in Stephen K. Wegren and Dale R. Herspring (eds), *After Putin's Russia*. Boulder, CO: Rowman & Littlefield.

Sakwa, Richard (2011), *The Crisis of Russian Democracy: The Dual State, Factionalism, and the Medvedev Succession*. Cambridge: Cambridge University Press.

Sakwa, Richard (2012), 'Modernisation, Neo-Modernisation and Comparative Democratisation in Russia', *East European Politics*, vol. 28, no. 1, March, pp. 43–57.

Salmenniemi, Suvi (2008), *Democratization and Gender in Contemporary Russia*. London: Routledge.

Salmenniemi, Suvi (ed.) (2012), *Rethinking Class in Russia*. Burlington, VT: Ashgate.

Sandle, Mark (1997), *A Short History of Soviet Socialism*. London: UCL Press.

Saunders, Peter (1986), *Social Theory and the Urban Question*. 2nd edn, London: Hutchinson Education.

Schedler, Andreas (2002), 'The Menu of Manipulation', *Journal of Democracy*, vol. 13, no. 2 (April), pp. 36–50.

Schedler, Andreas (2013), *The Politics of Uncertainty: Sustaining and Subverting Electoral Authoritarianism*. Oxford and New York: Oxford University Press.

Schmidt, Victoria (2012), 'Orphan Care in Russia: Cause for Dismantling the Down Staircase', in Joanne Bailey, (ed.), *Orphan Care: A Comparative View*. Sterling, VA: Kumarian Press.

SCO (2011), Statement by SCO Observer Mission on Preparation and Conduct of Parliamentary Election in Russia, at http://www.sectsco.org/EN123/show.asp?id=314.

Sergeyev, Mikhail (2013), 'Goskorporatsiya Rossiya', *Gazeta.ru*, 12 July.

Service, Robert (2005), *A History of Modern Russia: From Nicholas II to Vladimir Putin*. Cambridge, MA: Harvard University Press.

Shabdurasulov, Igor' (2008), 'Otsy-Osnovateli', *Novoe Vremya (The New Times)* (April 14), pp. 18–19.

Sharafutdinova, Gulnaz (2013), 'Gestalt Switch in Russian Federalism: The Decline in Regional Power Under Putin', *Comparative Politics*, April, pp. 357–76.

Sharlet, Robert (1992), *Soviet Constitutional Crisis: From De-Stalinization to Disintegration*. Armonk, NY: M.E. Sharpe.

Sherr, James (2013), *Hard Diplomacy and Soft Coercion: Russia's Influence Abroad*. Chatham House, Royal Institute of International Affairs.

Shevchenko, Olga (2009), *Crisis and the Everyday in Post-Socialist Moscow*. Bloomington ,IN: Indiana University Press.

Shevtsova, Lilia (2007), *Lost in Transition: The Yeltsin and Putin Legacies*. Washington, DC: Carnegie Endowment for Peace Press.

Shevtsova, Lilia and Mark H. Eckert (2000), 'The Problem of Executive Power in Russia,' *Journal of Democracy*, vol. 11, pp. 32–9.

Shleifer, Andrei and Daniel Treisman (2004), 'A Normal Country', *Foreign Affairs*, vol. 83, no. 2, pp. 20–38.

Shpil'kin, Sergei (2011), 'Statistika issledovala vybory', *Gazeta.ru*, 10 December, available at http://www.gazeta.ru/science/2011/12/10_a_3922390.shtml.

Sigal, Yevgenii (2013), 'Rakety strategicheskogo naznacheniya', *Kommersant*, 22 July.

Silverman, Bertram and Murray Yanowitch (2000), *New Rich, New Poor, New Russia: Winners and Losers on the Russian Road to Capitalism*. Armonk, NY: M. E. Sharpe.

Slider, Darrell (2005), 'The Regions' Impact on Federal Policy: The Federation Council', in P. Reddaway and R. Orttung (eds), *The Dynamics of Russian Politics*. Washington, DC: US Institute of Peace, pp. 123–43.

Slider, Darrell (2009), 'Putin and the Election of Regional Governors' in Ross and Campbell, pp. 106–19.

Smith, Steven S. and Thomas F. Remington (2001), *The Politics of Institutional Choice: Formation of the Russian State Duma*. Princeton, NJ: Princeton University Press.

Smyth, Regina (2006), *Candidate Strategies and Electoral Competition in the Russian Federation: Democracy without Foundation*. Cambridge: Cambridge University Press.

Smyth, Regina, Brandon Wilkening and Anna Urasova (2007), 'Engineering Victory: Institutional Reform, Informal Institutions, and the Formation of a Hegemonic Party Regime in the Russian Federation', *Post-Soviet Affairs*, vol. 23, no. 2.

Sokolov, Mikhail (2013, 19 October), 'Lev Gudkov: "Rossiya dlya russkikh?" Uzhe ne stydno', *Radio Svoboda*.

Solomon, Peter H., Jr. (1987), 'The Case of the Vanishing Acquittal: Informal Norms and the Practice of Soviet Criminal Justice', *Soviet Studies*, vol. 39, no. 4, pp. 531–55.

Solomon, Peter H., Jr (2007), 'Informal Practices in Russian Justice: Probing the Limits of Post-Soviet Reform', in Ferdinand Feldbrugge (ed), *Russia, Europe, and the Rule of Law*. Leiden: Martinus Nijhoff, pp. 79–92.

Solomon, Peter H., Jr, and Todd Foglesong (2000), *Courts and Transition in Russia: The Challenge of Judicial Reform*. Boulder, CO: Westview Press.

Solovyov, Vladimir (2008), *Putin: putevoditel' dlya neravnodushnykykh*. Moscow: Eksmo.

Sovet Bezopasnosti Rossiiskoi Federatsii (2009), *Strategiya national'noi bezopasnosti Rossiiskoi Federatsii do 2020 goda*, in *Sobranie zakonodatel'stva Rossiiskoi Federatsii*, no. 20, item 2444, 12 May.

Sovet Bezopasnosti Rossiiskoi Federatsii (2010), Voennaya doktrina Rossiiskoi Federatsii', *Rossiiskaya gazeta*, 10 February, p. 17.

Stalin, I. V. (1937), 'Rech' na predvybornom sobranii izbiratelei Stalinskogo izbiratel'nogo okruga goroda Moskvy', *Pravda*, 12 December, pp. 1–2.

Stephenson, Svetlana (2006), *Crossing the Line: Vagrancy, Homelessness and Social Displacement in Russia*. Aldershot: Ashgate.

Stephenson, Svetlana (2008), 'Searching for Home. Street Youth and Organized Crime in Russia', in Dave Brotherton and Michael Flynn (eds), *Globalizing the Streets. Cross-Cultural Perspectives on Youth, Social Control, and Empowerment*. New York: Columbia University Press, pp. 78–92.

Stephenson, Svetlana (2012), 'The Violent Practices of Youth Territorial Groups in Moscow', *Europe-Asia Studies*, vol. 64, no. 1, pp. 69–90.

Steven S. Smith and Thomas F. Remington (2001), *The Politics of Institutional Choice: Formation of the Russian State Duma*. Princeton, NJ: Princeton University Press.

Suny, Ronald Grigor (1998) *The Soviet Experiment: Russia, The USSR, and the Successor States*. Oxford: Oxford University Press.

'Sudebno-arbitrazhnaya statistika o rassmotrennykh delakh arbitrazhnymi sudami Rossiiskoi Federatsii v 2002–2005 godakh' (2006), *Vestnik Vysshego Arbitrazhnogo Suda Rossiiskoi Federatsii*, no. 5, pp. 22–3.

Surkov, Vladislav (2006), 'Suverenitet – eto politicheskii sinonim konkurento-sposobnosti', in Nikita Garadzha (ed.), *Suverenitet*. Moscow: Evropa.

Sutela, Pekka (2012), *The Political Economy of Putin's Russia*. Abingdon: Routledge.

Swint, Brian (2012), 'Rosneft Buys BP's TNK-BP Stake for $26 Billion in Cash, Shares', *Bloomberg*, 20 October.

'Tablitsya osnovnykh pokazatelei raboty arbitrazhnykh sudov Rossiiskoi

Federatsii v 2008-2012 gg.'(2012), available at http://arbitr.ru/_upimg/9A722CAA5045E32D46304A764C9D449B_5.pdf.

Taylor, Brian D. (2011), *State Building in Putin's Russia: Policing and Coercion after Communism*. New York: Cambridge University Press.

Thomas, Timothy L. (1996), 'The Russian Military and the 1995 Duma Elections', *Journal of Slavic Military Studies*, vol. 9, no. 3, pp. 519–47.

Thomassen, Jacques and Henk van der Kolk (2009), 'Effectiveness and Political Support in Old and New Democracies,' in Hans-Dieter Klingemann (ed.), *The Comparative Study of Electoral Systems*. Oxford: Oxford University Press.

Thorun, Christian (2009), *Explaining Change in Russian Foreign Policy: The Role of Ideas in Post-Soviet Russia's Conduct towards the West*. Basingstoke: Palgrave Macmillan.

Tovkaylo, Maksim (2013), 'Voenniye otbili byudzhet', *Vedomosti*, 10 July.

Treisman, Daniel (2011), *The Return: Russia's Journey from Gorbachev to Medvedev*. London: Simon & Schuster.

Trenin, Dmitri (2004), 'Moscow's Realpolitik', *Nezavisimaya gazeta*, 16 February.

Trenin, Dmitri (2007), *Getting Russia Right*. Washington, DC: Carnegie Endowment for Peace.

Trenin, Dmitri (2013a), 'Vladimir Putin's Fourth Vector', *Russia in Global Affairs*, no. 2, April/June.

Trenin, Dmitri (2013b), 'Putin's Syrian Game Plan', *World Today*, October/November, p. 11.

Trochev, Alexei (2006), 'Judicial Selection in Russia: Toward Accountability and Centralization', in Kate Malleson and Peter H. Russell (eds), *Appointing Judges in an Age of Judicial Power*. Toronto: University of Toronto Press.

Trochev, Alexei (2008), *Judging Russia: The Role of the Constitutional Court in Russian Politics 1990-2006*. Cambridge and New York: Cambridge University Press.

Troxel, Tiffany A. (2003), *Parliamentary Power in Russia, 1994–2001: President vs Parliament*. New York: Palgrave Macmillan.

Tsvetaeva, Roza (2011), 'Sistemnyi lobbizm dumskikh forvardov,' *Nezavisimaya gazeta*, November 29.

Tsygankov, Andrei (2013), *Russia's Foreign Policy: Change and Continuity in National Identity*. Lanham, MD: Rowman & Littlefield.

Tucker, Joshua A. (2006), *Regional Economic Voting: Russia, Poland, Hungary, Slovakia, and the Czech Republic, 1990–1999*. Cambridge: Cambridge University Press.

Tyler, Tom R. (2006), *Why People Obey the Law*. Princeton, NJ: Princeton University Press.

Urban, Joan Barth and Solovei, Valerii D. (1997), *Russia's Communists at the Crossroads*. Boulder, CO: Westview.

Urban, Michael (1994), 'December 1993 as a Replication of Late-Soviet Electoral Practices', *Post-Soviet Affairs*, vol. 10, no. 2 (April–June), pp. 127–58.

VCIOM (Russian Public Opinion Research Center) (2007), 'Russia Has Two Allies: The Army and the Mass Media', Press Release no. 831, 11 December, available at http://wciom.com.

VCIOM (Russian Public Opinion Research Center) (2013), 'Ratings of Social Institutions', available at http://wciom.com/index.php?id=123.

Vinogradova, Elena, Kozina, Irina, and Cook, Linda J. (2012), 'Russian Labor: Quiescence and Conflict', *Communist and Post-Communist Studies*, no. 45, pp. 219–31.

Viola, Lynne (2002), *Contending with Stalinism: Soviet Power and Popular Resistance in the 1930s*. Ithaca, NY: Cornell University Press.

Volkov, Vadim, Arina Dmitrieva, Mikhail Pozdnyakov and Kirill Titaev (2012), 'Rossiiskie sud'i kak professional'naya gruppa: sotsiologicheskoe issledovanie', available at http://pravo.ru/store/doc/doc/Pozdnyakov.pdf.

Voltmer, Katrin (2000), 'Constructing Political Reality in Russia: Izvestiya – Between Old and New Journalistic Practices', *European Journal of Communication*, vol. 15, no. 4, pp. 469–500.

Voltmer, Katrin (2013), *The Media in Transitional Democracies*. London: Polity.

Vybory deputatov Gosudarstvennoi Dumy Federal'nogo Sobraniya Rossiiskoi Federatsii shestogo sovyza 2011. Sbornik informatsionno-analiticheskikh materialov (2012), Moscow: Tsentral'naya izbiratel'naya komissiya Rossiiskoi Federatsii.

Walker, Charles, (2010), *Learning to Labour in Post-Soviet Russia: Vocational Youth in Transition*. London and New York: Routledge.

Walker, Charles (2012), 'Re-Inventing themselves? Gender, Employment and Subjective Well-being amongst Young Working-Class Russians', in Suvi Salmenniemi (ed.), *Rethinking Class in Russia*. Farnham: Ashgate, pp. 221–40.

Way, Lucan (2005), 'Authoritarian State Building and the Sources of Regime Competitiveness in the Fourth Wave: The Cases of Belarus, Moldova, Russia, and Ukraine,' *World Politics*, vol. 57, no. 2, pp. 231–61.

Webber, Stephen L. (2006), 'Introduction: The Society–Military Interface in Russia', in Stephen L. Webber and Jennifer G. Mathers (eds), *Military and Society in Post-Soviet Russia*. Manchester and New York: Manchester University Press.

Webber, Stephen L. and Jennifer G. Mathers (2006), *Military and Society in Post-Soviet Russia*. Manchester and New York: Manchester University Press.

Webber, Stephen L. and Alina Zilberman (2006), 'The Citizenship Dimension of the Society–Military Interface', in Stephen L. Webber and Jennifer G. Mathers (eds), *Military and Society in Post-Soviet Russia*. Manchester and New York: Manchester University Press.

Weber, Max (1978), *Economy and Society: An Outline of Interpretive Sociology*. Berkeley: University of California Press.

Weber, Max (1990), 'Politics as a Vocation' [1946], in Peter Mair (ed.), *The West European Party System*. Oxford: Oxford University Press, pp. 31–6.

Wegren, Stephen, (ed.) (2013), *Return to Putin's Russia*. 5th edn. Boulder, CO: Rowman & Littlefield.

Westwood, John (2002), *Endurance and Endeavour: Russian History, 1812–2001*, 5th edn. Oxford: Oxford University Press.

White, Stephen (1991), 'The Soviet Elections of 1989: from Acclamation to Limited Choice', *Coexistence*, vol. 28, no. 4 (December), pp. 513–39.

White, Stephen (1994), *After Gorbachev*, revised 4th edn. Cambridge and New York: Cambridge University Press.

White, Stephen (2000), *Communism and its Collapse*. London: Routledge.

White, Stephen (2011), *Understanding Russian Politics*. Cambridge and New York: Cambridge University Press.

White, Stephen and Valentina Feklyunina (2014), *Identities and Foreign Policies in Russia, Ukraine and Belarus*. Basingstoke: Palgrave Macmillan.

White, Stephen and Ol'ga Kryshtanovskaya (2011), 'Changing the Russian Electoral System: Inside the Black Box', *Europe-Asia Studies*, vol. 63, no. 4 (June), pp. 557–78.

White, Stephen and Ian McAllister (2007), 'Turnout and Representation Bias in Postcommunist Europe', *Political Studies*, vol. 55, pp. 586–606.

White, Stephen and Ian McAllister (2008), 'The Putin Phenomenon', *Journal of Communist Studies and Transition Politics*, vol. 24, no. 4, pp. 604–28.

White, Stephen and Ian McAllister (2010), *Public Opinion in Russia, 2010*. Aberdeen: Centre for the Study of Public Policy, SPP 479.

White, Stephen *et al.* (2012), *Russia's Authoritarian Elections*. Abingdon and New York: Routledge.

White, Stephen, Ian McAllister and Sarah Oates (2005), 'Media Effects and the Russian Elections, 1999–2000', *British Journal of Political Science*, vol. 35, no. 2 (April), pp. 191–208.

White, Stephen, Richard Rose and Ian McAllister, Ian (1997), *How Russia Votes*. Chatham, NJ: Chatham House.

Whitefield, Stephen (2002), 'Political Cleavages and Post-Communist Politics', *Annual Review of Political Science*, vol. 5, pp. 181–200.

Whitefield, Stephen and Geoffrey Evans (1999), 'Political Culture Versus Rational Choice: Explaining Responses to Transition in the Czech Republic and Slovakia', *British Journal of Political Science*, vol. 29, no. 1, pp. 129–55.

Willerton, John P. (2007), 'The Putin Legacy: Russian-Style Democratization Confronts a "Failing State"', *Soviet and Post-Soviet Review*, vol. 34, no. 1, pp. 33–54.

Willerton, John P., Mikhail Beznosov, and Martin Carrier (2005), 'Addressing the Challenge of Russia's "Failing State": The Legacy of Gorbachev and the Promise of Putin', *Demokratizatsiya*, vol. 13, no. 2, pp. 219–39.

Wilson, Andrew (2005), *Virtual Politics: Faking Democracy in the Post-Soviet World*. New Haven: Yale University Press.

Wolff, Stefan (2012), 'The Transnistrian Issue: Moving beyond the status-quo', European Parliament, Directorate-General for External Policies of the Union, Policy Department Study, https://www.gov.uk/government/uploads/system/uploads/attachment_data/file/224472/evidence-stefan-wolff-the-transnistrian-issue.pdf, accessed 14 October 2013.

World Economic Forum (2012), *The Global Economic Competitiveness Report 2012-2013*, Geneva: WEF (http://reports.weforum.org/global-competitiveness-report-2012-2013/#=).

Wyman, Matthew, Stephen White, Bill Miller and Paul Heywood (1995), 'Public Opinion, Parties and Voters in the December 1993 Russian Elections', *Europe-Asia Studies*, vol. 47, no. 4, pp. 591–614.

Zalessky, Vladimir (2007), 'Sistema "fal'shvybory', *New Times*, no. 42, 26 November, pp. 16–18.

Zayavlenie no. 4 Assotsiatsii 'Golos' po itogam nablyudeniya v den' golosovaniya ot 4 dekabrya 2007 g., at http://files.golos.org/docs/2399/original/2399-zayavlenie-4.pdf?1311920807.

Zenkovich, Nikolai (2006), *Putinskaya entsiklopediya*. Moscow: OLMA-Press.

Zorkaya, N., (ed.) (2012), *Russian Public Opinion 2010–11*. Moscow: Levada Analytical Center. Available at: http://en.d7154.agava.net/sites/en.d7154.agava.net/files/Levada2011Eng.pdf

Zubarevich, Natalia (2012), 'Sotsial'naya differentsiatsiya regionov i gorodov', *Pro et Contra*, vol. 56. no. 4-5, pp. 135-52

XIX Vsesoyuznaya konferentsiya Kommunisticheskoi partii Sovetskogo Soyuza, 28 iyunya – 1 iyulya 1988 g.: Stenograficheskii otchet (1988) 2 vols (Moscow: Politizdat).

Index